Praise for Dan Baum's

GUN GUYS

"[A] wonderfully guileless and open-minded guide to American gun culture. . . . [Baum] has done a public service."
—*The Christian Science Monitor*

"Baum sets out to understand what motivates so many Americans to be 'gun guys'. . . [and] depicts these people and their different motives with genuine empathy."
—*The New York Review of Books*

"On Baum's road trip, he became more deeply immersed in the gun culture, and the resulting journey inside his head is . . . fascinating." —*The Seattle Times*

"As a writer, Baum doesn't have it in him to lay down a dull sentence. [*Gun Guys*] is wise, considered, delectably written, fun to read and wholly lacking in tendentiousness."
—Bloomberg.com

"An accomplished nonfiction storyteller. . . . Baum's also more much articulate than the average gun-lover—or hater." —*Tampa Bay Times*

"It is interesting and funny. But most of all it is enlightening." —*Beaufort Observer* (North Carolina)

"His descriptions of the frequently awkward encounters are pitch-perfect." —*Richmond Times-Dispatch*

"For every yahoo in the gun culture prattling on about world government there are nine guys (and girls) who simply like to shoot." —*The Wall Street Journal*

"The strength of Baum's book is that he doesn't drink from the tap of conventional wisdom."
—*The Gambit* (New Orleans)

"A provocative, probing and frequently funny journey deep into the mentality of the approximately 40 percent of Americans who own guns." —*The San Diego Union-Tribune*

"Thoroughly entertaining and provocative."
—*The Plain Dealer*

"Fascinating, intelligent. . . . *Gun Guys* is . . . necessary, insightful." —*Minneapolis Star Tribune*

"Thank goodness we have Dan Baum to guide us through this morass." —*Chicago Reader*

"Baum stretches across the divide like few others."
—*Maclean's*

"A fascinating look at a part of our culture often vilified without recourse." —*Florida Times-Union*

"Vivid. . . . Schlepping among the gun lovers with this guy is unfailingly diverting as well as illuminating."
—*Newsday*

Dan Baum

GUN GUYS

Dan Baum is the author of *Nine Lives, Smoke and Mirrors,* and *Citizen Coors*. He was a staff writer for *The New Yorker* and has written for *Rolling Stone, Playboy, The New York Times Magazine,* and many other publications.

www.danbaum.com

Also by Dan Baum

Nine Lives: Death and Life in New Orleans

Citizen Coors: An American Dynasty

*Smoke and Mirrors: The War on Drugs
and the Politics of Failure*

GUN
GUYS

Dan Baum

GUN GUYS

A Road Trip

VINTAGE DEPARTURES
VINTAGE BOOKS
A DIVISION OF RANDOM HOUSE LLC
NEW YORK

FIRST VINTAGE DEPARTURES EDITION, DECEMBER 2013

Portions of this work were originally published, in a different form, in
Harper's Magazine (August 2010) and online as a Kindle Single titled
Guns Gone Wild (September 2011).

Grateful acknowledgment is made to Steve Lee for permission to reprint an
excerpt from "I Like Guns" from *I Like Guns* by Steve Lee (November 2005).
http://ilikeguns.au/. Reprinted by permission of the artist.

The Library of Congress has cataloged the Knopf edition as follows:
Baum, Dan.
Gun guys : a road trip / Dan Baum.—1st ed.
p. cm.
1. Firearms owners—United States. 2. Firearms ownership—United States.
3. Firearms—Social aspects—United States. I. Title.
HV8059.B38 2013
683.400973—dc23
2012028767

Vintage ISBN: 978-0-307-74250-6
eBook ISBN: 978-0-307-96221-8

Author photograph © Michael Lionstar
Book design by Michael Collica

www.vintagebooks.com

Printed in the United States of America
10 9 8 7 6 5 4 3 2 1

For my brother, Andy

I like guns I like the way they look
I like the shiny steel and the polished wood
I don't care if they're big or small
If they're for sale, Hell, I want 'em all
I like guns, I like guns, I like guns.

. . .

I don't really get all the fuss
Why they're trying to take guns off of us
'Cause I ain't going to shoot anyone
No one shoots at me 'cause I've got a gun
I like guns, I like guns, I like guns.

> —*Steve Lee, from his 2010 CD,* I Like
> Guns, *which also includes the songs*
> *"I'll Give Up My Gun," "Gun Shy*
> *Dog," and "She Don't Like Guns"*

CONTENTS

GUN
GUYS

PROLOGUE: BIG BANG

Dick Cavett: I always wanted a Luger.... The Luger is a sexy object;
there is something about that design that is genius and appealing.
Randy Cohen: We don't have any say in the objects we find seductive.

−On the public radio show *Person Place Thing*, February 15, 2012

Within days of arriving at summer camp, it was clear I'd be forever consigned to right field, ignored by quarterbacks, left jiggling and huffing in the rear during capture the flag. At five, I was the youngest kid ever at Sunapee: a pudgy, overmothered cherub amid a tribe of lean savages. Though I'd begged to follow my brothers to camp, my first week in Bunk 1 was a fog of humiliations large and small. I knew nothing of baseball, tits, or rock and roll; I was quick to tears; I wet the bed. At the end of the first week, I feigned illness for the raw relief of the cool, sympathetic touch of the nurse's hand on my forehead.

At the edge of the woods loomed a mysterious monolith that was both exciting and vaguely disturbing: a giant white boulder neatly cracked in two. It must have stood five feet high—much taller than my head. The two sides lay just far enough apart that a person could slip between them, and I occasionally saw bigger boys disappearing along the path through the rock—it appeared to be some kind of portal.

One hot day in the second week of camp, Bunk 1's counselor led the ten of us through. The broken rock faces sparkled in the sunlight, and as we stepped in, a thick mantle of cool air enveloped us. I was disoriented for a moment, as though I'd entered into another dimension. Then the boy in front of me moved, the boy behind me shoved, and we emerged onto a sparsely wooded hillside.

The ground sloped gently away, through white birch saplings, to a wooden platform floating on a sea of ferns. On the platform stood a big man with his fists on his hips. We trotted down the path and clattered aboard. Five urine-stained mattresses lay at the big man's feet. On the mattresses lay rifles.

Real guns! It was 1961, and, like many kids, I'd seen lots of gunfights on TV. I'd played cowboys with Mattel cap pistols and ambushed friends with primary-colored squirt guns. These rifles, though, were long and serious-looking, their burnished wood warmly reflecting the dappled sunlight. The big man, a crew-cut Rutgers footballer named Hank Hilliard, scooped up a rifle and opened its bolt with a *slick-click* that I felt in my spine. He pointed to the various parts and spoke their names, extending blunt fingers to show how to line up the sights. He sternly repeated the range rules. Then he eenie-meenied five of us to lie on the mattresses and warned us not to touch the rifles until he gave the go-ahead.

I lay on my side, hands clasped between my knees, gazing at the steel barrel two inches in front of my eyes: MOSSBERG 340 KA NORTH HAVEN, CONNECTICUT .22 SHORT LONG OR LONG RIFLE. I cannot remember the names of my neighbors' grown children or the seventh dwarf, but to this day I can summon every detail of that rifle and its metallic, smoky, chemical aroma: *guns.*

A cartridge plopped onto the mattress—slender shiny brass with a rounded gray tip. "Pick up your rifles," Hank boomed, and I hoisted the Mossberg into my arms. Across the far end of the clearing stretched a board fence on which he'd tacked sheets of white paper, each with a black dot at the center. "Open your bolts." I worked the knob up and back. *Slick-click.* "Load." I poked the nose of the cartridge into the breech and mashed it forward with my thumb. "Close your bolts." I pushed the bolt forward and locked it down, the most determined thing I'd ever done. "Aim and fire at will."

The kid next to me grunted as his rifle popped off. The other three shot nervously in the next two seconds. I ignored them. For days, I'd enviously watched these boys swing bats and tennis rackets, throw spirals, and execute high dives. Now I tuned them out and squeezed the world down to my front sight, a bead-topped post looping tighter and tighter around the black dot. The rifle gave a slight jump against my shoulder and a distant crack. Hank dropped another cartridge on the mattress.

We each shot five bullets and, after an elaborate ceremony of opening bolts and clearing chambers, pelted across the clearing to retrieve our targets. One kid's was completely untouched. The rest had two or three holes, the shots scattered widely.

All five of mine were inside the black dot, which I now saw was divided into five concentric rings. Several of my bullet holes touched; one nicked dead center. When I handed the target to Hank, he rocked his head back in surprise. "Damn," he breathed, touching each hole with a pencil point. "Thirty-six out of fifty." He handed back the target and gave me my first-ever man-to-man look. "Nice shootin', Tex."

Was that my personal Big Bang? Did I get hooked on guns because I discovered I was good at shooting at precisely the moment I was experiencing my first feelings of masculine inadequacy? Is this why I've spent a lifetime carrying around an enthusiasm that has made me feel slightly ashamed? Or did I just think the guns were cool and fun, the way other kids fell for fishing rods and ant farms? All I knew at the time was that the rifle range replaced the nurse's office as my refuge. By day I was forced to trudge through ball sports with the rest of my bunkmates, but when the shadows grew long and we were allowed an elective, I invariably chose riflery. I learned to breathe evenly, listen to my heartbeat, and let the shot go between beats, when the muzzle was steadiest. I learned to place the pad of my index finger against the trigger and squeeze so slowly that the shot came as a surprise. I came to love the snap of the rifle, the rich aroma of burned cordite, the magical geometry of a bullet's razor-straight trajectory connecting to a tiny, distant point. I even came to enjoy the faint aroma of ancient urine soaked into cotton batting, because that, too, was part of the Camp Sunapee rifle-range experience. Ten targets of twenty-five-plus points won me a tiny bronze Pro-Marksman medal that first summer and a National Rifle Association patch to sew on my melton wool camp jacket. *The National Rifle Association!* Cool! Ten of thirty-plus points made me a Marksman the following year, and I soon moved on to forty-plus points: a Sharpshooter. As I returned to Sunapee summer after summer, I worked my way from prone to sitting to kneeling to standing, and my skill and enthusiasm got me invited to the range at off-hours—during rest period or meals—for one-on-one instruction and the high honor of cleaning the rifles with rags, bore brushes, and banana-smelling Hoppe's No. 9 Solvent.

It was, however, a confusingly bifurcated gun life. Aside from Hank Hilliard, I had no gun mentors. Neither my parents nor anybody in their circle of suburban New Jersey Jewish Democrats had ever hunted or owned a gun. None, I am certain, would have dreamed of touching one. "Jews make guns and sell guns," my mother's friend Bubbles Binder said with a gravelly laugh. "We don't shoot guns." I don't know if there were gun ranges in or near South Orange, because taking me to one would have been the last thing my gentle, mercantile father would have dreamed of doing. So while riflery was a serious sport at camp, for the other ten months of the year my gun thing was allowed to spin off into the kind of violent fantasies that, in the mid-1960s, were not considered at all odd for a little boy.

One whole aisle of E. J. Korvette's toy department was given over to nothing but guns—Monkey Division bazookas, Johnny Seven One Man Army guns, Mattel Shootin' Shell rifles, Hubley snub-nosed .38s, Okinawa Guns, G.I. Joes with all their lethal accoutrements, Zero-M secret-agent weapons, fabulously realistic Johnny Eagle gun sets, Fanner 50 cap pistols, Sound-O-Power M16s, Secret Sam folding-rifle spy briefcases, *Man from U.N.C.L.E.* guns, and on and on, all of them advertised relentlessly and unabashedly on *Wonderama, Sandy Becker,* and every other children's television show. I can sing those commercials still. When I wasn't running around the neighborhood in a plastic helmet with Chucky Blau and my Dick Tracy tommy gun, I was studying *Combat!*—"starring Vic Morrow as Sergeant Saunders"—with the devotional zeal of a Talmudic scholar. I slept with toy guns under and in my bed. I was always either holding a gun or pantomiming doing so, my hands aching for the rich fullness of stock and handgrip. Every few days, I looked up "rifle," "pistol," or "machine gun" in our 1960 *World Book,* lingering over photos and diagrams—the intricate sweep of bolt and trigger—memorizing make, model, caliber, muzzle velocity, and cyclic rate of fire. James Bond burst into my life in 1964 like a newfound god, and I began looking forward to the rare occasions on which our parents would drag my brothers and me to Temple Israel, because services gave me an excuse to wear a suit jacket like a grown-up, which meant I could conceal a plastic shoulder holster and Luger, with a Magic Marker jammed into the muzzle as a silencer. That delicious bulk under my arm could sustain me through an entire Kol Nidre.

And then every summer it was back to Sunapee's rifle range, where the merest suggestion of James Bond or Sergeant Saunders would get a kid banished, because the range was about marksmanship, not fantasy. Year by year, guns were working their way into my chromosomes from two directions—the manly discipline of precision shooting, rooted in the coldest imaginable reality; and the wildly sexy mythology of soldiers, cowboys, gangsters, and spies that made firearms overwhelmingly glamorous. I didn't stand a chance.

All of this was fine until about 1967, when, like the sun passing behind a cloud, my gun thing went vaguely dark. The signals were subtle but unmistakable: Guns were uncool, my obsession with them icky. At eleven years old, my friends were outgrowing Army playing; I remember precisely the day the nickel dropped. Chucky, Arthur Lewis, and I were up at the vacant lot on Irving Avenue, assaulting the same Nazi pillbox we'd been trying to take for longer than the duration of the real Second World War. I ran my heart out, serpentining like a demon to avoid enemy fire, biting my fist and heaving air grenades, *k'tow-k'tow*ing sound effects. I could tell, though, that Chucky and Arthur were simply going through the motions, slow and listless as we advanced under enemy fire. As I looked back to signal them to flank left, I found them sitting off to the side, talking and tossing pebbles at a can, their guns resting casually in their laps. It hit me like a rock in the forehead—*they're humoring me.* And walking home, the death blow: We ran into Susan Stern and Caroline Bell, both of whom we'd known since kindergarten. They looked different now; slinkier, wiser—*pretty.* They wrinkled their foreheads at our toy guns as though to say, "Really, guys. . . ." Chucky and Arthur instantly began swinging their rifles like baseball bats, as though, surprised to find these long things in their hands, they'd discovered something reasonable to do with them. I was losing my lifelong platoon buddies to baseball and football—precisely the kind of impossible athletics that had driven me to the Camp Sunapee rifle range in the first place. I felt like a baby the size of a parade balloon—not merely abandoned: humiliated.

The other tsunami flooding my gun obsession with disgrace was Vietnam. Opposition to the war was nearly universal in our suburb, where regiments of allergists and orthopedists stood ready to write young men excuses. The task of lining up a way out of the draft was preoccupying my oldest brother, and the war was becoming an unignorable presence in our lives. The cool kids in school were way out in front with flamboyant opposition, even in sixth grade, adopting the peace-and-love aesthetic that was blooming across America. To be seen with a toy gun, to be drawing war pictures, to be playing with toy soldiers: All of it was completely wrong. I was against the war, too, and aspired to the hippie aesthetic as much as any sixth grader. But that didn't keep me from liking guns. To me, they were separate.

I tried to make the transition with Chucky and the others; really, I did. I trooped off to Little League tryouts, hoping to wear one of those uniforms with BECK'S HARDWARE or SHOP-RITE on the back. Alas, I was shunted off to the so-called Pee-Wee League, a uniformless sump of the halt and uncoordinated known informally as "Fat-Kid League." I gamely stuck with it for a season, playing right field for the Washington Senators, and my parents did all they could to encourage me. My father even had one of those fake front pages printed with a headline: DAN BAUM GIVES UP GUNS, BECOMES BASEBALL STAR.

But I didn't give up guns any more than I became a baseball star. I merely transitioned to the kind of guns a bigger kid might reasonably justify—a spring-loaded BB rifle and a CO_2-powered air pistol. These verged on acceptable because they were more about hitting targets than fantasizing battle scenes. I couldn't play Army anymore, but setting up paper targets in the backyard reawakened the pleasure I'd taken at camp in the disciplined practice of squeezing down a gun's tremendous force and delivering it precisely to a distant point. Air-gun shooting let me keep guns in my life. It satisfied my hand's urge for stock, grip, and trigger.

In the rural South or the Rocky Mountains, nobody would have thought twice about my gun thing. I'd have gotten a shotgun for my twelfth birthday, taken hunter safety at fourteen, acquired a deer rifle for Christmas, and spent autumn tramping through the outdoors with my dad and uncles. Guns would have become a normal part of growing up, like chasing girls and learning to drive. In my New Jersey suburb, though, they made me a mutant, and my hobby was equally verboten at the private colleges I attended in the 1970s. When I bought my first real gun, during junior year at New York University—an elegant old Remington .22 rifle much like the ones I'd shot at camp—I kept quiet about it.

By the time I was a voting adult, I'd begun to perceive the gun lover in me as some kind of malevolent twin. My upbringing, reading, and experience kept me believing in unions, gay rights, progressive taxation, the United Nations, public works, permissive immigration, single-payer health care, reproductive choice, negotiation rather than preemptive force, regulation of business to protect workers and the environment, and scientifically informed rather than religion-based policies. Guns were as firmly delineated a political battlefield as abortion or school prayer, and guns belonged to the other guys. When gun-control measures passed, my people won; when gun rights expanded, the other team won. Because I wasn't yet thinking very seriously about the issue, I went along with my side, reliably lending my support to the calls for background checks, registration, assault-rifle bans, and waiting periods. None interfered with my enjoyment of guns because, aside from my .22, I didn't own any.

What did bother me, though, was the gut reaction of my friends to any mention of guns. "Ugh. I *hate* guns," was the way they usually expressed it. And my friends' contempt went beyond guns to the people who liked them. They wouldn't have dreamed of saying "nigger" or "fag," but they laughed at "gun nuts" or "gun loons." I'd stay quiet during such talk, like Tom Hanks chuckling along at the anti-gay jokes in the first reel of *Philadelphia*.

In my early thirties, I taught myself to hunt deer, partly as a new way to experience the outdoors but also as a "legitimate" reason to keep guns in my life. Unfortunately, applying for licenses and buying ammunition put me on the radar of the National Rifle Association, which pestered me endlessly to join. By this time, the NRA had transformed itself from the marksmanship-and-safety organization of my youth into what sometimes seemed like the armed wing of the Republican Party, bent on stirring up class resentment against those who, in the words of the NRA monthly magazine, *America's 1st Freedom,* "sip tea and nibble biscuits while musing about how to restrict the rest of us." The NRA wasn't my only problem. The diatribes of the gun-rights movement often came wrapped in appeals to limit government, deport immigrants, cut taxes, and elect conservatives—everything I opposed. I felt like the child of a bitter divorce with allegiance to both parents.

I was a gun guy, but I didn't belong to gun culture, and I didn't know much about how guns fit into people's lives. Did the gigantic megaphone of the NRA reflect gun culture? Distort it? Create it? I hadn't a clue.

The winter the Obamas moved into the White House seemed a good time to start learning. Gun-owning America had reacted to the prospect of an Obama presidency by buying up guns and stockpiling ammunition in a panic. Prodded endlessly by the NRA, the gun industry, and the gun press, gun owners had come to believe that confiscation was nigh. Along with all the other divisions the United States suffered, America seemed to be cleaving along the gun-guy fault. And there I was, straddling it.

To begin figuring out my fellow gun guys, I read a tower of books on the history of American gun culture, mined FBI crime data for trends, ground through books arguing for more and less gun control, perused studies on the dangers and benefits of gun ownership, and hung out on countless gun-guy websites. At a certain point, though, I realized what I was avoiding. The overwhelming majority of gun owners didn't show up in crime statistics, weren't players in gun policy, didn't hang out on the Internet's vitriolic gun forums, and didn't physically threaten anybody. A lot of assumptions were made about gun people—by the NRA and Fox News on one side and by the editorial board of *The New York Times* and a slew of Democratic politicians on the other. What nobody seemed to be doing was *listening* to gun people—asking the questions that most puzzled me about myself: Why do we like these things? Why do they move us so deeply?

I didn't want to rewrite the history of America's unique relationship with guns that other writers had plumbed so thoroughly. Nor did I wish to wallow in the minutiae of gun control and formulate my own policy proposals. I was after something more visceral: the essential quality that, like anchovies on pizza, impassioned some people and disgusted others. Guns were beyond reason; either you loved them or hated them. But why? And why, as surely as the shopping network came with basic cable, did a fondness for guns come with political conservatism?

Gun owners were, in any case, almost half of our population—worth knowing because their enthusiasm for firearms said something about us as a people, worth listening to because nothing lasting or decent could happen in gun policy without them.

If I was going to get to know my fellow gun owners, I would have to approach them one by one, at ranges and gun shows, at contests and auctions, in the woods and in garages. A look in the mirror, though, told me that it wouldn't be easy. A stoop-shouldered, bald-headed, middle-aged Jew in pleated pants and glasses, I looked like a card-carrying biscuit nibbler. So I held my nose and joined the NRA, which brought me not only subscriptions to its monthly magazines, *American Rifleman* and *America's 1st Freedom,* but also a snappy blue-and-gold NRA cap and lapel pin—excellent camouflage.

The best place to observe social behavior is in a species' natural habitat, so one blazing autumn morning, I went looking for a gun range.

1. BARBIE FOR MEN

I *am* compensating. If I could kill stuff with my dick from 200 yards I would not need a firearm, would I?

−Posted by Zanther on AR15.com

A gun range is an odd place. It's communal, in that it gathers people to engage in a shared activity, but it's solitary, because when you're behind a gun, you're on your own. The practice is sort of like hitting a bucket of golf balls on a driving range, except that instead of whooshing balls onto a quiet greensward while chatting with people waiting their turn, you're blasting copper-jacketed bullets downrange at 2,900 feet per second, wrapped in hearing protectors and a cocoon of ear-shattering noise. I always preferred to do my shooting deep in the woods or out in the desert, where I didn't have to listen to anybody's gunfire but my own.

But I had to start my gun-guy walkabout somewhere, so I drove down to the Family Shooting Center, a private gun range within Cherry Creek State Park, about an hour south of my house in suburban Denver. I found my way around a man-made pond and parked in front of a chain-link fence. No doubt I was at the right place. From beyond the fence came a racket like the Battle of Fallujah.

At the end of a long chain-link corridor stood a tall range officer in an orange vest and earmuffs, hands on hips and feet slightly spread—that same all-business, slightly forbidding stance that Hank Hilliard had assumed on Camp Sunapee's range. On his vest, one button read, BLESSED BE THE INFIDELS, FOR THEY SHALL ENJOY FREEDOM, ART AND MUSIC. Another said simply, MOLON LABE.

"What's that?" I asked, shouting to be heard through our hearing protectors and above the gunshots.

"You know your history?"

"Some."

"Battle of Thermopylae?"

"No."

"Four-eighty B.C.: Xerxes of Persia asked Leonidas I, king of the Spartans, to lay down his spear. Leonidas said, *'Molon labe.'* 'Come and take it.' You hear what I'm telling you?" He stared into my eyes for a long moment. I blinked. He said, "Please take firing position four."

I took my place at a wooden shooting bench and unpacked my rifle, a .30-40 Krag-Jørgensen made in 1900 for the Spanish–American War. I'd bought it twenty years earlier at a Montana gun show for $115, when I was broke and needed something to shoot at deer and antelope. I'd figured that someday I'd be financially solvent beyond my wildest dreams. That's when I'd buy myself a proper hunting rifle. But the Krag fit me well and shot so straight that I'd never needed to trade up. Showing up at hunts with a 110-year-old rifle made me something of an oddball. But everybody who liked guns grooved on their longevity; it was hard to think of another consumer product that, a century after its manufacture, was as functional as on the day it was made. I got points, too, for hunting with plain iron sights instead of a scope.

I stepped up to position number 4 and, like a boy in the junior high gym shower, furtively looked over the other guys' equipment. Out of six men shooting—two old guys like me and four in their thirties or younger—I was the only one with a traditional wooden rifle. Everybody else was shooting a black AR-15—the civilian version of the military's M16. I might as well have been on the range at Fort Benning.

I'd seen these guns creeping into stores and ranges and had never understood the attraction. With their plastic stocks and high-tech man-killer look, they lacked the elegance of traditional firearms. The most common reason that people bought guns was for protection against crime, but shotguns and handguns were best for close-order shooting. The second most common reason was target shooting, like here at Cherry Creek. Hunting came third, but rarely with the AR-15. Most states didn't allow the taking of deer with the tiny .223 bullet fired by the basic AR.

The AR was excellent at what it was designed for: killing people at medium range on the battlefield, which was not something the average retail gun buyer needed to do. Yet more and more rack space in gun stores seemed to be given over to AR-15s, and at this range on this day, they had taken over completely.

At the bench next to mine, a cherubic young man with a round, close-cropped head and plump fingers held an all-black rifle that looked ready for SEAL Team Six. Everything that was wood on my rifle was plastic on his. Instead of a horizontal stock, the gun had a vertical foregrip, as on a tommy gun. A rubber-encased telescopic scope the size of a salami lay along the top. Wired-up cylinders of some kind encrusted the barrel. The young man slapped in a banana-shaped magazine and, peering through the scope, fired four slow shots at a bull's-eye a hundred yards off. Then he touched a button on the side of the gun, and the foregrip split into a bipod, which he rested on the bench to continue his deliberate firing. The man's sweet, plump-cheeked baby face contrasted so thoroughly with the rifle's flamboyant lethality that I almost laughed aloud. Instead, when he paused to reload, I broke gun-range protocol and invaded his space. "Will you forgive an ignorant question?" I asked. "I mean, look at the old iron I shoot. What do you use that gun for?"

"This!" he said with a laugh. "Shooting!"

"You're, uh, not thinking you're going to *need* it or anything . . ."

He laughed. "Oh, no. I know what you mean. No. None of that. I just like it. And it's a little piece of history, what our boys are using in the Gee Wot."

"In the *what*?"

He laughed again. "The GWOT. The Global War on Terror. It's what they call the whole thing—Iraq, Afghanistan, all the shit we don't hear about everyplace else. You ever shot one of these?"

"No."

"Then come on!" He laid the rifle on the bench and gestured me over. I hesitated. Shooting another man's gun was like dancing with his wife. Some guys got offended if you asked, yet here he was offering it up unbidden.

"Here's the deal," he said excitedly, licking his lips like a five-year-old showing off his favorite toy truck. "The bullet's only sixty-four grains, but it goes superfast." He held up a cartridge much smaller and pointier than mine—a beer bottle, say, to my wine bottles. The sixty-four-grain—four-gram—bullet looked like the tip of a ballpoint pen. The kid ran his finger along the black plastic buttstock of the rifle. "In here's a big-ass spring. It takes up most of the recoil. And feel how light." I picked it up. It felt like a BB gun, especially after the Krag. "You starting to get the attraction? Now look through that." I put my eye to the scope, and the target trembled on the tip of my nose. "That's an ACOG," he said. "It costs more than the rifle, to tell you the truth. It's what every guy in Iraq and Afghanistan who can afford one is using."

I lifted my face from the scope. "They have to buy it?"

"Not the rifle. The Army gives them a stripped-down rifle with iron sights. But everybody uses optics. Some get them issued to them, but most bring them with them, or have their parents send them over."

It hadn't occurred to me that the military allowed soldiers to modify their rifles. Talk about a captive market: What mother wouldn't sell a kidney to send her son a twelve-hundred-dollar rifle scope that might keep him alive?

"Not like I've been over there or anything," the young man was saying. "I see them on TV. Look at the guns next time you're watching the news. Everybody uses optics. Go ahead. Fire a few."

My trigger hand gripped what felt like a pistol, while my left hand clutched the vertical foregrip. I suppose it was more ergonomic than the Krag. To grip the Krag, I had to tilt both hands. On this genetically modified organism of a gun, both fists stood straight up, as though I were boxing. It fit nicely into my shoulder, too, and my eye fell naturally into position behind the scope. I put the crosshairs on the chest of the silhouette target and squeezed.

There was a light bump against my shoulder and an odd sensation of the rifle's insides sliding around as the floating parts compressed the big spring and soaked up the recoil. My own rifle punched me like a prizefighter, and to fire a second shot, I had to throw a heavy bolt lever up and back, forward and down. With this gun, I barely brushed the trigger, as gently as flicking crumbs off a tablecloth. *Bam!* And a third flick—*Bam!*

I shot four times more, as fast as I could move my finger— *Bambambambam*—feeling little more kick than I would from a garden hose. An AR-15 is semi-automatic, meaning it fires one shot for every touch of the trigger, while the M16—and other true "assault rifles"— can fire continuously, like a machine gun. The distinction seemed pretty meaningless, though—this AR could rock and roll faster than I could properly aim.

"How many shots do I have?"

"The magazine holds thirty, but, uh, ammo's kinda expensive."

Understood. This roly-poly, diffident youth was the perfect gentleman: I could dance with his wife, but I couldn't use his wallet to buy her jewelry.

One of the devices clamped to the barrel was a powerful flashlight whose on/off switch lay precisely where my left thumb met the foregrip. It nudged on and off as gently as the trigger. I asked about the other cylinder.

"Look through the scope," the kid said. "Now press that button with your left index finger." I hadn't noticed the other button. When I pressed it, a red dot appeared a hundred yards away, on the chest of the silhouette target. "Laser," he said. "Pretty cool, right? Wherever that light is, that's where your bullet will go. The laser, the ACOG; I got this one set up like they had them in *Transformers*."

I could see through the scope that my first three shots—the ones I'd taken a second to aim—had landed in a group about an inch and a half across on the silhouette's shoulder—a bit high and to the right, but good shooting, considering I'd never fired an AR.

The young man was beaming like a soccer dad as I handed it back. "It's something, ain't it?"

I had to admit that it was. It was effortless, like shooting a ray gun. If ARs made everybody as good a shot as the kid's made me, it was easy to see why they were popular. Imagine a guitar that made you play like Eric Clapton.

"I have to ask, though. What's a rifle like that cost?"

He looked sheepish. "Altogether, I probably have in it about . . ." He trailed off in a mumble.

"Excuse me?"

"Thirty-five hundred dollars, more or less." He uttered a short laugh, as though he'd been Heimliched.

"May I ask what you do for work?"

"I work for a company that manages home-owner agreements."

"Must pay well."

He shrugged, and his gaze flitted about, looking for someplace to fall. "Well, I usually only get about eight hours a week."

"How do you live on that?"

He paused, looking at his shoes. "I live with my parents," he said quietly.

"You . . ." And I stopped myself, tamping down the urge to go all Hugh Beaumont on him, to preach the idiocy of throwing money at a pricey toy when he couldn't afford an apartment. The kid was another man's son; to me, he was a shooting mentor.

I thanked him and punished myself for a while shooting my antique, which, after the AR-15, felt as awkward as a piece of furniture. I pressed cartridges one by one into the five-shot magazine while the men

around me slapped in magazine after magazine and popped off shots—
Bambambambambambambam—showering the cement floor with tin-
kling brass casings. At my next birthday, I would turn half the age of my
rifle. Working its bolt made me feel old, but not as old as when I realized
that an AR-15 was, to a twentysomething, "a piece of history"—a history
stretching all the way back to the advent of the GWOT, on September 11,
2001, or perhaps even to the dim prehistoric reaches of the Vietnam War.

The kid was right about one thing. I'd become familiar with the
AR-15—without even knowing it—from watching the news on Afghanistan and Iraq. On TV and in the paper, the AR's military version was
ubiquitous, gripped in the hands of every soldier and Marine, in a million dolled-up configurations. Whatever else the Gee Wot was achieving,
it was producing a high-budget, twenty-four-hour advertisement for the
AR-15.

Which, as I thought about it, seemed pretty weird. The M16 was not
a hot consumer item during the Vietnam War, nor was the M1 Garand
during the Second World War. The Vietnam-era draft didn't inspire dab-
bling; young men didn't know when they'd be handed one of those black
rifles for real. And World War II wasn't televised. It turned out that com-
bining a volunteer army with twenty-four-hour cable-news war coverage
was, inadvertently, a potent strategy for marketing firearms.

The kid was loading up the trunk of his teal Chevy Cavalier as I left
the range. On the bumper, a McCain-Palin sticker had been pruned, the
McCain half scissored off. I invited him to lunch, and he suggested I follow him to a nearby Burger King.

As we waited in line, I asked about his bumper sticker. "I wrote in
Palin. I'm not sure why I didn't trust McCain."

"Obama?"

He snorted. "I have a conscience."

It was a strange and depressing lunch. I had to keep reminding myself
that he was less than half my age. He was twenty-four—I call him "the
kid" because of his full pink cheeks and because he asked me not to use
his name—but he talked like a washed-up man of seventy, looking back
wistfully on a life of screwups, cop-outs, and missed opportunities.

His boyhood dream of becoming a pilot, for example, was already
doused. He had gotten into home-computer flight simulators and, at fif-

teen years old, successfully "piloted" a real-time—six-hour—flight from Anchorage to Seattle that required him to monitor fuel consumption, avoid bad weather, and cope with unexpected mechanical problems. He'd joined Air Force Junior ROTC in high school and enjoyed wearing the uniform every Tuesday. September 11, 2001, was a Tuesday. But instead of sharing with his JROTC buddies a surge of pride in the uniform and martial fury, he became so weepy and trembly that he had to ask the school to call his mother. He spent the rest of the day in bed.

The Air Force isn't the thing anyway, his cousin Jimmy told him. They didn't have enough pilot slots. *Let's go Army and fly Black Hawks!* The Army, embroiled in two wars, would have been happy to have them—not as pilots, because they weren't college grads, but as the true hot dogs on a combat chopper: crew chiefs. They could have stood in back, manned the door gun, and managed everything going on behind the cockpit. The Army would have given a rank for every year of JROTC, so the kid could have gone in as an E-3. Hell, yes, Jimmy had said, it'll be awesome. And Jimmy had signed up, shipped out, and done three tours downrange.

"I chickened out," the kid told me listlessly, pawing damp fries from their waxed-paper bag. "Makes me feel I missed out."

I wanted to take him in my lap, chuck him under the chin, and tell him to buck up. "It's not for everyone," I said. "Are you still interested in flying?" His voice went flat as he told of enrolling at a commuter college in Denver to study aviation. Each semester had cost two thousand dollars in tuition and twice that again for flying lessons. His grades weren't good enough to win him scholarships, so after three semesters he'd found himself five thousand dollars in debt, with no clear prospect of digging out. He'd said the hell with it and dropped out. And there went his dream of becoming a pilot.

"So now what?"

"I worked at a Burger King for a while, and as a contractor for Dell, until that ran out. I'm taking courses at the community college. In IT. You know." The kid balled up his sandwich wrapping and licked a tomato seed off his ring finger. The conversation was spiraling toward dark matter. To wrench us up, I asked about the AR.

"Well," he said, sitting up straight again, animated. "Honestly, I really got into firearms because of computer games. I play the *Battlefield* series. You know that one? *CounterStrike* really got me into it." He talked for a long time about the shooter games he liked—*Battlefield 1942, Armed Assault II,* and *Call of Duty 4.* Each was a point-of-view Internet fight game, in which the player was not merely controlling a digital proxy but was *there*. Human players operated every other soldier on the screen, he explained; that was the miracle of it. He was playing against real people, all over the world, each seeing the battlefield from a different perspective. Kids' gun fantasy had morphed from Mattel Shootin' Shell cap guns to *Call of Duty,* but otherwise this kid was a lot like my childhood self.

It was *Call of Duty 4* that got him interested in the AR-15. As he accumulated points, he earned the right to use and modify progressively deadlier weapons. Descriptions of ACOGs, lasers, and other gadgets appeared on the screen for him to choose. The descriptions were ads, really, extolling the virtues of brand-name devices.

Video games may have explained why the AR-15 was the hope of a firearms industry worried about its aging customer base. My nephew, for example, who had lived his entire life within a few blocks of his Greenwich Village birthplace and had less experience with guns than almost anybody, knew AR-15 terminology—ACOGs, Magpuls, etc.—better than I did because he played video games. He didn't transfer his virtual enthusiasm to a real AR-15 the way the kid in Denver did, but in one of its endless gun-market surveys, the National Shooting Sports Foundation found that lots of young people apparently had. While gun guys overall showed up in the gun-industry surveys as mostly over forty, rural, middling educated, and white, the people who shot AR-15s tended to be younger, more urban, better educated, and more racially diverse. In other words, they looked more like where America was going than where it had been.

The NSSF found that not only were AR shooters younger and more diverse, they also took their guns out to the range and shot them more often than owners of other guns did. They'd made the AR-15's .223 cartridge the biggest-selling caliber of rifle ammunition. AR shooters could be counted on to buy, with real dollars, in real life, the endless stream of parts and accessories that they earned playing *Call of Duty 4* in cyberspace. And AR shooters did the thing the industry most depended on: They *evangelized the pleasures of shooting,* just as the kid had done when he held out his rifle for me to try.

On his twenty-first birthday, the kid had been home alone, bored. Federal law prevented gun stores from selling handguns to anyone younger than twenty-one, and this gave the kid an inspiration. "I think to myself, *I have a wad of cash. I want a gun.*" He drove to a nearby gun store and, after a fifteen-minute computerized background check, walked out with a .40-caliber Smith & Wesson Sigma pistol. "It was impulsive," he said. "I didn't do any research. I just saw it, liked it, and bought it." Four months later, he sold the pistol at a gun show for fifty dollars less than he'd paid for it and went to a pawnshop to buy a nine-millimeter Hi-Point 995 carbine—another impulse buy, he said, because it was "cool looking." Eric Harris had thought so, too; he wrote that it looked like the gun in the video game *Doom,* right before he fired ninety-six shots from one at Columbine High School.

"Did the video games have anything to do with your decision to buy a real gun?" I asked.

"Everything!" he said. "I wanted to take the next step—feel the recoil and pull the trigger." He cocked his head, studied me for a moment, and seemed to realize that it sounded a little odd. He dropped his voice a manly octave. "In a world of stuff you throw away, firearms are something you can hand down for generations, right?"

The day after he bought the Hi-Point carbine, he went to another pawnshop and bought a Springfield XD pistol, also in nine-millimeter; it seemed cool to own two guns of the same caliber. "I still wasn't telling my parents I had these." He giggled and sipped his Sprite. "I kept them in my closet."

He was home alone again one day, bored, playing with the pistol in his bedroom. He was dry-firing, pulling the trigger on an empty chamber, which normally is a fine way to practice a trigger pull. With a loaded magazine in the gun, though, it's textbook stupid. He pulled the trigger and racked the slide to recock the gun. Alas, racking the slide scooped a cartridge from the magazine into the chamber. He pulled the trigger again.

"It took me about ten seconds to realize what had happened," he said. "I was completely deaf, but I could smell the powder. I'm running around in a total panic, looking for the bullet. Then I stop, take a deep breath. I go upstairs and I can see the drywall punched out of the floor of my parents' dressing room. I go back downstairs, and I can see that it's gone through a vent in my ceiling, missing the ceiling fan by this much. Ultimately, it lodged in a wall stud." He laughed and sucked at the ice at the bottom of his Sprite. "I explained to my dad when he got home. I told him, 'I just had a negligent discharge. This is for you—it's a pistol, and a bag with forty-nine rounds.' He was like 'Oh, okay, thank you.' He didn't show any emotion. That was it. My mom still doesn't know." His face burned scarlet; he looked like a pomegranate. Equally sodden with gun fantasy as a kid, I might have made a similar mistake—but for my rigorous range time with Hank Hilliard.

"And the AR-15?"

He sighed, relieved to be back on that subject. "I started building that after getting into the game *America's Army,* which is released by the Army for recruiting purposes. I liked it. You've got to go through basic training, marksmanship, and an obstacle course before you can actually play." In that game, he'd used the shortened, commando version of the M16— the M4. And once again, he'd set down the gaming console and gone to the gun store—this time, to buy a real AR-15. In his telling of the story, he was switching back and forth from virtual gun to real gun so quickly that I had trouble keeping track. I wondered if he sometimes had the same problem.

Pushing aside the detritus of our lunch, he told of the parts and accessories he had swapped on and off of his AR-15 in the year since he'd bought it. He kept lapsing into such phrases as "At that point I got the new railed hand-guard from LaRue Tactical, which made me replace the gas block." I found the details hard to follow. In my experience, about the only things you could change on a rifle were the sights and the sling that hung it from your shoulder. But I gathered that he had changed something on the rifle about every four days since he bought it, the way I'd swapped derailleurs and hubs on and off my ten-speed bike back in the seventies. "I like the shooting," he said. "I like shooting as cleanly as possible. But I really like the engineering—the springs, the detents, the catches. I sometimes think, *Hmm, this piece hangs a bit,* or *This roller pin wobbles.* I like taking the whole gun apart in my room. Whenever I shoot, I roll out my cleaning mat and take it all down. I take the bolt apart every time, cut off small pieces of patch, and run them through the firing-pin channel." The kid kept talking, losing himself in the arcana of direct impingement and chamber pressure, recoil spring and trigger pack. His eyes were sparkling. The light on his face had grown rosy, and I realized we'd been sitting there for hours.

"Sounds like you really dig it," I said. "Have you thought about designing guns for a living?"

His eyes went flat. "I've thought about it," he said, his voice sliding back down the drain, "but I'm not very imaginative."

An app called Gun Store Finder on my iPod Touch directed me to two Denver stores, but one was boarded up and the other had become a nail salon. The afternoon was so crisp, and the sight of the aspens turning in the mountains was so lovely—great yellow brushstrokes across the pines—that I ended up driving all the way to Colorado Springs, ninety minutes out of Denver. They'd had snow already, and it lingered in the shadows thrown by trees. As I pulled into a slushy parking space at Specialty Sports & Supply, a black Lab stuck his head out the window of a huge Ford pickup and gave me a baleful stare, as though to ask, "What are *you* doing here?" He wasn't fooled a minute by my NRA cap.

Most gun stores in my experience were intimate, cluttered, invitingly musty little shops, the owner leaning on the counter, talking football or ballistics, while customers ambled freely among racks of used rifles. Specialty Sports & Supply, though, smelled like the future—a vast, airy big-box gun store with the fragrance of hand sanitizer.

All the rifles stood in racks behind counters, out of reach. Employees in matching blue vests leaned on the counters, waiting, under bright fluorescent lights. The only things customers could touch without permission were the nonlethal merchandise: clothes, cleaning kits, targets, beef jerky, and 5-Hour Energy Shots—which seemed about as appropriate to sell in a gun store as pints of Jack Daniel's. I'd once made the mistake of drinking an Energy Shot and spent a day ricocheting around the inside of my own skull.

When I visited stores, I always looked for guns from the early to mid-twentieth century. Besides the Krag (made in 1900), I had a Savage .32 pistol from 1907; Smith & Wesson revolvers in both .45 and .38, from 1917 and 1921; a 1920 Luger; a Chinese army Mauser rifle from 1934; a Hungarian Femaru pistol from 1937; and a Colt Detective Special made in 1956—the year I was born. Guns of that era were usually milled from solid steel rather than cast. They were knurled with an eye to artistry, and their stocks glowed with the kind of deeply grained woods no longer affordable to gunmakers. They evoked an era that I enjoyed thinking about, an era smelling of coal smoke and damp wool overcoats. And they usually fell into the sweet spot, price-wise, between modern guns and the genuine antiques of the nineteenth century and earlier. At Specialty Sports & Supply, alas, the racks of rich brown walnut stocks gave way within a few yards to vast ranks of coal-black plastic.

I stood at the counter waiting for one of the many clerks to wait on me. None did. Several looked at me and turned away. Finally I motioned to a blue-vested clerk with a pimpled, hatchet-shaped face and a red, high-fade haircut, and he walked over with a vaguely quizzical look. NRA cap or no,

I wasn't his typical customer. Too old, perhaps. Too urban. I introduced myself as a newcomer to the AR-15 and asked what he would recommend. He cocked an eyebrow, as though to say, *Seriously?* But he was polite.

Running a finger along a line of what looked to be identical rifles, he selected one, slid open the breech to ascertain that it was unloaded, and handed it over. Like the kid's, it was toy-gun light, almost hard to take seriously.

"How'd you pick this one?"

"Price, mostly, sir. That one's a DPMS." He looked at the tag dangling from the trigger guard. "Eight hundred dollars."

"How high do they go?"

"Oh, you can spend a lot, sir." He listed attributes—metal thickness, barrel twist, direct impingement versus piston, and competition triggers—none of which meant a thing to me. After he'd called me "sir" about five times, I asked whether he was ex-military. "Yes, sir. Marine Corps."

"Iraq?"

"Afghanistan."

"And you like these?"

"It's the only rifle I'd carry into combat, sir."

"But I'm not going into combat. Why would I want it?"

"Accuracy. Shootability. Compared to others, the ammo is cheap and available."

From over my shoulder came a rumbling whisper: "Don't do it, man."

I turned, and there stood Mutt and Jeff—one slight and compact in a short high school athletic jacket and pressed jeans, the other an unshaven giant in open galoshes, an earflaps hat, and a quilted, olive-green coat over coveralls. "Excuse me?" I said.

"Don't do it," the big man said quietly. "That eight hundred bucks is just the beginning. Once they got you, they got you."

"Yeah," said his wiry friend, gazing raptly into a case full of gun parts. "It's like heroin; the first taste is cheap."

The clerk laughed nervously. "Yeah, there's a lot of cool pieces-parts to buy, that's for sure."

The big guy snorted. "I bought that same rifle right here in this store back in September for eight hundred dollars," he said. "I've spent, what, another two thousand? Three?" His friend nodded. "I'm not saying I'm sorry. I've got a very cool rifle, and I love to shoot it. But you open *Guns & Ammo,* or just walk in here, and every month there's something else you gotta have."

"Like what?" I set the rifle on the counter, and the big guy launched into a techno-rap like the kid's.

"What'd I do?" he asked his friend, and began bending back carrot fingers. "First it was the Magpul stock; that was like a hundred and a half. Then the Command Arms grip—another forty. Then the forearm with the Picatinny rails, another hundred and something . . ."

"And then you're in real trouble," said the friend, getting down on one knee to peer into the case.

"Right. Because then it's all the stuff you can hang *on* the rails. Your lasers, your lights. There was that SureFire Universal WeaponLight I saw in *Blood Diamond* and had to have . . ."

"It fucking never stops."

"It fucking never stops. Scopes, trigger packs, sights. You get one on there, and the next week they come out with something even cooler, and you have to get that."

"Wait," I said. "You're saying you change the *stock*?" The stock is the body of a gun—on a traditional rifle, it's the wooden part. The idea of modifying a rifle that way seemed as bizarre as customizing a car by replacing the chassis.

"The stock, the barrel, the trigger, the grip—anything," the little guy said, his face still pressed to the glass. "I even changed the caliber on mine—bought a 6.5 Grendel upper so I could hunt deer. That cost me, shit, almost seven hundred before I was done." The red-haired clerk turned to the rifle on the counter and began snapping it apart. In about ten seconds, using no tools, he'd reduced it to six or seven components, a disassembled Lego toy.

"It's like that small-block Chevy," the clerk said. "You could take and use it for almost infinite applications by changing the intake manifold, the cylinder heads, the pistons, and the cranks."

As they chattered on, I couldn't tell whether they were describing an undiagnosed gear addiction or merely a reasonable affection for a device as versatile as a Leatherman pocket tool. Shooters could not only trick out ARs, they explained; they could turn them into entirely different guns. Swap this part and that part, and your basic .223-caliber AR-15 could shoot everything from a diminutive .22 rimfire up to a deer-killing 6.5 Grendel. Swap parts again and the AR could shoot the AK-47 round favored by every third-world army and guerrilla movement from Venezuela to the Congo. Swap again and it could shoot the .50 Beowulf, whose cartridge, proportioned like a ChapStick, had shattered Taliban Land

Rover engine blocks in Afghanistan. You could even buy parts to trans-
form an AR-15 into a shotgun or a crossbow. In one afternoon, you could
knock tin cans from a fence, hunt rabbits, kill a bear, and shoot skeet—all
with the same gun. It seemed both weird and revolutionary—like grocery
shopping in a Toyota Prius, then pushing a button on the dash and transforming it into a Dodge Ram to haul trash to the dump. It let a gun guy
do all his different kinds of shooting and always be handling the same
grip and stock. "Beware the man with one rifle," the red-haired clerk said,
quoting an old saying. "He probably knows how to shoot it."

The unshaven giant sighed loudly and gazed at the parts counter with
red-rimmed eyes. "You know what it is, right?" he said. "It's Barbie for
men."

2. CONDITION YELLOW

People who argue for the banning of arms ask for automatic rule by
the young, the strong, and the many, and that's the exact opposite of
a civilized society.

—Major L. Caudill, USMC (Ret.)

I knew one thing: as soon as anyone said you didn't need a gun, you'd
better take one along that worked.

—Raymond Chandler, *Farewell My Lovely*, 1940

Back home, I kept replaying that quizzical look from the clerk at Specialty Sports & Supply. My NRA cap clearly was not the perfect camouflage. Slapping it over my pointy bald head was likely to camouflage me at gun venues in Arizona and Kentucky about as effectively as sticking a sprig of parsley on a Panzer. I was likely to get frozen out, if not run off the property with a shotgun, as I ambled around asking people about their gun lives.

Clicking around the gun-guy websites one day, I blundered into a conversation about something called "open carry"—the practice of wearing a pistol in plain sight. In almost all states, no permit was needed to carry a gun that was holstered and visible. It took me awhile to get my head around that, but once I did, it seemed a spectacular solution to my problem.

The thinking, which went back to the Old West, was that if you could see a man's gun, he had less chance of doing mischief with it. Open carry was the new front in the nation's perpetual war over gun rights. Activists were holding armed picnics, video-recording encounters with police

("Hey, bud, what's with the gun?" *"I know my rights!"*), and wearing guns openly to Starbucks in hopes of being refused service or, better still, arrested. (Starbucks refused to take the bait, serving the gun toters with a smile.) A few gun wearers had even shown up outside of rallies in New Hampshire and Arizona attended by President Obama. If they'd hoped to martyr themselves and file false-arrest lawsuits, they were disappointed: The Secret Service, knowing perfectly well that open carry was legal, left them alone.

Mike Stollenwerk, the retired Army lieutenant colonel who ran OpenCarry.org—"A Right Unexercised is a Right Lost!"—told me when I called him that he thought displaying a gun at a presidential event was for "Tea Party nutties." He wanted more people showing guns not at political events but in supermarkets and at kids' soccer games, because "we want everybody to have that right." Wearing guns openly so that you could wear guns openly sounded to me like the old Firesign Theatre joke about the mural depicting the historic struggle of the people to finish the mural. Open carry was already legal almost everywhere. But Stollenwerk said the movement was more about changing culture than about changing the law. "We're trying to normalize gun ownership by openly carrying properly holstered handguns in daily life," he said. *Good luck with that,* I thought. My guess was that Stollenwerk's strategy would backfire—that, instead of acclimating people, the open-carry movement would frighten them, and they would eventually ask their legislators to put a stop to it.[*]

Regardless of what it did for the gun-rights movement, open carry, I figured, could be the answer to my camouflage problem. NRA caps were nice, but nothing said "gun guy" like a gun. A loaded revolver on my hip would make my bona fides beyond question. I took from the safe the biggest, most ostentatious handgun I owned—a 1917 Smith & Wesson .45 revolver—slid it into its holster, hung it on my belt, and checked my look in the mirror. Unironed blue oxford shirt, thrift-store wool pants, crewneck sweater with snowflakes, and an antique Army pistol the size of a trumpet. The muzzle almost reached my knee.

Colorado law may have been fine with me walking around with a hogleg on my hip, but I answered to a higher authority: Margaret. We had been married since 1987, and she was a boy's pal—willing to camp in the snow, hitchhike across Tanzania, and swim naked at inappropriate places and times. She was devoid of material cravings, could hold her liquor, and

---

[*] California's did, in October 2011.

deployed her brain to devastating conversational effect. She was, above all, as willing as I was to risk a tenuous fortune on a harebrained scheme. I couldn't have asked for a more supportive partner—as long as my proposals weren't extravagantly stupid or potentially catastrophic. Strutting about displaying a loaded gun, I worried, might qualify.

It's safe to say that my gun thing was not the quality that Margaret found most attractive in me. Born of deep peacenik, Northern California stock, she had an instinctive aversion to firearms. She was willing to shoot with me on occasion and even hunt, but the less she had to see and acknowledge my guns, the better. Also, we lived in Boulder, a university town so achingly liberal that its city council once argued for three days over whether people were "owners" or "guardians" of their pets. (Guardians won.) The thought of me strolling around Boulder with a loaded handgun as plumage did not go over well with Her Majesty.

"For Christ's sake," she said as I headed for the door, strapped.

"Gotta try it," I said.

"Don't get killed. Don't get arrested. Don't cause a riot."

"Keep your phone on in case I need bail money."

I rode my bike first to Home Depot, a manly place where I figured my gun was least likely to scatter people in panic. I removed my coat, draped it over my left arm to make my right side completely visible, and strode through every aisle: tools, electrical, housewares, plumbing. Bracing to be tackled by the burly guys in lumber, I got no reaction at all. People walked by me, chatting to each other, paying no mind. Maybe the big leather holster looked too much like a carpenter's belt. After twenty uneventful minutes, I pedaled over to Target, which was full of women and children, and got the same nonreaction. I watched people's faces. If they even noticed the enormous pistol hitched over my thigh, they didn't let on. It was getting a little frustrating. I planted myself in front of a uniformed security guard by the cash registers and fumbled around in the bargain bins. He had to have seen the gun, but he said nothing. Apparently a balding, middle-aged man in scratchy pants and glasses rummaging through Post-it notes and leftover Halloween decorations with a tired old gun on his hip was not a particularly threatening sight. Maybe he figured I was some kind of cop or a ranger from the city's vast open-space parks system.

I tried the Apple Store next, where young clerks in rectangular-framed glasses and identical blue T-shirts stood right beside me as I played with an iPad for half an hour. It wasn't possible that they didn't see the big handgun. My guess is that it simply didn't interest them. A World War I revolver is pretty dull technology compared with a touch-screen device running a 1GHz A4 chip and 802.11a/b/g/n Wi-Fi.

Finally, I steeled myself for the toughest test of the day: Whole Foods. If I couldn't get a rise out of that crowd, I might need to try a rifle on my back. I drifted slowly through the entire store, from the six-dollar pints of açai berries to the salmon-and-scallop sausages, and reached high—gun hip facing flamboyantly outward—for a bag of muesli. I sat for half an hour on a high stool sipping an Odwalla Mango Tango Smoothie, gun hip out. Men in bicycle-racing Lycra, women in yoga pants, children with flickering lights on their shoes came and went. I watched their eyes. If anybody noticed the gun, I missed it. Nobody said anything, or stared, or alerted store management. I felt like a ghost. Perhaps their eyes saw the pistol but their brains discounted it: *This is Boulder; that can't be a gun.*

Fed up, I headed home to ponder the odd results. On the way, I stopped at a gritty little Mexican grocery to buy some tortillas and *crema*. As I locked my bike, a chubby boy ran up and asked, in breathless Spanish, if my gun was real. I assured him it was. Inside the store, everybody swiveled toward the scrawny gringo with the gun. They peered at it, whispered to each other, took their children by the hand. I tried to relax, breathing in the mingled aromas of meat, onions, and votive candles that constitute the Mexican national fragrance. But I couldn't relax any more than they could. *"¿Por qué la pistola?"* a man in line for the register finally asked. *"¿Por qué no?"* I answered. He shrugged and turned away, shaking his head—not as if I was dangerous, but more to say, *gabacho* fool.

Maybe the Hispanics in the grocery were simply more candid than the Anglo Boulderites, and more socially relaxed. Maybe they figured I was an agent of *la migra*. Or maybe they tuned in to the handgun because in Mexico almost nobody gets a license to own one, let alone wear one.

I did not repeat the experiment. I don't know how many Whole Foods shoppers had started down the overpriced-cheese aisle, only to spot the gun and reverse course toward the overpriced tea, but I'd made people in at least one store anxious. Wearing a visible gun made me feel obnoxious.

To say nothing of unsafe. The idea that wearing a gun in plain view was a smart precaution now felt completely crazy. I'd worried the whole time that someone would knock me on the back of the head and steal it, or that a nutcase would challenge me to a draw. And that was in genteel, urbane Boulder. I couldn't imagine carrying openly in places like Phoenix or Detroit.

Which brought me, inevitably, to the place where, all along, I'd secretly hoped to arrive: concealed carry.

Gun guys don't talk about it much, because we don't want to seem weird, but a huge part of the attraction of guns is the sensual pleasure of handling them, whether shooting them or not. They are exquisitely designed and beautifully made, like clocks or cameras. To manipulate a gun's moving parts—its "action"—is deeply satisfying to hand and ear. Guys like machines, and guns are machines elevated to high, lethal art.

Most of us, though, seldom enjoy the pleasure of handling them—perhaps only when we take them from the safe for hunting season, plus a few sessions of target practice. The rest of the time, we read about them, think about them, and watch movies full of them. But we don't handle them. Imagine a musician who got to touch a guitar for one week a year. Short of joining a police department, shipping out to a combat zone with the Marines, or being willing to carry openly, about the only way to live the quotidian gun life was to go through the trouble of getting licensed to carry one concealed.

For most of American history, that was hard to do. Laws requiring a license to carry a concealed weapon go back to the early nineteenth century in places like New York City. And right up to the end of the twentieth century, almost every jurisdiction in the country made people prove a need for carrying a hidden gun. Merchants in rough neighborhoods and the well-connected could usually manage that; everybody else went unarmed or carried illegally.

Then came the *Miami Vice* days of the mid-1980s. The crack cocaine epidemic was heating up, and crime was on the rise. Miami was the worst of the worst—which is why the era's emblematic hyperviolent cop show was set there. Most places ravaged by gun violence reacted by passing increasingly strict gun laws, on the theory that making it harder for law-abiding residents to get guns would make it harder for criminals, too. Florida, though—suffering a murder rate almost half again higher than the national average—went the other way. Bad guys would always be able to get guns, the legislators figured, so law-abiding citizens should have the means to defend themselves.

In 1987, Florida created a state agency to issue carry permits to any adult who wanted one, provided there was no good reason to deny it. The Florida law was nicknamed "shall issue"—as in, state officials shall issue the permit and not apply their own discretion. I was living in Atlanta at the time and sneered at the bumpkins to the south. *Oh, that's a good idea,* I thought. *Let's put more guns in circulation. That'll stop the killing.* There was a whiff of Wild West machismo to Florida's move, like handing out guns to a posse. I predicted that every Florida fender bender would turn into a gunfight.

The majority of Americans, though, saw it differently. Or, perhaps more accurately, a majority of the people who cared one way or the other about it saw it differently and made a lot of noise. From Maine to Arizona, they clamored for the right to defend themselves. Or maybe they clamored for an opportunity to live the gun life, to handle a gun every day. Whatever the case, once gun guys heard about what Florida had done, they asked their legislatures to follow suit. And, one after another, they did.

It was a big moment in the history of gun politics. The gun-rights movement had won just about every battle it had engaged since coalescing in the late 1960s, but most had been defensive battles against new gun-control laws. Reversing the burden of proof on carry permits *expanded* gun rights. For the first time, the movement was on offense.

By the time I was embarrassing myself by carrying a blunderbuss down the aisles of Whole Foods, thirty-seven states had gone shall-issue—including my home state of Colorado. Many recognized the permits of other states. So I had an alternative to displaying my firepower. I could carry discreetly and show the gun only when I needed to—like flashing a Masonic pin or giving the secret handshake.

I still faced, of course, the Margaret hurdle. She never said no to anything, but she had infinite power to make me feel like an idiot and a weenie. She would surely do so when I mentioned a carry permit. The responsibilities of literature, however, were great.

"You want to wear a concealed *gun,*" she said when I brought it up one night at dinner. Across the table, our sixteen-year-old daughter, Rosa, put down her fork and said, "Dad."

I explained that I needed to look like a gun guy. I explained that I needed to get into the gun-guy mind-set. I explained, and I explained. Margaret and Rosa looked at each other in a way that no woman ever looks at a man. It was a look that said, *We have to share the planet with men; let's make the best of it until we find a use for them.*

By this time it was no longer necessary to speculate, as I had in Atlanta, as to what kind of mayhem widespread concealed carry might unleash. We had two decades of experience demonstrating that the short answer was: None. The national murder rate had fallen to about half what it had been when Florida started the shall-issue revolution; rape, robbery, and aggravated assault had also fallen sharply. Not only were "bad guy" murders way down—those committed in the course of other felonies—but so were the kind of spur-of-the-moment shootings that turned law-abiding people into murderers. Depending on how you did the math, 1989 to 2010 may have seen the fastest and steepest drop in crime ever recorded in the United States. To ice the cake, most kinds of gun *accidents* had also decreased. Maybe the country had simply been lucky.

The theories as to why crime rates were falling ranged from data-conscious policing to stricter sentencing. The authors of *Freakonomics* went so far as to suggest that the drop in crime was a by-product of legalizing abortion in the 1970s: Fewer unwanted, underparented babies yielded fewer desperate young men. Whatever the cause, the decrease in crime had brought a new twist to gun politics.

Usually, the NRA and the gun business preferred to maintain the fiction that crime was out of control and everyone should own a gun for self-defense. But after the shall-issue revolution, they claimed credit for the drop in crime. Criminals were afraid to prey on people who might be armed, they argued, so more gun ownership meant less crime.

It was easy to argue that crime was falling everywhere, not just in shall-issue states, and falling faster in some restrictive states than in some shall-issue states. The back-and-forth over the effect of shall-issue laws demonstrated precisely why statistics are almost useless when debating gun policy; people read into identical data what they want to see. Few are going to be shaken off their fondness or antipathy for guns by a page of statistics.

This much, though, was beyond debate: Almost seven million people had obtained carry permits in the two dozen or so years since Florida had risen up, and when you ran the numbers, legal gun carriers committed murder at a quarter the rate of the general population.

A subset of the "more guns, less crime" debate erupted in 1995 over how often law-abiding citizens used guns to defend themselves. It was an important question, because if lawful defensive gun use happened often, that would support the movement to make carry permits easier to get. If it was rare, it would weaken the need for permissive carry. Everybody agreed that defensive gun use rarely ended in shots fired and usually involved nothing more than brandishing the gun or announcing, "I've got a gun." Beyond that, nobody agreed on anything.

Two prominent gun researchers squared off. In one corner was Gary Kleck, of Florida State University, a longtime critic of most gun-control laws. Relying on a collection of telephone and questionnaire surveys, he came up with a breathtaking 2.5 million defensive gun uses a year, or more than 6,800 a day. Across the ring from Kleck was Harvard's David Hemenway, who throughout his career had been as consistently anti-gun as Kleck was pro. Using the government's National Crime Victimization Survey, Hemenway came up with only 80,000 defensive gun uses a year.

I interviewed both men on the phone, and each predictably disparaged the other's work in the harshest terms, as though *no gentleman* would consider using the data the other had chosen. Their pissing match went on for years in academic journals. Each had his defenders. The NRA weighed in on Kleck's behalf, citing his 2.5 million number as proof that guns were important to public safety. The Brady Center to Prevent Gun Violence, the country's leading proponent of stricter gun laws, backed Hemenway's number as evidence that the utility of private gun ownership was over-rated. In 2004, the National Research Council stepped into the ring as referee and essentially called off the match. "Ultimately, the committee found no comfort in numbers: the existing surveys do not resolve the ongoing questions," it wrote.

I slogged through all the arguments, and what came through most clearly was that both sides had lost track of the obvious: Even Hemen-way's lower number was huge. "Only" 80,000 a year meant that 220 times a day, Americans were protecting themselves with firearms one way or another. This meant that eight times as many Americans were defend-ing themselves with guns every year as were being murdered with them.

It seemed crazy to me that guns could be used harmlessly so often with-out us ever hearing about it, until I considered what I would do if a thug threatened me on the street, I pulled my gun, and he ran away. Would I call the police? Only if I was in the mood for spending the rest of my evening answering questions—and perhaps being booked for assault, being held in a cell overnight, and losing my gun. More likely, I'd shut up. And even if I did report the incident, how likely is it that a reporter would find it newsworthy?

It's possible, of course, that in both surveys a lot of those who reported using their guns to stop a crime were inventing a story to make themselves feel cool or had brandished a gun needlessly at a panhandler or harmless bump in the night. But even if only an eighth of Hemenway's already "low" number were genuine life-or-death situations, guns were still quietly saving as many lives as, or more than, they were taking. For someone like me, who started out thinking widespread concealed carry was a bad idea, this was rattling.

In any case, my sneering at Florida had been misplaced: Shall-issue may not have caused crime to drop, but neither had it uncorked rivers of blood. And let's be honest—I found that a little thrilling. Because now I could get a concealed-carry permit of my own and start handling my gun every day without feeling as though I were contributing to a virulent social pathology.

Colorado required people who wanted a carry permit to get trained, but it left the details up to county sheriffs. Mine, a jovial and popular Democrat named Joe Pelle, required only proof of training by an "NRA-approved" instructor. Knowing how Boulder's pleasures tended toward qigong and Pilates, I expected to drive some distance to find a shooting school. So I was surprised to find in the phone book something called the Boulder Rifle Club, whose NRA-approved concealed-carry classes were booked an astonishing two months out. The number of carry permits Sheriff Pelle issued annually had risen eighteenfold in the previous decade. Nine hundred Boulderites applied every year. Maybe the aging hippies in Whole Foods hadn't blinked at my gun because they were packing themselves.

"There's Brazilian music tonight at the Laughing Goat," Margaret said one afternoon as we returned from yoga class. "Rosa and I are going." She snapped her fingers theatrically. "Oh, that's right. You have your *gun thing* tonight."

And off I slunk, to join the legion of the armed.

Boulder can be an uncomfortably high-tone place—wealthy and possessed of a higher concentration of advanced degrees than any town in America. The club turned out, though, to be down-home in the extreme: naught but a couple of ranges bulldozed from the sagebrush, and a cement-floored, cinder-block-walled "clubhouse" that was about as elegant as a boiler room. I was glad; this was what a shooting place was supposed to look like. Red school lockers lined one wall, and a lone flickering fluorescent tube gave the room a sickly middle-school pallor. The bulletin board carried ads for gunsmithing, taxidermy services, guns, and car insurance. Posters taped to the wall, I was relieved to see, were all about gun safety; nothing in the room was political—no NRA posters.

Three big thirtysomething guys dressed in identical black hoodies— hoods up—whispered and chuckled to each other like a band of Jawas en route to capture R2-D2. The rest of the students had already found seats at the cheap folding tables that would serve as desks: an elegantly dressed elderly gentleman, a middle-aged husband-and-wife team, and, at a table with an empty chair, one of Rosa's teachers from middle school.

"What are *you* doing here?" I asked, taking a seat.

His eyes didn't quite meet mine; he seemed mortified to have been recognized. "I've never owned a gun," he said softly. "I've hardly ever shot a gun."

"And now you want to *carry* a gun?"

"I don't know," he mumbled, and busied himself with the paper handouts.

The twelve-hour class was to be spread over four consecutive weeknights. This first night would be a general introduction to firearms and the social realities of carrying one. Night two: live firing. Night three: the legalities of self-defense. The last night would cover strategies for carrying.

Our teachers called us to order. Dick was a big man in his sixties with a boxer's nose and a Jersey City stevedore's accent. Judy was short and sturdy, also in her sixties, with cropped auburn hair and a wry, tough-gal way of talking out of one side of her mouth. From the moment they started making Obama and illegal-immigrant jokes, they made it clear that they were not of Boulder's dominant culture and that for the next four nights we were on their turf. They also made it clear that they were not bumpkins; Judy was a lawyer, and, while Dick didn't tell us his profession, he let drop that he lived in an expensive part of town.

So they weren't teaching this class for the money, which was a good thing. Assuming the other seven people were paying a hundred dollars for the class, as I was, the Rifle Club was taking in eight hundred dollars. Divided by twelve hours and two teachers, that was a little more than thirty-three dollars an hour to stand in a cold, dimly lit cinder-block room for four nights running—and the Rifle Club was no doubt taking

GIFT RECEIPT

Barnes & Noble Booksellers #2614
2100 North Snelling Ave
Roseville, MN 55113
651-639-9256

STR:2614 REG:005 TRN:7579 CSHR:Mikaela B

BARNES & NOBLE MEMBER   EXP: 01/26/2014

Mekong First Light
9780891418160   11
(1 @ B.RH)
                                 B.RH G

Thanks for shopping at
Barnes & Noble

101.32A   12/15/2013 06:10PM

within 14 days of purchase from a Barnes & Noble Booksellers store or Noble.com with the below exceptions:

A store credit for the purchase price will be issued (i) for purchases made by check less than 7 days prior to the date of return, (ii) when a gift receipt is presented within 60 days of purchase, (iii) for textbooks, or (iv) for products purchased at Barnes & Noble College bookstores that are listed for sale in the Barnes & Noble Booksellers inventory management system.

Opened music CDs/DVDs/audio books may not be returned, and can be exchanged only for the same title and only if defective. NOOKs purchased from other retailers or sellers are returnable only to the retailer or seller from which they are purchased, pursuant to such retailer's or seller's return policy. Magazines, newspapers, eBooks, digital downloads, and used books are not returnable or exchangeable. Defective NOOKs may be exchanged at the store in accordance with the applicable warranty.

Returns or exchanges will not be permitted (i) after 14 days or without receipt or (ii) for product not carried by Barnes & Noble or Barnes & Noble.com.

Policy on receipt may appear in two sections.

Return Policy

With a sales receipt or Barnes & Noble.com packing slip, a full refund in the original form of payment will be issued from any Barnes & Noble Booksellers store for returns of undamaged NOOKs, new and unread books, and unopened and undamaged music CDs, DVDs, and audio books made within 14 days of purchase from a Barnes & Noble a cut. Dick and Judy were here because they believed in the cause. They wanted to help more citizens get licensed to carry guns.

We went around the room introducing ourselves and saying why we'd come. Two said they weren't sure they wanted to carry; they mostly wanted to learn how to live safely alongside a firearm. I said the same. The other five all said they wanted to carry—but not when they were on city streets, only when they were out in the woods.

This was a new one for me; I'd always thought of concealed carry as an urban thing. I was accustomed to taking a gun along when car camping by the roadside, because one never knew who would be prowling the highways. And I'd carried a rifle or a shotgun in the Alaskan wilderness, because of the grizzlies. But Colorado trails were the last place I'd ever felt unsafe. Some people, apparently, are creeped out by the forest. "What happens if someone comes into camp to steal from us and takes my husband out?" the woman asked, and I wondered what she might have in a campsite that someone would be willing to kill for. A camp stove? A sleeping bag? Maybe she was imagining some sort of hideous *Deliverance* scenario. Which wasn't completely unreasonable, I supposed, just different from my own ideas about when a concealed gun might be necessary.

Dick started, in barely disguised boredom, describing the parts of a gun. "This is the trigger. This is the muzzle." I looked at my watch. Two and a half hours to go, with three more nights to come. For people teaching a skill on which lives could depend, Dick and Judy seemed lackadaisical, drifting through prescribed material, turning pages lazily, often losing their train of thought. It wasn't until two hours into the evening that Dick let drop why he seemed to care so little. "I don't have a carry permit," he told us casually. "I don't believe I should have to ask the government's permission to exercise my constitutional rights."

"So you carry illegally?" I asked.

He said he did not. He kept a gun in the armrest of his pickup truck and several in his home, but he didn't carry concealed, because he wanted neither to break the law nor approach the government on bended knee for permission to do something already guaranteed to him in the Constitution.

"But you think we should."

"Really, it's the only rational thing to do, given the way crime is these days."

"Out of control," Judy said. "Absolutely out of control."

Say what? Just that day I'd been looking at the figures on America's stunning drop in violent crime—one of the few pieces of unalloyed good news out of the previous two decades. I put up my hand, but the lights went out.

Judy started a video produced by the NRA. It opened on a suburban street of landscaped McMansions, "a neighborhood probably not very different from yours," according to the narrator, which made me wonder whether they showed this same film in, say, downtown Oakland. We watched as a white guy in chinos and a ski mask jimmied a window, let himself in, and, even though the woman in the negligee told him she had a gun and was calling the police, kicked open her bedroom door. She shot him twice. Then we watched another scenario: the same white guy in chinos and a ski mask threatening a businessman in the alley behind his store and suffering the same fate. I was convinced: Ban chinos.

"The way crime is simply out of control, you can't afford not to be prepared," Judy said. Dick handed around a color police photo of a man slashed open with a knife. Both Dick and Judy insisted repeatedly that crime was "out of control." I kept track; they used the words "out of control" nine times. The disconnect between their ironclad belief and the reality was so stark, it was disorienting.

This first night, then, wasn't about teaching us gun skills. It was about recruiting us into a culture animated by fear. Because until we bought in, the very idea of carrying a gun was ridiculous. I could understand the NRA and the firearms business wanting everybody convinced that crime was out of control; it was good for membership, and good for business. But Dick and Judy?

Maybe it wasn't enough for them to say they liked guns and wanted to carry one around and handle it every day. Maybe they felt they needed more justification. I was always looking for a reason to have guns in my life; why wouldn't they?

During a break, I asked Dick if he wasn't being a tad misanthropic. "I'm an optimist," he said, "but we live in a world of assholes."

The first night was not, for the record, worthless. They taught us the eminently sensible Five Cardinal Rules* and made us repeat them back aloud.

---

* The Five Cardinal Rules: 1. Treat all firearms as though they are loaded. 2. Never allow your muzzle to cross anything you are not willing to destroy and pay for. 3. Keep your finger off the trigger until your sights are on the target and you're ready to fire. 4. Be sure of your target and what is around and behind it. 5. Maintain control of your firearm.

And Judy kept returning to what may have been her best piece of advice: "You can't call back the bullet. You own everything the bullet touches. You have to ask yourself: 'Can I afford to pull the trigger?'" Dick chimed in, "You have to let anger issues go. If you have anger issues, perhaps concealed carry isn't for you." Judy stepped around him, put her fists on her hips, and fixed us with that gun-moll squint. "You need to decide whether you're willing to take a life. Make your decision in advance and review it often. Don't wait until you're in a situation. If you can't do it—if you can't take a life—*don't get a gun.*"

By eleven o'clock, my legs had frozen from the knees down from sitting with my feet on that frigid cement floor. As we stood, I expected to chat a bit with my fellow students. To my surprise, everybody put his head down and headed for his car in silence.

On the second night, we were to bring our guns in bags, unloaded. I selected my Colt Detective Special, a snub-nosed .38 revolver that had starred in every black-and-white cops-and-gangsters movie since the silent era.

A door at the front of the clubhouse stood open, leading to an indoor range. We each took a lane, about twenty feet from a man-silhouette target. In the lane beside me, one of the Jawas unpacked a huge Sig Sauer P226 semi-automatic with a bright nickel finish. In his hand, it looked as big and shiny as the bumper of a 1966 Buick, and I wondered how in the world he would be able to wear it concealed. I asked, but all he said was, "It's the one Woody Harrelson carried in *Zombieland.*"

Each of us was assigned a range officer, trained by the NRA and paid little or nothing; they served for the same reason Dick and Judy were teaching the class: because they believed in gun culture and wanted it to be safe. My range officer was a gentle anesthesiologist named Charlie who wore a gun every day to work. "It's a habit," he said with a shrug. "I don't mind carrying it, and if I need it, I have it."[*]

Charlie taught me the isosceles stance—arms straight ahead—and

---

[*] Though I've done no scientific survey, a disproportionate number of gun carriers I've met seem to be physicians. Usually they say that their jobs have them walking across hospital parking lots late at night, and junkies think the doctors might be carrying drugs in their black bags. One, though, told me he believes the impulse to carry a gun derives from the same source as the impulse to be a doctor: "We get off on managing death."

then the Weaver stance, in which the left edge of the body angles toward the target; the right hand pushes the gun forward while the left hand isometrically pulls it back. He discovered I was cross-eye dominant, meaning that although I was right handed, my left eye was stronger. Standing calmly shooting at targets, I'd learned to compensate. But in a sudden gunfight, Charlie taught me, my cross-eye dominance might throw off my shots, with fatal results. "Shoot with both eyes open," he suggested, "or consider learning to shoot left-handed."

We dutifully punched holes in paper, as required by Sheriff Pelle. We didn't practice anything that might come in handy during a gunfight, such as drawing our guns, shouting commands, finding cover, reloading, or—best of all—running away. But it was a reasonably useful evening; I hadn't fired a handgun with an instructor at my shoulder in a long time.

It reminded me, too, how deeply unpleasant target practice can be, especially in an indoor range with five or six other guns going off. Earplugs and oversize muffs didn't cut it; I felt like I'd spent an hour with my head in a spaghetti pot while a two-year-old beat on it with a ladle. We scurried in stony silence to our cars, which was fine with me, since I was deaf.

If I was really going to carry the thing, I wanted to be sure I didn't end up in prison. So I most looked forward to the night with a police officer as our teacher. We drew a burly detective named Gary, from one of Denver's far-flung suburbs. He had a straw-colored bristle mustache and looked like a young, fit Captain Kangaroo. "Any lawyers here?" was the first thing he said, and when no hands went up: "Cool." He played a videotape—the Pillsbury doughboy farting. "Just a little humor to start," he said.

"The Supreme Court says that if you have time to reload, you have time to think, so any killing you do after that is premeditated," he said. "That's why I carry the FN Five-Seven; it holds twenty rounds." He reached around behind him and came up with a bright orange plastic gun—an inert replica of an FN. Holding it out with both hands, he aimed, whispered *"pshew,"* faked the recoil, like an eight-year-old playing cops and robbers, and reholstered.

Like Dick and Judy, Gary was an acolyte of the Church of Out-of-Control Violence. And as a policeman, he seemed oddly eager for us to partake of it. "If you're in a place you're legally allowed to be, you are *not* required to withdraw!" he barked. He'd rather we draw down and shoot it out if the alternative was backing away from a fight. Good people cowering from bad ones was a recipe for social decay. He drew his orange gun again, brought it to firing position, said *"pshew,"* and reholstered.

"In Massachusetts," he said, "you're required to withdraw *from your own home*."* He shook his head and chuckled as he tucked the orange gun away—those wacky East Coast liberals. It seemed to me that dashing out the front door as a burglar came in the back was a pretty good strategy, if the alternative was a shoot-out. But it wasn't question time.

"Within twenty-one feet, an attacker with a knife can get to you within 1.5 seconds," Gary said, and I could sense us all remembering that photo Dick had shown us of the disemboweled stabbing victim. "Remember that the next time you hear people bitching that a cop shot someone who 'only' had a knife."

One of the hooded Jawas asked whether he could legally shoot someone who came into his house. "There are some prohibitations about that," Gary said as he drew, pointed, and reholstered his orange gun yet again. I wasn't even sure he knew that he was doing it. "It could be bad if you shot a burglar who turned out to be unarmed. It would depend on the jury."

"What about if he's, like, on the way out the door with my flat-panel TV," the Jawa said.

Gary chuckled. "I don't think anybody here would let a guy walk out of their house with their forty-eight-inch flat-panel," he said. "You can say 'Stop!' and if he sets it down and comes at you, you're justified."

"And if he runs away?" the Jawa asked.

"Now he knows you won't shoot, and he's going to come shopping at your house again."

I raised my hand. "So shoot him?"

Gary chuckled again, drawing and reholstering, drawing and reholstering. "If your aim is good, you have time to get your story straight before I get there."

On the fourth and final night, Dick and Judy talked about various ways to carry guns. Dick had on cargo pants and a jacket, under which he said

* Not true.

he was concealing thirteen of them. "These are unloaded, and there is *never* any live ammo in this room," he said. He drew his guns, one by one, and laid them on a table in a kind of weird lethal striptease: five from his belt, inside and outside the waistband of his pants, two from his ankles, two from his front pockets, two from hidden pockets in a spandex undershirt designed for concealed carry, and two from a wide elastic band that wrapped around his midsection like a truss. It was like watching clowns tumbling out of a VW; it went on and on. "Really, though, I think two would suffice," he said.

For the benefit of the woman in the class, Judy used her .38 snub-nose to model various holsters made to fit the female body. She waved the gun around, showing it at her hip, at the small of her back, and in her purse, then stopped suddenly and peered closely at it. "Oh shit," she said, her face reddening. She opened the revolver and dumped out five live cartridges.

Into the appalled silence, Dick ventured: "Object lesson in rule number one: All guns are always loaded!" He grinned, as though they'd planned all along to have Judy wave a loaded gun at us.

Carrying a gun was only one component of the new lifestyle Dick and Judy wanted us to adopt. The world into which they had invited us required us to keep on our nightstand our gun, glasses, cell phone, and flashlight. If we didn't like the idea of keeping an unsecured gun in the open, we could bolt to the wall beside the bed one of several available electronic safes that opened with a push-button code. "Every night before closing my eyes, I repeat the code aloud," Dick said.

"Make your house uninviting," Judy said. "Put up good exterior lighting. Clear away shrubbery where someone could hide."

"But plant thorny bushes under the windows," added Dick.

I was conjuring an image of my house on a denuded lot, bathed in halogen light, with thornbushes bunched under every window like barbed wire, when Judy carried my imagination inside.

"In your home you should know where your safe-fire zones are," she said. "Figure out where you can stand and shoot without the bullet going outside or into the neighbor's house."

"You men, if you sleep in the nude, might want to rethink that. Men aren't comfortable fighting naked. It's something to consider."

"Always expect the worst."

If there was a line here between preparing for something awful to happen and praying for something awful to happen, I was having a hard time finding it.

But Dick and Judy left us with a piece of good advice: Concealed means *concealed*. You don't show people your gun, you don't tell people you're carrying. If someone asks about it, you change the subject. "If someone goes to hug you," Judy said, "make sure your arms are in the inside position so they don't feel the hard lump on your hip. Guns make people react in unpredictable ways. If the wrong person learns you're carrying a gun, he might whack you on the head to get it." For the same reason, we were not to put up one of those PROTECTED BY SMITH & WESSON lawn signs or, on the car, the bumper sticker KEEP HONKING, I'M RELOADING. "A guy who sees one of those is likely to follow you to a parking lot," Judy said, "and when you leave the car, smash the window to get your gun."

As we were getting ready to pack up at the end of class, Dick handed around a card with what I first took to be a Transportation Security Administration threat assessment. It was, in fact, a way of thinking about readiness when carrying a gun. Condition White was total ignorance of one's surroundings on the street—sleeping, being drunk or stoned, losing oneself in conversation or—the ultimate in modern oblivion—texting while listening to an iPod. Condition Yellow was being aware of, and taking an interest in, one's surroundings. This was akin to the mental state we were encouraged to achieve while driving: keeping our eyes moving, checking the mirrors, being careful not to let the radio drown out the sounds around us. Condition Orange was awareness of a possible threat. Condition Red was responding to one.

"You should be in Condition Yellow whenever you're on the street, whether armed or not," Dick said, "but especially if you are wearing your gun. When you're in Condition White, you're a victim. You're a sheep."

The role Dick wanted us to play when out in public was that of "sheepdog"—alert, on guard, not aggressive but prepared to do battle on behalf of the defenseless. A handout from the American Tactical Shooting Association noted that the only time to be in Condition White was "when in your own home, with the doors locked, the alarm system on, and your dog at your feet. . . . The instant you leave your home, you escalate one level, to Condition Yellow." The instant? Really? Like if I'm riding to the store in the morning for the paper and a carton of milk? Or on my way to a PTA meeting in the middle of the afternoon? And what's this about alarms?

It turned out I was the kind of person who was contributing to a dangerous softening of society. Just as the Red Cross would have liked everybody to be qualified in cardiopulmonary resuscitation, gun carriers wanted everybody prepared to confront violence—not only by being armed but by maintaining Condition Yellow. "I believe that in my after-life I will be judged," Dick said solemnly. "Part of the judgment will be: Did this guy look after himself? It's a minimum responsibility."

I submitted my certificate of instruction to Sheriff Pelle, allowed a deputy to take my fingerprints, and settled in for a wait that could last, under Colorado law, as long as ninety days. "Due to the high volume of concealed-carry-license applications," a recording on the sheriff's phone line said, "do not expect your license before ninety days and do not call this office to inquire." In Boulder!

While waiting for the permit, I went shopping for a holster in which to carry the Detective Special. Colt stopped making my particular model in 1972, so a holster wasn't something I could order from Amazon. I figured I'd find heaps of old holsters at the monthly Tanner Gun Show, at the Denver Merchandise Mart, and drove down one snowy Saturday to rummage the offerings.

I never got inside. As I approached the desk to pay my entry fee, a young woman handed me a piece of paper and said, "Concealed-carry class beginning *right now*!" I looked at the paper. A company called Equip 2 Conceal was offering a class right here at the gun show that would qualify pupils to get a Colorado concealed-carry permit—in three hours. This I had to see.

She directed me across the parking lot to the Aspen Room of the Comfort Inn, where tables had been lined up classroom style and a dozen people sat filling out forms. "Before we begin, I'll tell you right off that I'm an NRA recruiter," said a dark-haired young man named Rob, in an Equip 2 Conceal golf shirt. "My job is to get as many people into the NRA as possible, because we really need it now. They're doing a lot of things to protect our rights." He motioned to a pretty young woman in a company shirt, who put a membership form in front of me.

Rob used the first hour to run through the "This is the trigger, this is the muzzle" drill. What he really wanted to talk about, though, was something he called "home invasion"—people coming into your home not to steal things but for the sheer maniacal pleasure of torturing you to death. "They"—white guys in ski masks and chinos, presumably—"have been watching what time you come home, what time do you get up to go to the bathroom. They know where your bedroom is, and they're there to kill you. Make sure you have your gun loaded. I live alone, and I always have my gun near me. I carry 24/7. I'm ready."

The Aspen Room had Wi-Fi. By going to several websites and juxtaposing numbers, it took me about ninety seconds, while Rob was talking, to discover that Rob wasn't entirely paranoid. Robberies in peoples' homes had increased by almost half from 2004 to 2008—one of the few crime stats that was growing worse. Seventy-two thousand American households had been struck, or about one in sixteen hundred. On the other hand, only eighty-seven Americans had been murdered in such incidents in 2008. I was literally more likely to be struck by lightning.

The young woman was passing out another set of forms. "In addition to your Colorado permit, you can get a nonresident carry permit in the state of Florida," Rob said. "That's right: Florida will issue you a carry permit even though you don't live there. Why do you want one? For one thing, three states—Washington, Virginia, and West Virginia—honor a Florida permit but not your Colorado permit. So that's three extra states where you can exercise your constitutional rights. Second, let's say you lose your Colorado permit. You couldn't carry here, because Colorado doesn't recognize a nonresident Florida permit, but you'd still be able to carry in thirty states."

The only reason I would "lose" a Colorado permit would be if, say, I committed a violent felony or beat up Margaret and had a restraining order placed on me. Florida was willing, even then, to step in and allow me to continue to carry a gun.

For the live-fire portion of the class, we got into our own cars and followed Rob across metro Denver—thirty minutes of our three hours—to a grimy shooting range in a shopping center. Five of the six lanes were taken up by young black guys teaching their girlfriends to shoot, with lots of whooping and laughing amid deafening blasts of nine-millimeters and .45s. My classmates and I filed to the sixth lane and, one by one, snapped off twenty shots from a long-barreled .22 target pistol. As preparation for defending ourselves with a gun, it was about as useful as learning to cook an omelet. We emerged, heads ringing from the concussions of the nine-millimeters and .45s, and Rob was there to hand us a certificate, xeroxed onto faux parchment.

"You can't possibly believe this class has prepared me to carry a gun," I said.

"This class has met the *legal requirement* to carry a gun," he said. "There's a difference. I strongly recommend more training."

The shooting portions of the classes had reminded me why I rarely took my guns to the range. I hated the noise. So, in for a penny, in for a pound: As long as I was going to carry a gun, I decided to look into getting a silencer for it.

The first silencer I ever saw was the one Oddjob used to dispatch Solo—before having him crushed inside a Lincoln Continental—in *Goldfinger*. I was eight years old. The elegance of that long tube protruding from the muzzle of the pistol, and the deep *thud* the shot made, moved me the way the first *slick-click* of Hank Hilliard's Mossberg .22 rifle had. For years I saw silencers in every cylindrical object I found—toilet paper rolls, Magic Markers, apple corers—and affixed them to every toy gun I had. I know how that sounds, but to paraphrase Freud: Sometimes a silencer is just a silencer. When it was time to put away childish things, I tried making real ones by duct-taping two-liter soda bottles over the muzzle of a .22 pistol. They worked, sort of. A crude silencer is naught but a chamber in which exploding gases depressurize before escaping. In a commercial silencer, baffles—which look like a stack of washers separated by tiny spaces—tamp the sound even more. My homemade ones were nowhere near as cool as screw-on silencers. They made it impossible to aim and often flew off with the first shot. But they did give the gun more of a *snap* sound than a reverberating bang.

They were also felonious. The first federal gun law, in 1934, required people who wanted a silencer to apply for a permit, submit to a background check, and pay a two-hundred-dollar federal tax—big money at a time when the average farmworker earned less than a dollar an hour. The same rules applied to machine guns and sawed-off shotguns, which, when Pretty Boy Floyd, Baby Face Nelson, Ma Barker, and the Barrow Gang were tearing up the country, were the era's weapons of mass destruction. Silencers got thrown into the law not because they were gangster weapons but because, in the depths of the Depression, people were using them to poach wildlife. For me to make a silencer without paying the tax was like applying to go to federal prison.

By the time I was in the market for a real silencer, two hundred dollars and a bit of paperwork made applying for the permit little more onerous than applying for a passport. In the decade since 2000, the number of permit applications had grown sixfold. Silencers were becoming so popular that the National Shooting Sports Foundation—the gun industry's trade association—sent a flyer to its retailer members alerting them to this growth opportunity.

When I told my friends I was in the process of getting a silencer, they were appalled. "You can buy silencers?" "Why does anybody need a silencer?" "An assassination weapon?" It turned out to be a very American attitude; in Europe, it was hard to get a license for a gun, but in most countries you could buy a silencer over the counter. In some, you were required to do so. Europe was crowded—who wanted to listen to gunfire?

"We in Finland have no legislation which regulate or ban the use of silencers, not the hunting legislation, not the firearms legislation," wrote Klaus Ekman, of Finland's Hunters' Central Organization. "But you have to remember that before you can buy a gun in Finland, you have to explain to the police the purpose you are buying the gun."

Peter Jackson, a designer and manufacturer of silencers in Scotland, sent me what amounted to a scholarly treatise on European silencer law, which included the remarkable news that silencers were completely unregulated in France; that silencers for shotguns and air rifles could be sold freely through the mail in the United Kingdom (I hadn't known that shotgun silencers existed); that rifle silencers were available in Britain with minimal paperwork; and that Article 5 of Directive 2003/10/EC, a European Union law, *required* silencers to be issued to anyone, such as a gamekeeper, who used a gun at work. "Although this obligation only applies to the employers of people who are 'at work,'" Jackson wrote, "it is a fair bet that our courts would award heavy damages against any official who denied a recreational hunter the protection against exposure to noise which is mandatory for a professional." He also reminded me that silencers protect the sensitive ears of hunting dogs, who cannot wear earmuffs like their human masters can—a very British concern.

"The great majority of the people get their image of firearms silencers from those special agent movies," he wrote. "That is why people resist using silencers on firearms. If I knew only the movie image of silencers, I would resist them, too."

The agency that issued the permits in the United States was the Bureau of Alcohol, Tobacco, Firearms, and Explosives—the ATF. I called to ask whether the ATF disagreed with the Europeans—whether they believed that silencers were a public safety risk.

"If the police find a body with a hole in it, they can't tell if a silencer was used," said the official in the appropriate department to whom I was passed, who asked that I not identify him. But, he added, "If we thought there was a problem, we'd do something about it. And we don't."

The first step in getting a silencer was to find a "Class III dealer"—someone specially licensed to sell weapons covered under the 1934 law. That led me to the most enthusiastic gun guy I'd ever met: Oliver Mazurkiewicz.

His shop was hard to find. It had no sign out front. MapQuest took me to a locked, smoked-glass door in a Longmont, Colorado, office park, next to something called White Rose Herbals. I buzzed, and a grim-faced man opened the door six inches and peered out at me suspiciously.

"I'm here to see Oliver," I said, and he opened just enough to let me in, then relocked. It was like entering a speakeasy. "I'm here to buy a silencer," I said.

"He'll be back soon."

I looked around and understood the security precautions. We were standing in a small, windowless showroom that looked like a set from *The Man from U.N.C.L.E.* On the walls hung the most terrifying collection of battle weapons I'd ever seen: twenty-five or so black or desert-tan AR-15s crusted with scopes and lasers, each with a big tubular silencer screwed to its muzzle. I took one of the rifles from the wall, noticing its full/semi switch. It was a machine gun—a silenced, scoped, fully automatic weapon.

"You military contractors?" I asked the sour-faced man.

"Not yet. Hope to be."

"So who buys these?"

"Who doesn't?" He went back to a workshop where two other guys were working on guns at a long bench.

I sighted through the machine gun's big scope out the smoked-glass door. A ladder on a rooftop two blocks away shimmered on the bridge of my nose; I could have hit a fly crawling on it. The door flew open, and a broad-shouldered, sandy-haired man burst through, his face filling the scope.

"Whoa!" he said with a laugh, looking down the barrel. "You Dan?"

I hung the rifle back on the wall. Oliver was a burly man in his early forties, with a handsome Slavic face and a handshake like Oddjob's car crusher. "That's a two-stamp gun," he said, pointing at the rifle with two index fingers. "You need one federal stamp for the machine gun and one for the silencer. I'll sell it to you right now for fifty-six hundred, which is an incredible deal."

He started doing many things at once—checking his computer, making phone calls, fixing the printer, rummaging through paper files, and unpacking two guns from holsters concealed in his waistband: a snub-nosed Smith & Wesson .357 Magnum and a compact .40-caliber Glock. While talking on the phone, he handed me a small cardboard box in which I found a black anodized tube about six inches long, with TEC-65 and a serial number etched on the side. As he kept up his manic phone call, he took my credit card and ran it for $325—$250 for the silencer and a $75 "transfer fee." With the phone clamped between his ear and his shoulder, he carried what was now my silencer into the workshop and locked it in a huge gun safe. I wouldn't see it again for three months. The same time limit applied to background checks for the silencer as for the concealed-carry permit; I'd get them at about the same time. Oliver ended his call and addressed himself to me. "Sorry. It's just nuts!"

"Silencers?"

"Silencers, guns, everything!"

"How'd you get into this?"

"My mother grew up in Germany during the war and hates guns," he said. "She wouldn't let me have a squirt gun, wouldn't let me have a rubber-band gun. Wouldn't let me point my finger and go 'Bang.' Well, Mom?" He gestured at the firepower surrounding us on the walls. "Look what you did."

"And the silencers?"

"The majority of my customers are like *you*." He swung both arms back, up and over, to point two index fingers at my nose. "They want a silencer because it's such a taboo. But then they discover that it makes sense to quiet it all down. You try to teach a kid to shoot, and if he's wearing hearing protectors, you have to yell so he can hear you. Kids get tired of people yelling at them! They tune them out! Silence the gun, you don't have that problem.

"I won't shoot without a silencer anymore," he continued. "Why should I? Why put up with the noise when you don't have to? Most guys don't start out thinking that way. They start out thinking just, *It's cool. It's James Bond.* You can fault Hollywood for that. You want to hear what it's going to sound like?"

He scurried into the back room and came out with a scoped .22-caliber rifle that had a six-inch cylinder screwed onto the barrel. We walked across the parking lot to where a plow had pushed a big pile of dirty snow. Oliver worked the bolt, pointed the rifle into the snowbank, and pulled the trigger. The gun made a faint *phut*—much like in the movies—and a handful of snow leapt from the pile.

"Is that cool or what?" he asked as we walked back inside. Only .22-caliber silencers, like the one I was buying, are as quiet as Hollywood silencers, he said. A nine-millimeter or .45—to say nothing of a full-size hunting rifle—makes a pretty loud pop, though still a lot less than an unsilenced gun. And then there's the issue of the bullet's speed. A silencer only reduces the bang of powder exploding. Most bullets, .22s included, travel faster than sound and make a distinctive *crack*. That can be eliminated only by using subsonic ammunition, as Oliver had used in his demo.

"Where do you get *that*?"

"Everywhere. I need to see your driver's license." He copied down the information, signed and stamped the form, and handed me a sheaf of papers.

"Go over to Kinko's and get two passport pictures taken. Take them and these papers to your sheriff and get fingerprinted. You also need him to sign off; he has to give his *permission*." He rolled his eyes theatrically. "When you get the papers back from him, you send everything to the ATF with a two-hundred-dollar check. It's all bullshit, but it makes us rich."

"Then what?"

"Then you wait. Probably the full three months. The paperwork will come back to me. I'll call you, and you can come pick up your silencer."

His phone started ringing, and he reached for it with his left hand. At the same time, he extended his right to me to shake, flicked his eyebrows, and smiled wickedly. "Welcome to the dark side."

My concealed-carry permit came right on time, and I picked it up from the county clerk. It was the size, shape, and texture of a credit card. As with most IDs, the photo made me look like someone who shouldn't be carrying a gun. I went home and loaded my .38 with 125-grain hollow-point cartridges. I slipped it into a holster and tucked it inside the waistband of my trousers, over my right kidney. Then I put on a sport coat and went out for a walk on Boulder's quaint downtown pedestrian mall, expecting at any moment to hear someone yell, *"He's got a gun!"* and tackle me. Nobody, of course, paid me a blind bit of notice.

I found that I wasn't so much in Condition Yellow as Condition *Day-Glo* Yellow. Everything around me appeared brilliantly sharp, the colors extra rich, the contrasts shockingly stark. I could hear footsteps on the pavement two blocks away. As people around me went about their business, utterly relaxed, I experienced a weird amalgam of envy and pity. Their bliss seemed ignorant, almost irritatingly obtuse. There was an undeniable sheeplike quality to them as they licked their ice cream cones and swung their shopping bags. Utterly blithe and vulnerable, they looked like extras in the first reel of a disaster movie. And there I was, striding among them, uniquely capable of resisting whatever violence might be their portion. It surprised me that it made me feel rather noble.

Dick and Judy needn't have hectored us to remain in Condition Yellow; there was no way to lapse into Condition White when armed. Carrying a gun is uncomfortable; my fat little revolver, with its bulging six-shot cylinder, felt, by day's end, like a baseball digging into my love handle. More than that, its phenomenal lethality made it unignorable.

I didn't tell anybody that I was embarked upon an experiment in going armed. "Concealed means *concealed.*" One afternoon during that first week of carrying, I ran into a friend downtown. As we stood and talked, the gun on my hip felt as big as a toaster oven. She told a long, complicated story about her teenage son; I tried to follow it, but all I could think about was how freaked out she'd be if she knew the gun was there.

I was fine with the strict secrecy rule, because in the world I inhabited, carrying a gun would have made me a social outcast. Most of my friends would have kept their distance or felt it necessary to tell me that a gun wasn't welcome in their house. For reasons I had a hard time identifying, I felt a particular need not to let on to any of Rosa's male friends—or the sons of any of our friends, whatever their age—that I was living alongside a gun. *What a weenie,* shouted one side of my brain. *Guns are a natural part of a young man's education, and you should be proud to be a responsible role model.* But the other side shouted, *Of course you don't want to be a gun-carrying role model for young men. They're the ones who do most of the killing with guns and are most often killed by them.* I didn't have to go far to learn about the nation's conflicted attitude toward guns. I could just tour the inside of my own skull.

Whatever I was doing, during those first months, the Colt on my hip seemed to occupy half my brain. In supermarkets, I had to be conscious of keeping the gun covered up when reaching for the high shelf or stooping for the low one. On the street, I looked people over in a whole new way.

Where are his hands? What does his face tell me about his intentions? The gun kept me in my own little movie, glancing at the door when a person walked in, evaluating, in a microsecond, whether a threat had appeared, and weighing my options for response—roll left and take cover behind that pillar? Some nights, I dreamed gunfight scenarios over and over and woke up bushed.

Carrying the gun even changed my relationship with Margaret and Rosa. Although they'd known in a general way that I'd been planning to get a carry permit, I hadn't kept them up on specifics, and I certainly hadn't told tell them that my experiment had begun. Getting ready to go out with them, I'd make for the little electronic safe stowed on a closet shelf behind my stack of sweaters and punch in a three-button code. The safe's door would pop open, I'd slip the loaded gun inside my waistband, and off we'd go, with nobody the wiser. If Margaret put her arm around me while we were walking, I'd shift so her hand wouldn't fall on the business. In a family accustomed to keeping no secrets, going armed became a perpetual sin of omission.

My instructors' crime paranoia wasn't my style, but the weight on my hip left me no choice. It was hard not to see attackers everywhere, or at least in the places they might be hiding—like *behind that Dumpster!* Not that I thought Boulder had become Dodge City, but the darkness at the center of my vision was hard to shake. My fellow man had become a threat. I didn't like it. Nor did I like my new relationship with Death; now that I was equipped to do his bidding, I couldn't help feeling that I'd joined his payroll.

But wearing the gun and staying in Condition Yellow also had positive effects. It made me more organized. I stopped doing stupid things like leaving credit cards on store counters or sunglasses on restaurant tables. I got better about remembering to lock the house at night. (If I was equipping myself to shoot an intruder, locking the door seemed a reasonable first step.) I became a more astute driver. I seemed to be more punctual, as though I'd subtly rearranged my life so that I was a little less frazzled, a little farther in front of the eight ball. Wearing the gun, I was Mr. Together. There was no room for screwing up when I was equipped to kill. Existential catastrophe lurked as close as the time it would take to draw.

———

A couple of weeks after getting my carry permit—and three months to the day after I sent in the silencer paperwork—Oliver called to say that my federal tax stamp had arrived and the silencer was legally mine.

The silencer's impending arrival had forced me to buy a new gun, because, Hollywood be damned, there was no way to silence a revolver: The gap between the cylinder and the barrel made it impossible to seal. (The Nagant M1895 revolver was the sole exception. Pulling the trigger both rotated the cylinder and pushed it against the end of the barrel, making a seal.) My silencer, then, was not for the Colt Detective Special. On GunBroker.com—the eBay of firearms*—I had bought an Argentine Bersa .22 semi-automatic pistol with a threaded barrel. At Walmart, I'd bought some subsonic .22 cartridges. After picking up the silencer at Oliver's, I drove up Left Hand Canyon to a spot in the national forest that people had turned into an informal shooting range.

Because Boulder was culturally hostile to guns, it hadn't created a proper county-owned range. What it had instead, for those who didn't belong to the Rifle Club, was a miserable arroyo strewn with broken bottles, shot-up cardboard boxes, flattened shotgun shells, and mountains of expended brass—an environmental disaster that would have offended most Boulderites' sensibilities if they'd ever deigned to visit. The arroyo was narrow—it didn't allow for a shot of more than about twenty-five yards—and it was all rock, which made it dangerously prone to ricochet.

It was one of those eerily warm days Boulder gets in February, and, in the middle of a workday, two groups of people were banging away with their guns. One group consisted of three tattooed men and two women, and they were a fine advertisement for gun control, drunkenly whooping and hollering as they threw glass bottles into the air and smashed them with shotguns. Farther along, a group of young men speaking Spanish snapped off rounds from semi-automatic handguns. I walked behind both groups, carefully, up to the end of the arroyo, to be as far away from the shooting as possible. Still, I was unpacking my guns when someone caromed a bullet off a rock; there was a terrifying whine, like a finger

---

* Relax. You could bid for and buy a gun online, but it had to be shipped to a licensed gun dealer, who was required to perform the background check. All the usual rules applied. While GunBroker.com participants could in theory have simply mailed guns to one another illegally, the online sale and the shipping both created records of the transaction, which were incentives to play by the rules. That GunBroker.com had been operating since 1999 indicated that the ATF hasn't found reason to shut it down.

sliding up a guitar string, and a *whack* as the bullet smacked into a patch of snow about six feet from me. Such was the nature of this wretched, informal range. In its aversion to guns, Boulder had created conditions that made guns more dangerous.

I drew a black spot on a cardboard box and set it up about thirty feet away. Picking up the Bersa, I experienced the sensual thrill—part cinematic and part onanistic—of screwing the black cylinder to the muzzle. When I pulled the trigger, about all I heard was the pistol's slide reciprocating. I kept firing—*phut, phut, phut*—and realized I was hearing something else: my bullets hitting the cardboard box. This was new. Hearing the bullets strike the target connected me afresh to what I was shooting at, which made me a lot more aware of the power of what I was doing. And the silencer did more than reduce the noise. It funneled the concussion downrange and weighted the muzzle, which reduced recoil. Noise, concussion, and recoil: The silencer had removed everything unpleasant about shooting, and it may have made me a safer shooter, because I was more cognizant of what I was throwing downrange.

I wasn't wearing big acoustic earmuffs, so I could hear the Hispanic guys talking. I could hear people's footsteps. Another thing that makes gun ranges dangerous is that a bad guy who wants a gun knows he can find one there. Shooters' lore is full of stories of people murdered at ranges for their guns. This very spot had, in 1990, been the setting for such a tragedy. People who were focused downrange and deafened to their surroundings by hearing protectors were especially vulnerable. Shooting unmuffed, I was safer.

I had no plans to mix the silencer with carrying concealed. Although it was technically legal, it would be awfully difficult explaining *that* to a jury. But for ordinary sport shooting, using the silencer was so pleasant for me, and presumably for the people around me, that it suddenly seemed crazy to put up with the racket of *unsilenced* firearms. It was the twenty-first century, for heaven's sake; why should anybody—shooter or bystander—have to be annoyed by, or risk hearing loss from, the eight-hundred-year-old sound of exploding gunpowder? If we were a little less hysterical and polarized about firearms, we could have had such a discussion, and perhaps made silencers a matter of etiquette—if not law—for those who like to shoot, the way they were in Europe. For a while, I thought of getting all the required licenses and opening a business in yoga-centric Boulder—Namaste Guns: Fine Silent Firearms. Margaret thought it was funny. To a point.

3. THE iGUN

With our technology . . . literally three people in a garage can blow
away what 200 people at Microsoft can do. Literally can blow it away.

—Steve Jobs

ully armed, the car loaded with ammunition and camping gear, I was
ready to set off in search of gun-guy America. Boulder felt as though
it had been swept under a rug of clouds the day I pulled out of town.
I drove south toward Arizona, planning a short stop in Colorado
Springs, not to visit a gun store this time but to see a city councilman. The
relationship between Boulder and Colorado Springs illustrated the depth
of my ignorance about American politics. A child of the Great Society,
raised by New Dealers, I'd grown up with the bedtime story that Democrats were the party of the workingman, while Republicans carried the
cudgel for the rich. That, of course, was outdated wisdom. Boulder, for
example, was simultaneously among the richest cities in the nation and
the bluest imaginable stronghold, while Colorado Springs, a hard-luck
town with more tattoo parlors than latte shops, was nationally known as
a red-meat conservative redoubt and home to Focus on the Family. The
GOP's capture of working-class America was a thirty-year-old story by
the time I got on the road with my Colt, but it never failed to surprise
me when I encountered it. Guns were part of the story of that shift, and
on my way through Colorado Springs, I wanted to meet Bernie Herpin,
who had made a name for himself after the Columbine High School massacre, in 1999. Coloradans had responded to the tragedy by approving a
ballot initiative to "close the gun-show loophole," requiring at gun shows
the same kind of computerized background checks that were mandated

at gun stores. The new law probably wouldn't have changed anything at Columbine—where a law-abiding adult had bought the guns for the teen-age shooters—but still, it sounded good to many in the traumatized state. Herpin was among those who'd taken an unpopular position against it.

I also looked forward to meeting Herpin because it was thanks to him that Colorado Springs was one of the few cities in America where I could carry a gun into City Hall. Keeping Americans from being armed in the places where their laws were made was un-American, he'd argued. He'd won that one, so I was surprised to find a metal detector standing between me and the elevators in the City Hall lobby. I walked through, and it warbled like a canary.

"Empty your pockets, please," said the female security guard. She wore the uniform of a private security company and a holstered .357 Magnum. I put my keys and watch in the plastic dish and walked through again. *Beeeep!*

"Anything else in your pockets?" she asked. I patted them.

"No."

"No other metal?"

"Just my gun."

She didn't laugh, but neither did she reach for the .357 Magnum. "You're going to have to return that to your vehicle."

I opened my mouth to assert my rights but decided I was unwilling to risk a gunfight to defend Bernie Herpin's regulation.

Herpin was a stolid man in his fifties, with a broad, unexpressive face and old-fashioned, large-framed glasses that added to an overall ranine aspect. "I'm unarmed, by the way," I said. "I hope that's okay." I told him about the encounter downstairs, and he rolled his eyes. Passing the ordinance had been one thing; enforcing it was another. He still thought regulating gun shows was wrongheaded.

"What's next?" he asked as we took seats in his office. "The bulletin-board-at-work loophole, the ad-in-the-paper loophole, the sell-to-your-neighbor loophole?"—all of which were legal ways to buy guns.

Herpin told me how the 1994 assault-rifle ban had woken him up to the need to defend the Second Amendment, and how he'd fought to allow licensed adults to carry guns into K–12 schools because someone checked out and licensed was no threat, and might be able to stop a school shoot-ing. He went on to say that President Obama's bailout of General Motors was on the same spectrum as gun control: government taking power from the people, and as his rhetoric devolved into standard-issue right-wing

Obama bashing, he became less interesting than I'd hoped. I glanced at my watch and the window; I still had a few hours in which to make miles before the sleet closed in. I thanked him for his time. But as I stepped out the door, he called to me in a new tone—almost hurt. I paused at the door, half in and half out.

"You're from Boulder, so maybe you can explain something to me," he said. "The Democrat party used to be the party of the workingman, who is the hunter, the gun guy. How can it now be anti-gun, anti-ATV on the public lands, anti-hunting? The leadership of the Democrat party criticizes conservatives for our *tastes*."

I told him I was the last person who could explain that, and he waved me off with one hand while lifting the phone with the other to chew out the security guard downstairs.

In that last moment, Herpin had finally said something interesting. Most proponents of gun control doubtless would argue that their position was based on public safety. But to Herpin, the pro-gun-control position felt like an attack on his tastes, on who he was as a person. Maybe he was wrong, but that was how he heard it. There are two steps to a message, I remembered: the sending and the receiving.

Outside of Walsenburg, Colorado, I saw a sign for Hollowpoint Gun Shop. My plan on the trip was to stop at every gun store I saw, so I pulled over and checked my look in the rearview. NRA cap: check. Worn leather jacket: check. Gun on hip: check. I was about to walk armed into a gun store; if I didn't get cut down in a blazing crossfire, everything should go swimmingly.

Hollowpoint was a cozy little place—low-ceilinged, stocked mostly with fishing rods—overseen by a beautiful, petite woman named Erin Jerant. She wore a crocheted vest, her gray hair in a bun; I half expected her to offer me a cup of tea. Gun guys dream of finding, say, an 1897 Bergmann No. 5 pistol in the shop of a sweet old lady who says, "Oh, I don't know why anybody would want that old thing. I'm glad to see it go." I thought maybe I'd hit the jackpot.

Alas, Erin was not that sweet old lady. A quick look at her price tags indicated that she'd been up late at night scanning the prices on GunBroker.com. Her guns were as expensive as any. And there weren't many dusty old rancher's rifles but, once again, a rack of AR-15s that wouldn't have looked out of place in the armory at Fort Polk. "Everybody wants one now," she said, touching the muzzle of a black rifle. "You've got your end-of-the-world types who buy them. For ranchers dealing with prairie dogs and coyotes, they're great." She looked up into my eyes and recited the gun-guy liturgy. "The way crime is just out of control, you can't blame people."

I mentioned that I'd found a couple of gun stores closed and asked how business was.

"Last year was good, when Obama got in. I am sure that as soon as he knows this term is over and he's not going to get reelected, he'll try to push through all kinds of gun bans, and we'll have another good few months. But long-term, no, it doesn't look good. Only people I see in here anymore are almost as old as I am. I'm giving myself five more years and then retiring."

She leaned on the counter, and a dreamy look came over her. "Last year, though," she sighed, "I had them standing five deep in here filling out their 4473s;* you could smell the testosterone."

The specter of a new assault-rifle ban had become, to some gun guys, what the Holocaust was to some Jews: the organizing dread of their lives. The original ban came in 1994, after the country had been brutalized by the crack-cocaine murder wave of the late eighties and early nineties. It was aimed at the AK-47, which was being disgorged by the tens of thousands from China and the collapsed Soviet empire, and at the American-made AR-15. Sponsors of the ban, in their haste to "do something" about gun violence, made enough gaffes to give their opponents endless political ammunition and make the entire exercise as polarizing as possible. They mangled brands and model numbers—a couple of proposed laws would have banned guns that didn't exist—and garbled gun parts. When Senator Dianne Feinstein said of assault rifles on national television, "They have light triggers, you can spray-fire them, you can hold them with two hands, and you don't really need to aim," gun guys were paying attention. They knew that assault rifles didn't necessarily have lighter triggers than other guns, and any gun could be held with two hands, fired rapidly, or fired without aiming. Feinstein and her allies were trying to ban something

* The federal form required to buy a gun.

they didn't even understand. Instead of listing every conceivable variant of the AR-15 and AK-47, the law banned characteristics deemed too military for civilian possession, such as pistol grips, bayonet lugs, collapsible stocks, and barrel shrouds that protect shooters' hands from heat. Banning guns by characteristic turned out to be like banning Pontiacs for their chrome pipes and death's-head shift knobs. Smart entrepreneurs simply churned out "post-ban" AK-47 and AR-15 knockoffs that lacked the cosmetics but were every bit as lethal. Ironically, it's entirely possible that the bill's mostly Democratic sponsors ended up putting *more* assault rifles and high-capacity magazines on the street, rather than fewer. The long debate in 1993 and 1994 that led to the ban, and the additional months before the law took effect, gave everybody who wanted such things, or thought he might someday, ample time to stock up. I was living in Montana at the time; gun stores were selling AK-47s off pallets for $110 apiece—along with hastily manufactured thirty-two-round magazines by the case. It was like watching people preparing for a zombie invasion.

A sunset provision, in any case, gave Congress and President George W. Bush the chance to let the ban expire a decade later. When Representative Carolyn McCarthy of New York was pushing to reinstate it, the conservative commentator Tucker Carlson asked her on television if she knew what a barrel shroud was. After trying to evade the question, she eventually blurted, "a shoulder thing that goes up," a line that instantly became infamous. Senator Charles Schumer was given to declaring that machine guns, assault weapons, and cheaply made pistols were available "in cyberspace for the taking." In truth, you could find guns through the Internet, but actually buying one required following all the standard background-check and paperwork rules, and machine guns weren't available that way at all. Once again, gun guys were watching. They saw the ban supporters' inability to demonstrate even a passing familiarity with the things they were presuming to ban as the height of elitism. They convinced Congress to block reinstatement, and "pre-ban" AR-15s and AK-47s returned to gun stores.

Whether the short-lived ban saved lives is a topic of unending contention. What is undeniable is that it contributed to one historic death—that of the Democratic majority in Congress. The November after President Clinton signed the assault-rifle ban, gun guys helped give the Democrats their worst drubbing since 1946, ending their hold on both houses.

Even though they beat reinstatement, gun guys did not stand down from red alert. The ban had so permanently inflamed their outrage

gland—an organ prodded ceaselessly by the NRA and the gun press—
that when it looked as if another Democrat was going to win the White
House in 2008, the gun industry had its best year ever. A common nov-
elty at gun stores was a poster of Obama's smiling face over the words
FIREARMS SALESMAN OF THE YEAR. And in fairness, the petite Erin Jerant's
fear may not have been entirely irrational. Soon after the election, the new
attorney general, Eric Holder, let slip that reinstating the assault-rifle ban
was one of "a few gun-related changes that we would like to make." The
comment set off such a shitstorm that within weeks he was mumbling
that all he'd meant was "enforcing the laws we have," exactly the NRA's
position.

The AR-15 was so prevalent everywhere I'd been so far that it was starting
to feel like one of my story's protagonists. The more I read about it, the
more it seemed like the future—the iGun, perhaps. Even the business
surrounding it was different from the gun industry of the past. While the
big traditional firearms companies—Smith & Wesson, Ruger, Remington, and Colt—made AR-15s, they were hardly the whole game. At least
thirty American companies, some of them two- and three-man shops,
were making them. It was an industry that lived not in huge, smoky factories, but largely among the engine shops, custom extruders, and welders in
edge-of-town industrial parks. When I reached the Grand Canyon State,
I went looking for one.

I showed up in Phoenix the week that Congress passed President
Obama's health-care bill, and the city was undergoing a collective nervous
breakdown. It made it hard to talk to Arizonans about anything else, even
their guns. In the airless waiting room of a Jiffy Lube, an elderly gentleman became so distraught over the new law that he was making himself
short of breath; I feared he might suffer a stroke. "It's been socialism for
the past fifty years, but now it's out-of-the-closet, bare-assed naked!" he
cried, as overture to a twenty-minute monologue delivered at top volume
to an audience of two—me and a heavyset woman glancing nervously
over her copy of *Prensa Hispana*.

"Sir," I finally said, reaching over to pat his seersucker knee. "Allow me
to reassure you: All that has happened is that you lost one. It happens to
my side all the time. Believe me; the republic is fine."

He refused to be consoled.

I had some time to kill before an appointment, so I roamed Phoenix in my freshly lubricated car, following the lead of Gun Store Finder. The first store it sent me to was out of business—the GUNS sign creaking in the hot breeze but the windows were whitewashed over—and so was the second. Peering through the glass door, I could see that it had been vacated recently: A poster on the wall advertised the Taurus Judge revolver, which had been a hot new item that year. I was beginning to feel like an epidemiologist on the trail of a mysterious plague that was leaving behind a string of desiccated gun-store corpses. At a time when gun sales were strong, something was killing off the stores.

But it was time to get to Glendale, so I hacked my way through the traffic to a vast grid of gray, unlandscaped, steel-sided buildings adorned with vaguely technological but opaque corporate names like Technotron and Tronotech. I drove around and around until I was sure I was lost, and at that moment, directly in front of me, a sign appeared for the place I was seeking: Patriot Ordnance Factory. I parked and banged on an unmarked steel door.

After a rattling of locks, the door swung open, and Frank DeSomma looked me up and down. "You found me," he said, waving me into a cheaply furnished office and locking the door behind us. DeSomma looked less like an Arizona gunmaker than a discount-electronics salesman on Flatbush Avenue. Short and soft, he wore a powder-blue leisure suit, gold chains, and a big, knobby gold ring. His dark hair was slicked back, and a Vandyke adorned his meaty features. In an accent so heavily Brooklynese I could practically smell the pickles, he launched into a predictably despairing monologue about President Obama's health-care bill. I let him go on for ninety seconds, tapping my foot; it was the cost of doing business in Arizona that week. Finally, I held up a palm. "Spare me. Let's talk about guns."

DeSomma shrugged, smiled, and got down to the story of his business. His family had moved to Arizona from Brooklyn when he was eight. All his friends had firearms, and as a budding aerospace machinist in his twenties, he was as enchanted by guns' mechanical perfection as by the flash and boom. In 2002, with the ten-year assault-rifle ban soon to expire, DeSomma sensed that the market for the AR-15 was about to take off. He sold an apartment building and asked his wife if he could use $25,000 of the proceeds to start a gun-parts business.

All AR-15s are functionally identical; it's the interchangeability of their parts, after all, that makes them so thrilling. But DeSomma thought he could make a better gun. The AR-15 had been known since the Vietnam War for being lightweight and accurate but finicky and prone to jamming. DeSomma figured the problem was the way it used gases from one firing round to eject the casing and insert the next round into the chamber. Pushing the bolt directly with hot gases meant covering it with dirt, eventually fouling the rifle, so DeSomma revived an idea from semi-automatic rifles that predated the M16. He engineered a way to use the gases to push a rod, or piston, and have the rod push the bolt, adding a little weight but keeping the bolt cleaner. He took his invention to the big gun-industry trade show in 2004, and people thought he was crazy for taking AR-15 development in a reverse direction.

Thus began one of those signature stories of ingenuity and pluck that crop up often enough to sustain the American dream. For the first four years, DeSomma paid himself zero, plowing every available nickel back into the business. By the time I met him, he was paying himself a meager $250 a week but had twenty-five employees making a thousand rifles a year, which sold for a breathtaking $1,900 to $2,600 a pop. He was selling a few to police departments every year, but the bulk of his sales went to civilians. And he was banking on the wars in Afghanistan and Iraq.

"You sell to the Army?" I said.

"No, but every guy who comes home is used to the platform and is going to want to continue with it." Continue with it? The last thing that the Vietnam vets I knew wanted was to "continue" with the M16. Was it because they hadn't been lionized during their war the way soldiers were nowadays? Was it because so many more of them had died? Or was it simply the times?

DeSomma unlocked a safe and handed me one of his rifles. It was heavier, beefier, and tighter-feeling than the kid's AR-15 I'd shot in Denver. The reviews had been phenomenal. Many considered it the finest AR-15 on the market. *Gun Digest* had called it the "ultimate AR," capable of firing an unbelievable 100,000 rounds between cleanings.

DeSomma wore his emotions close to the surface and kept lapsing into standard, ugly comments about liberals, Obama, and the "gun grabbers." But he was also a man with a deeply felt vision of the America in which he wanted to live and a commitment to using his business to bring it about. The miracle of the U.S. Constitution, he told me, was that it went out of its way to give ordinary citizens the means to unseat a tyrannical government. "Name me another country that ever did such a thing," he said, turning his sweaty head sideways and inserting it enthusiastically between my face and my notebook as I tried to jot notes. The way he put it, enshrining an armed citizenry into a country's founding document did seem to imply a rather extraordinary amount of trust in ordinary people. DeSomma believed the framers of the Constitution wanted every American to have, hanging over his fireplace as a bulwark against tyranny, the latest battlefield technology: a flintlock musket. Its equivalent today, he said, was the AR-15. Far from banning it, we should consider the AR the firearm *most* protected by the Second Amendment. To manufacture AR-15s was a privilege, almost a sacred calling; it gave DeSomma a role in realizing the dreams of the founders. Sure, he was proud of how well and how quickly he'd built his business. "But this isn't about money; it's not even really about guns," he said, sweeping a hand to take in the factory grounds. "This is about the power of the states and the people!"

As a gunmaker, DeSomma paid an 11 percent excise tax on top of his income and business taxes, the same as someone making booze or cigarettes, products whose consumption the government wanted to discourage. His gripe with the excise tax wasn't about parting with money; it was about the insult. "It's as though we're something evil, something dirty," he said, with an emotional catch in his gravelly voice. When he'd applied for a line of credit at Chase Bank, which held all his accounts and knew his excellent credit rating, they'd told him they didn't conduct "that type of business."

"Like I'm running a whorehouse or something!" He thrust out his arms in a classic sue-me gesture. "Last year I had a twelve-million-dollar backlog, and Chase wouldn't give me a line of credit!"

DeSomma seemed more than hurt. He was genuinely, deeply confused: Chase and the people who'd decided that the gun business should pay an excise tax—to say nothing of those who wanted guns banned or restricted—seemed *wrong* about guns. They seemed to think that guns were *bad* and, by extension, that the people who liked them should be punished.

DeSomma's friends, all gun guys, were among the finest, safest, most upstanding and law-abiding people in Greater Phoenix. Their guns were simply a piece of equipment, designed ingeniously and—DeSomma's especially—manufactured with a jeweler's precision; anybody who'd ever held and fired one could see that. The police and military needed high-quality firearms to keep the country safe, but DeSomma didn't want to hide behind that argument. *Private* gun ownership was what made America unique; the Second Amendment was what separated a citizen from a subject. The people who reviled DeSomma's products—who placed sin taxes on them, discriminated against them in business dealings, and wanted them banned as "assault rifles"—were either massively ignorant or held a genuine disdain for the freedom such weapons represented. They were either the worst kind of elitists—trying to control something they couldn't be bothered to understand—or fundamentally un-American. They boggled his mind.

He dug his iPhone from his pocket. "Watch this," he said, and punched up a YouTube video of Ronald Reagan delivering his first inaugural address. "We have a country with a government, not the other way around," Reagan's tiny, stern image said. "The federal government did not create the states; the states created the federal government."

"That man was like a grandfather to me," DeSomma said sadly as he put his phone away. "He was the only president of my lifetime who really cared about America."

Sensing he'd harangued me enough, he motioned me to follow him into the factory, a warren of windowless warehouses. Despite the suburban setting, I expected to see throngs of men in leather aprons forging gun parts amid deafening noise and showers of sparks. Instead we found ourselves in a nearly silent hangar full of computerized-numerical-control (CNC) machines—cube-shaped, ten-foot-tall behemoths of steel and glass. Before each stood a man studying code, the computer screen silently reflected in the lens of his safety glasses. These guys looked less like factory workers than like air-traffic controllers.

We approached one of the CNC machines. "The receiver is designed on a computer and transmitted digitally to these machines," DeSomma said. The receiver is the body of the gun, a hollow metal box about the size of a videocassette. The gun's trigger parts are fitted inside, and the barrel, buttstock, and everything else is attached to it.

The operator opened the hatch of the CNC and clamped in a short board of silver-gray metal—an aluminum blank. He consulted an LCD screen bearing a long list of numbers—the computerized instructions—and pushed a few buttons.

Behind the glass, robotic drills and routers bored into the blank, sending up curls of aluminum, transforming it, in about twenty-five minutes, into an AR-15 receiver. DeSomma handed it to me; it weighed nothing.

Legally, the hollow metal slab I was holding—the receiver—was a firearm. It would be the only part of the rifle that would carry a serial number. To buy one—even an empty, naked, harmless, and inert one like the one I was holding—would require filling out a federal 4473 form and submitting to the same background check as for a fully functioning Glock or shotgun. But after that, all the bits that made an AR-15 shootable were, under the law, just parts. The bolt, barrel, magazine, stock, trigger, and so on could be bought, sold, and sent through the mail as freely as fishing gear or kitchen supplies. So once a shooter owned a receiver, he could build himself a nearly infinite variety of weapons without ever again encountering a background check or a federal form. Despite shooting, essentially, a variety of guns, an AR-15 owner had to confront state and federal bureaucracies only once. On the flip side, the ATF no longer knew what caliber weapons were out there. The AR-15 made that impossible. It was constantly shape-shifting.

It was easy to see, then, why the AR-15 was so popular. It was fun to shoot. It was a geek's dream of limitless high-tech parts. It made everybody a bit player in the global war on terror and the march of American history. It worked for whatever kind of shooting a gun guy might want. It limited a shooter's exposure to the federal firearms bureaucracy. And it made life harder for the ATF. It was the perfect gun for the Tea Party era.

DeSomma walked me to my car. I removed my jacket before climbing in, revealing the holstered Colt in my waistband. "Look at *you*!" DeSomma said, beaming. He placed his hand on his heart and closed his eyes. "You honor me by wearing your gun to my place of business."

Never had I encountered a business or a hobby as tangled up with a political worldview as firearms and shooting. From the range officer with the *Molon labe* button to Erin Jerant to Frank DeSomma, just about everybody I was meeting lapsed, sooner or later, into a conservative aria. It wasn't as if every tennis player in America was a Jabotinsky Revisionist, or everybody in the tire business was eager to lecture you on the virtues of Peronismo. I decided to make one more stop before leaving metro Phoenix: the Goldwater Institute. Senator Barry Goldwater scared me to death in 1964, but I retained a secret soft spot for him. He may have been a wild-eyed missile rattler, but he was an intellectually consistent wild-eyed missile rattler. He wanted government out of citizens' lives—and that included homosexuals, women who needed to end their pregnancies, and marijuana users. If anybody could explain to me why a fondness for firearms was so often found on the same chromosome as political conservatism—how a natural

Democrat like the working-class, debt-saddled, and dead-ended kid at the Family Shooting Center could have voted for Sarah Palin—it would be here in the hypothalamus of the conservative movement.

The institute was a modern white-brick building on a leafy side street in central Phoenix. A big bronze bust of the late senator dominated the lobby, and the walls displayed black-and-white photographs of Goldwater posing with a pantheon of the conservative movement: Friedrich Hayek, George Will, Ronald Reagan, Clarence Thomas, Margaret Thatcher, and Arthur Laffer. Goldwater's forbidding signature glasses glowered from every direction as I approached the receptionist to introduce myself.

"I have just the guy for you," she said, and pointed me down the hall to Nick Dranias.

In a city of people dressed Western casual—pearl-snap shirts or the golf-shirt-and-yellow-pants uniform of the retiree—Nick, in a blue dress shirt and necktie, looked like the Ambassador from Back East. He occupied the usual politico's cage—paneled walls covered with handshake photos, certificates of appreciation, and patriotic tchotchkes.

Nick could have been anywhere from thirty-five to fifty, with deep-set eyes and a face held studiously immobile, as though emoting would be somehow *liberal* or amount to giving something away for free. He was gracious about receiving an unscheduled visitor, but I got the feeling that he had a button under his desk that would drop my chair into a spiked pit if I irritated him.

He wrote amicus briefs for a living, injecting a conservative and libertarian viewpoint into legal battles involving everything from election laws to aquarium subsidies to guns. I asked about the relationship of guns to the conservative movement, and he began winding up to DeSomma's Second Amendment argument that an armed citizenry is a bulwark against tyranny.

"Stop," I said, holding up a palm. "A bunch of guys with rifles in their closets isn't going to do much against an army with tanks, helicopters, and jet planes."

He sat back and regarded me down his nose with a faint smile, as though he'd been waiting years for someone to blunder into such a trap. "That's an odd thing for someone of your age to say," he said. "What year were you born?"

"Nineteen fifty-six."

He sat forward, folded his hands, and leaned forward over them, glowering at me. "Vietnam is the defining war of your lifetime, and the mighty

U.S. military was defeated by an enemy with little more than rifles. Our two current wars are much the same, and neither is looking good. And look at the Russians in Afghanistan." He leaned back luxuriously in his swivel chair. "Don't tell me that people with nothing but rifles can't take on a modern military."

We looked at each other in silence for a moment. I opened my mouth to respond, and he leaned forward slightly like a panther ready to strike. I closed my mouth and sidestepped.

The Supreme Court had recently struck down Washington, D.C.'s long-standing handgun ban, which conservatives were celebrating as a great victory. Nick himself had written a brief arguing that the ban should go. "I thought conservatives were all about states' rights," I said. "Don't you think the people of Washington, D.C., have the right to decide what gun laws work best for them locally?"

He smacked that one away. "I think we need to get rid of the concept that local government is sacrosanct. If anything, the government that knows where you live is even more dangerous than the government far away in Washington."

"Tinfoil hat!" I said, and I could feel his finger inching toward the button. Instead he glanced at his watch.

"You on the left look at a problem like gun violence and say, 'We have to do something,'" he said with a kind of bemused sadness, as though describing the pitiable behavior of primitives. "We on the right are more inclined to say, 'We're a big, messy, polyglot nation with an extraordinary amount of freedom, and a certain number of bad things are bound to happen.' Where did you get the idea that you can limit gun violence without infringing on people's rights?"

Thirty thousand gun deaths a year was a terrible thing, as Nick saw it, but not as bad as limiting the gun rights of Americans—just as 136,000 dead American soldiers had been a heartbreaking catastrophe, but not as bad as letting Europe fall to the Nazis. Freedom had a price. It suddenly seemed less odd that the father of the kid I'd met at the Family Shooting Center had let his son keep guns after the accidental discharge inside the house. Depriving his grown son of firearms after the scary lesson of the accidental shot must have seemed worse to him than letting him keep the guns: His son had learned a lesson, and if he hadn't, he'd pay the price. This was at the opposite pole from the way I'd always thought about risk and personal sovereignty—whether of a son or of a populace.

"You carry a gun?" I asked Nick.

"I have one; I don't carry it."

"Why not?"

He shrugged and stood up, letting me know our time together was over. As he opened the door, he coughed into his fist and lowered his voice. "I have to tell you this, though. I and a lot of us conservatives are appalled at our reaction after 9/11. We got caught up in the bloodlust, and it took us a year or two to recover our principles. The Patriot Act, Guantánamo, the renditions . . . we should have been out there objecting, and we weren't. So if today, as you're traveling around talking to what seem like angry gun owners, and you perceive conservatives doubling down on these principles, our failure after 9/11 may be why."

4. BLOWBACK

We cannot but pity the boy who has never fired a gun; he is no more humane, while his education has been sadly neglected.

—Henry David Thoreau, "Higher Laws," *Walden*

Robert had a terrific childhood. His family was midwestern Jewish royalty, grown wealthy beyond measure by processing worn-out milk cows into hamburger. Robert and his brother, Justin, had the run of a sprawling operation, from the wood-paneled office where his dad and grandpa sat at facing desks to the macabre excitement of the killing floor. At the cooperage, gray-bearded craftsmen hammered iron staves to bind wooden barrels; they taught Robert the trick of spinning thirty-five-pound monsters across the floor on their edges. Everybody knew little Robert. Everybody loved him.

Home was a gigantic Southern colonial with a pool, not far from Lake Michigan. Dad had a den to himself, with a big wooden desk and glass cabinets that held a fine collection of early U.S. military pistols. He'd call Robert over and invite him to run a finger along the page of a musty-smelling reference book. "This .65-caliber light dragoon pistol was important at the Battle of New Orleans," Dad would begin, settling into an action-filled history lesson. He often took Robert with him to gun shows. While Dad inspected Scottish Highland flintlocks, Robert bought trinkets—a Nazi armband for two dollars, a bayonet for a buck, cartridge belts, holsters, insignia—nothing that cost more than a few dollars. His parents eventually let him take the bookshelves out of his bedroom and install glass cases like Dad's for his collection.

Weekends were the best. Robert would sit on a split-rail fence while Mom and Dad swung shotguns skyward from their lakeside gun club, scattering clay-pigeon fragments across the water, laughing and joking like best friends. Few women shot at the club, but Mom had a more expansive sense of fun than most. She was Texan—the granddaughter of Jewish covered-wagon pioneers—and lived her heritage large. When she built her house in the cold, flat North, Texas governor Allan Shivers sent her a box of Kinney County dirt to pour into the foundation so that she could raise her boys on Texas soil. Once a year, the family boarded the Texas Chief, and Uncle Buddy would flag the train down at the hamlet of Sugar Land, where, between Hanukkah and New Year's, Robert Justin lived the cowboy life with a slew of cousins on the family ranch.

That Uncle Buddy—he was a character. He'd commanded a Negro machine-gun unit during the war and would have made the Army his life but for a car accident that locked his knee. During one visit, when Robert was nine and Justin eleven, Uncle Buddy took the boys for a bumpy ride on his tractor—always a treat—and they chugged along until they reached a big cottonwood. At its base stood a rusted fifty-five-gallon drum. Uncle Buddy hopped down awkwardly, with his stiff-straight leg, and, with a tug that would change the course of little Robert's life, opened a wooden box bolted to the tractor. From a tangle of tools and rope he brought up a submachine gun.

It was an M3—a short, crude weapon made entirely of stamped steel. The Army had bought them by the thousand during the Second World War, for a few dollars apiece; soldiers called them "grease guns," because they looked more like mechanic's tools than weapons.

Uncle Buddy loaded up a long magazine with .45-caliber cartridges and stood behind Robert, wrapping his arms around him, helping him tuck the bent-wire stock into his shoulder. Robert tightened his right hand around the pistol grip and his left around the magazine. "Okay," Uncle Buddy said, and the short, fat gun bucked wildly in Robert's hands, with the roar of Robert's future splitting open.

It clicked empty in two seconds, the fifty-five-gallon drum thoroughly perforated.

Even with the copious spending money Robert was earning in the cooperage by then, he couldn't buy a shootable machine gun; he was only nine years old. But he could buy one that was deactivated, and the next time he went to a gun show with his dad, he found a Sten—a British submachine gun made of cheap stamped steel, much like the M3—with a bolt welded through the receiver to render it harmless. The price was $25—a lot of money in 1963, but Robert had it. He mounted the Sten proudly in his display case. Robert was hooked.

Reading gun magazines, he learned that until 1934, anyone could walk into a hardware store and buy a live Thompson submachine gun for about $250, with no paperwork to fill out and no questions asked—which helped explain why the only figures Robert could name from the twenties and early thirties were the likes of Al Capone, Baby Face Nelson, Machine Gun Kelly, John Dillinger, Bonnie Parker, and Clyde Barrow. Then came the National Firearms Act, which placed the same background-check requirement and two-hundred-dollar tax on machine guns as it did on silencers.

For a long time after the gangster era, most people had no idea that it was legal to buy a machine gun. The government certainly didn't publicize it. Machine-gun enthusiasts were a small, quiet club, selling each other guns for a few hundred dollars apiece, buying their two-hundred-dollar tax stamps, and keeping out of trouble. At age nine, Robert parted the curtain on this hidden world.

The tax, background check, and restrictions didn't apply to deactivated guns, and little Robert was interested in any he could get for two hundred dollars or less. He supplemented his income at the cooperage by bringing back from Texas for his private-school friends two treasures unobtainable in the upper Midwest: fireworks and Fritos.

In 1964, when Robert was eleven, he placed a person-to-person call to the dean of American machine-gun dealers: J. Curtis Earl. Robert wanted to buy a deactivated MP40—a German submachine gun from the Second World War—but he knew that Mr. Earl might hang up the phone as soon as he heard a squeaky prepubescent voice. So he did his homework carefully and got a lot of in-the-know language into his first sentences. He was looking for a DEWAT, he said—collectors' jargon for a deactivated war trophy—and while he'd love an MP38, because of its machined receiver and the longitudinal grooving on the receiver and bolt, he'd settle for the less expensive MP40, with its stamped-steel parts. Oh, and he didn't necessarily need the Bakelite foregrip.

There was a pause on the line. "Yes, I can help you," Mr. Earl said.

As soon as Robert had the MP40, he wanted the MP44, another Nazi weapon, and Mr. Earl sent him one, deactivated, for another two hundred dollars. "I know you can't put a drum on the A-1 Thompson, and it has the fixed firing pin," Robert said in his next appeal, "but does it still have the Blish lock in it?"

A Thompson, it turned out, was too expensive, but no sooner had he recited his Torah portion at his bar mitzvah than he unwrapped a DEWAT M1 Thompson, the wood-and-steel queen of submachine guns. Mom was the best.

Robert didn't want to be an architect or a veterinarian; he wanted to work in the family business and enjoy the good life. He put in time at unpleasant jobs in the rendering plant, on the killing floor, and in the blood room, where ring driers desiccated blood for the fertilizer shop. No matter how long you showered after working in the blood room, the odor would leach out of your pores the minute you began to perspire. He learned to tell a sick cow from a healthy one: Is her head swinging? Is she salivating? Does she have lumps in her brisket? He went to Burger King's Whopper College and spent a year running a Burger King in London, to see how the downstream industry operated. He worked for months on a gigantic deal to sell hamburger meat to the Moscow school system and walked away without clinching it, disgusted with the breathtaking graft.

By the mid-1970s—married, with small children—he was earning only eighteen thousand dollars a year. But his salary was irrelevant. Standing behind him was a slaughterhouse empire that he and his brother were in line to inherit. He could ladle up endless amounts of money for whatever he liked. What he liked was machine guns.

The more he read about them, the more fascinating their hold. Not so much the killing they did—military history wasn't his thing. What he loved was their gorgeous engineering, which said worlds about the mentality, technology, metallurgy, and international patent law of the late nineteenth and early twentieth centuries. Although Hiram Maxim of Maine had invented the machine gun (and the mouse trap!), it was John Browning of Ogden, Utah, who had pretty well perfected it by the time World War I broke out. His design was so simple, reliable, and elegant that it was still being used in Vietnam.* The other great powers of the turn of the century couldn't—for reasons of patent law, national security,

---

* The .50-caliber machine gun that Browning designed in 1918 was still the standard heavy machine gun of the U.S. military in 2012.

and jingoistic pride—simply copy Browning's design. So Britain, France, Germany, and Russia each went to sometimes comical lengths to dance around Browning's patents. The French, for example, created, in the St. Étienne Mle 1907, a blow-*forward* mechanism that used a pinion to transfer energy. It was ridiculous, guaranteed to foul in muddy conditions, but it was France's own design, and the French military proudly fielded it.

Robert loved all the Brownings and all the copies, the ones that worked and especially the ones that didn't. For him, the joy of collecting was seeing the march of technology through time. But he was also ready to move beyond DEWATs, to dip into the family fortune and buy a live machine gun. He called a man he knew at a police supply business and for $2,250 bought a never issued Model 1921 U.S. Navy Thompson with a fifty-round drum.

It was a blast to grind through cases of .45-caliber ammo at the gun club, until he realized with horror that he'd shot a virtually new gun down to about 93 percent condition. He hung the Thompson on the wall, retired. Collecting still mattered more than shooting.

He wangled himself an invitation to the exclusive York Arms and Armor Museum auction, in Las Vegas, where, at twenty-five, he was by far the youngest person in the room. He stood in the back, listened, kept his mouth shut until the right moment came to bid, and walked out the owner of a Browning Model 1917A1—the tripod-mounted, water-cooled .30-caliber machine gun on which the U.S. Army relied from the first World War through Korea. Not long after, he snagged a Vickers gun from Britain—another tripod-mounted, water-cooled giant—for a mere $2,500, and he followed that with a pair of 1920s-vintage water-cooled Swedish Brownings, each emblazoned with the king's crest and mounted on an anti-aircraft stand.

Taking the guns apart was pure joy. Their designs were ingenious, their internal parts beautifully wrought, and every gun had a universe of accoutrements to track down: ammo belts, ammo cans, carts, tripods, canvas covers, sights, cleaning kits, and manuals. He collected voraciously and gradually amassed a fully automatic arsenal worth many millions of dollars: an 1895 Argentine Maxim gun with a gleaming brass water jacket; an Austro-Hungarian Schwartzlose 07/12, which used the weight of the bolt to delay blowback; a nineteenth-century Nepalese Bira, a huge two-barreled, crank-operated contraption, seemingly of pig iron and covered with Devanagari script; a Soviet-made Maxim "snow gun," with its signature white-painted ricochet plate in front; a rare seawater-cooled

.50-caliber Browning, from the deck of a U.S. World War II destroyer; an Italian Fiat-Revelli that looked as though it would fall apart if sneezed on; Uzis; Schmeissers; a 1930s Soviet Pulemyot Degtyaryova Pekhotny, its round pan of ammunition mounted on top like a Frisbee. He arranged them in a bunker the size of a tennis court and decorated like an English gentlemen's club—pale yellow carpet, leather easy chairs, oak-paneled walls. But Robert was just about the only person who went down there. His guns were not for public display.

Robert's stack of machine-gun licenses grew as thick as a Manhattan phone book. The passport-size photos affixed to each license testified to the passage of his years, from a smooth-cheeked young scion to a jowly baron of commerce. Machine guns were an expensive hobby: Plugging gaps in his huge collection meant buying rare guns that cost $50,000 or more, sometimes *lots* more. He was becoming what machine-gun collectors call a "black hole," a guy who never sells a gun. He prided himself on being a true collector, not just an accumulator. He didn't hoover up every gun he found to demonstrate how rich he was, the way some people did. Each had to represent a unique moment in the technology's advancement.

Money wasn't a problem. Robert and his brother sat at the face-to-face desks their father and grandfather had used and grew a big business into a gigantic one. They diluted their shares to raise capital, packaged meat for Costco under the Kirkland label, expanded into deli meats and precooked dinners, and became the meat supplier for the McDonald's Steak, Egg & Cheese Bagel.

With bigger money, though, came bigger headaches. The science of looking for *E. coli* had gotten better since Robert and Justin had taken over, and the harder the government inspectors looked, the more they found. One week, the grinding line was closed; the next week, the killing floor. One government inspector would tell the plant to do one thing; another, the opposite.

Robert and Justin built a million-dollar laboratory to do their own testing and stay ahead of government scientists, but it wasn't only the scientists they had to watch; it was also regulators, who seemed to come up with a new requirement every fifteen minutes, and lawyers. The business never had a serious *E. coli* violation, thank heaven, but you never knew when it might come. Even a small violation could cost a fortune, exposing the company to the caprice of FDA inspectors or the mercy of plaintiff's attorneys.

The ATF, with its persnickety rules about machine guns, seemed to Robert a lot like the FDA; between the hobby and the business, he had no peace. There came a day, late in the Clinton years, when Robert and Justin looked at each other across the pushed-together desks and asked, "Who needs this?"

Justin was fifty, Robert getting close. They had all the money they would ever need. To continue the business would mean expanding yet again—there is no standing still in American industry—and that would mean starting all over: diluting shares and selling stock to raise capital, inventing new products, and finding new customers.

If any of their children had wanted to take over, Robert and Justin might have gone forward. But none did. So in August 2001—a month before the attacks of 9/11—they sold to Cargill the business their grandfather had built from nothing, and walked away loaded.

Retirement afforded Robert the time to ferret out artifacts of machine-gun culture—antique lead-soldier machine gunners, machine-gun-unit insignia, memoirs of machine gunners, machine-gun beer steins, one-sixth-scale working models of historic machine guns—and to fill the lacunae in his gun collection. He began writing technical articles on historical machine guns for one of the more scholarly firearms magazines. He became a well-known elder in the community of machine-gun enthusiasts, a gentleman collector, and a generous source of technological and historical information. He traveled each year to the big machine-gun shoots to see who had what on the firing line, reconnect with old friends, and perhaps find something new for his collection.

In the spring of 2010, he flew to Las Vegas, rented a car, and drove three hours south to Wikieup, Arizona, to one of his favorite shoots. There, amid the racketing gunfire, he met a stoop-shouldered middle-aged man in pleated pants and glasses, looking ridiculous in an NRA cap.

We stood atop a bulldozer-flattened ridge, in front of which spread a dry swale about half a mile wide, with a line of low hills rising beyond it—a perfect place to shoot. The hills beyond the swale made a backstop, and we were miles from the nearest house. As the sun came up, men in hoodies and camo pants were setting up a firing line on the flattened ridge, unpacking tools and ammunition boxes, rubbing their hands against the chill, talking in the kind of easygoing, jargon-heavy language you'd hear beside a NASCAR track. Dozens of machine guns stood on bipods and tripods or in racks, under makeshift sunshades made of blue tarp. We could have turned back the Wehrmacht.

Down in the swale, people moved about, erecting targets of various kinds: steel drums, junked cars, and dozens of odd-looking wooden stakes with orange tips, like enormous strike-anywhere matches.

Robert—with dashing black eyebrows, animated eyes, and a rakish smile—was holding forth on the technical problems of the nineteenth century. "The first machine guns were black powder; you can imagine the cloud of smoke they made," he said, dragging on a cigarette. He was short, so in his crisp insignia-covered leather jacket he looked like a ten-year-old boy playing fighter pilot. "What you needed was powerful, uniform, well-fitting cartridges to make the machine gun really work. It was the imprecision of cartridges that held back their early development." He'd have gone on, but an old friend, "Doc," called him over to help iron out a Vickers-gun problem.

An aroma of coffee drew me to a trailer manned by the Kingman, Arizona, 4-H club; since I'd last looked, the Department of Agriculture had broadened its mission of agrarian youth empowerment to include waiting on machine gunners. I bought a breakfast burrito and a cup of hot, coffee-flavored water from high schoolers who were suspiciously cheerful, given that the sun was barely up.

I'm not sure what I expected from the machine-gun crowd. But as I took a place at a picnic table with some gloriously unshaven shooters, I found myself in a history colloquium, a round-robin of martial arcana. Slurping up my burrito, I learned that the Viennese captain Baron Adolph von Odkolek had sold Hotchkiss its machine-gun design in 1893, but of course it was Laurence Benet who came up with the gun's signature heat-dispersing doughnut rings. Not until 1909, it turns out, did Argentina abandon the 7.65×53 Belgian round for the Maxim gun, replacing it with the 7.65×53 Spitzer—obviously for the flatter trajectory!

Holding burritos in their solvent-stained hands, the men debated whether Vickers had improved on Maxim's design when it bought the company in 1896, and whether the Blish lock was an advance or a dangerous step backward. Without so much as a pause, the conversation segued into machine guns seen in movies. The HBO series *The Pacific* had just begun, and everybody at the table agreed that its producers had gotten uniquely right the distinctive *clink-clink-clink* made by the reciprocating bolt of the Browning Model 1917A1 water-cooled machine gun.

Most of my companions were in their fifties or older, many with gray ponytails hanging from beneath ball caps, and dressed like day laborers. Yet they talked like professors—or patent freaks—and, given the value of the guns on the firing line, no doubt earned like bond traders.

A wizened man of about sixty in a Marine piss-cutter cap asked me to scoot over so he could sit down, and he brought the conversation down to where I could graze. "What you see in the World War One movies, machine guns mowing down rows of advancing soldiers? That's not how it was," he said. "The British called it the 'wall of fire.' What you did was, you shot your machine gun in the air so the bullets fell in a line in front of your own advancing soldiers. You shot over their heads, and the bullets came down in a curtain. The *cone* of fire was something else. You needed a forward observer for that. You done with this?"

He crumpled up my burrito wrapper. "Here's your machine gun," he said, one hand on the wrapper. "Over here"—my paper coffee cup—"is the enemy, camped behind a hill where they think they're safe." He laid his forearm between the cup and the wrapper to represent the hill. "You fire *over* the hill and rain the bullets down on them. *That's* how a machine gun should be used."

There's an image for a sleepless night: bullets raining silently out of the sky, straight down, so that not even a foxhole is cover.

I asked the men whether they minded paying the two-hundred-dollar federal tax. Wasn't that kind of steep? They laughed.

"I'll tell you steep," said a guy named Walter, who'd trekked to Arizona from Staten Island. "I got a 1917 Browning over there. I paid fifteen hundred for it back in the seventies. You wanted to buy that now, it'd be thirty grand. *Thirty grand!* And you're talking a two-hundred-dollar tax stamp? Shit, my gun will eat up two hundred dollars' worth of ammunition in thirty seconds. Two hundred dollars . . ."

"Used to be, it was a barrier to ownership. The tax was more than the gun."

"Those days are over."

"*Long* gone."

"So if I wanted to get into this, what's the cost of entry?" I asked. "What's the least expensive machine gun I could buy?"

"Sten gun," three men said in unison, and gave each other weary high fives. The stamped-steel British submachine gun with which nine-year-old Robert had started his DEWAT collection had cost the British government about four dollars apiece during World War II; now, if you could find one, it would go for a thousand times that much. And that was the cheapest machine gun on the market.

What had first jacked up the price was a piece of pet legislation from the National Rifle Association, the grandly named Firearms Owners' Protection Act of 1986. The law, signed by Ronald Reagan, repealed a lot of what the NRA considered bothersome 1960s-era gun regulations. At the eleventh hour, though, someone slipped in an amendment that banned the sale to civilians of any machine gun registered with the ATF after May 19, 1986. Suddenly the number of legally tradable machine guns was fixed at about 186,000. But what made the price skyrocket, about seven years later, was the advent of the World Wide Web. Pretty soon, Web crawlers all over America were finding sites catering to the full-auto hobby and saying to themselves, "Holy shit! I can buy a *machine gun*!"

"In the early days, it was working guys, guys interested in mechanical things," said Walter from Staten Island. "They'd buy one for a few hundred bucks, shoot it awhile, sell it, and buy another. Back then—we're talking the fifties and sixties—machine-gun people were the lower-class shooters, looked down on by the skeet shooters, the marksmen, the collectors. This is an era, remember, when skeet shooters wore neckties. We machine-gun guys were a little fraternity with dirt under our fingernails. Then, in the nineties"—he clapped his hands loudly—"prices go crazy. It becomes a yuppie thing. Now it's the owner of the muffler shop instead of the guy working in the muffler shop, you hear me?" He leaned in close. "Me, no way I could buy that gun today." He glanced over both shoulders. "More rich guys here than at the Kentucky Derby."

The men stood, threw their foil wrappings into blue plastic trash barrels, and made their way to the firing line. The people had cleared out of the swale, and the air was alive with the *clickety-clack* of guns being loaded and locked. Everybody clamped on hearing protectors. A Freon boat horn sounded, and all the guns opened up at once with a sound like the universe splitting in twain.

Puffs of dust danced over the swale, green-and-red tracer bullets scratched the air, brass cartridges leapt in twinkling streams from smoking receivers. The oversize strike-anywhere matches turned out to be posts with sticks of dynamite strapped to them. Each time a bullet found one, it exploded with a sinus-popping boom and a house-size ball of sulfurous yellow smoke.

Robert stood watching with his hands in the pockets of his leather flight jacket, grinning widely around a cigarette. "I love this shoot!" he yelled above the din. "Look how few spectators! It's just for the shooters. It's a gentlemen's shoot!"

"Are there other shoots?"

"Lots! They've become popular as Republican fund-raisers! You going to shoot?"

"I don't have a machine gun!"

He motioned me to follow him, and we strolled down the line to a blue-tarp booth with a hand-lettered sign: MACHINE GUN RENTALS. Listed on the board, like sandwiches at a deli, were guns available to rent. THOMPSON $25. PPSH $20. STEN $20. BAR $50. The prices listed were to fire a single magazine of ammunition. I stepped forward and told a young woman—one of the few women I'd seen all morning—that I wanted to shoot the Thompson. She took my money and motioned me forward to the lip of the swale.

It was an inferno down there—tracers bouncing everywhere, junked cars aflame, dynamite bursting. The prairie dogs and lizards must have been wondering, *What in the hell?* A buff man in his sixties, his high fade looming like a granite cliff, stepped up beside me, clutching a Thompson submachine gun. He inserted a thirty-round magazine, pulled back the bolt, set the safety, and held it out to me.

"Could you undo all that?"

He cocked an eye suspiciously.

"Could you take out the magazine and uncock it?" I shouted above the din.

He frowned.

"I want to do all that myself!" It was the *feel* of a gun I liked most— hefting the weight, working the mechanism. I'd been watching soldiers, cops, and gangsters manipulate tommy guns since before I could remember. I could have gone through those insouciant moves in my sleep. And here was my one chance to do it myself.

The man shrugged and removed the magazine. He ejected the chambered round, pressed it back into the magazine, and put the gun in my arms.

Holding it by its pistol grip, I fitted the magazine into the slot and slapped it home with the heel of my hand, like Sergeant Saunders on

Combat! or Eliot Ness on *The Untouchables*. With my left hand, I grabbed the bolt on top of the gun and slicked it back. Clenching an imaginary stogie between my teeth, I raised the gun to my cheek.

It kicked far less than I'd imagined. With the stock beating against my shoulder, I was able to direct a line of dust clouds across the desert floor and onto one of the orange sticks. *Ka-boom!*

The gun clicked empty—twenty-five dollars gone in about four seconds. Robert was grinning enormously. "You get it now?" he asked with a laugh.

I did. Choose the most adamant anti-gun peacenik you know and give him a tommy gun to shoot at a stick of dynamite. Then strap him to a polygraph and ask him if it was fun.

Roger Sprava, one of the youngest shooters on the line, was hammering away with a tripod-mounted Browning Model 1919 belt-fed .30-caliber—a gun you practically needed a mortgage to buy—making a small mountain of empty brass shells. In a wooden rack behind him stood more guns, a collection that probably topped $100,000. I figured he was a trust-fund baby.

"Rich? Me?" he said, when he took a break. He had short hair and a thin, boyish face, which he wrinkled up as he fanned smoke away from his gun's hot breech. "I work for a semiconductor company in Phoenix. I just save up." He'd bought his first machine gun in 1997. "All I wanted was an eight-hundred-dollar MAC-10, after that two-handed thing Arnold Schwarzenegger did in *True Lies*," he said. But after that, one thing led to another. "I got an M16 next . . ." He gestured sheepishly toward the collection beside him: an M2 carbine, an Uzi with a silencer as big around as a whiskey bottle, and a Thompson. Their long steel barrels glinted in the intense Arizona sunlight. Sprava was glad he'd put his money into these instead of, say, mutual funds—an understandable sentiment in the recession-darkened spring of 2010. "I know these are always going up in value," he said. "And you can't take your mutual funds out on Saturday and play with them." I asked what had attracted him to the guns. Their mechanical elegance? The story of their patents? The history of the battles in which they were used? "Naw," he said. "They're fun to shoot." He figured he'd probably go through six thousand dollars' worth of ammunition at the two-day event.

The shoot lasted all day and into a blazing, tracer-streaked night. About once an hour, the guns fell silent so that range officers could replace and refresh targets and shooters could collect brass in big barrels for reloading. New guns kept showing up. A couple of guys spent an hour setting up a six-foot-long Soviet DShK 12.7-millimeter anti-aircraft machine gun that sucked everybody's attention away from the ordinary Vickers and Brownings. When those guys finally started firing off a belt of cartridges the size of small flashlights, I could feel my clothing flutter.

Reporters can be cynical, but in thirty years of encounters, I'd had plenty of moments to marvel at the freedom of information that Americans enjoy. I'd challenged powerful government officials in interviews without having to think about the consequences. I'd received packets of sensitive documents in the mail, not from thieves but openly, in response to Freedom of Information Act requests. I'd published accounts of official wrongdoing and expected only accolades (as opposed to a midnight interrogation and summary execution). Day to day, I'd taken it for granted. Every now and then, though—especially when working in Latin America, Asia, and Africa, and even in Europe—I'd felt awe for the uniqueness of America's compact with its citizens. The power we enjoyed to *know* implied an amazing amount of trust in the people. Go ahead, the system seemed to say, discover and denounce the most explosive misdeeds of your government. The republic can take it. The republic depends on it.

I found myself thinking that way on the flattened mesa outside Wikieup, where ordinary Americans, some rich, some not so much, were playing with incredibly powerful weapons, blithely taking them out and blasting away on a sunny Saturday with no kind of official supervision. No other functioning country on earth trusted its people with such weapons. And the trust seemed well placed. An ATF official I'd met told me that, in the seven decades since licensing began, not a single licensed machine gun had been used in a violent crime. The people who got permits were thoroughly checked out, had thousands of dollars invested in their toys, and didn't want to risk losing them.

If you bought the argument that the private ownership of firearms demonstrated America's exceptional trust in its citizens, then to be one of the people who owned and used firearms was to make that trust manifest. To do so with a machine gun—well, that was the ultimate.

This was how the NRA and the firearms industry encouraged those of us who liked guns to think, at any rate. It was how they'd managed to raise an otherwise ordinary hobby to the exalted plane of patriotic duty.

During the next break in the gunning, I found myself standing next to Roger Sprava in line for a cup of that watery 4-H coffee. His face flecked with powder residue, his hands streaked with angry red blisters from brushing against a red-hot barrel, he was one happy-looking man.

"Let me guess," I said. "You're not married."

"No," he laughed. "If I was married, I'd probably have a fancy bathroom instead!"

5. FUDD LIKE ME

A peculiar virtue in wildlife ethics is that the hunter ordinarily has no gallery to applaud or disapprove of his conduct. Whatever his acts, they are dictated by his own conscience, rather than by a mob of onlookers. It is difficult to exaggerate the importance of this fact.

—Aldo Leopold, *A Sand County Almanac*

All the anger about guns mysteriously evaporated when the subject turned to hunting. Even the most ardent gun-control advocates knew that too much tradition lay aback of hunting to think of meddling with it.* Hunting could even be useful to them; it afforded the opportunity for some political jujitsu. By acknowledging hunting as a legitimate use of guns, gun-control advocates could offer an olive branch while condemning other guns and gun use. Politicians hoping to reimpose a ban on assault rifles could establish that they wouldn't dream of interfering with the good guns with which Americans hunted, only with the bad guns with which they killed each other. Howard Dean: "I never met a hunter who needed an AK-47 to shoot a deer." John Kerry: "When I go out there and hunt, I'm going out there with a twelve-gauge shotgun, not an assault weapon." Bill Clinton: "You don't need an Uzi to go deer hunting, and everybody knows it." If the only gun use you countenanced was hunting,

* Not a universally held view, of course: Harvard Law professor Cass Sunstein made himself famous in 2007 by saying in a speech, "We ought to ban hunting now, if there isn't a purpose other than sport and fun. That should be against the law. It's time now." The remark, along with his assertion that animals should have standing to sue in U.S. courts, almost cost him his Senate confirmation as President Obama's regulatory czar.

the comments made perfect sense. If, though, you were into self-defense, competitive shooting, Walter Mitty fantasy, historical collecting, end-of-the-world preparation, tyranny prevention, machine-gun meet-ups, or you just thought guns were cool and fun, holding up hunting as the sole legitimate use of guns sounded either ignorant or offensive or both.

Still, the firearms industry recognized that the path to firearm legitimacy ran through hunting, and it was making a feverish attempt as I drove around Arizona to rebrand the AR-15 from "assault rifle" to "modern sporting rifle"—the firearm with which everybody was likely to be hunting in a few years. Most states didn't allow people to hunt deer with the .223-caliber bullet that the basic AR-15 fired, but the cartridge was great for small game, and because of the gun's unique modularity, it was easy to make it fire hunting-caliber cartridges. The website of the National Shooting Sports Foundation offered a video of a kindly old gent in flannel shirt and Elmer Fudd hat hefting a camo-painted AR. "Anti-gun folks insist on calling these rifles 'assault weapons,' to label these 'bad guns,' as opposed to more traditional-looking 'good guns,'" he said, as soothingly as Wilford Brimley in a Quaker Oats commercial. "Truth is, it won't be too long before lots of hunters call one of these rifles 'Old Betsy.'"

As I traveled around talking to gun guys, "modern sporting rifle"—or MSR—was becoming the new term of art for the AR-15. Though I never once heard anybody use the term while speaking, the gun press used it universally. It was easy to get the sense that a kind of race was under way: Could the AR-15 lose its assault-rifle stigma and become thoroughly legitimized as a modern sporting rifle before the forces of gun control could mount another assault-rifle ban?

The truth was, a lot of gun-rights activists didn't even consider hunters allies in the cause. They called them "Fudds" and dismissed them as dilettantes who lolled comfortably in their privileged status as the only legitimate gun users. Fudds couldn't be bothered to raise a ruckus over handguns, concealed-carry rights, or the Second Amendment. As one gun-rights activist put it to me in an e-mail, "I don't need phony gun owners, like the American Hunters and Shooters Association, muddying the waters." What's more, Fudds had dropped the ball on inducting a new generation into the gun life; the number of hunters was dropping, and their average age was increasing.

Hunters were a diverse group, attracted to the sport for myriad reasons, and hunting was a lot more complicated—physically, socially, ethically, and spiritually—than I could have imagined before trying it. I came to it as a way back to guns, many years after leaving my high school air guns. It was, as they said, a legitimate way to keep guns in my life. I could feel their weight and shape in my hands as I walked the woods.

My first hunt was in Georgia, in 1985. I'd crossed the Mason-Dixon line to take a job as a police reporter for the Atlanta *Journal-Constitution,* whose newsroom was a vast cavern of cigarette smoke, with green-screen computer terminals the size of small refrigerators. The Internet lurked just over the horizon, and newspapers like the *Journal-Constitution* were snoozing through the lazy, corrupt twilight of their media dominance. The city desk may have been anchored by good ol' boys who packed their cheeks with tobacco and put salted peanuts in their Co'Cola, but the reporters with whom I spent my days were largely cynical, urban Yankee transplants like me.

With nobody in my life who could teach me to hunt, I bought an ancient copy of *How to Hunt Deer and Small Game,* a 1959 hardcover full of terrific black-and-white photos of men in checkered duffel coats and Elmer Fudd hats trudging through the Maine snow. I pored over utterly unfamiliar concepts ("Slice through the anus-end of the lower intestine and carefully lift it free of the body cavity . . ."). I wasn't sure if, when the moment came, I'd be able to kill a big mammal with a gun.

The spindly Remington .22 I'd bought in college wouldn't reliably knock a deer over and wasn't legal for hunting, so I paid a pawnshop sixty-five dollars for one of the rifles I loved from old war movies: a British .303 Lee-Enfield, a blunt-nosed monster of wood, iron, and brass that was made in 1916 and weighed slightly less than a grand piano.

Thus equipped, I drove south one autumn evening to the Oconee National Forest, expecting to pitch my little tent in the silent woods and wake in solitude before dawn of opening day. As my headlights swept the forest's campground, though, I beheld the pandemonium of a miniature redneck Woodstock: dozens of tents pitched side by side, roaring camp-fires, gigantic jacked-up pickup trucks rumbling through, and hundreds of skinny white men whooping and hollering and passing around bottles of Evan Williams bourbon while boom boxes balanced on truck hoods blasted George Strait and Ronnie Milsap. This was obviously an annual ritual. I wedged my tent between two others and joined a nearby camp-fire. "Hey, man," a ropy Confederate said, offering the bottle. "You from

Atlanta, ain't you." To these guys, Atlanta—forty minutes away—was another planet; not quite Yankeeland, but close.

"Worse, actually. I'm from New Jersey, and I *live* in Atlanta."

"Yankee boy!" one of the men laughed, spinning the cylinder on a long-barreled .357 revolver. "Well, you're welcome here if what you come for is to hunt deer. That's what we're about tonight: hunting deer."

"I'm here to hunt deer," I said. "But it's my first time. What do I need to know?"

Everybody started talking at once: *You want to take and hold just back of the point of the shoulder. Spray your legs with this here deer estrus to mask your scent. Get you a place to sit while it's still dark so you're there when the sun first comes up. Deer can only see motion; sit still enough and they'll walk right up on you. Get in a tree if you can; deer don't look up. Cut the scent glands out the hind legs first thing so they can't taint the meat, and then be sure to wash your knife. Keep the wind in your face. Watch you don't cut the gut getting it out the deer or your meat will taste like shit.*

It was too much to absorb, especially with that bottle of Evan Williams going around, but what came through was how sincerely the guys wanted to initiate me into their world. A man who hadn't grown up hunting must have been an oddity for them—and a Yankee certainly was—but they didn't pay that any mind. What mattered was that someone wanted to know how to hunt, had bought himself a rifle and a fistful of deer tags, and had come to try it. They took me in like a kid brother, not in a condescending way but with tenderness and concern. What they were doing, I'd come to understand years later, was *recruiting.* Like the baby-faced kid who would insist I shoot his AR-15, the guys in hunting camp were doing what they could to widen and strengthen the circle of gun guys—or at least of Fudds. When people talk about a "brotherhood of arms," it isn't just soldiers they mean.

I finally staggered off to bed and woke in darkness to the *tweedle-deet* of my pocket alarm clock. The camp was stirring, bacon and coffee heavy in the air. I felt my way down a dirt road in blackness, walking for twenty minutes or so before turning into the woods. I crunched through the dry leaves until I guessed I'd put plenty of distance between me and everybody else. It felt like the heart of the forest primeval. By starlight I could make out a broad swale ahead of me. I sat with my back against a tree, with a good view of any animal that might pass.

It took a long time for the sun to rise. An eerie mist rose from the rotting leaves. The squirrels began to stir and the birds to chirp. Voles scurried beneath fallen leaves. Gradually I discovered that I could see color—the yellow of the leaves on the forest floor, the bright orange of my vest, everything slowly morphing from shades of gray. I looked at my watch: 5:59. One minute to the start of my first-ever deer season.

Out of nowhere, the woods exploded with gunfire—a great ripping wave roaring from every direction. It seemed that every man from the campsite had opened fire the second it was legal to do so, whether he had a target or not. I slid lower on the tree, lest a stray bullet find me. I heard a *thump-rustle* in the swale below, and trotting through, about seventy yards away, was a panicked yearling, no bigger than a German shepherd, looking to get out of the bullet storm. Like a cat on a mouse, I fixated. Whatever doubt I'd had about my ability to kill vaporized in a flash of predator energy. I'd come out to kill something, and here something was. I hoisted the Enfield to my shoulder and sighted on the deer's rib cage. When I pulled the trigger, the gun thudded hard against me; the shot must have sounded, but it hardly registered. I looked over my gun barrel and the yearling was gone. Had I disintegrated the tiny animal with my enormous rifle? A second passed, and another *thump-rustle* in the brush told me he had fallen.

I walked down the hill with my hand wrapped around my mouth in horror. The little deer lay with its front leg twisted under it, eyes open, stone still. A big red hole glowered from its rib cage like an angry third eye, and vivid red blood splashed the yellow leaves. My face was hot, as though I'd smashed a priceless vase; my first impulse was to run away in shame and tell nobody what I'd done. But I took a breath, removed the magazine from the rifle, and jacked the cartridge out of the chamber. Then I knelt beside the deer and did exactly what *How to Hunt Deer and Small Game*—and my drunken brothers from hunting camp—had taught me to do. It was remarkably easy, and very quickly the remorse and disgust I'd felt gave way to a sense of wonder at the complexity of a mammal's anatomy and—as corny as it would have sounded to my colleagues in the newsroom—gratitude to the deer for letting me take him. The whole job took less than twenty minutes. I dragged him from the woods, laid him in the trunk of the car, drove him home, and, after a day of taking him apart, cooked him three different ways and held a dinner party at which my friends ate every bit of him.

It's one thing to handle guns and shoot them at paper targets. It's another to blow a ragged, bloody hole through a large warm-blooded animal. A week later, in my capacity as a police reporter, I sat in on an autopsy and was dumbstruck at how similar we are, internally, to a white-tailed deer: same pink-and-purple organs, same striated meat. Shooting that deer changed my relationship to guns. I'd killed something with a firearm, which both connected me to guns' history as tools and made me forever a dealer in gun death. I felt oddly freed to start buying them and discovered that I liked the ones from the early twentieth century. I found a 1918 British Webley revolver as a companion piece to my big Enfield, a 1942 Victory Model Smith & Wesson .38, and a Marlin pump-action shotgun from the Pinkerton strikebreaker era. Like a dope, I hung them on the wall of my Atlanta cottage, envisioning myself as the great out-doorsman, and was promptly burgled. For months, I imagined arriving at a homicide, reporter's notebook in hand, to peer over a detective's shoulder and find my Webley lying in a pool of blood.

It was around this time that I fell in love with Margaret, who was also a reporter at the paper. She'd spent her childhood summers hiking the Sierras from a phoneless, unelectrified family cabin three miles from the nearest road, so her appetite for the woods was a given. I worried that my gun thing might be a problem for someone reared by Berkeley-educated Unitarian academics who worshiped at the altar of logic and reason. But I was encouraged when, on a hike, I pointed out a deer about the size of the one I'd shot, and she said, "Yum!"

Margaret was not a girly girl. The second of four children, she'd spent her childhood trying to keep up with a big brother. It was encoded in her DNA: If the boys were doing it, she had to do it. On a reporting trip to southern Georgia, I wandered into a pawnshop looking for old, cheap guns, as usual, and found on the rack a beat-up .30-30 Winchester, the basic cowboy saddle rifle, for $140. Margaret had been a horse-crazy kid and had learned lots of cowboy songs on the guitar during her off-the-grid summers. I wondered if a gift of weaponry too early in the relationship might queer it, but the Winchester's size and history seemed perfect.

"I have something for you," I told her that evening, and gingerly placed the rifle in her hands. "Cool!" she said, working the lever—*click-clack*—and sighting down the barrel. When I told her that she could learn to use it and come along hunting with me and the rednecks, whatever anti-gun instincts had been imprinted on her yielded to the need to keep up with the boys. We went to a range, and although the rifle's concussion made her burst into tears after the third shot ("I'm okay, I'm okay"), she put ten bullets through a five-inch paper plate at a hundred yards.

She wondered, as I had, whether she could bring herself to shoot a deer. "If, at the moment, you don't want to," I said, "don't. This isn't for everybody." All the lead-up, though—packing gear, studying maps, learning regulations—she enjoyed. She drank bourbon with the rebs in hunting camp and rose the next morning in the dark without complaint. We trooped farther into the woods this time, to get away from the gunfire, and found a couple of spots along a narrow creek. It was a cold morning; I kept my ungloved hands away from the rifle's metal parts as I waited for dawn. I blew on my fingers to keep them warm and ready, until finally, orange sunlight caught the frosted tips of the tall grass.

Gunshot. Gunshot. I took off running. As I approached, Margaret called through the forest, with an admirable lack of euphemism, "I killed a deer."

She hadn't—yet. The deer, which lay about fifty yards from where she had hidden, raised its head and looked at her. Beyond, frozen in wonder, stood the deer's fawn. For the first time, Margaret was upended. "Which do I shoot?" she asked, her voice trembling.

"Finish the one you shot," I said, and lifted my rifle to shoot the fawn, which to my great relief bounded off into a motherless future. Hurrying, Margaret fired. Her deer kicked around in the leaves and sat back up. I aimed at the deer's head, but Margaret said, "Let me." She stepped in closer, held her rifle out in front of her with two hands like a pistol, looked the deer right in the eye, and fired again. The deer went over and didn't move.

"Whew," Margaret said, panting clouds of steam, openmouthed and wide-eyed. We stood for a long moment saying nothing, then she sighed, jacked the remaining shell from her rifle, knelt beside the deer, and drew her knife. She ran her hand along the doe's flank and said, "Soft." She lifted its hind leg to roll it onto its back and began the incision. "Look," she said, "she's lactating."

Margaret worked with single-minded concentration, taking as long to gut her dead doe as it would have taken to perform a heart transplant on a live one. With her hands deep in the steaming cavity, she asked questions about the butchering. But when I moved to help, she said, "I'll do it. It's kind of nice. She's warm inside."

She'd had the same reaction I'd had on my first hunt. After she'd waited, listened, and watched, unmoving forever in the cold, something primal had taken over when the prey stepped into view. For better or worse, we of the twenty-first century are held to a much narrower range of animal emotion than our forebears. Few of our stresses involve death. When you shoot a mammal as big as you are and bury your hands in its hot viscera, your spiritual-emotional seismograph swings like crazy: raw, chest-beating triumph, horror, gratitude, pride, shame . . . It is a brief and tiny taste of what it means to be a link on the food chain. A mammal's open eyes going cloudy as the life drains out, piles of steaming entrails on golden autumn leaves: Hunting is in a different category from tennis or windsurfing—or even other gun sports. You know you're really into it when you walk up on your dead animal and your stomach rumbles.

Thus did my childhood fascination with guns become my adult fascination with guns. I didn't yet understand the many ways that hunting—and the guns essential to the enterprise—moved other people. But for me, guns had become entangled with death and the outdoors and the woman I eventually married.

Mostly, I've hunted with a guy who doesn't care much for guns at all. Craig Menteer was raised in the dark woods of Washington State by a logger father so strong, stocky, taciturn, and stubborn that behind his back his stepsons called him "the Stump." He taught them everything there is to know about the woods—particularly how hard a man has to work to make them mean anything. Hunting trips with the Stump were businesslike affairs. The purpose was to gather meat, not clown around, drink, or show off. It wasn't about the guns, either; it was about the woods—understanding them well enough to navigate without getting lost, finding animals, surviving the unexpected, taking home the bounty. Craig also earned an Eagle Scout badge, expanding his familiarity with ropes and tools and the ways of Northwestern nature.

Hunters are warned never to take loaded firearms in a car, but some are so familiar with their equipment—and so sure of their own abilities—that they write their own rules. One night on the way home, with Craig behind the wheel and his brother in back, the Stump sat up front, unloading a lever-action .348 Winchester, a giant of a gun popular in Alaska for killing bears. As he worked the lever to jack the shells free, his finger touched the trigger. The blast, encased in the car, was so loud that Craig's ears swallowed it as a thick, high-pitched silence. By luck, the bullet missed Dad's foot, the steering apparatus, and the brake lines, making a harmless hole in the floorboard. The car filled with the smell of burned cordite and the appalling realization that the Stump had screwed up. Nobody yelled, though, and nobody apologized. Craig muttered, "It's okay. It didn't hit the tire." They drove on in silence and never discussed it again.

By the time I started hunting with Craig in Montana in the early 1990s, he was a carpenter and performance artist, gray-haired, broad-chested, and strong as Samson. He was more at home in the woods than anyone I'd ever known, with a natural command of their rich lexicon. We'd "work a drainage" to "jump up" an elk. He'd have me sit by a "swale," stake out a "coulee," or climb to a "park." We'd separate for the morning, and when we met up, he'd draw in the dirt a map of everyplace he'd been. Being an Eagle Scout, he built hunting camps that looked like illustrations from *Boy's Life*—the tents squared, with drainage ditches cut around them, a neat fire ring with grill and coffeepot atop, ample firewood in stacks segregated by size, and a hatchet planted in a stump at the regulation 45-degree angle.

What impressed me most when I started hunting with Craig was the solemnity that attended the harvest. Montana's hunting regulations were published in a thick booklet that divided the state into more than a hundred tiny hunting districts, each with its own fussy rules about species, sex, weapon, the permissibility of vehicles, day of month, time of day, and antler points. Forms had to be filled out and boxes checked. A tiny mistake could invalidate the application. Getting a deer tag was as complicated and tedious as doing taxes, but the process imparted a message: Deer were a precious resource, to be managed with care.

Craig extended the ethic into the field. He taught me to stalk on tiptoe, "glass" animals through binoculars for their legal characteristics before placing a shot, and butcher with the exactitude of a surgeon so as not to waste a mouthful of meat. The hip thing to do in those days was to rub a little tobacco on the dead animal's fur to thank its spirit for the offering. The whole exercise was wrapped in reverence.

For all of his love of hunting, Craig's rifle was the most woebegone piece of shooting equipment I'd ever seen. It was an old bolt-action Savage .30-30, a low-end gun to begin with, and in miserable shape. A hose clamp held the rear sight to the barrel. The olive-green cloth strap of a Boy Scout canteen was tied on as a sling. He kept it clean and oiled, being an Eagle Scout, but he cared little for it.

He didn't shoot it much, either. We'd go to the range before the season began, and he'd bang away a few times to make sure it was sighted in properly, but I never knew him to shoot for fun. He didn't troll pawnshops with me in search of old guns. During hunting season, he rarely shot. Many years, he bagged no deer at all. He never seemed to care, though. What he liked was hunting—reading the woods, searching for signs, sensing where the animals might be feeding by how the snow fell and the wind blew, cooking and sleeping among the trees. When the season ended, he cleaned and oiled his rifle, put it in the basement, and didn't think about it again until the following October. When I finally persuaded him to buy a new rifle, he made an odd choice: a lever-action .444 Marlin that shot a monstrous straight-walled, blunt-nosed cartridge. It was designed to hunt bear in dense woods, not deer in the kinds of fields and open forest where we hunted. Guns move people in mysterious ways. The Marlin was heavy, expensive to shoot, and terrible beyond a hundred yards. It did, however, recall the Stump's big lever-action .348.

Craig was on my mind as I drove back to Boulder after the Arizona machine-gun shoot. Margaret and I were planning to canoe Utah's Green River with Craig and his wife, Laura, in a few weeks, and I looked forward to being in a new kind of wilderness with the old Eagle Scout.

I tried telling friends in Boulder about the Wikieup machine-gun shoot, but few of them could get past their horror that people were allowed to own machine guns. I also wrote an article about it for *Men's Journal,* one of the magazines owned by *Rolling Stone* publisher Jann Wenner, and for the first time in my twenty-five-year career had an article killed for explicitly political reasons. The editor had quibbles with the piece as editors always do, but wouldn't give me the chance to fix them. "I can't even show this to Jann," said the editor. "It's not anti-gun enough."

Not anti-gun *enough*? Machine gunners were a colorful male subculture that did nobody any harm. Why did an article about them have to be *anti* at all? I tried explaining to my editor that gun owners felt vilified by the media and that this was a good opportunity for *Men's Journal* not only to run a story appealingly full of bang-bang and idiosyncratic characters but also to buy some goodwill from the 40 percent of American households that owned guns. He wouldn't budge. Jann had his position on gun stories, he explained. Only one point of view was welcome.

I broke my "concealed means *concealed*" rule only once, and was instantly sorry. A few days after returning from Arizona, I went to hear a lecture at Naropa University, the Buddhist college in Boulder. Naturally, I had my gun under my jacket, and I later made the mistake of mentioning that to a friend. He went white with rage. "You wore a *gun* into a peace-building institution?" I might as well have told a Hasid that I'd smuggled a crucifix into his shul. Our relationship was strained for months.

I was looking forward to taking a break from the gun; I wasn't plan-ning to bring it on the canoe trip with Margaret, Laura, and Craig. Nor were we planning to take Rosa. She was deep in the swale of high school's junior year and the dreary approach of college application essays. Also, she had recently gotten her driver's license and was eager for a vacation from parental supervision. She was a responsible kid; we had no reason not to trust her. After heaping upon her the obligatory mountain of rules and admonitions, we kissed her on the forehead and ditched her for the desert.

The Green River was a thick chocolate brown, silty with winter runoff. The stretch we were floating had no rapids, and we could paddle or not as we saw fit. We spent many hours holding the canoes together by the gunwales, pinwheeling gently downriver, the scenery gliding past. No e-mail, no cell phones, no automobiles . . . nothing but river, sky, and the soughing of the breeze. By the middle of the third day we were floating through a Road Runner cartoon; walls of red rock three hundred feet high towered over us like great slabs of raw beef. We paddled close along-side and ran our fingers over their smooth scarlet faces, and when ravens flew by, the sound of their wings echoed off the rock like vorpal blades going *snicker-snack*.

We came upon a pair of newlyweds on a honeymoon float; they offered us leftover wedding canapés and slushy margaritas, so we lashed our canoes to their raft. Suddenly: a gunshot. A hundred yards ahead, a bul-let splashed into the river. A second later came another shot and another splash. Firing at water is the act of a madman; there's no telling where the bullet might ricochet. So much for being away from guns for a few days. We back-paddled, yelling.

"Hey! Hey!" Craig stood in his canoe and waved his arms.

The shooting stopped. The cliffs gave way to sagebrush flats, and we could see men standing beside a jeep that had big lights mounted on the roll bar. For a minute I thought they were cops or rangers, but they were only off-road motorheads who'd bounced into the canyon on a rutted trail. We stopped back-paddling. There was no alternative but to drift past them. Two of them, young and tattooed, in sleeveless shirts, ball caps on backward, eyeballs swimming in beer, seemed the type who showed up in YouTube videos, drunkenly firing at propane tanks. The other two, in golf caps and camouflage pants, could have been their fathers. I addressed myself to the oldest, who had steel-gray hair and a big hard belly. "Please don't shoot at the water!" I yelled. "Those bullets can bounce anywhere!"

"We weren't shooting at the water," he called back. "We were shooting at those cliffs up there!" He pointed across the river at a magnificent thousand-foot tower of red rock. I was shocked into silence. Laura—accustomed, from living in Montana, to the antics of armed chowderheads—turned away discreetly and guffawed into her hand. They'd shot at the rock, and the bullet had bounced back to hit the water thirty feet in front of them. Instead of absorbing the wee physics lesson, *they'd shot at the rock again.* How long would they have kept it up if we hadn't floated by? Until one of them ended up in the emergency room, probably. It was like watching someone try to win a Darwin Award.

Calling a man a fucking idiot when he's holding a gun a million miles from civilization is unwise, so I requested merely that they hold fire until we'd rounded the bend. They agreed, and sure enough, as they dropped out of sight behind us, we could hear the shooting start up.

"You see what I'm talking about?" Margaret said. "A gun is not like a knife or a golf club. You can project idiocy a long ways with a gun."

I couldn't disagree. My sporting enjoyment over here could sever your aorta way over there. Most gun guys were careful, but chuckleheads had Second Amendment rights, too. We dropped the subject. By the time we reached our Mineral Springs takeout, two days later, we'd all but forgotten the incident. We were sunburned, sweaty, and relaxed down to the cellular level.

As we pulled into Green River in Craig's pickup, we came under cell-phone coverage, and my phone beeped. Twenty-one messages. First thought: Rosa.

Rosa was fine. Brandon Franklin was dead.

6. FLICKED OFF

I like shooting them, Judge. I don't know why. I feel good when I'm
shooting them. I feel awful good inside. Like I'm somebody.

—Bart Teare, played by fourteen-year-old
Rusty Tamblyn in *Gun Crazy*, 1949

We'd met Brandon in February of 2007, eighteen months after Hurricane Katrina, in the band room of O. Perry Walker high school, in New Orleans. It was in some ways the city's darkest moment since the storm. Whole neighborhoods were still dark and muddy. Barely a quarter of the inhabitants had returned. Nobody was sure the city would even survive. And New Orleans had long since dropped out of the news. The initial excitement was over, and the long slog was under way. I was in town to write about the recovery for *The New Yorker*.

Fully a quarter of O. Perry Walker's kids were living on their own, bunking together in FEMA trailers or abandoned buildings. Their parents, if they had any, had been unwilling or unable to return, and an atmosphere of emergency pervaded the school. That day, though, the band room—grimy, windowless, and stuffy—was a maelstrom of excited teenagers honking their horns into tune, searching for their caps, playing grab-ass. They were getting ready for the highest-profile performance of their young careers—a march down St. Charles Avenue in a nighttime Mardi Gras parade.

The band director, Wilbert Rawlins Jr., an enormous chocolate-brown man, pulled over a broad and stolid boy named Joshua, a baritone player with a face that never changed expression. "This man walked out of the

Lower Ninth Ward all by himself, water up to here, with nothing but his mouthpiece in his pocket." He massaged Joshua's chest with a big hand. "Heart, you hear me? This boy has heart." He released Joshua, grabbed a wispy, light-skinned boy, and pulled up the boy's sleeve to reveal a pocked scar. "Tell Mr. Baum what happened." The boy looked uncertain. "Go ahead," Wilbert said.

"I got shot."

"Tell him who shot you."

"My dad."

"Who else did he shoot?"

"My mom and my sister."

Wilbert let him go, and he drifted off. "You see?" Wilbert said. "That's what I'm talking about."

Wilbert told us that he would never put a kid out of band, no matter how bad the kid's behavior. Years before, when he was teaching at another school, he'd had a kid who was so disruptive during practice that he'd had no choice but to throw him out—and a week later the child was dead, shot down on the street after school. "During band practice!" Wilbert said with stunned, breathy wonder in his voice. "We were in the band room when he got shot! If I hadn't put him out, he'd have been there with us!"

The band-room door opened and a handsome young man loped in, swinging his shoulders in that gangster-casual figure-eight. Into my head leapt the word: "trouble." He swaggered through the swirl of teenagers toward the front of the room, and I worried that an attitude like his might infect the band. But it was all an act. He stopped, turned, and raised his right arm, and the room fell silent. "Yo," he grunted, and horns snapped, in unison, to lips. He pulsed his arm in time, pulling the band through its scales. "That's a little bit flat. Leviticus, that's you," he said above the racket to a tall boy with a trombone. "Sit up," he said. "Put a little bit into it." They shifted in their seats, sitting straighter. The next round of scales sounded loud and crisp.

"Brandon Franklin," Wilbert told me. "I've had him since seventh grade. Excellent saxophone player. But more than that, he's got something." He was Wilbert's drum major, which involved a lot more than wearing a big furry hat and waving a baton at the head of a parade. The drum major was essentially a band's equivalent of a master sergeant. Far from being a troublemaker, Brandon held the band together for Wilbert.

Margaret and I invited him to lunch. "Anywhere you want to go," we said, and he chose Popeyes Chicken. Over a pile of dusty popcorn shrimp, he told a story as woebegone as they came: the Desire Project, divorced and indifferent parents, an older sister dead already, constant moving from one dilapidated rental to another. What he really wanted in life was to be a high school band director like Wilbert. "But I got a baby on the way and stuff," he said. "I got to work. I got to provide. I might go to welding school. That's where the money at."

We were clearing away the paper residue of lunch and heading for the door when Brandon, behind me, said something so softly that I missed it. I turned and said, "What?"

"I like to be listened to," he said, looking at the floor. "That's all I need: a little attention."

He managed not only to graduate—we watched him do backflips across the stage to receive his diploma—but to get himself accepted into the band program at Texas College. ("Brandon Franklin is not going to be no welder," Wilbert told us proudly.) But being that far from home, with a baby—and then another—was too hard, and he eventually dropped out. Wilbert turned Brandon's homecoming into an opportunity, making him an assistant band director, putting him up in the guest room of the house that Wilbert and his wife, Belinda, had rebuilt after the storm, and inducting him into the wildly competitive domino games that were Wilbert's recreation. When you beat a fellow at dominos in Wilbert's crowd, you got to stick a Band-Aid on him as a mark of defeat, and Brandon often had the pleasure of doing so to Wilbert. "That boy has become Wil's son," Belinda told me more than once. "Actually, it's more like he's become Wil—a younger version of his own self."

A lot of those twenty-one voice mails waiting for me in Green River were from Belinda. In the first one, she was crying so hard I could barely make out the message that Brandon was dead; she'd just seen the news on television as she dressed for work. "Wilbert is still asleep," she sobbed. "I don't know how to wake him. I don't know what he'll do."

Brandon's killing was one of those unspeakably stupid incidents that show up in FBI homicide statistics as "other": The mother of his children squabbled with her new boyfriend, and when he stormed out, she called Brandon to come over and change her locks. The boyfriend returned with a gun and, finding Brandon, shot him dead—New Orleans's eightieth murder that year, and it was only May.

The shooter's name was Ronald Simms; he turned himself in to police that night. He was no gangbanger, but rather seemed to be a decent, hard-working guy who for reasons unknown had spun momentarily out of control. Where had he gotten the gun? Nobody knew. Truth is, nobody seemed to be asking that question, either at the funeral or in the voluminous comments about the shooting posted online. Everybody seemed to assume that if a young man wanted a gun in New Orleans, plenty were available. He could have borrowed it from a friend. He could have bought it out of the trunk of a car in a back alley.

Or he might have paid retail for it, with a credit card, in a brightly lit suburban gun store. New Orleans had no gun shops within its city limits, but several lay in the outlying parishes. Gun laws were loose in Louisiana; stores had to follow federal laws about performing background checks and not selling handguns to people under twenty-one, but no further restrictions applied. Simms was twenty-two and had no criminal record. It's possible that he'd stopped at a store on his way to his girlfriend's house, waited fifteen minutes for his background check, and continued on his merry way to do the killing.

If a background check wouldn't have prevented Brandon's murder, might a waiting—or "cooling off"—period have done the job? From 1993 to 1998, federal law required anybody buying a handgun in a store to wait three days before picking it up. That federal rule was replaced by the requirement to perform instant background checks, but ten states retained waiting periods of their own. Had Louisiana had such a law in place, might Brandon have survived his encounter with Simms?

It's impossible to say. In 2005, a group of nine physicians and public health academics collected every study they could find on the effect that various types of gun laws—bans, registration, background checks, and waiting periods—had on rates of violent crime. They published their results in the *American Journal of Preventive Medicine,* which often published articles on the negative public health implications of widespread gun ownership. When it came to waiting periods, the seven studies evaluated by the team found a statistically significant reduction only in suicide among people over age fifty-five, with no reduction in murder or assault.

Whether a cooling-off period would have saved Brandon's life was yet another excruciating mystery.

The funeral was, even by New Orleans standards, a doozy. There must have been a thousand people in the stifling warehouse of the New Orleans East church. It was the fashion, at the funeral of a murdered young person, for mourners to wear T-shirts garishly printed with the deceased's image, his date of birth ("thugged in"), and his date of death ("thugged out"). But nobody was wearing such a thing at Brandon's funeral; he was no thug. He lay in an open white coffin, wearing his blue band uniform.

"In the past month, I've buried six boys this age!" the pastor shouted from the pulpit. He paused for a long moment as a roomful of Majestic Mortuary paper fans beat furiously against the rising heat and the sobbing reached a crescendo. "Nineteen years old! Twenty-one! Twenty! Nineteen! Eighteen! Twenty-two! Six of them!"

At the end of the service, a thousand people filed past the coffin, and Wilbert, burying a "younger version of his own self," leaned over and spoke to Brandon in words I couldn't hear, and did something to the boy's jacket. When I reached the coffin, I saw that he'd put a Band-Aid on Brandon's lapel.

Sweating in his stiff funeral suit and talking in a kind of trance, as though he still couldn't believe it, Wilbert fleshed out the story for me. "When the boyfriend came back with that gun, he didn't know Brandon was going to be there. He was coming to kill the girl and them kids. She told me Brandon spent about fifteen minutes trying to talk him out of it, saying, 'Come on, man, you don't want to kill nobody; put up the gun.' But it went on and on, and she told me Brandon finally lost patience with the guy and said something like, 'Punk-ass motherfucker, you ain't going to kill nobody.' And that's when the guy flicked off, and shot Brandon like fifteen times. He was dead right there."

On the long walk to the cemetery, several dozen people danced behind the horse-drawn hearse, parasols held high, because that's what the tradition required. People clapped hands; sang along; bought bottles of water, beer, and Sprite from the inevitable vendors pulling coolers on wagons. The photographers were there, as they always were, endlessly reaching for the perfect shot of New Orleans culture on display.

Since Katrina, New Orleans had been undergoing a slow-burn freakout that made shootings even more widespread and unpredictable than they had been before the storm. You didn't have to be a gangbanger to catch a bullet; Brandon's death made that clear. The broken levees, the ruined neighborhoods, the loved ones drowned and displaced—all that had been inflicted upon New Orleans. The violence was the city's own doing. Guns were, as New Orleanians might have put it, a lagniappe of misery. As I trudged along behind the hearse, with Brandon's band blaring and people dancing beneath parasols to celebrate a life cut short by a handgun, it was a little awkward to have a .38 Colt secretly digging into my sweaty back.

Much as I loved New Orleans, its breathtaking murder rate lent a dark undertone to my visits, as though a bow were being drawn, just at the edge of hearing, across a low E contrabass string. It wasn't as though the violence was relegated to "those" parts of town or to "those" people, either. One friend, a lawyer, had been shot in the back in a "good" part of town. Another, a Tulane English professor, had been robbed at gunpoint in front of his house. He'd had only seven dollars in his pocket, and as the robbers walked off, a neighbor heard one say to the other, "Seven dollars! We should have shot him."

Ever since hearing that story, I'd made a point of carrying $300 in cash whenever I walked around New Orleans. But now, of course, I also had a .38 Colt—awkward at Brandon's funeral, perhaps, but rather comforting elsewhere.

New Orleans at Condition Yellow: I was picking up every detail. That man emerging from the alley with his hands in his pockets—what was he up to? That dude over there wearing sunglasses at night—where were his hands? Whose running feet were those coming up behind me?

Even in the Big Easy, where one's default condition is relaxed and maybe a little tipsy, I found I'd come to like the sheepdog feeling. Like the militant gun carriers, I discovered I was proud of that coolness of head, presence of mind, and courageous acceptance of responsibility.

But five months into my gun-carrying experiment, I was becoming increasingly aware, with increasing discomfort, that I was participating in a profoundly political act that didn't square with my own pre-armed worldview. Inveighing against the oblivious sods who drifted around in

Condition White was one more subtle way to gin up resentment toward the airy-fairy elites who lived in gated communities and enjoyed the luxury of musing, sipping tea, and nibbling biscuits while the good people of the world had to work for a living and keep their guard up. And those who armed themselves to ensure their own safety intrinsically devalued the role of the police—the government—to do that job. Gun-rights activists never tired of quoting a 2005 case, *Castle Rock* v. *Gonzales,* in which the U.S. Supreme Court held that police had no constitutional duty to protect citizens from crime. "When seconds matter," snarked the gun-rights bumper sticker, "the police are only minutes away." Smarter policing was probably behind the big national drop in crime during the two decades bracketing the turn of the twenty-first century, and cops certainly played a role in keeping the public safer in general. But in the *particular*—in the unlikely moment when a lunatic lunged with a knife—a cop almost certainly wouldn't be there. Furthermore, went the argument, if your life wasn't important enough for you to meet the "minimum responsibility" of defending it, why should a $31,000-a-year cop risk his life to do it for you?

Once you started thinking that way, it was easy to make the jump to believing that a government that couldn't protect its citizens shouldn't pass gun-control laws that hindered their ability to protect themselves. From there, it was an easy jog to grokking the rest of the conservative/ libertarian worldview. "My prediction," wrote a particularly articulate blogger with whom I sparred for a while by e-mail, "is that a substantial proportion of people who come to the realization that they need one or more firearms to protect self and family, because they cannot rely on the government to do so, will eventually come to question whether they should be relying on the government for such things as retirement, medical care and the education of their children."

Oh, goodie, I thought when I read that. If I don't carry the gun, I'm turning my back not only on my own safety but on my duty to participate in the security of my community, and if I do carry the gun, I'm betraying my commitment to Social Security, Medicare, single-payer health care, and public education.

On my last full day in New Orleans, a friend offered to take me to lunch at Commander's Palace, one of the city's famous high-end restaurants. It was a rare treat, and after the rigors of Brandon's funeral, I was ready to be pampered. Commander's Palace was locally famous for offering twenty-five-cent martinis at lunch, so I left the gun in my hotel room.

Riding the streetcar uptown through the Garden District, I realized how different I felt without the gun on my hip: lighter, dreamier, more cheerfully conscious of how the afternoon light slanted against the gleaming white antebellum mansions. I was enjoying the faces around me instead of scanning them for threats. Hopping off at Washington Avenue and walking toward the river, I found myself composing lines of prose. I took a few minutes to wander Lafayette Cemetery No. 1 at the corner of Coliseum Street, grooving on the ornate, decrepit mausoleums and imagining New Orleans at the time of the Louisiana Purchase.

I was lapsing into Condition White. And I was loving it.

Condition White may make us sheep, but it's also where art happens. It's where we daydream, reminisce, and hear music in our heads. I realized, as I ducked under the blue-and-white awning of Commander's Palace for my four-martini lunch, that Condition White wasn't something I was willing to give up indefinitely. And yet, the thought of giving up the gun completely zinged an unexpected pang of guilt through me.

What, I wondered, *is my responsibility now?* Was a certain level of situational awareness—call it Condition Pale Yellow—a reasonable mind-set to expect of an adult, whether armed or not? I was always going on about the collective good, while my counterparts at gun factories, stores, and ranges were all about individual sovereignty. Was maintaining a certain situational awareness while out in public not only smart for staying safe but also a service to the collective? Loafing along in Condition White, focused comfortably inward, how ready was I to, say, pull a child from in front of a speeding car, spot someone across a restaurant silently choking, or notice an elderly lady who needed help with a heavy parcel—to say nothing of intervening should someone get violent? Not that I'd ever argued *against* maintaining such vigilance, but it was the gun guys who made a virtue of it. One didn't need to wear a gun to act like a Boy Scout—alert, responsive, and civic-minded—but I was discovering that with gun on hip, it was impossible *not* to act that way. And until I started wearing a gun, I'd never thought much about my minute-to-minute responsibilities to the strangers around me.

———————

Late that night, I was crossing the corner of Dauphine and Kerlerec Streets, on my way back to the French Quarter, with the gun in place under my jacket. I wasn't smelling the sweet olive, grooving on the architecture, or even mourning Brandon. I was in Condition Yellow and fully aware of two scruffy guys lounging in a doorway up ahead. "Can you help us out?" one asked. I made my usual demurral and walked on. When I'd gone about fifteen feet, one of them yelled, "Faggot!"

I'd never been one to throw down because someone called me a name. But it's possible that in the old days I'd have yelled something back—especially if I were in the kind of funk that Brandon's death had lowered over me. At the very least, I'd have felt my blood pressure spike.

This time, though, I didn't become angry or even annoyed. To my great surprise, a Zen-like calm overtook me. I felt no need to restrain myself; my body didn't even gesture in the direction of anger. Taking offense wasn't an option, because I had no way of knowing where it would end, and somehow my brain and body sensed that. I yell something back, they come at me, and I'll have shot someone because he called me a faggot. Gun guys loved quoting Robert Heinlein: An armed society is a polite society. Having the gun made what might have been a tense and unpleasant moment pass with a weird kind of sweet peacefulness. I began to understand why we hadn't been hearing a lot of stories about legal gun carriers killing one another over parking spaces. That sheepdog sense of guardianship imparted a kind of moral superiority. I was the vigilant one, protector of the flock, the coiled wrath of God. To snatch out a gun and wave it around would have not only invited catastrophe but also sacrificed that righteous high ground and embarrassed me in the worst possible way.

Of course, the gun hadn't had a calming effect on Brandon's killer. But he hadn't been checked out for a permit and trained to carry. Nor had he been the one on the defensive. The unknowable that really tortured me as I retreated from the name callers on Kerlerec Street was this: If Brandon had been formally inducted into the sheepdog cadre and had had a legal gun concealed upon his person, would he have called Ronald Simms a "punk-ass motherfucker"? Might the gun have saved his life without ever being drawn?

7. THE RUBBER-GUN SQUAD

All you need for a movie is a gun and a girl.

—Jean-Luc Godard

Brandon's funeral was just about the only place I'd been since start-ing my gun project where nobody had mentioned Hollywood—as though only a genuine violent death could divorce the firearm from the movie camera. Gun guys could talk all day about precision and workmanship, history and tradition, the Second Amendment and self-defense. But any who denied that movies and television played a part in our infatuation had to be fooling himself. And ever since Camp Sunapee, I'd been as guilty as anybody of conflating movie guns with real.

The camera adores everything about the gun—the flash, the smoke, the menacing *slick-click* of a hammer being cocked, the power the gun bestows upon the weak to inflict third-reel redemptive violence on the strong. Movies don't need guns to be exciting, but add a gun to a story and the emotional temperature rises. Moviemakers have known this since at least 1903, when *The Great Train Robbery,* a twelve-minute-long silent shoot-'em-up, ended with an actor firing a revolver straight at the camera.

After the heavy dose of gun reality at Brandon's funeral, I needed a break. So it seemed a good time to make a side trip to the Dream Factory. The mystery to me was not that gun guys caught the bug from watching movies but that more people didn't. Everybody went to the movies and watched television, yet only some of us fell in love with the cinematic gun—which reinforced my growing belief that a fondness for firearms was somehow etched in the DNA, like hammertoes or blue eyes.

In 1913, a vaudeville performer named Jesse Lasky went into business with his brother-in-law, a thirty-four-year-old Polish Jew who had been born Schmuel Gelbfisz but had anglicized his name to Samuel Goldwyn. Along with a middling-successful thirty-two-year-old Broadway producer named Cecil Blount DeMille, they formed a movie company, the Famous Players—Lasky Corporation, and moved into a rented barn near the corner of Vine Street and Hollywood Boulevard, on the outskirts of Los Angeles.

A year later, when DeMille was directing the first movie made in Hollywood, a Western called *The Squaw Man,* the actors hired to play soldiers gave him fits. "Can't anybody here teach these men to look like soldiers?" he yelled in exasperation. A reedy young laborer stepped forward and said, "I can." He was James Sydney Stembridge, a Floridian who, before migrating to California, had served in the Philippines during the Spanish–American War as an Army drill sergeant. He did a fine job teaching the actors to look like soldiers; DeMille kept him around.

Two years after that, the Famous Players—Lasky Corporation was absorbed into a new studio called Paramount Pictures. Stembridge noticed that directors were having trouble finding guns to put in their movies; World War I was on, and even civilian guns were tough to scare up. He proposed to the bosses at Paramount that he scour the country for guns and establish an arsenal that Paramount and other studios could use in their films. Stembridge Gun Rentals was born on the Paramount lot and for the rest of the century furnished the guns for just about every movie made in Hollywood.

This was the temple of firearm mythology I headed for upon landing in Los Angeles. By all accounts, Stembridge Gun Rentals had never sold a gun; it was said to house John Wayne's guns from *Stagecoach,* the machine guns used to shoot King Kong off the Empire State Building, and the rifles seen in *Beau Geste.* When Robert Downey Jr., shooting the biopic *Chaplin* in 1994, had his company call Stembridge for a rifle similar to what Charlie Chaplin had used in the 1918 film *Shoulder Arms,* Stembridge not only had one like it—an employee pulled from stock the same gun the Little Tramp himself had used.

By the time I got to L.A., Stembridge Gun Rentals had decamped to Glendale, far from the Paramount lot. The scrubby brown San Gabriel Mountains jumped up, stunningly clear in the cool California sunlight, as I threaded from the 405 to the 118 to the 210. I turned onto Magnolia Avenue and immediately figured I'd misread the directions: a dead-end street of mechanics, welders, and, at the end, what looked like a feed-and-seed store with a bunch of old cars parked out front. This couldn't possibly be the throne of the Hollywood firearm. But the address was right, so I parked, snaked my way among the dilapidated cars, and pushed open a screen door. It took my eyes a moment to adjust to the gloom. Yes, it was a feed-and-seed store, with sagging boxes heaped on top of each other and a lot of old farm implements stacked up higgledy-piggledy. But wait: Those weren't farm implements. They were guns.

"Hello?" I called. In the back, some kind of machinery clanked. I moved slowly inside, through a messy wood-paneled office that might have come from a 1943 movie set: wooden desk, overflowing wooden in- and out-trays, yellowish papers strewn over pocked, coffee-ringed surfaces. Tacked to the wall, a black-and-white poster showed Humphrey Bogart in *Sahara,* clutching a 1921 Thompson submachine gun with a gangster foregrip and a round ammo drum. "Hello?" I called again. No response. I started gingerly back through the mess, a little uneasy, worried that someone would mistake me for a burglar in this firearms trove and shoot me to pieces.

Beyond the office, I stepped into a drafty barn of a room. The underside of a corrugated steel roof soared high above exposed rafters. I moved among stacks of old files, bundles of what looked like Victorian costumes, and glass display cases heaped high with ragged cardboard boxes. I peered into a couple: a single-action Colt, a nine-millimeter Beretta—valuable guns, just lying around. More cardboard boxes littered the floor—pistols and revolvers had been tossed into them. Gaudy but cheap glass-fronted gun cabinets of the type you'd find in rural double-wides stood at random around the room, overstuffed with rifles and shotguns. A minigun—a modern, six-barreled machine gun that looked like the weapon Arnold Schwarzenegger had wielded so effectively in *Terminator 2: Judgment Day*—hung from nails high on a wall.

I crept alongside a rack of Civil War muskets and a Spencer repeating carbine, all falling over onto each other, looking as though they hadn't been touched in years. In my hands, the Spencer revealed itself to be no Hollywood reproduction but the real thing, worth tens of thousands of dollars, seemingly forgotten. I set it down carefully.

High above my head, steel shelves bulged with rifles from the Spanish–American War and the Second World War, priceless pieces piled up like cordwood. Only their muzzles and buttstocks were visible, coated in dust. Strips of dried masking tape curled from the shelves, hand-lettered .30-40 KRAG and 98 MAUSER.

The buzz of machinery grew louder as I tiptoed deeper into the dim vastness of the barn. In a lighted alcove at the far back, a man in a work shirt operated something that looked like a drill press. I forged ahead and extended my hand. He switched off the machine, wiped his hand on a rag, and gave mine a strong squeeze. He was in his fifties, balding, with a leathery face; he looked like a character from *The Grapes of Wrath*. I took him for a maintenance man.

"Syd Stembridge," he said.

"Related to James Sydney Stembridge?"

"My great uncle."

I noticed now that the machine he'd been operating wasn't a drill press but some sort of ammunition loader. A row of brass cartridges stood in ranks on a conveyor belt, like soldiers.

"I'm making blanks," he said. "That was the bulk of the family business for years: blanks."

"They hard to make?"

"Tricky. A gun ain't made to fire blanks. And when you're shootin' bullets, it don't matter what the flash looks like, but in the movies, that's everything."

"You make all the blanks for Hollywood on that little machine?"

He laughed. "No, we've been out of the Hollywood business for four years. These are for Disneyland, for the jungle boat cruise."

"Where they shoot the hippo? I loved that as a kid!"

"They don't shoot the hippo anymore. Too many people complained. Can't be shooting a *hippo*. Oh, no. Now they shoot in the air. For a while, they stopped shooting altogether, but they got too many complaints about *that*. It didn't have the same drama. People expected the shooting on the jungle boat cruise. They just didn't want the gun pointed at the hippo."

"At the *mechanical* hippo."

He shrugged. "You know, it's funny about the jungle boat cruise. People love guns and people hate guns. Usually at the same time. When you work with actors and actresses, a lot don't like the guns at first, but then they get into it. God, I remember working on shows, and you go out with a gun and the actor don't want to touch it. Marthe Keller in *Black Sunday*: Did you see that one? She plays a terrorist. She was completely afraid of the guns. Came into the gun room when we were at Paramount, and I could see she was uncomfortable. Didn't want to touch it. But watch her at the end, shooting from the helicopter with a Madsen or a Smith & Wesson 76—I can't remember. But watch her face. She's really into it."

I looked around at the ramshackle warehouse. "I've got to say, I'm a little surprised to find Syd Stembridge in the back of a shop making blanks with his own hands," I said. "I mean, aren't you Hollywood royalty? This is the great Stembridge arsenal!"

"No, we auctioned that off in 2007. Oh, we kept a few things. But most of this belongs to Mike Papac." Papac was legendary, the armorer on such gun-heavy movies as *Lethal Weapon, Die Hard, Con Air,* and *We Were Soldiers.* "We let him keep his things here," Stembridge said.

As we made our way back to the office, he told stories from the set—of stripping the huge magazine from a twenty-millimeter cannon so that the audience could see Richard Crenna's face in *Rambo III,* of failing to talk Sylvester Stallone out of twirling his .45 automatic in *Cobra,* of the day in 1982 when a helicopter blade killed Vic Morrow (who'd been Sergeant Saunders on *Combat!)* on the set of *Twilight Zone: The Movie.*

He kept telling stories, but my eye had fallen on the hand-lettered cards in one of the glass cases, and I crossed the room to look closer. Under a nickel-plated Colt Detective Special: EFREM ZIMBALIST JR., 77 SUNSET STRIP. Under a Colt Official Police: ROBERT STACK, THE UNTOUCHABLES. Under a P38: FRANK SINATRA, THE MANCHURIAN CANDIDATE.

"Good God," I whispered.

"Yup," Syd said proudly. "Those are Papac's now, from our collection."

It went on and on, from case to case. Steve McQueen's .45 from *The Getaway.* Kevin Costner's Star automatic (standing in for a .45 Colt) from the 1987 version of *The Untouchables.* William Holden's pistol from *The Wild Bunch.* Holy relics.

"We sold off a lot of the good stuff," Syd said. "Mel Gibson's guns from *Payback* and *Lethal Weapon,* that shiny .45 from *Titanic,* Harrison Ford's ray gun from *Star Wars* and his revolver from *Raiders of the Lost Ark . . ."*

"I remember the *sounds* those guns made in *Raiders* as well as I remember anything about it," I said. "It was the first time I noticed that gun sounds had gotten good in the movies."

Syd brightened. "I worked on that! I flew up to Skywalker Ranch with Ben Burtt, who did all the sound for that show. I had a Thompson up there, and we fired it next to a cement wall. Not *at* the wall, but next to it, so you'd get the noise off the wall. That's how we got that big sound. And the scene in the bar, the big shoot-out? What they wanted was to re-create a Warner Bros. 1930 ricochet. Ben always said that Warner had the best ricochet sound. He didn't know how they did it. So we're out there trying to re-create it. We get out on a dirt road, a straight road. We put up hay bales with a slot down the middle, an alley, and we set up microphones all along the way. I'm inside the slot with a Smith & Wesson 76 submachine gun, firing single-shot at the road, trying to glance bullets off the ground at the right angle to get that whine."

We were back in the front office by now, standing next to a framed black-and-white photo of a professorial gent of about sixty in a three-piece suit and horn-rimmed glasses, smiling at a pretty young woman holding two enormous single-action Colts. Behind them, the walls were covered with revolvers—the old Stembridge warehouse. J. S. STEMBRIDGE WITH PATRICIA FARLEY, said a yellowed strip of paper typed on a manual Royal, and, taped to the frame, PICKING GUNS FOR "SUNSET PASS," A ZANE GREY FILM WITH RANDOLPH SCOTT. Patricia Farley, plump, laughing, and lavishly dressed in a plumed hat, had no idea that her career would last only two more years. I pointed to the picture of Humphrey Bogart holding the Thompson.

"A Stembridge gun?"

"Of course. That may be one of the ones referenced here." He tapped his fingernail on the glass of a framed letter, and I bent close. It was from the Harbor Defenses of Los Angeles, dated September 3, 1944, signed by Colonel W. W. Hicks of the Coast Artillery Corps.

"Our appreciation is extended to you for your generous cooperation without compensation in loaning automatic weapons to the Harbor Defenses of Los Angeles at the beginning of the war," it read. "Due to the critical shortage of such weapons on 7 December 1941, those provided from your stock were a most welcome addition to our defenses."

"They didn't have any guns!" Syd said. "The Japs bombed Pearl Harbor, and for all anybody knew, they were coming here next. Stembridge had more guns than anybody. They called up here from Fort MacArthur, and Fritz Dickie drove down there with five Thompsons."

"Weren't yours all set up to fire blanks?"

"I think we'd just gotten a load that hadn't been converted yet. So that put us in good with the Army. During the war, they'd do these war shows at the L.A. Coliseum. You know, stage a mock battle in the stadium, with planes flying over and all that, to sell war bonds. We helped them with that, and after the war we got the guns. Speaking of Thompsons, I was cleaning up and found this." He handed me a piece of yellow paper—a telegram:

Bell twx 710 82209247

Mr Gerald Benedict

Request permission to transfer the following to joe lombardi, special effects unlimited, 752 n. Cahuenga blvd., Hollywood, calif., Class 3 permit #94191, calif permit 318r

2 Thompson submachine guns for blank ammunition

Cal 45 model 1921

#4090 5035

Title will not be transferred. Guns are to be used in new york city on paramount productions "godfather" and will be returned upon completion of episode.

"These were the guns they used to kill Sonny at the tollbooth," Syd said reverently, smiling at the paper. After all the stars he'd worked with, all the magic he'd undertaken, even Syd recognized the telegram as a sacred artifact—the Hollywood equivalent of a scrap of the Dead Sea Scrolls.

"So Syd," I asked, "if Stembridge had all the guns that Hollywood used for eighty years and sold them all off, where are they now? Who's got Hollywood's guns?"

A lot of them, it turned out, were sixteen miles away, in the farthest reaches of the San Fernando Valley, at Independent Studio Services, "the largest movie armory in the world."

A lot of Hollywood's guns had been converted to fire blanks, but that didn't mean they weren't real guns or couldn't be converted back. Given the lethality of what lay inside ISS, I expected a fenced compound, German shepherds, and an armed gatehouse guard scanning a clipboard for my name. Instead, ISS looked like a suburban medical practice—a three-story brick-and-glass box just off the Foothill Freeway, landscaped with oleander. Inside, no metal detector, no ID check, just a slinky receptionist who offered me coffee and sent me unaccompanied down a hall decorated with framed movie posters and mannequins dressed as everything from Civil War soldiers to jet pilots. For a movie buff, it was like visiting Santa's workshop.

Finally, I came to something locked—a steel-mesh door—and through it spied what looked like a counter in an auto-parts store. A man in a greasy baseball cap stood behind the counter, writing up paperwork, while a couple of customers leaned on the counter, chatting. The counter was piled with all kinds of junk—tools, boxes, coffee cups, stacks of paper. Advertising posters covered its front and climbed the walls behind it, where inventory poked from high shelves or hung on display.

The difference, of course, between what lay behind the mesh door and an auto-parts store was that all the merchandise was firearms, from flintlock muskets to AK-47s. The advertisements weren't for FRAM air filters and Duralast brake pads, but for Glocks, H&Ks, and Springfields. Yet nobody could mistake the place for a gun store. Behind the counter, on massive tripods, stood an M19 grenade launcher capable of firing five forty-millimeter shells a second and a Hughes M230 Chain Gun designed to tear up tanks. In the parlance, heavy shit—post-1986 hardware that not even the richest and most ardent collector could obtain. I pressed the doorbell and was buzzed in. Larry Zanoff bustled out to greet me.

He was a baby-faced man in his forties, somewhere between buff and roly-poly, with a buzz cut and glasses, jeans and a black T-shirt. I'd gotten his name from the credits of Steven Spielberg's *War of the Worlds*—he was listed with the enticing title of "armorer"—and he'd handled the guns for many other films, including *Collateral, Iron Man 2,* and *Thor.*

"You have one cool job," I said.

"You have no idea." He gave a little laugh, as though discovering anew what a fun gig he'd blundered into.

Strictly defined, an armorer is a gunsmith for a military unit or police department. "Here, it means you're the guy on the set responsible for the guns," he said, ushering me into a spare, windowless office on whose single shelf stood a Hanukkah menorah, a row of blank cartridges, and two life-size pistols made of glass—awards of some sort. On the walls were articles—from the *Los Angeles Times, Guns* magazine, and others—about the ISS armory, and Zanoff spoke with the practiced ease of a guy used to explaining his world to reporters. The armorer's job starts, he said, with the script. Sometimes a screenwriter specifies a character's gun, but usually not; usually the script just says something like "Murray pulls a gun," and it's up to the director to decide what kind of gun Murray pulls. Some, like John Milius and Michael Mann, really knew guns and would come to Larry already wanting a Sig Sauer P232 or a Walther P5. Sometimes an actor had an idea of what he wanted. Most actors and directors, though, had in mind only an image and a mood they wanted to re-create on-screen. Then it was up to the armorer to find the gun that fit the bill.

Zanoff clapped his hands together and leapt from his chair like a fullback coming off the bench. He led me down a series of narrow hallways to a room dominated by a wooden table long enough to seat thirty people. On the table lay sheets of computer paper printed with characters' names—The Ranger, Old Pete, Jesus—and atop each paper lay two or three Old West revolvers. "This is what we call a show-and-tell for a Western we have coming up," Larry said. "The director's coming in today. We've read the script and thought about each character, and we'll suggest these." Larry and his colleagues were offering a plain-Jane Colt Peacemaker for the Ranger—a subtle way to signal that the Ranger was not a man of violence. He'd carry a gun, but he wouldn't fetishize it. But from what was laid out for Jesus, I had a bad feeling about him. Atop his name lay a shiny nickel-plated Smith & Wesson Schofield with an eight-inch barrel—the kind of flamboyant gun that tells the audience, without the audience even being conscious of it, that this character is an egomaniac who loves killing people.

"What if the director wants something anachronistic?"

"You bring it up. If he overrides you, that's okay. He wants to tell a story, and sometimes that overcomes reality. It's like, you'd never bring a real gun near your face in a gunfight. Sometimes, though, the director wants both the gun and the actor's pretty face in the frame. That's fine. The thing is, if you don't bring it up, and he reads on the blog that he made a mistake, it'll be, 'Why didn't you tell me?'"

"So how much of what we see is realistic?"

"A lot more than used to be. With the blogs and the Internet, everybody's an expert, everybody's commenting. Back in the Tom Mix movies, they're shooting double-action revolvers. Totally anachronistic. You'd never get away with that now. One thing's still totally fake, though: People don't fly backwards when hit with bullets. We call it the river of damage. You crumple up around the wound. Even with a shotgun blast. People flying backwards looks good in the movies, but it's not realistic."

I was a little sorry I'd asked, and was starting to wonder if all this looking behind the curtain was going to spoil the movies for me.

Larry apologized for returning me to his office by a roundabout route. Two LAPD detectives were in the house, on a spot inspection of ISS's inventory—something that happened two or three times a year. "We had the ATF here last week," he said. "We told the LAPD guys, 'Hey, we just had ATF here,' but no, they have to do their own thing. The guns we have here, they're real guns. Some of them have been modified to fire blanks and will never fire live ammunition again. But they're still real guns." We threaded our way past the enormous modern tripod-mounted military guns I'd seen through the steel-mesh door.

"How do you get stuff like this?" I asked, being careful not to touch them, lest I inadvertently kill everybody in the room.

"We are firearms dealers. Really, you have to be, to be an armorer, because you have to be able to go out and buy what you need for a show, and you have to be able to transfer it legally to the people who will use it."

Back in Larry's office, he handed me a blank; it looked like a cartridge, except instead of a bullet it had a crimped-down tip. "A revolver, you can take and just put in the blanks. But a semi-automatic or a machine gun? To make one fire blanks can take twelve hours of work, because they rely on the explosion of the powder and the resistance of the bullet to cycle the gun. With a blank, you have no bullet, so you have to use more powder, and you also have to alter the gun to make it work."

"You just plug the barrel, right?"

He snorted. Was there no end to ignorance about the art of Hollywood gunsmithing? "I could take ten Beretta 92Fs straight from the factory, and each one might require something slightly different to make it work right firing blanks. . . . Barrel plugs, changing the recoil spring—if I told you exactly what we do to guns to make them fire blanks, I'd have to kill you, because we have our own proprietary system. It's protected technology."

But the first thing he wanted me to remember about the guns I saw in movies was that most of them are rubber. "Unless you see it fire, of course." He thought a moment. "And even then."

Once again, I wasn't sure I wanted to hear this.

"Cops standing around a squad room with guns in their holsters? Rubber. Cowboys on horseback? Rubber. Soldiers marching, or the ones in the background? Those guns will be rubber." A rubber gun didn't require having an armorer on the set, he said, so it could be rented from a prop house without paperwork. Even a protagonist's "gun" was really, on the set, five or six different versions, depending on the scene. "In the scenes where you're just seeing it in his holster, it's probably rubber. If he's just loading it, it might be a nonfiring replica." If the logistics of sets and costumes allow it, a director will often shoot all the scenes in which the guns are visible but don't fire, and then bring in an armorer with the real guns for a couple of days of shooting nothing but the firing scenes. "If you see the actor firing the gun, it might be one set up to fire quarter-flash blanks. But another scene might require full-flash blanks, so that might be a completely different gun. The audience thinks it's always the same gun. . . . When the actor's going to hold the gun close to the guy he's shooting, they might use a rubber gun and CGI the flash in later"—CGI being computer-generated imagery—"or they might use a non-gun."

"A non-gun?"

He opened a desk drawer and took out what looked like a Glock pistol. Upon closer inspection, it was solid metal, like a paperweight, with a button where the trigger should have been. With a screwdriver, Larry removed the front half, showing me the electrical mechanism that created a big, harmless spark at the muzzle when an actor pushed the button. The gun looked incredibly blocky and fake. "Later, you enhance the flash, you add the bang and the tinkle of the casing hitting the floor, and it looks very real, believe me," Larry said. "You've seen it a million times and didn't know it."

I groaned. Now he'd done it; I would never enjoy a gun movie the same way again.

The door opened, two young men walked in, and Larry leapt to his feet and, to my great surprise, began speaking fluid Hebrew. One of the men was slight, with glasses, the other a matinee idol, with shiny hair swept straight back. They chatted awhile in Hebrew, which, to my secular-Jewish ears, sounded like praying. I'm pretty sure they weren't praying, though, because they kept laughing and dropping in such English words as "muzzle flash" and "ejection port." Finally, the slight one extended me his hand. "Lior Chefetz," he said, in that peculiar Israeli accent that manages to be both whiny and aggressive at the same time. "I directed *The Godmother.* Perhaps you saw it?" I hadn't. The matinee idol introduced himself only as Nitsan—he was not an actor after all but a needlessly handsome handgun instructor for the Israel Defense Forces. I looked at Larry. "I was born in Philadelphia," he said, "but I grew up in Israel." He hooked a hand at us. "Come."

Larry led us through a warren of narrow hallways to a chamber about the size of—but hardly decorated as—a child's bedroom. Hundreds of revolvers encrusted the walls, their barrels slipped over dowels that stuck straight out, their grips pointed outward. The six-guns seemed to be loosely grouped by age, with those from the early twentieth century mounted low on the wall, the newest far above our heads. "This," Larry said, "is the revolver room."

Unlike semi-automatics, revolvers don't depend on the blast of a cartridge to function, so everything in the room could fire live ammunition. "Some of these, though, have been to Mexico on shoots, so they have their barrels pinned," Larry explained. "Mexico requires any gun coming into the country to have a pin driven through the barrel so it can't fire live ammo." *Except,* I thought, *the ones going to the drug cartels.*

Larry led us to the Western room—single-action revolvers protruding from one wall, lever-action rifles and Spencer carbines stacked against another, and, in the middle, a gigantic brass Gatling gun. The Colt that Russell Crowe used in *3:10 to Yuma* hung on a peg at nose level—I recognized it by the silver cross on the handle—and leaning in a corner was the gigantic eight-gauge shotgun lugged around by Viggo Mortensen in *Appaloosa.*

"It's just an ordinary twelve-gauge," Larry said. "We built pipes around the barrels to make them look bigger." I looked close: Sure enough.

Onward we went, to semi-automatic pistols, perhaps eight or nine hundred of them, from 1896 Broomhandle Mausers to 2011 Jordanian Vipers. All had been modified to shoot blanks and would never again fire live ammo. "Oh, baby!" yelled Nitsan, the handgun trainer. A big sign on the wall warned, DO NOT HANDLE THE GUNS, but Nitsan couldn't help himself. He snatched one off the wall, hefting its weight, then tucked it into his armpit so he could grab another, and another. He was like a child in a candy store; Larry finally had to ask him, in singsong Hebrew, to put everything back.

After the rifle room—hundreds of M1 Garands and German Mausers, the backbone of any World War II picture, stacked butt to muzzle to save space—Larry took us to the largest room of all, the grand hall of machine guns. Robert, the midwestern machine-gun collector, had drawn a distinction for me between collectors and accumulators. ISS was an accumulator. Full-auto weaponry covered every inch of every surface. *"Ohhh,"* Nitsan sighed, and muttered something reverent-sounding in Hebrew. Lior rotated on his heels, head back, eyes wide. Gangster guns, Army guns, Nazi guns, police guns. Piles and piles of machine guns. From Robert and my Wikieup, Arizona, buddies, I had a sense of what machine guns cost; the ISS collection had to be worth several tens of millions of dollars.

"This is *not* a collection," Larry insisted. "This is a *working inventory.*"

On a table in the middle of the room lay three futuristic ray guns. "From *Avatar,*" Larry said, putting one in my hands. It was green, bizarre, but for all that it appeared completely functional. "We built these."

"Out of what?"

"All it is inside is a Ruger Mini-14," Larry said—a common sporting rifle. He opened the side of my green vanquisher of Na'vi to reveal the quotidian gun beneath. "We went through a bunch of designs on the outside, and when we got to where James Cameron liked it, we built them out of plastic." He pointed to fictional manufacturers' logos on the barrels. "I especially like this touch; our graphics department made those."

"Why do you even need the real gun inside?" I asked. "Couldn't you make the plastic one and let the actors use that? The flash and the sound is added later anyway, right?"

"You could do that, but it wouldn't feel real to the actor. He's got to feel the thing shoot. He's got to hear it go bang and see the flash. Otherwise he's just faking it, and it wouldn't look right."

"So this is for the actor's sake?"

"Absolutely. He's got to get into it. He's got to be feeling it."

I must confess: It hadn't occurred to me. On the stage of a theater, sustained by a live audience, sure. But in a ten-second take, the movie actor has to be feeling it? So much of what went into the movies was fake—the rubber guns, the digitized effects—that I'd assumed the acting was a delightful sham.

Larry crooked a hand, and we followed him into a room that looked like a vast art studio in a high school. A dozen or more people worked at long benches; on the one in front of me, a big box brimmed with some kind of foamy blue plastic imprinted with the negative image of a submachine gun. "This is studio art and technology," Larry said. "These are the people who make the rubber guns. I mean, that's not all they do—they make everything—but with the guns, if I'm using a new one, one that we don't already have rubber for, I bring it to them and they'll make it." He pulled us over to another bench, where a woman was pressing a branch of a tree, about three feet long, into a box of blue plastic. "We have a show coming up in which a character is beaten to death with a tree branch. She's making the branch." At another bench, a man flicked an airbrush to make the stock of a rubber M14 rifle look like wood. Even up close, it was hard to tell that the rifle was a fake.

But it was the next room—the rubber-gun room—that most blew my mind. If the real revolvers, semi-automatics, and machine guns had numbered in the hundreds, these hung from the wall by the thousands. A single protruding dowel dangled perhaps two dozen identical pistols by their trigger guards, and there must have been five hundred such dowels between the floor and the fourteen-foot ceiling. On the floor by my feet sat an M60 machine gun that looked for all the world like the real thing. I picked it up; it was spongy and weighed hardly anything. The shiny surfaces, I saw, had been painted on.

"So you have a scene where soldiers are running through the jungle, they flop down and start shooting," Larry said. "When they're running, when they're flopping down, this will be the gun. Only when they start shooting will we swap in a blank-firing gun."

Lior and Nitsan, having seen what they needed, shook our hands and left, and Larry and I headed back to the office for a second time. I settled again into the straight-backed chair across from his desk and asked, "What's it take? What's the difference between a good armorer and a mediocre one?"

"You need the foundation of real guns, but you have to switch a switch in your brain to make them run right with blanks. Here, we're taking something that someone else designed and making it do something it wasn't designed to do. That's a challenge."

"What does it cost a movie to rent these guns?"

"A revolver, like in the Western room, fifty-five dollars a week. It goes up from there."

"That doesn't seem like much."

"The average movie takes thirteen weeks to shoot. Usually, they need a lot more than one gun. Then there's ammo. And then there's me."

"You're on the set with the guns?"

"Always."

"Making sure they don't walk away?"

"That's part of it. I load them, put them in the actors' hands. The director yells, 'Cut!' and Makeup and Hair want to rush onto the set. But in the safety brief, we make clear that nobody moves until I gather up every gun and yell, 'The weapons are cold.'"

"So an actor doesn't go to lunch with his gun in his holster."

Larry laughed. "Well, maybe if it's a rubber gun."

"Are all armorers gunsmiths?"

"No, you could have a props guy run the guns on set, but if something breaks, he can't fix it. If you can't fix the gun on set, you're not really an armorer. Guns break. Actors drop them—a gun gets dropped in the mud, you have to take that one and set it aside and have a replacement, and then that night you have to take that muddy gun completely apart and clean and oil it, because they're going to need it in the morning."

"Do they ever use real bullets? Like if an actor is shooting bottles off a fence?" I was thinking of Warren Beatty in *Bonnie and Clyde* shooting bottles, then smashing the windows in an abandoned farmhouse.

"There are never, ever live rounds on a set. If you see an actor shooting bottles off a fence, there's a charge in the bottle timed to explode with the shot."

"So what happened with Brandon Lee?" I asked quietly, and Larry sighed. Armorers, it seemed, got asked this a lot.

Lee, the son of martial arts great Bruce Lee, was twenty-eight years old in 1993, a budding martial arts film star in his own right, when he signed on at a studio in North Carolina to shoot a movie called *The Crow*. The script called for Lee to be shot at close range with a revolver. The bullets in a revolver (unlike a semi-automatic) are visible in the front of the cylinder, so when a camera angle calls for a front view of the gun, an armorer will load it with dummy cartridges. Dummies have bullets on the end, so they look real from the front, but no powder charge or primer, which is the tiny explosive capsule that the firing pin or hammer hits.

"What happened was," Larry said, "it was a non-union armorer who didn't know what he was doing and made every conceivable mistake. They showed up on the set without dummy rounds, and instead of saying, 'Okay, let's shoot this scene tomorrow and get dummy rounds over-nighted,' he went to a gun store, bought live ammunition, and took the rounds apart in his motel room to get the powder out. They popped out the primers, but missed one. So on the set, they shoot the scene with the dummy rounds, and then to be safe, they point the gun at the floor and click the trigger six times. They don't hear the pop when that one primer goes off and pushes the bullet into the barrel. They put the gun away without checking it, and the next day they load it up with blanks for the scene. Nobody thinks to look in the barrel; if they had, they'd have seen it was plugged by the bullet. Now you have a blank in the cylinder and a bullet in the barrel—essentially a gun loaded with live ammo. They do the scene; Brandon's blood pack goes off like it's supposed to, and he falls, but he's saying, 'I don't feel good, it doesn't feel right.' They walk him over to his trailer, and they're cleaning him up, trying to figure out what is fake blood and real blood, and in those twenty minutes he bleeds to death."

"Yikes."

"It's every armorer's nightmare. But I've never had an actor get hurt. You almost never hear of anybody getting hurt on set with a gun. I once packed up all my guns and walked off a set because the director wanted something done with a gun that I didn't think was safe. By the time I got to the bottom of the road, there was a PA with a radio waving me down, telling me to go back up. They did it my way."

His phone buzzed—time to go. "Tell you this, though," he said as we stood. "No matter how many times I do this, I have butterflies until the guns are locked up and everything's done and finished."

He wanted to get on with his day, but I couldn't quite let him go. Here, in the flesh, was a high priest of gun culture. Neither Wayne LaPierre of the NRA, nor Dennis Henigan, the arch-gun-controller at the Brady Center, would ever have a tenth of the influence that Larry did over how Americans felt about guns. By making them sexy and powerful on-screen, this stocky, self-effacing Jewish boy was arguably as responsible as anybody for our national conflicted romance with firearms. Blocking his exit from the office, I blurted out the story of my own beginnings as a gun guy, telling how guns had colored my identity ever since. "What is it?" I implored. "What keeps us so firmly in their thrall?"

He rocked back on a heel, folded his arms, and looked at the ceiling. "My own philosophy?" he said. "There was a ruler of Japan in the 1500s: Nobunaga. This is in the era of bows and arrows and swords. Nobunaga had the flintlock and used it to conquer the country. Then he gathered them all up, destroyed them, and outlawed them. Japan is the only society that ever had a weapon of mass destruction and voluntarily stepped back. Why? Because it took years to get good with a bow and arrow and sword, but with a gun, you could train a peasant in a month. For me, that's part of the fascination with the gun. You can be the poorest peasant in a land of samurai or the fat kid at summer camp, and with a little practice you're equal to anybody." Or, as the Colt's Patent Fire Arms Manufacturing Company put it in its ads a century and a half ago, "God made all men, but Samuel Colt made them equal."

Maybe that helped explain why American movies tended to have more gunplay in them than those of other countries—and maybe even why America itself tended to have more real-life gunplay in it than other countries. Yes, as historians never tire of reminding us, we are a young country with a violent frontier tradition and a unique Second Amendment. But there's also this: We're equality freaks. We endlessly congratulate ourselves for our Equal Protection Clause and our founding mythology of classless society. If equal is good, and guns make men equal, then by extension guns are good. They make each of us sovereign and inviolate. An armed man is a little republic unto himself. An armed woman, especially one who blows away the big, strong villain in the third reel, strikes the ultimate blow for innocent weakness over unjust strength.

Guns on-screen pushed lots of buttons; I was glad to know all that went into getting them there. Guns were so sexy, so powerful, and so central to screen drama that it was a wonder to me that there wasn't an Oscar for Best Gun in a Supporting Role. Hell, for certain guns—James Bond's silenced PPK, Dirty Harry's .44 Magnum, Little Caesar's tommy gun, the Jackal's collapsible rifle—they could practically give an Oscar for Best Gun in a Leading Role.

8. BRING IT ON, GOD DAMN IT!

Be nice to white men. One of the besetting sins of many in the progressive and liberal movements is that they have made white men the enemy. In fact, no ethnic group in history gave up so much power so quickly and so peacefully.

—Sam Smith, editor of *Progressive Review*,
in his *Post Empire Survival Guide*

Boulder sits at the place where the Rocky Mountains jump up from the Great Plains at a nearly ninety-degree angle. To find a place where the topography changes as suddenly, you'd probably need to stand on a beach. Twenty-eighth Street is on the plains. Nineteenth Street is in the mountains.

Full of mountain bikers and rock climbers, Boulder is culturally oriented toward the mountains. But as I packed the car for the next leg of my gun-guy walkabout, I looked forward to heading out into the big, flat open. For one thing, the Plains presented a gun-policy conundrum. Guns were plentiful out there, gun laws were loose, and gun violence was rare, whereas places with superstrict gun laws, like Chicago and Washington, D.C., suffered tremendously from gunfire. Those who supported tougher gun laws said that that made sense: The places bloodied most by guns would want to control them more stringently.

But arguing it that way reversed cause and effect. Tough gun laws were sold to the public on the premise that they would have an effect on violence, not the other way around. Moreover, the high level of violence in places with strict gun control didn't speak well for gun control's effectiveness. Yes, things might have been even worse in Chicago and Washington without tough gun laws, but it was impossible to know. Further confusing matters was that New York City had tough gun laws and relatively low violence. Didn't that suggest that perhaps other factors went into reducing violence, such as policing strategies, urban design, class differences, and who knew what else? As was often the case when it came to gun policy, the logical path between cause and effect was a hall of mirrors. Maybe I was just being contrary, but since it was the guns in cities that hogged the limelight, I wanted to see the guns that nobody talked about.

I also had a sense—or maybe just a hope—that on the Plains I'd find a calmer variety of gun guy than I'd encountered in the Southwest or on the Internet. Frank DeSomma had been so inflamed by political outrage that he'd had a hard time staying on the subject of his own gun business. Even kindly old Erin Jerant, in her small-town gun shop, had felt the need to get in her digs at President Obama. *Oh well,* I figured, *the Southwest has always been a flinty, individualist place.*

As for the Internet, its anonymous nature no doubt amplified the worst of gun-guy anger. Like a drain at the bottom of the sink, it concentrated the most unpleasant elements. Lots of topics attracted hateful language on the Web, but it was different when the topic was guns. It may have been hot air, but gun-guy hot air was always more disturbing, because there was no forgetting that gun guys had the means to act out their fury. There is no need for an extended tour through the cesspool, but here is an example—rougher than most but by no means unusual—by someone calling himself SinCity2A on AR15.com, in response to a question about whether a UN small-arms treaty could infringe on Americans' Second Amendment rights:

> The UN can suck my constitutional cock and lick my bill of rights balls! Hey UN, you don't want none of this! Come try it motherfuckers. The last thing you will see is the muzzle flash of my rifle as the bullet rips into your face and the hydrostatic shock turns your brain into mush and blows it out the back of your skull! And you'd better pray for death, cuz if you are still barely alive after I give you lead poisoning, I will use my tactical ax I bought at Big 5 on sale to chop off your head and use it as a shitter! THAT'S RIGHT, I WILL MOTHERFUCKING SHIT IN YOUR

EMPTY MOTHERFUCKING HEADS! I will use my machete to lop off your arms and beat the fucking shit out of the survivors of my motherfucking apocalyptic second amendment wrath! I will reach down your fucking gullet, rip out your fucking entrails, and fucking strangle you with them! FUCK YOU GLOBALIST COLLECTIVIST AUTHORITARIAN ASSFUCKS, THE FIERY GATES OF MOTHERFUCKING HELL WILL BE OPENED UP ON YOUR BITCH STANKIN ASSES! The fucking arfcom army is gonna give you child raping atrocity enabling two bit dictator supporting illiterate disease ridden shit water drinking third world pieces of pigeon shit a g—–damn motherfucking insurgency you won't fucking believe! If you want to see what's in store for you, read the Book of Revelation! My fucking trigger finger is getting too damn motherfucking itchy! I NEED TO KILL ME SOME BLUE HELMET MOTHERFUCKERS, I NEED TO SATISFY MY FUCKING BLOODLUST WITH THE FOOTSOLDIERS OF THE ILLUMINATI! FUCK FUCK FUCK FUCK FUCK, I AM RIP MOTHERFUCKING ROARING READY TO MOTHERFUCKING HELL GO! I will use my baseball bat to bash in your heads and warpaint my face with your blood and brain matter before I rack up a body count greater than Vlad the Impaler! And UN, all this that I just laid out for you, will not just be dealt you by me, but by TENS OF MILLIONS OF OTHER CONSTITUTION LOVING MINISTERS OF DEATH! Bring it on, BRING IT ON G—–DAMNIT!

In fairness, one forum participant responded, "Jesus Christ. Tighten the ol' tin foil hat down," but others called the post "most excellent." Nobody seemed to take it as a joke.

It amazed me when I read SinCity2A how thoroughly Timothy McVeigh had dropped down the national amnesia hole. Had a Muslim been raving online this way about jihad, he'd have found himself on an unmarked Gulfstream in short order. The Department of Homeland Security was keeping an eye on people like SinCity2A; it issued an intelligence assessment in 2009, listing reasons to expect a resurgence of militia activity: economic downturn, illegal immigration, a black president, and, interestingly, disgruntled veterans. In the summer of 2010, though, it was hard to know whom to worry about, with Sharron Angle talking of

"Second Amendment remedies" during a U.S. Senate run in Nevada and Sarah Palin telling supporters, over and over, to "reload."*

Anyway, SinCity2A was listed on AR15.com as being from Nevada, and I wrote off his rant as just more sunbaked, dust-maddened Southwestern spleen. Out on the grassy, watered prairies, I hoped to find the kind of gentlemen who talk quietly across their back fences, wouldn't dream of shooting guns at people, and could describe their gun lives to me politely. Sure enough, I found one on my very first day.

I'd become accustomed to finding gun stores boarded up, so the blue, steel-sided building outside McCook, Nebraska, was a welcome sight, sporting not only a banner announcing GUNS in letters six feet high but an OPEN sign on the door. I suited up—NRA cap, holstered gun—and walked inside.

Outdoor Sports was a small shop in a huge space, airy and understocked. Behind the counter, all by himself, sat a man of about sixty, wearing plastic-framed glasses, a bristle mustache, and an orange T-shirt that said FIDDLER ON THE ROOF. He looked more like a philosophy professor than a gun merchant. I half expected him to speak with a British accent when he stood up to introduce himself as Greg Hepp.

Greg's face lit up when I owned that I was working on a book about why people like guns. "I've wondered about that myself," Greg said, "and I'm in the business." I picked up a pre-1964 Winchester Model 70 hunting rifle, whose style and workmanship made it, for gun guys, the equivalent of a 1955 Chevy Biscayne.

"This is one beautiful weapon," I said.

Hepp held up a palm. "I have a degree in English, and I must take exception to your rhetoric," he said. "Don't call it a 'weapon.' Do you know what the dictionary definition of a weapon is? 'A device used either offensively or defensively.' That means against humans. Not all firearms are weapons. That one there, for example, is a hunting rifle."

From a rack, I hefted an M1 Garand, the American infantry rifle from the Second World War and Korea. Lord knew how many people this one had killed. "This is a weapon, though, right?"

"That *was* a weapon. Now it's a historical artifact." He picked up a Civil

---

* Kudos to the gun guys who organized TheHighRoad.org, which described its mission thus: "This board is called 'The High Road' for a purpose. Its reason to exist is to be a place for a higher grade of discussion than is found on some other gun forums. Posts consisting of personal attacks, group stereotyping, macho chest-thumping, and partisan hackery are low road."

War Zouave musket. "Just like this. It *was* a weapon. But would you call it that now?" He set it down and folded his hands on the counter.

"People use firearms for all kinds of things that have nothing to do with offense or defense," he said. As though to prove his point, he handed me a flyer from a stack. The Southwest Nebraska Rifle and Pistol Club was holding a small-bore bench-rest contest that weekend. Each shooter would have fifteen minutes to fire ten .22 rifle bullets at a paper target fifty feet away. It was gentlemen's shooting, slow and precise. "You have skeet shooters," Greg said. "They wouldn't dream of pointing a shotgun at a person. Their shotguns are sporting goods, like tennis rackets. I get collectors in here who don't even shoot the guns they own. The idea that every gun is a weapon is most destructive."

I looked at some price tags. Nine hundred dollars for that Garand, eleven hundred for the Winchester, five hundred for an ordinary Stevens twelve-gauge side-by-side—all pretty high. "People around here can afford eleven-hundred-dollar guns?"

"All the time."

"No recession?"

"Not here. People have to eat. The government pays farmers to grow and it pays farmers not to grow. It pays them in good times and it pays them in bad times." He laughed good-naturedly. "It's you Democrats. Agriculture is the biggest welfare program there is." I hadn't mentioned my politics; so much for my camouflage. Perhaps I needed to wear belts of ammunition across my chest.

The door opened and two women entered—a mom in her late thirties with a teenage daughter. The mom took from a folded piece of paper an enormous gold-colored coin about four inches across and as light as cardboard: an aluminum reproduction of a 1930s-era twenty-dollar gold piece. "We dug this up in our yard," she said. "Can we pawn it? It's bullion. That's what my father said when I showed it to him. Some of these were gold, but some were bullion."

I put my hand over my mouth. The only kind of bullion that would make a coin that light was chicken bouillon.

Greg was the model of politeness and respect. "I'm not really a pawnshop. Guns and tools are all I take." The thing was worthless, but he wasn't going to say that. "Let me see what you have there," he said. He unfolded the paper in which she'd wrapped the coin, a Wikipedia printout on the original. It described the coin as thirty-four millimeters across.

"This is quite a bit bigger than thirty-four millimeters," Greg said—

five times bigger, at least. "Also," he explained gently, "bullion is 99.5 per-cent gold. A bullion coin this big would be quite heavy."

"Can I pawn it?"

Greg chuckled. "I wouldn't be able to give you anything for it. It's not a real gold coin, you understand."

"Mom, let's go," the teenager said.

The woman put the heel of her hand against her forehead and paused. "It would sure help. I don't know how I'm going to . . ." She let the sentence hang.

"Mom."

The woman let out a sigh and turned to go. Greg called her back to take the coin.

As they passed through the door, a young man came in, wearing a John Deere cap and overalls with no shirt. He carried a Marlin .22 rifle with a black plastic stock.

"Do you buy guns?"

"Yes."

"I want to sell this one."

Greg picked up the rifle and examined it with care. It was clearly the type sold at Walmart for about $129, but Greg inspected it as judiciously as he might have a 1920 Holland & Holland double .500.

The kid reached out and touched the focusing ring on the scope, which fell free and clattered across the counter. "That's broke," he said.

"Yes, I can see that," Greg said. He set the rifle down. "How much would you like for it?"

"I don't know," the kid said. "How much you want to give me?"

"I never make an offer," Greg said. "I might make you an offer and fif-teen minutes later someone else might offer a thousand dollars more and then you'll think I ripped you off. How much would you like?"

"I don't know."

"Son, when you walk into a store, there's a price tag on every item. You don't make an offer; you pay the price that's being asked or you don't. Tell me the price of this rifle and maybe I will buy it from you, but maybe not. That depends on the price."

"Well," he mumbled. "I got to get some money in a hurry. How about three hundred?"

Greg cocked his head to one side sympathetically. "I can buy this gun new for less than half that."

"What about the scope?"

"Forgive me, but the scope would be worthless even if it wasn't broken."

The kid looked down sadly at the rifle. He chewed his lip with anxiety. Greg said, "Why don't you do a little research and see what kind of price you're likely to get." The kid picked up his rifle and left, forlorn.

"I've been thinking about your question," Greg said, gliding past the irony of those two visits immediately upon his extolling the area's wealth. "About why we Americans like guns so much. For some people, I'm sure it's just to tick off the liberals. You know: Liberals hate guns, so I love them—that kind of thing. But I also think it's visceral. You like them or you don't. My sister can't be around guns. They give her the willies, and she gets all nervous and upset. She knows that's not rational, but there it is. Over in Palisade a few years ago, there was a man with a rattlesnake in a bell jar—a live one. He'd set it up on the bar and bet you that you couldn't keep your hand on the glass when the snake struck. He made a lot of money on that bet. Everybody knew the snake couldn't bite through the glass, but nobody could keep his hand there. They had a visceral reaction. It's the same with guns. I couldn't tell Barbara Boxer not to hate guns. She hates them, and that's all there is to it. Maybe something happened to her once that makes her feel that way, but she can't help it. It's just how she's made."

This is the genetics argument—that each of us is born hardwired either to love or hate guns. That more men than women love them suggests that it's a sex-linked trait. That more conservatives than liberals love them suggests it's . . . what? That one's politics are also hardwired, commonly coupled with a love or hatred of guns the way blue eyes often come with blond hair? Why, then, if one's likes and preferences are indelibly etched on our mitochondria, bother with politics at all? It would be no more possible to talk people out of their views than to talk them out of their shoe size. I suspected that Greg Hepp was trying to be a gentleman and allow everybody his or her own worldview. But I left his store feeling strangely hopeless.

Determined to stay off the interstates, I took US 6/34 east from McCook. The highway followed a rail line, punctuated every ten miles or so by an identical settlement: grain elevator, gas station, bar. As soon as I passed one elevator, the next hove into view in the hazy distance. The hamlets and the flat terrain between them were so similar that I might as well have been driving around the tiny planet of *The Little Prince,* passing the same raised landmark again and again.

The distances were disorienting. I realized that over the years my eyes had become close-range instruments, focused on things as far away as the length of my arms—newspaper, computer screen, handlebars of bicycle. Out here, I locked onto the horizon and felt my eyeballs stretching—bulging from my head as in a Warner Bros. cartoon—trying to cope.

It was hard to get a handle on conditions out on the Plains. Some farmhouses looked prosperous, freshly painted and surrounded by great swaths of perfectly mown lawn, but others appeared abandoned. The unsettling encounters in Greg Hepp's store echoed around in my skull. The grocery stores and bars looked like something out of a Walker Evans photograph, and the billboards along the highway told a hard-luck story of their own: SPEND TIME WITH YOUR KIDS, KIDS NEED BREAKFAST, AVOIDTHESTORK.COM, POUR FAT FREE OR I PERCENT FOR KIDS 2 AND UP, and, near an Indian casino, 1-800-BETS-OFF, advertising a treatment center for gambling addiction.

With the setting sun behind me, the yawning tedium of sun-blasted corn morphed into a glorious Van Gogh. Pink light slanted among the cornstalks, and each stood out vividly from the rest. Grain elevators were transformed from monochromatic plinths of cement into delicate sculptures of light and shadow. Houses that had looked forlorn at noon waxed stately and inviting at sundown. Unable to find a state park in which to camp, I pulled in behind a farmhouse that looked as though it had been abandoned in the 1980s. I scraped a mountain of rusted tin cans aside with my foot and set up my tent. It was too hot to eat, so I dug out the .22 pistol and silencer, lined up some of the old cans on a split-rail fence, and amused myself plinking them off.

An entire freight train slid across the prairie: 104 cars, and I could see all of them at once. Beyond that, a thunderstorm reared up, a foaming black cloud the size of Pluto, pulsing with lightning, dragging misty tentacles of rain across the horizon like a Portuguese man-of-war. The people under that, I figured, must think it's a rainy evening everywhere. Out here, it was just another feature of a landscape too big to grasp. The thought gave me the creeps, and I crawled into my tent.

The next morning, Gun Store Finder directed me to a boarded-up gun shop in Hastings. Then I found a live one in town, but a hand-lettered sign taped to its locked door said, MEET ME AT THE GUN SHOW AT THE GRAND ISLAND CONV. CENTER.

The gun blogosphere and magazines were lit up that spring with fearful rumors of the feds "closing the gun-show loophole," and my in-box had been filling with equally hopeful memos from the Brady Center to Prevent Gun Violence and Mayors Against Illegal Guns. The loophole at issue was a gap in federal law that allowed people to sell guns at gun shows without computerized background checks. Gun *stores* had already been tamed. In 1968, Congress—spurred by assassinations and riots—passed the first gun law that affected the average gun owner: the Gun Control Act of 1968. It banned mail-order gun sales, prohibited in-store sales to felons or lunatics, and imposed a waiting period on handgun sales. For nearly three decades, though, the law largely ran on the honor system. A buyer signed an affidavit saying he wasn't a "prohibited person," but who knew? Not until 1994 did the Brady Law give the Gun Control Act teeth, by requiring stores to run a computerized check on a buyer's record, in lieu of a waiting period.

The background-check requirement applied to federally licensed gun dealers at shows as well as in their stores. The "loophole" applied to everybody else. People without licenses could, under federal law, set up tables at gun shows and buy, sell, or trade as many guns as they liked without background checks or paperwork.

I'd started going to gun shows in 1989 in Montana and had bought any number of interesting old guns with nothing more than cash and a handshake. One particularly great find—a 1933 Remington Model 8—I'd snagged in the parking lot of the University of Montana field house before even walking inside to the show. Spotting the rifle in a guy's trunk, I'd dickered with him a little and clinched the deal for $130—a happy transaction between consenting adults. It had never occurred to me that it might be unreasonable.

Since then, a few states—post-Columbine Colorado among them—had closed the loophole by requiring everybody at a gun show, dealer or not, to run background checks. Nebraska had closed it halfway, allowing the free-and-easy sale of rifles and shotguns but requiring a background check for handgun sales. In most states, though, gun shows were utterly unregulated. Felons, drug addicts, wife beaters, and schizophrenics who couldn't buy a gun at a store could in theory buy all they wanted and unleash mayhem.

"In theory" was the operative phrase. Professors from the Universities of

Maryland, Michigan, and London studied crime data from the vicinities of 3,400 gun shows—including those in loophole states—and found that the shows, loophole or no, had no effect on local homicide or suicide rates. Still, to those most worried about gun violence, letting people buy guns with no background check seemed crazy.

In truth, though, a much bigger loophole existed, one neither side wanted to discuss. Under federal law and in most jurisdictions, ordinary people—those who weren't licensed gun dealers—not only could sell guns at shows; they could sell guns anywhere they liked. I had sold a lot of guns, including that Remington 8, through classifieds in *The Missoulian*. A buyer came to my house, put cash on the kitchen table, and off he went—no questions, no paperwork, and no one the wiser. A gun is not like a car; there's no title. I'd purchased most of my guns in the same casual way. A guy showed up at my house with a Walther PPK, I gave him three hundred dollars, and he drove away; we didn't even exchange names, let alone sign papers or run a background check. A seller was not supposed to deal with a buyer who he had "reason to believe" was prohibited from purchasing guns. Each of us, under federal law, was to decide whether those prison tats on a buyer's neck, those claw marks on his face, or his incoherent babbling made him a prohibited buyer. By some estimates, nearly a third of the *legal* gun sales in the United States took place with no background check or paperwork—and only a tiny percentage of those were at gun shows.

Gun guys didn't talk about this, because they didn't want to set off a call to ban private transactions. Gun controllers didn't talk about it, either, because banning private gun sales was politically—to say nothing of practically—impossible. So both sides were hollering themselves hoarse about the gun-show loophole.

By the time I pulled into the vast parking lot of Grand Island's convention center, the loophole was a red herring the size of a blue whale. I paid my five dollars to enter and got a black ink stamp on my hand that said, in inch-high letters, GUN. So much for attending a Quaker meeting anytime soon.

At their best, gun shows are real *shows*—exhibitions of old, unusual, or idiosyncratic firearms collections. But so many firearms were being manufactured every year that the new ones—with their black plastic furniture—were crowding out the old gems of lustrous steel and deep-grained wood. So I was delighted to find, just inside the front door, a middle-aged man with a genuinely strange gun on his back. It looked like some kind of futuristic carbine, but instead of a straight magazine protruding from the bottom it had a plastic cylinder the size of a Quaker Oats box laid across the top. The cylinder, the man explained, was designed to hold a hundred rounds of nine-millimeter ammunition, which was impressive, since most carbines held thirty shots at most. A weirdo gun—just the kind of thing I went to gun shows to see. This was promising. As he talked to me about the gun—its made-in-America space-age design—I studied his face. Up close, I could see that he wasn't middle-aged. He probably wasn't much older than thirty. Exhaustion had added twenty years to his face.

"Why are you selling it?" I asked.

"It's this or the house," he said with a weary laugh. I wished him luck.

The vast room was un-air-conditioned and stuffy, which might have explained why so few people milled about. I'd been expecting the collegial hubbub of like-minded enthusiasts gathered without their wives, but instead, a leaden, almost funereal silence lay over the room. The few shoppers were squarely positioned in the middle-aged, white, rural bulge of the gun-guy demographic, and hardly any of them seemed to be buying. "Sell anything?" I heard one vendor call to another. *"Nada."* The carbine at the door looked like it would be the most interesting firearm here; the rest were mostly variations of the AR-15, J.C. Penney–grade shotguns, and modern semi-automatic pistols no more unusual than those you'd find in a pawnshop. And if I'd thought driving across the Plains would be a relief from gun-guy rage, I was in for a disappointment.

A hard-looking man with a table full of AR-15s was also selling envelopes containing two plastic yellow pellets. 'BAMA BALLS, said the card stapled to the envelope. "They'll raise your taxes, take your guns, leave your border unprotected, and surrender two wars." Beside them lay baseball caps emblazoned with JOHN 3:16.

"What's that passage say?" I asked.

"For God so loved the world that He gave His only begotten Son, that whoever believes in Him should not perish but have everlasting life."

I opened my mouth to point out the irony of quoting the gospel of Jesus while deriding policies that might assist the poor or turn swords to plowshares, but then I remembered I was in a room full of armed Nebraskans and let it go.

A heavyset couple ambled by holding hands, the man's T-shirt showing a television set and the motto MORE WATCHIN', LESS TALKIN'.

A skinny young man at a table full of AR-15s had on a T-shirt that said INFIDEL—a common fashion statement that year in gun-guy America.

"How's business?" I asked him.

"Terrible," he said. "I need Obama to say the word 'gun' one time on television. He doesn't have to say anything else. Just 'gun,' to get people buying again." He took a pull from a twenty-four-ounce Mountain Dew.

"This your full-time gig?" I said. "Got a gun store?"

"Nope. Work in a body shop. Can't get the hours, though. Anymore, unless it's hit so bad you can't drive it, people don't come in."

Stuck to one of Infidel's gun cases was a McCain-Palin sticker. I told him about the AR-loving kid at the Cherry Creek State Park Family Shooting Center who'd written in Palin for president. "He thought McCain would be no better than Obama on guns," I said.

"Really? McCain? As bad as Obama?"

"That's what he said."

"Democracy, man."

"What don't you like about Obama?"

He gestured grandly across the table of rifles.

"Really?" I asked. "All he's done is let us wear them in national parks"—for that had been the new president's only action on gun policy, much to the frustration of his pro-control constituency.

"He's just waiting," said Infidel. "Trust me. Second term, that's when he'll make his move. They're all the same." That hung in the air for a second, until he realized how it sounded. "Democrats," he added quickly.

I picked from a stack a fake trillion-dollar bill—"Federal Debt Note"—emblazoned with Obama's smiling face. "I'll take one of these."

"Two dollars," he said. "Thank you."

I spotted an oasis of Old West guns amid the black plastic—single-action Colts and Winchester rifles—and made my way gratefully in that direction. As I drew close, the man behind the table was telling a friend, "All the federal government has the right to do, according to the Constitution, is secure the borders, make war, and control international trade, and the liberals are doing everything but!"

I veered away and nearly bumped into a haggard-looking man in a T-shirt that read IF GUNS CAUSE CRIME, THEN SPOONS MAKE ROSIE O'DONNELL FAT. And here was a whole table of bumper stickers and T-shirts: I'LL KEEP MY FREEDOM, MY GUNS, AND MY MONEY. YOU CAN

KEEP THE CHANGE. OBAMA WANTS YOUR WALLET AND YOUR GUN. IF 10%
IS ENOUGH FOR GOD, IT'S ENOUGH FOR THE IRS. WELCOME TO AMERICA,
SPEAK ENGLISH OR GET THE HELL OUT. KEEP WORKING: MILLIONS ON WEL-
FARE ARE DEPENDING ON YOU.

Next to it was a table of Nazi memorabilia, and another piled high
with cheaply printed books—on such topics as how to make silencers at
home—and tracts: *Can You Survive? Guidelines for Resistance to Tyranny
for You and Your Family.* The cover of that one depicted a blood-dripping
Commie sickle slicing through a U.S. map—two decades after the Soviet
Union disappeared.

I picked up *Modern Weapon Caching: A Down-to-Earth Approach to
Beating the Government Gun Grab,* by Ragnar Benson, published by Paladin Press in, of all places, Boulder. "Today, many Americans realize the
United States is in a race against firearms confiscation in which the lessons of the past will play a significant role," he wrote. I thumbed ahead.
"The media will fry gun owners if they get any chance at all." I found
diagrams showing how to pack guns into watertight PVC tubes before
burying them. "If possible, bury chunks of steel in the vicinity of your
cache—pieces of scrap, large bolts and nuts, whatever will confuse metal
detectors."

The young man behind the book table said, "If it's time to start burying them, it's time to start digging them up."

"People really bury guns?" I said.

"People really *don't* bury guns?" he said.

We looked at each other for a minute.

"Dude, if you don't get it, you don't get it," he said.

"Don't get *what*?"

He screwed up his face. A big man sitting on a rolling office chair at
the next table rolled over to listen.

"Seriously," I said. "Say I walk over there and buy myself an AR for nine
hundred dollars. You want me to bury it in the ground?"

"I don't want you to do anything, man."

"But why would I bury it in the ground?"

"Why wouldn't you?"

"I don't know," I said. "So I could shoot it, maybe? So I could enjoy it?"

"You shoot your *other* one. The one they're going to take away."

"Who's 'they'?"

"Your duly elected government. Look, man, I don't have time to explain
it all to you."

The man in the swivel chair was chuckling wryly, as though to tell me not to get started with this nutcase. But when I smiled at him, he stopped chuckling and his face darkened. It wasn't the other guy he'd been laughing at.

"Where you from?" he growled.

"Colorado."

"I don't know how they do things in Colorado, but here, we take our 2A rights very seriously. If you don't think the government's coming for your guns, you need to reread your history."

I always forgot this part of gun shows until I got inside. The T-shirts, the bumper stickers, the printed harangues, and the palpable bitterness had started showing up at about the same time as the plastic-handled guns—and at about the time of the Clinton-era assault-rifle ban. Gun guys had derived two lessons from the ban, the first being that Democrats were willing to restrict freedoms without having the slightest idea of the construction or function of the tool they sought to ban—the "shoulder thing that goes up." Even worse, though, was that Democrats had shown themselves willing not just to place rules on the buying of guns but to ban an entire class of weapon. If you could make some guns illegal, went the thinking, it was but a short step to making all guns illegal.

The thing is, the assault-rifle ban had lasted only ten years and had already been gone for six. Aside from the anemic attempts at closing the meaningless gun-show loophole, the country hadn't seen a serious run at gun control in years. Why weren't these guys celebrating their victory over the forces of gun control instead of hunkering down in a defense crouch?

A University of Virginia sociologist named James Davison Hunter had published that spring a book called *To Change the World,* which argued that modern American Christianity was mired in the "language of loss, disappointment, anger, antipathy, resentment, and desire for conquest." Reviewing it, the conservative *New York Times* columnist Ross Douthat wrote that because modern Christianity "mobilizes but doesn't convert, alienates rather than seduces, and looks backward toward a lost past instead of forward to a vibrant future . . . [it] punches way below its weight."

The gun-rights movement was equally mired in the language of loss, disappointment, anger, antipathy, resentment, and desire for conquest—and poorly serving its constituents. In its incessant whining about the gun grabbers and the liberals, in its obsessive nurturing of inchoate anger, and in its all-or-nothing worldview, the NRA and the rest of the organized gun-rights movement was likewise punching below its weight. The tactical strategy was transparent enough; the specter of a renewed assault-rifle ban, like the myth of "out-of-control crime," kept the contributions rolling in, and by never declaring victory, they could keep it going forever. The NRA could play endlessly to its limited constituency, but that constituency was aging rapidly. And it could swing a bully's club when it needed to. But its white-hot combativeness and inflexibility put a scary face on the American gun guy, and this was hardly the way to win people over and expand the circle of firearms-tolerant Americans, which seemed to me a much more worthwhile exercise. As a gun guy, I kept waiting for the NRA—which understands guns and their use better than any other entity—to make itself an honest partner in the national effort to reduce further gun violence and gun accidents. Merely shouting "More guns for everybody!" didn't qualify—to me anyway.

The NRA no doubt had its own interests in being naught but a perpetual-combat machine. The mystery was why ordinary gun guys—with plenty else to worry about in that recession-stressed summer—were so eager to go along.

9. CONDITION BLACK

The only times an Afro-American who was assaulted got away has
been when he had a gun and used it in self-defense.

—Ida B. Wells, *Southern Horrors: Lynch
Law in All Its Phases*, 1892

ick Ector was born in northwest Detroit two months after the 1967
riots and six years before the first oil crisis began shifting the auto
industry's center of gravity to Japan—before free fall, in other words.
The Ectors' neighborhood of single-family homes between Seven
Mile and the Southfield Freeway was calm and hardworking. The world
appeared orderly to Rick—full of kind, steady neighbors, safe streets to
play in, and teachers who cared. Detroit was balkanized according to auto
manufacturer; the Ectors, a Chrysler family, attended Plymouth Congregational Church. Living in an orderly world, Rick was an orderly child;
he got good grades in school, babysat three younger siblings, and cooked
dinner for them on nights when his parents worked overtime.

Through her protective goggles at Chrysler's Mack Avenue stamping
plant, though, Rick's mother could see the future. Neither Detroit nor the
auto industry would stay safe for a black man with nothing but high school
behind him. "Do *not* count on a factory job," she'd say. "There won't be
any. You *will* go to college." And as predicted, disorder descended. Rick's
father, tired of being harassed by Detroit's edgy and racist police, gave
up his autoworker job and joined the force. Now he came home at night
with a revolver on his hip and an increasingly broody nature. Rick's mom
endured that until Rick was ten, then packed up the children and took
them to live near relatives in Evansville, Indiana. A year of that—square

dancing in school instead of basketball!—was plenty for Rick; the family returned to Detroit shortly before his estranged father shot himself dead with his departmental revolver.

As Detroit's young black men came to realize that the riots hadn't helped, and the auto jobs were vanishing, their lives slid into what felt like a perpetual riot. Nighttime gunshots intruded on Rick's once upright neighborhood. Holdups, shootings, murders: The buzz of violence became part of the backdrop. Rick steered clear of it all, invoking Martin Luther King's doctrine of nonviolence and pressing his face ever more firmly into schoolbooks. First chance he got to vote, he chose Michael Dukakis. As a black man and the son of union autoworkers, Rick had two iron bonds to the Democratic Party. Without thinking about it too much, he agreed with the party and Detroit's black leaders that the city had too many guns and should make them harder to get. Rick didn't want a gun anyway. Guns were for other people—the kind who couldn't wait for their rewards, weren't willing to work for them, and couldn't rise above their fears.

At Wayne State, Rick studied industrial engineering with the same placid, methodical discipline that had kept him straight through adolescence, and went on for a master's degree from the University of Michigan. He married his girlfriend, Martha, at Plymouth Congregational. He became president of the campus chapter of the National Society of Black Engineers and a member of its national board, never doubting that when he was ready, an executive position—not a factory job—would be waiting for him within the bosom of the Chrysler family. When he showed up for his interview in 1994, he made the mistake of wearing a necktie.

"Please remove it," the interviewer told him. "A tie is a power symbol here." In feverish imitation of Toyota, Chrysler had switched to a Modern Operating Agreement, which meant that the company needed not executives but "facilitators"—a buffer layer between workers and management to coax and cajole, not force and threaten, better work on the factory floor. There would be no executive lunchroom for Rick at the Jefferson North Assembly Plant, the way he'd expected all his life. No reserved parking space. No necktie.

On his feet all day, walking the floor among half-built Jeep Cherokees, Rick memorized every face by "name and last four." The aching egalitarianism of the Modern Operating Agreement deprived him of the stature he'd expected, but he found that he loved the work. He was not only troubleshooting bad paint jobs and misfilled fluids; he was also slapping backs and keeping people cool and happy. When something needed doing, Rick could simply ask a man to do it; nobody got his back up about union rules. For a while, the Toyota way seemed to work.

Rick was taking home twenty-thousand-dollar profit-sharing checks on top of a fine salary, ample overtime, and gold-plated benefits; at only twenty-seven, he was making more than a hundred grand a year. He and Martha were able to buy a pretty Tudor house with a detached garage on a corner lot, among the black middle managers of North Rosedale Park. They filled it with furniture, appliances, and four children. Life was good.

When Rick got passed over for promotion, he figured that staying on the factory floor would only leave him bitter, so he took a cut in pay to transfer to Chrysler's growing information technologies department. Instead of surfing the floor's wild wave of technical challenges and intense personalities, he sat in a cubicle gazing at a screen, untangling an endless matrix of servers and terminals, matching projects to capacity, and combing the system for bugs. It was okay, really. Figuring out servers and Web protocols felt more like the future than debugging steering columns and upholstery. But it wasn't nearly as much fun. Life felt pared down. The new job carried no overtime, so Rick and Martha had to budget carefully. The whiff of having been passed over—of having yielded his fate to others—lingered.

North Rosedale Park wasn't what it used to be, either. The houses were as neatly kept and the lawns as finely manicured as ever, but a neighbor's car was stolen one night, and then someone broke into Rick's car and wrecked the steering column trying to start it. A house up the street was burglarized. Blue flashing lights started showing up on nearby streets, their cold glare pulsing off houses he and the kids often visited. One evening after dinner, Martha looked up and said, "Was that a gunshot?" Rick drove to Kmart the next day and for two hundred dollars bought a Mossberg twelve-gauge pump-action shotgun. "Fella hears this sound," said the salesman as he worked the gun's mechanism with a loud *clack-clack,* "he's going to take off before you even see him."

Rick had never fired a gun, and he didn't fire the Mossberg. It was a shotgun, after all. If he ever had to shoot, he'd be just steps away, and a shotgun would spray enough pellets to get the job done. He slid it under the bed and instructed his children in the protocol: That's Daddy's. Don't touch.

They were sensible, as he'd been. He only had to tell them one time.

A grim advantage to living through Detroit's economic collapse was that an unbelievable stream of antiques and collectibles became available as families' fortunes imploded, and Martha seized the opportunity to start a business. She combed the paper for auctions and estate sales, snapped up treasures for pennies on the dollar, and resold them. Often, a family's collapse was so quick and thorough that their belongings were simply left on the sidewalk. Rick and Martha spent a lot of weekends driving through hard-hit neighborhoods, finding Gustave wardrobes or Arts and Crafts bureaus given up to the rain. Neighborhoods were being abandoned at breathtaking speed to drug addicts and gangbangers; Rick and Martha were careful to be out by nightfall. Often, toughs eyeballed them from the corner as they poked through piles of belongings; Rick sometimes found himself wishing he had the Mossberg with him, or a handgun up under his clothes, but he pushed those thoughts aside. What would he do with a gun out here? Guns were the scourge of the city.

Besides, to get a carry permit, you had to give the state gun board a good reason. Antiques hunting wouldn't qualify.

In 2000, so many people were dying from gunfire every week that when the legislature began considering whether to make Michigan a shall-issue state, like Florida, the debate pegged the needle on the city's emotion meter. Democrats and Detroit's black preachers inveighed against it; how could making guns easier to get possibly help? White suburban leaders made the Florida argument—that bad people had all the guns they wanted, and good people deserved the right to protect themselves.

Rick felt odd new feelings stir. At the giant Pentecostal Apostolic church that he and Martha now attended, he'd just answered an altar call and given his life to Jesus, wading into a vast pool with dozens of others to be immersed in the cleansing water. Rick knew that guns violated Jesus's teachings to love one's enemy as oneself, and he still felt that if black preachers and Democrats were against the shall-issue law, that was enough for him. At the same time, though, he'd been reading: All the while that Jesus was preaching love and forgiveness, he kept armed guards. Didn't Scripture describe Peter slicing an ear off one of the Roman centurions who came to arrest the Lord? What did he use for that? A loaf of bread? A fish?

It was confusing. The nightly news showed hundreds of people lining up to get carry permits. A lot of them were black. A lot were probably Christians. Probably Democrats. People like him. But the process was taking eight months at least. It seemed like a bureaucratic nightmare. Rick let it slip from his mind.

Meanwhile, he had more serious worries; Martha was contemplating divorce. She and the kids had decamped to her mother's house, across town. It was strange to wake up alone in the bed and to come home to an empty house after staring at a computer monitor all day. He hardly spoke a word to anyone some days, from sunup to sundown. The fat, fair era of a house flush with cash and alive with children was only a decade gone, but it felt like another lifetime. Rick's affability was draining away. He found himself shouting at drivers who cut him off on the freeway.

One chilly evening in September 2006, he pulled into his detached garage, exited its side door to the backyard, and started tiredly across the lawn to the house. Behind him, someone spoke.

Rick turned; a young man stood at the end of the driveway, wearing a dark hoodie, holding a gun. "You know what this is," he said.

"You've got to be kidding me," Rick said. He thought of the shotgun under his bed, an impossible thirty feet and two doors away.

The young man made a motion with his chin, and another man, identically dressed, stepped from the shadows. They ordered Rick to sit on the gravel, hands on his head. One held the gun to Rick's ear while the other went through his pockets, taking keys, wallet, and watch. Rick glanced up; the eyes of the man holding the gun looked dead. There was no way to read whether he intended to pull the trigger; it seemed it wouldn't matter to him either way. Rick squeezed his eyes shut, waiting for a bullet to crash through his skull. When he opened them, the men were gone. Shaking, he hurried into the house.

He paced—kitchen, living room, dining room, kitchen—trying to unclench his heart. It wasn't fear propelling him from room to room. It was rage. Not at the muggers—they were just knuckleheads. No, he was furious at himself, for putting off getting a carry permit and leaving it up to those thugs to decide whether he lived or died. If he'd had a gun, he'd have pulled it the minute he saw that boy at the end of the driveway.

Shot the motherfucker, is what he'd have done.

Rick's experience at the Northwestern District Police Station the next day only deepened his conviction to get a gun. He sat on a bench for hours. "We'll get to you when we get to you," a sergeant grunted whenever Rick tried to speak. The detective who finally took the report—black, exhausted, steel-haired—scribbled notes morosely. He didn't even pretend they'd follow up.

"This is an armed robbery," Rick finally pointed out.

"I know what this is."

"A serious crime, right?"

"One of many," the old detective said. He looked up. "You know what? You speak really well."

Rick had gotten the same bullshit at Chrysler: *You speak really well for a black man* was the subtext, as though an educated black man should be a rarity worth remarking on. That the detective was black only made it worse. "Well, thank *you*," Rick said. "Let me ask you: What do I need to do to buy a handgun?"

The detective put down his pen. "You don't want to do that."

"Oh, yes, I do."

"No, you don't." The old man fixed Rick with eyes so exhausted, they looked as though they'd been shellacked. "We got enough people running around with guns. You don't want to be part of the problem." He looked back down at his paperwork. "Leave it to the professionals."

"To the professionals."

"That's right."

"The police."

"That's right."

"Where were you when I had that gun up to my head?"

"Sir . . ."

"Where were you when that nineteen-year-old punk-ass was making up his sweet mind whether to leave my babies fatherless?"

"Sir . . ."

"Acey-deucey, like, 'Shoot him or no?'" Rick stood up, shaking with fury. "No, man, I'm serious. You can't protect me."

Rick spent a couple of days replacing the ATM card, credit cards, keys, and driver's license the muggers had taken, and as he moved around the house he found himself hyperaware, checking doors, windows, and closets for intruders. Out on the street, his eyes never stopped moving, scanning alleys, doorways, and parked cars. He couldn't stop thinking about those dead eyes, about how little his life meant to that thug. Martin Luther King's peaceful pieties seemed just that now, while Malcolm X made more sense to him, elaborating the right and responsibility of every man to defend himself by whatever means necessary.

Rick added to his list of errands that week a stop downtown at 1300 Beaubien—Detroit Police Headquarters—to pick up the paperwork for a concealed pistol license. The lady behind the window told him it would take about three months, and that if he wanted to buy a gun before then to keep in the house, he'd need a "purchase permit."

"How long does that take?"

"You take a seat on that bench, and I'll run your record. If it comes up clean, I can issue it right here."

"Let's do that."

An hour later, Rick was at Northwest Gun & Ammo Supply, on Grand River Avenue in suburban Redford, laying the paper on the counter. The clerk, a white guy about his age, sat on a stool reading the *Detroit News*. "I want to buy a gun," Rick said.

The clerk looked him up and down and made a face, vaguely annoyed. "What *kind*?"

Rick had no idea. His brother-in-law had mentioned owning something called a Smith & Wesson M&P, so Rick asked for one of those.

"You sound pretty sure."

"I am. Smith & Wesson M&P."

"I like the Glock."

"Smith and Wesson M&P." He wasn't going to let this supercilious white dude dissuade him. He wanted his brother-in-law's gun.

"What are you going to use it for?"

What do you think I'm going to use it for? he thought. *Tennis?* "I just got robbed. I'm getting a carry permit."

The man's face softened subtly. Rick seemed to have passed some kind of test. The man reached into a glass case full of guns—black ones and gray ones, big ones and little ones. He came out with one, gripped it in two hands as though to tear it in half. *Clack-click!* It stayed in one piece, but the whole top of it locked back, exposing the insides. He handed it to Rick. Rick had no idea what to think. His questions—How do you load it? What do I have to do besides pull the trigger? Does it kick?—got stuck in his throat, dammed up behind a wall of ignorance. All he said was, "Smith and Wesson M&P?"

"That's it."

"How much is it?"

"Five hundred and sixty-nine dollars."

Rick's chest thumped. He'd been expecting it to cost half that. He looked down, befuddled. The boxy black gun lay on the counter. It had all kinds of confusing buttons and levers. He picked it up gingerly. One thing was clear; it felt good in his hand. "Okay then."

"Okay?"

"I'll take it."

He drove from Northwest Gun & Ammo straight to Target Sports, a shooting range he'd noticed among the fast-food joints and car washes on Woodward Avenue. The man behind the counter was young and white; the whole legitimate shooting world, it seemed, was white. Behind the man, through a Plexiglas wall, shooters were aiming handguns at targets. Rick could hear muffled pops. "I just bought this gun and want to shoot it," he said.

The man laid a pair of what looked like stereo headphones on the counter. "Which target?" he asked. Rick took a step back. Pinned to the front of the counter were a dozen styles, including several man-shaped silhouettes and a photo of Osama bin Laden. Rick selected a silhouette. "Lane five," the man said, draping a target over the counter for him and turning away.

"Uh, I was wondering if you could show me how to load this."

The man turned and scowled.

He's trying to make me feel stupid, Rick thought, *like the guy at Northwest Gun & Ammo.* But he kept his gaze steady, insistent; if he didn't ask, how was he to learn?

Sighing, the young man took the gun from Rick's hands and showed him how to press cartridges into the top of the magazine until it was full. "Put it in there," he said, turning the gun over to show the slot in the grip, "and then do this." He yanked back the slide and let it snap shut. "Keep your finger off the trigger until you're ready to fire."

"That's it?"

"That's it. Line up the front sight with the back sight and put them both on the target. And put your ears on before you open that door; it's loud in there."

The range smelled of hot metal. He settled himself in lane five, at a waist-high carpeted shelf that served both as a barrier to walking downrange and a place to rest the gun. Every time the man in lane four let loose, Rick jumped inside his clothes. Even with his hearing protectors on, the gunshots were unbelievably loud. He pinned a target to a clip hanging from a cable in front of him and pushed a toggle switch. The target zoomed along the cable and came to a stop twenty feet down the gloomy alley. He pressed cartridges into the magazine until no more would go. He rammed the magazine into the pistol and yanked back the slide. He realized he hadn't drawn a breath in what seemed like several minutes, so he laid the pistol on the carpeted shelf, took a step back, and took several deep breaths of hot, smoky air. Then he stepped forward and picked up the pistol. It felt different loaded. Heavier, but also swollen, as if it were ready to burst. He wrapped his left hand around his right, like he'd seen in the movies, pointed the gun at the paper, and squeezed the trigger. The gun bucked, and he was conscious of a distant bang. A black dot appeared four inches to the right of the silhouette's head. He put the pistol down. Whew . . .

He raised it again and fired off all the bullets. When he brought the target up on its pulley, he saw what a poor shot he was. The holes were all over the place. Only about half his shots had hit the silhouette.

He sent the target downrange again, reloaded, and kept firing. Each time he pulled the trigger, he felt a little of the stress of the past twenty-four hours leave his neck and shoulders. Each time he fired, he felt a little less angry, a little less helpless. By the time he'd shot all fifty of his bullets, he was hitting the silhouette every time.

I am a gunfighter now, he thought. *I have a gun, and I know how to use it.*

Rick asked me to meet him at a Starbucks on Woodward Avenue in Royal Oak, a few hundred yards north of the Detroit city limit and the Target Sports range where he'd first shot his gun. I was freshly in off the road, having arced across Iowa and Wisconsin after Nebraska. "That Starbucks is my office," he said on the phone. Through the glass door of the Starbucks, I saw Rick before he saw me: a big man with bulging eyes and close-cropped hair perched at a tiny table, folders on his lap, cell phone cramped at his ear. He was typing on a big, old-fashioned Compaq laptop and pumping lots of energy into the phone conversation. Smiling widely and gesturing with his left hand, he radiated the desperation of a salesman whose client was slipping off the hook. He wore a loose-fitting, untucked, short-sleeved denim shirt—the kind I now thought of as a gun-guy shirt, easy to hide a pistol under. When he stood to shake hands, he saw my eyes go to his hip. "It's there," he said with a laugh. "Always."

We talked for a while, then walked down the block to shoot. Target Sports was as stuffy and hot as any indoor range I'd been to. A notice on the wall assured us that ventilators were replacing the air every few minutes, but I could taste atomized lead on my tongue. Even wearing hearing protectors, the blasting in the other lanes made it hard to appreciate the Zen geometry of shooting. As for socializing, forget it.

Gun carriers differed on how the range experience—standing still in a lane, gun ready in hand—prepared a person for a gunfight, which would involve clawing out one's gun in a panic and firing while dodging for cover. Rick agreed that running and gunning would be better practice, but he argued that any kind of practice handling a gun was valuable. "And any day shooting is a good day," he said, with that wide salesman's smile.

I was no longer wearing the Colt. Driving long days from Nebraska with that bulbous six-shot revolver against my back was like suffering a large, external kidney stone. So I'd bought a small Smith & Wesson .38 to keep in my right front pocket. Because it held only five shots, it was a little thinner than the Colt, and its aluminum frame made it light. But there were some trade-offs. It was so small that my pinkie dangled below the grip and so light that it stung my hand every time I shot it. Such is the defensive-gun dilemma. Any gun you'd want to have in a gunfight is unpleasant to carry and perhaps impossible to conceal, and a gun that's easy to carry is of limited use in a gunfight. The difference between my gun and Rick's said everything about the difference between Rick and me. Mine was all about carrying; I didn't really think I'd ever need it. Rick had had a gun pressed to his head; he was all about the moment when he'd shoot back. So the bigger the gun he could lug around, the better.

After fifteen shots with my tiny revolver, my hand felt as if it had been beaten with a ball-peen hammer. Rick cocked an eyebrow at my gun and said it was better than going unarmed. By that he meant, just barely.

"I like capacity, capacity, capacity," he said, sliding another sixteen-shot magazine into the Smith & Wesson M&P, banging them all off in one long staccato fusillade.

"But seriously, you don't think you're really going to get yourself into a sustained gunfight, right? I mean, you've read the stats; most gunfights are over in two shots."

"*Most* are over in two shots, but what about the ones that aren't?"

He let me shoot his gun, which filled my hand and pointed like a dream. I landed sixteen shots effortlessly in a three-inch group. But it was as charmless as it was efficient—a man-killer, with none of the history of my Colt or the jewelry elegance of my little Smith & Wesson. Concealing it would have meant dressing differently, and, as Henry David Thoreau said, beware any enterprise that requires new clothes.

Rick and I drove together into downtown Detroit, which looked at first as if it had been evacuated. Storefronts along Woodward Avenue were boarded up, and traffic was sparse. But the closer we got to the center, the more I picked up an edgy, offbeat energy that reminded me of New Orleans after Hurricane Katrina. The worst had happened, and now anything was possible. Espresso shops filled old bank buildings, informal art galleries occupied what once had been Ford dealerships. The sidewalk crowds were about equal parts beaten-down, middle-aged, unemployed autoworkers and hip young artists in groovy eyewear. A kind of backhanded revival was under way, with six-bedroom Victorians going for $7,000, abandoned auto plants converting into free studio space, and urban farms tended by nonprofits sprouting on razed lots in old autoworker neighborhoods. Rick and I parked—no problem finding a spot—and he took me to the Lafayette to eat "Coney Islands"—mediocre hot dogs slathered with chili and fluorescent mustard. The minibus of a retirement community was parked out front, and the place was crowded with doddering white men in lemon-yellow pants being guided by strong young black men holding their elbows: a pretty surreal scene. The room was grimy and hot. It must have been a beloved landmark, because I couldn't see any other reason for eating there.

A surly waiter plopped our plates before us, and I told Rick that he sounded like the cliché conservative—a liberal who'd been mugged. He didn't deny it. "Until I got robbed, I was a cog in the machine. I've seen the light now. The anti-gun people, they've been brainwashed. For me, getting a gun was like being born again."

When Rick left Target Sports that first day in 2006, he said, every cell in his body was quivering, fully in Condition Yellow. He had *capabilities*. Never again would he place his life in the hands of an evil stranger or be a victim. The course he took to get his concealed-carry license was as awful as mine had been; his instructor never even mentioned the laws that govern shooting an attacker. So Rick decided to become an instructor himself. He wanted to do it right and, in so doing, spread the gospel of armed self-defense. He sweated through the forty-hour NRA class to get his instructor's license, becoming a voracious student of the techniques, equipment, ballistics, and legalities of defending oneself with a firearm. He heard about something called the Gun Rights Policy Conference and drove five hours to Fort Mitchell, Kentucky, to attend. When he walked in, every face swiveled toward him, and every face was white.

"I've thought about that a lot," he said. "The gun-rights movement is very white, very Christian, and they don't do a lot of outreach to the black community. There's a lot of those people who don't want me, as a black man, to have a gun." He took a big bite of a Coney Island and laughed around it. "But hey, that's true of the NAACP, too!"

It wasn't only the NAACP. Every mainstream African American organization and public figure, from Jesse Jackson and the Rainbow Coalition to Al Sharpton to the National Urban League, was solidly in favor of ever-stricter gun control. Black America was perhaps the nation's strongest and most unanimous constituency for tougher gun laws. Even Bobby Rush, who'd gotten his political start as a Black Panther advocating "offensive violence against the power structure," was now, as a member of the U.S. House of Representatives, an advocate of more restrictive gun laws.

"I look at Bobby Rush and really have a problem," Rick said, reaching for a napkin to scrape a dab of mustard off his shirt. "Pushing that anti-gun agenda; I have no idea what he's thinking. All I know is there are members of our community pushing a cycle of dependency. If you're unarmed and on social welfare, then you're a slave. You're letting the government tell you how to live. I thought what we were fighting for all those years was to get people to stop telling us how to live!"

He balled up his napkin and threw it down onto the table. "There's a disconnect politically in the black community. We have been brainwashed into believing that guns are evil, and we continue to vote for candidates who are anti-gun. But gun-control laws got their start from pure racism. Read the history! The first gun laws were against recently freed slaves!"

It struck Rick as the worst kind of ahistorical self-hatred for blacks to deny themselves guns or agitate to make guns harder to get. The early denial of citizenship and the pattern of violence against African Americans made it a no-brainer. "For me, guns are key," he said. "You can't be considered a free man if you can't own a handgun. You are a slave. It's no coincidence that gun control is strictest where people of color live." To own a gun, and especially to carry one, he said, was ever a mark of full American citizenship.

I slid the chili off my hot dog. "It's easy to understand, though, why blacks who live in violent neighborhoods would want fewer guns around," I said. "They don't feel safe."

"Being free has nothing to do with being safe," Rick said impatiently.

"You want to live in a completely safe society? Go to North Korea. Malcolm X was more right about this than Martin Luther King. Freedom is not something that someone can give you. If you're a man, you take it." Inner-city Detroit was about as far as I could get from Phoenix without going through customs, but I could hear Nick Dranias at the Goldwater Institute making the same argument: that in a country as big, diverse, and free as ours, a certain amount of bad shit is bound to happen, and trying to engineer away all of it would do more harm than good.

What was unsafe, Rick said, given the violence whites had visited upon blacks, was for blacks to walk around unarmed in majority-white America. "I hear the pacifists say that real power doesn't need guns, that we should all do the Martin Luther King thing. But listen: King was successful in part because Malcolm X was waiting in the wings."

Rick's marriage to Martha ended in the spring of 2007, around the time he started augmenting his IT salary with a job as a firearms instructor. He managed to position himself as a Cadillac in a lot full of Edsels, charging $150 for a concealed-pistol class instead of the customary $90. He used a defense attorney instead of a police officer to teach the section on self-defense law. "I don't want a cop telling civilians what to do. A cop's job is to put you in damn jail." He began blogging, tweeting, and sending out a monthly newsletter, evangelizing—especially to African Americans—the gospel of self-defense.

On May 17, 2008, an e-mail appeared on his screen in the office at Chrysler, calling him and sixty of his co-workers to a mandatory meeting in the break room. Chrysler's chief technical officer walked in and announced, without preamble, "Bad news."

Chrysler was outsourcing its IT department.

Five years from when he would have retired on a Chrysler pension, Rick found himself working for an outfit he'd never heard of, doing the exact same job at the exact same terminal but for 20 percent less money and no benefits. He sold the Tudor house and moved to an apartment. "My marriage and Chrysler: That was my first life," Rick said as we headed back from the Lafayette to his car. "Divorced, outsourced, and a gun-rights activist: That's my second life."

A snarling purple Dodge Charger, jacked up in back and squirting black exhaust, cut us off at the corner of McNichols Road. Rick touched his brake and dropped back. "See that? My mind-set has changed," he said lightly. "Before I started carrying, I might lean on the horn if someone cut me off. I don't do that anymore, because if I lean on the horn and he gets pissed off and we stop and there's an altercation? It can go anywhere, and it would be, I shot someone because he cut me off on Woodward Avenue. I can't get mad if someone mean-mugs me. I don't have the luxury of fighting over a parking space at the mall. I tell students in my class that a concealed-pistol license is not a 007 license. It is a tool of last resort."

I walked him inside the Starbucks, where he nestled into a tiny table and unpacked his laptop and files. I looked back as I went out the door. He was performing into the phone again, balancing papers on his knees. All I could think was: Damn. Rick Ector once had a career with benefits and a pension, a Tudor house, a wife and four happy children. Now all he had was his gun and a scaffold of logic built around self-defense and self-reliance, black pride and American manhood. Standing in the exhaust-stinking humidity of Woodward Avenue, with the whole rusted skeleton of Detroit rattling around me, it looked like the shittiest imaginable comedown.

But something kept me standing there a moment longer, peering through the glass. Rick had lost everything, true, but so had a lot of people in Detroit—and elsewhere. Rick at least had his gun and the self-affirming philosophy, however brittle, of *Homo armatum*. If I didn't share it, maybe it was because I didn't live where he did, and hadn't had a gun pressed to my head. Rick had found a calling that returned some dignity and meaning to his life. And it wasn't likely to come to bad. Plenty of people couldn't be trusted with concealed weapons, but Rick Ector wasn't one of them. He knew his gun well, treated it with respect, and understood the law regarding its use. He wasn't likely to do anything mean or stupid with his pistol, and neither, in all probability, were the people who had been background-checked by the state of Michigan and were paying a premium to learn from him how to handle their guns. If they derived comfort and a sense of purpose from their concealed handguns, who was I to complain? They were probably making the city a little safer.

Rick did remind me, though, of arguments I'd had with missionaries while living in Africa in the 1980s, about the role of Jesus in Africans' lives. The poor needed the promise of a heavenly afterlife to endure their misery on earth, they'd say, and I'd argue that if the poor weren't so focused on the next life, they might organize to make this one more just and enjoyable. Perhaps Rick's gun was the same kind of consolation prize for a life radically pared down. If he hadn't had the comfort of a Smith & Wesson M&P's weight on his hip, he might have been working with his neighbors to better regulate the industries that had stolen his future and to make American society more equitable.

But then again, maybe not. Americans, whether armed or not, were still looking everywhere but at social class when parsing the texture of their lives. It wasn't so much that stressed-out blue-collar folks were clinging bitterly to their guns and religion, as Barack Obama had posited while running for president. It was more that guns and religion were keeping them from feeling bitter about the indignities inflicted on the middle class. From the ruins of the Motor City, that seemed worse.

10. IT'S NOT GOING TO BITE

I'm going to say what a blogger can and a politician can't. Guns suck. Guns are bad. I hate guns.

—*Huffington Post* blogger Mark Olmsted in a January 2, 2011, column titled "Recoil: A Sane Reaction to Guns"

Almost five hundred miles lay between Detroit and Bowling Green, Kentucky, and I was due there in two days to watch an unusual gun competition. It would be a fast dash through southern Michigan, Ohio, and Kentucky. Still, I was determined to stop at any open gun store I could find. So many seemed to be closed that it was becoming something of a personal challenge to find one that was up and running.

I made a rule for myself: not to be drawn into political discussions. The dose of gun-guy rage I'd endured at the Grand Island gun show would last me a while. Surely there was more to the attraction of firearms than resentment.

On the edge of Cincinnati, I discovered a really great gun store called Target World, which had a huge selection of both new and used guns and its own range to let customers sample the wares before buying them. The AR-15, in all its black plastic variants, crowded out the wooden guns here, as it had almost everyplace else, but I found an unusual pistol from the 1980s that I'd always wanted to handle: the Heckler & Koch P7, which wasn't cocked until the shooter's hand wrapped around the grip. I asked the young man behind the counter, who wore a name tag with "Todd" on it, if he would hand it to me.

I wasn't wearing either of my revolvers. Ohio did not recognize my Colorado permit, so for the first time on this trip I was unarmed. Not that Todd cared either way; very few customers were in the store, and he seemed glad to have someone to talk to. Neither did it matter to him that, not being an Ohio resident, I couldn't legally buy the pistol. Showing off an unusual gun to an interested gun guy was the pleasure of the job.

Beside me at the counter stood an impressively fit father in his sixties with a young-adult daughter. She was plump, with a bouffant and fuchsia stretch pants. I eavesdropped; the daughter, a schoolteacher, had just moved into her first house. They were at Target World to pick out a gun for her to keep at home. They laughed a lot as they looked over various revolvers and semi-automatics. They were having a ball and seemed as comfortable equipping the house with a gun as they might have been choosing a microwave oven.

On the other side of me, four young black men were handing around a nickel-plated Desert Eagle—a wildly powerful and flamboyant pistol that has no real sporting or self-defense purpose; it was just cool. I asked if they were planning to get carry permits, and they said no, they just liked looking at guns. Outwardly, they looked like the kind of people against whom the schoolteacher was buying a gun to defend herself—dreadlocks, gold teeth, neck tattoos, sagged pants, the works. The salesman helping them, as straight-looking as the young Pat Boone, was the model of politeness. If these guys were as bad as they looked, their records would come up on the background check and scotch the deal. In the meantime, no point in letting a seven-hundred-dollar sale walk out the door.

As I manipulated the P7, whose mechanism seemed ingeniously safe, I became aware of a voice behind me repeating softly but insistently, "No!" and a moment later, "No!" I turned, alarmed. A salesman was holding a thick-barreled stainless-steel revolver toward a young woman, butt first. She was small-boned and looked all the tinier for the huge man next to her, whose heavily tattooed arms bulged from a sleeveless T-shirt. They both wore wedding rings. She looked up at the big guy miserably and said, "Please."

"Just *hold* it," the big man urged, and she shook her head.

"Please," she said again, twisting her body as though to say, *Let's go.*

"Honey, hold it," the big man said, firmer.

Her face crumpled. The clerk holding out the revolver looked worried. "Honey," the big man said, trying to lighten his tone. "It's not going to bite."

She stared at the outstretched gun and finally put out her hand and took it, letting the gun and her hand drop to the counter with a thud, defeated.

"May I ask which of you is buying the gun?" the clerk asked nervously. Neither answered. "I mean, who is the end user? Because the person who is going to own the gun has to buy the gun. Legally, I mean."

"It'll be my gun," the big man said. "But I want her to be comfortable with it." As the clerk and the big man talked, the woman rested the hand holding the gun on the counter, her head bowed. I couldn't tell if she was looking at the gun, but her eyes were open and thoughtful; she seemed to be working through her options.

Her husband moved behind her, put his Popeye arms around hers, and helped her hold the gun straight out. She pulled the trigger once, and again. Then she turned her head back toward him and smiled tearfully. He kissed her on the nose.

Everything was okay.

The poor woman seemed to be suffering from what Greg Hepp might call Barbara Boxer's disease—a visceral aversion to firearms. "Hoplophobia" is what Jeff Cooper called it. Cooper, who died in 2006, was no psychologist. A Marine veteran from both the Second World War and Korea, he earned a political science degree at Stanford and a master's in history at the University of California, Riverside, and wrote prolifically on gun-related topics from combat shooting and firearm design to big-game hunting. It was Cooper who, in the 1970s, figured out that teaching policemen to stand erect and extend the revolver straight out with one hand was elegant, but useless in a gunfight. He invented the modern way of shooting with which we're all familiar from the movies—two-handed, in a crouch. Most of the wisdom I'd learned in my concealed-carry class, in fact, came from Jeff Cooper. It was he who set down the Five Cardinal Rules of gun safety* and invented the color-coded conditions-of-readiness chart.

Cooper coined the term *hoplophobia*—from the Greek *hoplon,* or

---

* I repeat them here because, really, they can't be repeated enough. The wording changes depending on who is teaching them, but the essence is the same. 1. Treat all guns as though they are loaded. 2. Never let the muzzle cross anything you're not willing to destroy and pay for. 3. Keep your finger off the trigger until your sights are on the target and you're ready to fire. 4. Be sure of your target and what is behind it. 5. Maintain control of your firearm.

"weapon"—in 1962, defining it as an irrational fear of weapons. "The most common manifestation of hoplophobia is the idea that instruments possess a will of their own, apart from that of their user," he wrote.* The NRA turned Cooper's thinking into a bumper sticker, GUNS DON'T KILL PEOPLE; PEOPLE KILL PEOPLE, which is often derided by gun-control advocates but which is also, strictly speaking, true. A firearm is a tremendously dangerous thing, but it can't do any harm until somebody picks it up.

Bumper-sticker slogan or not, *hoplophobia* as defined by Cooper is a pretty good way to delineate differences between what might be called the pro- and anti-gun camps. Gun-control advocates tend to focus on the gun, so when a terrible shooting happens—at a school, an office building, or a congresswoman's meet-and-greet—their first line of reasoning is, "We must do something about guns." To them, the gun is the actor. Control the gun and you ameliorate or solve the problem. To those on the other side, who favor fewer or no firearms controls, imbuing an inanimate metal object with that kind of agency seems genuinely crazy—as fanciful as conjuring up talking teapots in a Disney cartoon. To the extent they think about reducing gun violence, they tend to focus on the person behind the gun—by making the penalties for misusing one ever more severe. People, they argue, can be taught to think twice. Guns can't.

Being careful around guns is entirely rational, especially for people unfamiliar with them. But as someone comfortable with guns, I've always found rather precious those who get the fantods merely looking at one— and I've known plenty. I'm thinking in particular of a neighbor who was walking her dog past our house at the moment I was taking my hunting rifle from the trunk of the car. She gave a little yip, turned her head away, and held up a palm toward me at arm's length. It wasn't that she was afraid she'd be hurt by the gun; she was afraid to see it. Clinical hoplophobia in action or politically correct playacting? I had no idea. I confess, though, that I found it a little irritating, and vaguely insulting. What kind of monster was I, she seemed to be implying, who could handle something that she couldn't even bear her eyes to fall upon?

I couldn't entirely tell about the woman in the gun store. Clearly the gun was repulsive to her. But I also got the distinct vibe that her resistance

---

* Gun guys like to quote Sigmund Freud as saying, "A fear of weapons is a sign of retarded sexual and emotional maturity," although he never wrote that and there's no evidence he said it. Freud thought weapons seen in dreams represented the penis, but was otherwise silent on their psychological significance.

was as much about her husband as it was about the gun. The gun was his thing. When she seemed to be working through her options, it seemed like this was the math: To accept the gun was to accept the side of him she liked least. To accept the gun would be to give him an extra measure of power in the relationship. When she finally took the gun in her hand and clicked the trigger, and then smiled up at him, she seemed surprisingly serene. She seemed to have decided that she could do this, that in the long run doing this for her husband would be good for the marriage, and therefore good for her.

I wasn't so sure.

As I crossed the bridge over the Ohio River, the radio reported that thirty-seven-year-old Robert Reza had that morning followed his girlfriend to work in Albuquerque and shot her dead. He'd then turned his pistol on five others, killing one before killing himself. He'd had two drunk-driving convictions, and the police had several times paid domestic-violence calls on the home that he and his girlfriend shared with their twin five-year-old sons. None of that, however, had shown up in the records that New Mexico's instant background check could access. Reza had been able, five weeks earlier, to buy the pistol at an Albuquerque gun store called Precision Arms. Riven down the middle by the opposing cultures within me, I could easily derive both lessons: We must control access to guns more strictly, and, conversely, we must make it easier for the law-abiding to carry guns so that people like those Reza killed aren't defenseless. I could argue it eloquently both ways, and did, aloud and alone in the car, to alleviate the boredom of the drive.

As I reached Louisville under a charcoal sky, I found tucked into a small strip mall a gun store called Tilford's. Gun guys liked my old Colt so I dug it from the trunk and stuck it in my waistband before stepping inside to find a tiny, immaculate shop without much inventory, no animal heads on the wall, no endearing clutter. It felt more like an electronics-parts store than a gun shop. I noticed aloud that Tilford's had no AR-15s.

"Handguns," said the young man behind the counter. "Eighty percent is handguns, and it always has been. Now, though, what people want are the little ones, for concealed carry."

I could see at a glance that this was not the kind of store that would have baskets of old holsters, but my tactic for establishing my bona fides was to ask about holsters for my old Colt. I pulled open my jacket and swiveled so he could see it. "Got anything to fit this?"

His face lit up. "Nice! My dad had one of those."

"Okay if I draw to unload?" I asked.

"Sure!"

I took the gun from my waistband, dumped out the cartridges, and handed the revolver to him the proper way, butt first, with the cylinder open.

"Sweet," he said with a big smile, pointing it at the floor and clicking the trigger. "Old school."

"That's me." I reloaded and reholstered.

And then I made my mistake.

"Heard about the killing in Albuquerque?" I asked.

His smile vanished. His shoulders bunched up. He leaned both arms on the counter and released two big clouds of steam from his ears. "And they'll use that to argue for gun control, when we *both* know that if anyone else there had had a gun, it might have turned out different."

"Well, it seems a shame that the background check . . ."

"Oh, that's *bullshit,* man," he said, waving a hand at me and scowling. Suddenly I was no longer a new pal with a cool gun; I was some jerk making excuses for the gun grabbers. I groaned. Once again, I'd forgotten that a lot of gun guys are like the Taliban: Either you agree with them about absolutely everything or you're Satan. "Anytime there's a shooting, there's this blame-the-gun thing. This immediate jump, when there's a shooting at Virginia Tech or some school, it's immediately, 'Why do we let people have these guns?' rather than, 'Why didn't we see a problem with this person earlier, and get him proper medication?'"

The bell above the door tinkled, thank goodness, and two men entered—the younger one was thin and pale, with lank hair parted in the middle. He was wearing glasses, trousers many sizes too big, and an eerily blank expression. Around his neck hung a big plastic card identifying him as an employee of United Parcel Service. The older man was stocky, in jeans, work boots, a worn Carhartt jacket, and an air of impatient anger that, for once, had nothing to do with politics.

"His first gun," the older man said contemptuously. "Today's his twenty-first birthday, and *this* is what he wants." The pale young man floated up to the counter and silently extended a bony finger—like the Ghost of Christmas Yet to Come pointing at Scrooge's grave. What he seemed to indicate was a Taurus Judge, an unusual revolver that fired shotgun shells and was the hot product that summer in the gun press and on the blogosphere. Built around a comically elongated cylinder that could hold five shells of .410 gauge, it had a barrel only three inches long but its frame and cylinder looked as though they had been put in a vise and stretched. It was essentially a five-shot, handheld, sawed-off shotgun—at close range, devastating.

"I think it's too much for a first gun," the older man said. "I'd start him off on a .22. But it's his money, and this is what he wants."

I tried to engage the young man in conversation—"How does the shot spread from a barrel that short?"—but he stood mute, staring into the case as though lost in a world of his own. The man in the Carhartt jacket—his father, I presumed—answered for him.

"He don't know. He don't know *nothin'*. He just knows what he wants." The clerk removed the revolver from the case and held it out, unsure to whom he should hand it. The son stood like a mannequin; the dad sighed, took the gun, opened it to make sure it was empty, and handed it to him. The son held it briefly and, without examining it, handed it to the clerk. He didn't open the cylinder, cock the hammer, or pull the trigger. It was spooky; I'd never seen a man handed a pistol who didn't manipulate it somehow.

"Happy birthday," the dad said sourly.

"*How* old is he?" the clerk said.

"Twenty-one. Twenty-one."

"Well, then you got to take him to Trixie's, get him his first couch dance and a beer."

The birthday boy didn't smile.

"How will you celebrate?" I asked. He gave no indication he'd heard.

"He'll go shoot his gun," the dad said. "He's going to find out it costs a dollar-some every damned shot."

They were filling out the 4473 when I left the store.

If I had been that gun-store owner, would I have sold that kid that gun? The law not only allowed gun dealers to deny purchases to suspicious characters—it demanded that they do so. The National Shooting Sports Foundation was pushing a program that summer called "Don't Lie for the Other Guy," meaning, if you have a clean record, don't buy a gun for a friend who wouldn't pass the background check. Doing so carried a ten-year federal sentence. The NSSF was circulating to gun dealers a DVD showing what a dealer should do if he suspected that a customer was attempting what it called a "straw purchase." In the DVD, a couple enters a gun store, and, egged on by the man, the woman asks to buy a .22 rifle. As he's filling out the 4473, the dealer casually asks the woman what kind of shooting she plans to do. "Uh, hunting," she says.

"Oh?" says the dealer pleasantly. "What kind?"

"Uh, deer." In no state is a .22 a legal rifle for hunting deer. At that point, the dealer puts down his pen and politely tells the woman that he believes she is buying the rifle for someone else and that he refuses to make the sale. It's a powerful moment to watch, further complicated by the fact that the couple is African American. The unspoken implication is that the dealer, who is white, risks being accused of racism. Yet he is standing up for the principle that, background check or no, a dealer's intuition is the first line of defense against people getting guns who shouldn't.

Assuming the pale, silent young man at Tilford's passed his computerized background check, did he seem just too unstable to be trusted with a gun? Maybe the kid was just quiet. Quiet people have constitutional rights, too. I was glad I didn't have to make that judgment. Business didn't look terrific at Tilford's. Not only would it be hard to turn down a $350 sale, but the owner also would risk getting a reputation as a difficult guy with whom to do business.

My phone rang as I swung back onto Dixie Highway. The editor of a magazine called *The Oxford American* was on the line, with a kind of good-news/bad-news joke. Yes, he'd love to commission an article I'd recently pitched him. But the pay was what would have been standard in about 1993. And no, he couldn't help with expenses. I sighed aloud at the reminder that the hard times evident everywhere I traveled weren't just on the other side of the windshield. I accepted the assignment—work was work—but two decades into my freelance career, I felt like I was back at the beginning.

Before I could slip too far into a funk, another open gun store reared up alongside Dixie Highway, and this one, Biff's Gun World, looked like a gem. It was a big, rambling building, with all kinds of interesting junk on the porch—farm implements, a scarecrow, petroleum lanterns, old road signs. Inside, there was barely room to move. Aisles had been carved amid mountains of stuff—holsters, beer steins, ammo boxes, figurines, ancient copies of gun magazines . . . Hundreds of long guns lined two walls, and the glass counters held so many old handguns that they'd had to pile them on top of one another. The walls were a multilayered collage of framed hunting photos, gun posters, handwritten gun ads, and police department shoulder patches. I could have spent days wandering Biff's.

Eventually, I piled on the counter about two dozen copies of the *American Rifleman,* from 1960 to the mid-1980s. Biff himself waited on me.

He was a short, broad man with a big chest, a strong, flat belly, and curly white hair. He smiled when he saw the old magazines, and we spent a pleasant few minutes thumbing through them, marveling at the low prices in the gun ads. When I mentioned that so many gun stores seemed to have closed, I was intending to compliment him on his business acumen. But once again, I'd blundered. It was like kicking open a blast-furnace door; I practically had to grip the counter to stay upright under the force of his harangue.

"It's the paperwork!" he shouted. "You got to fill out the 4473 and keep it twenty years. And then after twenty years, they want you to keep it some more! Then they say, we recovered a gun at an armed robbery and we want to look at your paperwork, see if you sold the gun and who you sold it to! You think that's fun?"

"'They' who?"

"The ATF! Who do you think? They come in here, six of them, and they don't know their ass from a hole in the ground. They only give you about a week's notice before an inspection. They're not local guys. They're federal guys. One of them was from *California*."

Though delivered rather more forcefully than necessary, Biff's point wasn't unreasonable. ATF was both a gunned-up law enforcement agency, equipped with automatic weapons and bulletproof vests for taking down gunrunners, and the regulatory agency that oversaw the nation's legitimate gun dealers. (*F* is where all the action is; its *A* and *T* functions are largely moribund.) Biff wasn't the first gun dealer I'd heard complain that the ATF treated him like a crook. In his view, the agency's double mission was like giving homicide detectives secondary jobs as high school teachers; pretty soon they'd start seeing a killer in every teenager.

"They don't want us having guns!" Biff said, a vein throbbing on his neck. "Every year they make everything a little harder, a little more expensive. They're hoping people give up, say 'The hell with it!'"

"Whoa," I said, holding up my hands. "I come in peace."

He kept talking over me, as though in the grip of a spell he couldn't shake. "*Why* do liberals hate guns?" he yelled. "They don't believe in personal responsibility, that's why, and think the government should take care of everything!" He thrust his face across the counter like a barking dog, backing me into a tower of old computer speakers that shifted precariously. "Liberals think everybody can be perfected, everybody is good!" he shouted, straining to get his red face close to mine. "I disagree! I think there's evil in this world!"

To my relief, the door opened; another minute and Biff would have been vaulting the counter. I'm not sure I'd have sold Biff a gun, let alone let him get a dealer's license. A sallow young man with a tattooed neck approached, holding a fishing rod and preceded, at eleven-thirty in the morning, by a caustic cloud of alcohol fumes. "Will you give me something for this?" he said. "Ten dollars? My boss laid me off and I ain't got money for gas or cigarettes. I'll take anything."

Biff, still shuddering with fury, glanced at the rod, a little kid's Zebco that sold at Walmart for about eight dollars, and muttered, "It's worth nothing. I'll give you five dollars."

"I'll take it." Biff handed over a fiver and flung the rod into a pile of about thirty similar junk rods, a miniature monument to hard times in Kentucky—and to Biff's well-concealed soft heart.

The kid said he was a harbor dredger and used to working marinas as far off as the Chesapeake Bay. Now, though, there was no work. "It's our goddamn president," he drawled. "Somebody ought to shoot that guy. But then we'd get number two, and he's worse. And number three and number four."

"Don't you listen to the radio?" Biff said. "Everything's great!" He reached for a stack of cards on the cluttered counter and threw one contemptuously at each of us. I retrieved it from the floor. It said, "Psalm 2010":

> *Obama is the shepherd I did not want*
> *He leadeth me beside the still factories.*
> *He restoreth my faith in the Republican party*
> *He guideth me in the path of unemployment for his party's sake.*
> *Yea, though I walk through the valley of the bread line,*
> *I shall fear no hunger, for his bailouts are with me.*
> *He has anointed my income with taxes,*
> *My expenses runneth over.*
> *Surely, poverty and hard living will follow me all the days of my life,*

And I will live in a mortgaged home forever.
I am glad I am an American.
I am glad that I am free.
But I wish I was a dog . . .
And Obama was a tree.

That was it; I was done. Biff's tirade, coming on the heels of the scolding I'd gotten at Tilford's, had worn me out. I felt drained as I started the car and drove off. While I usually kept my eyes roving the roadside for gun stores, I found myself staring straight ahead. The last thing I wanted was another gun store. Another blast of gun-guy rage would have folded me up like a beach chair.

And I had another eight thousand miles of this to go.

What exactly was the complaint? As I picked my way down Dixie Highway, past the discount tire outlets and the Jiffy Lubes, I tried to remember all the gripes—from the Family Shooting Center through Arizona and the Grand Island gun show to Biff. Factually, none of them made sense. Gun laws were getting looser everywhere, public support for gun control was dropping, and even the dreaded Barack Obama had done his part to make life a little easier by allowing concealed guns in national parks.

But that didn't alter the gun-guy narrative any more than the huge drop in violent crime did. Gun guys were going out of their way to see the glass not as half empty but as shattered on the floor beneath their bare feet. Yes, certain media outlets were rather knee-jerk anti-gun—though certainly not Fox News. And if one considered American television—figuring in the cop, spy, and war dramas and reality TV shows like *Pawn Stars, Top Shot,* and *Sons of Guns*—the overall portrayal of firearms in the media was overwhelmingly positive. It was true that gun guys had to share the planet with people who supported stricter gun laws. But they were beating them just about every time. A certain slice of gun-guy America appeared to be suffering some kind of mass, self-inflicted anhedonia, choosing, despite all the evidence, to play the role of victim. *Christ almighty,* I thought, *isn't the Great Recession enough of a drag without needlessly manufacturing additional bummers?*

Maybe all the boarded-up gun stores were a clue.

Packed in my car was a thick booklet called the *Industry Reference Guide,* published annually by the National Shooting Sports Foundation. It was glossy, colorful, and in 162 pages deconstructed the firearms business from every conceivable angle. It tracked the number of hunting licenses for the past twenty years and the average money that each hunter spent. It charted trends in gunmaking by type of gun, caliber, and manufacturer; and import/export by source and destination. It mined excise tax data. It teased apart participation in the shooting sports by age, sex, income bracket, state, and region. It included polling about the public's attitudes toward guns and gun laws. All of it looked, at first glance, like good news for the gun industry.

Handgun, rifle, and shotgun sales had about doubled in a decade. The number of federal background checks grew every month. The average hunter was spending more every season. The public's appetite for gun control was weakening.

And yet . . . those shuttered gun stores I'd found all over America were not mere anecdotes. The number of licensed gun dealers had fallen by about half in twenty years. Walmart appeared to have been as toxic to mom-and-pop gun stores as it was to locally owned clothing stores, shoe stores, and hardware stores. But Walmart didn't entirely explain the disappearance of gun stores, because, except in Alaska, Walmart didn't sell handguns. Online shopping wasn't putting gun stores out of business, either. A shooter could buy a gun online—on the auction site GunBroker .com, say—but unless the gun was very old and/or the buyer had a special federal license, the gun had to be shipped to a gun store, where the buyer had to go through the same background check as anybody else—and the store collected a fee. Besides, gun prices tended to be high online; physical gun stores always seemed to have a price advantage.

No, the reason gun stores were closing was this: While more and more guns were being sold every year, they were going to the same shrinking group of aging white men. The NSSF's *Industry Reference Guide* showed that participation in every shooting sport except archery was down over the past decade; some—like skeet, trap, and rifle target shooting—by double-digit percentages. Despite a big industry push to get more women shooting, their participation had hardly budged since 2002. The average age of "avid" hunters was almost forty-four, and, as the guide put it, "the increase in gross dollar value . . . is coming out of the wallets of virtually the same amount of hunters." The average age of participants in all the shooting sports (except air-gun shooting) had gone up by as much as 5 percent just since 2002.

The table that really spelled doom, though, was the one that broke down gun purchasers by age. Two-thirds of handgun buyers were forty-five or older. For shotguns, the numbers were only slightly less dire; ditto for rifles, probably because of the AR-15. As the NSSF put it in another of its reports, "Data suggest that the future of hunting and shooting sports is precarious." To say the least.

Gun guys had a hard time accepting this. Whenever anybody mentioned online the statistical evidence that demographics were slowly whittling down gun culture, gun bloggers reacted furiously, talking about how crowded their local ranges seemed to be. At the same time, though, the standard gun-blogger shorthand for the typical shooter was "OFWG": old fat white guy. The longer I studied the *Industry Reference Guide,* the more it looked like the chart of a terminally ill patient.

I e-mailed Jim Curcuruto, director of research analysis for the NSSF, to be sure I was reading his numbers right. Perhaps he would tell me that older shooters had always done most of the buying, that cash-strapped young people were perpetually mediocre customers, and that they always started buying guns when they got older. Maybe nothing was new; maybe the industry would be just fine. To be sure, I asked him for parallel data from, say, ten, twenty, and thirty years ago—to demonstrate that what I was seeing was not the beginning of the end.

"We don't worry too much about the future," he wrote back, in a cheerfully brittle e-mail. "We're focused on the present. We don't want to predict anything." Don't want to predict anything? I had in my hand a 162-page effort to predict all kinds of things. Yet Curcuruto would have me believe that the one set of numbers the foundation didn't have was the historical evidence that the shooting sports and the industry that depended on them were withering away.

Maybe so. I could certainly understand the foundation not *wanting* those numbers. The *Industry Reference Guide* made it pretty clear: If the 2010 trends continued, the idea of bickering over gun policy was likely to look, in a few decades, as archaic as fighting over women's suffrage or temperance. After decades of bitter skirmishes over gun rights and gun control, it was looking as though the issue would be settled by nothing more urgent than fashion. Surely some folks would continue hunting and shooting, but by and large, young people wanted to be urban and digital, and guns were the opposite. For the consumers of tomorrow, guns were so yesterday.[*]

So perhaps at least part of the rage I was encountering everyplace I traveled was born of panic. The gun-rights movement, and gun culture in general, seemed to be making a flamboyant and belligerent show of themselves in precisely the way that a flower grows intensely fragrant just before it dies.

But that didn't explain everything, because what was also coming through again and again was that gun guys felt *insulted*. They had something they liked to do—own and shoot guns—and because of it they suffered, they believed, a continuous assault on their hobby, their lifestyle, and their dignity. The endless parade of nitpicky laws seemed to do naught but express disapproval of gun culture. And every time somebody went crazy with a gun, the mainstream reaction was always "We have to do something about guns," which the gun guys heard as "We've got to do something about gun guys." At precisely the moment they were sensing their numbers shrinking, gun guys were experiencing what they perceived as a nonstop attack on their very worth as human beings.

But how to tease apart everything that might have been making them feel that way? Many of the partially educated, rural, middle-aged guys in the bulge of the gun-guy demographic hadn't seen a real wage increase since 1978. And then there were the guys like the laid-off harbor dredger breakfasting on booze and the haggard young man at the gun show selling his futuristic carbine so he could hold on to his house. Job security: gone. Employer-provided health care: gone. Pensions: gone. House: underwater. They'd had their livers pecked out while women, immigrants, blacks, and gays all seemed to have become groovier, sexier, and more dynamic players in American culture than they were. If the ashen aftermath of the

---

* Cars, too. The number of nineteen-year-olds who'd bothered to get a driver's license fell by about a third, to below half, between 1998 and 2008, and those who had drove 12 percent fewer miles, according to the Federal Highway Administration. Almost half the drivers between eighteen and twenty-four said they'd choose Internet access over owning a car. "They think of a car as a giant bummer," a marketer named Ross Martin told *The New York Times*.

financial meltdown was making everybody feel like a loser, those guys must have felt like the bottom of the bottom.

The list of reasons to be angry was too long to get one's mind around. The cloud of indignities had no name. We had no vocabulary to describe it. There was no way to put one's hands on it, examine its contours, pick apart its elements. Even to examine it closely felt embarrassingly like making excuses for one's own sorry lot. And to the extent that I was different from them, it was only by a matter of a few degrees. If Infidel and Biff weren't where they'd hoped to be at this stage of life, well, neither was I.

It started to rain as the commercial strip petered out and turned to open country south of Louisville. I turned on my wipers, smearing days of smashed insects across the glass. I shifted in my seat and felt the solid bulk of the Colt against my kidney. It felt good. It reminded me that I wasn't merely an aging freelancer at a time of publishing-industry collapse; I was a member of the sheepdog cadre—vigilant, clear-eyed, sober, and true. I had the skill, courage, and maturity to manipulate a device of boundless lethality and keep its power safely contained. I didn't need to kill anybody for my gun to give me stature; the exact opposite was true. What bolstered my self-esteem was my ability to live alongside a firearm, day in and day out, without ever harming anybody. The gun made me useful, relevant, special. If that's what the pale young man at Tilford's had been after in asking his father to buy him that fat shotgun revolver, who could blame him?

Guns give us an identity. They make us supermen. A gun guy sees it this way: If you want to limit my contact with guns, you must be saying that you don't trust me with them. You, who may never have shot a gun and know nothing about what it means to handle and operate one, are presuming to make judgments about my ability to do so. You want to diminish me as a man, a citizen, a sovereign entity—and I've already endured quite enough of that, thank you.

11. SPIN DRIFT

The first time I saw Marcey Parker, she was happily firing a submachine gun through a window. This was a year before my gun-guy walkabout, and the window was in a freestanding plywood wall that stood by itself in the middle of a field of grass, like a set in a cowboy movie. Marcey hunched over her gun like a pro, sighting down the barrel, rattling off four-shot bursts, her brown ponytail bouncing from the recoil. After tearing up a row of steel targets with several loud *rat-a-tat-tat*s, she ran to the next window, dropping the magazine from her gun with a clatter and jamming in a new magazine from a pouch on her belt. Behind her ran a man in an orange safety vest, holding at arm's length a small box that I took to be a pocket camera. After shooting through all four windows, Marcey dropped the magazine, jerked the bolt open, and yelled, "Clear!"

The man in the orange vest looked at the box in his hand, which turned out to be a timer that could hear shooting begin and end, and called out her minutes and seconds. A small crowd, watching the subgun match from behind a rope at the Knob Creek Machine Gun Shoot, applauded politely.

Marcey laid her hot gun on the shooter's table with stylish, casual flair, removed her hearing protectors, and shook her long brunet hair free of a rubber band. It was hard not to stare. She was forty-six but looked to be in her thirties, with high cheekbones, large, wide-set eyes, and a strong, rounded figure—a total babe. She was as carefully made up here on the gun range as she'd have been at a cotillion—rouged, powdered, her lips painted deep rust with a hairline brown outline. She fluffed out her hair with painted fingertips, removed her shooting glasses, and replaced them with rectangular rimless ones. When she did that, and irradiated me with a wide smile, she looked strikingly familiar.

"How you doin'? You need anything? We got cold water and drinks in the truck," she said, as though *I* was the one who had just run a sun-blasted course firing three hundred rounds of nine-millimeter.

"What exactly is it you're doing out there?" I asked.

"What you got out there is a bunch of steel plates you got to knock down," she said.

"It's a machine gun," I said. "How hard is that?"

"Well, *one* of those plates is red, and if you hit *that* one, you get a penalty. What it is, is a balancing act. You shoot a long burst, that's quick—but you risk hittin' the red one. Shoot short bursts, you're more exact, but slower. See?"

Marcey's husband, Jeremy, walked up, cradling a Sterling submachine gun, and kissed her lightly on the lips. He had a craggy face with hooded eyes and a mouth that fell naturally into a soft smile. In my memory, she's bigger than he is, but I know that isn't true. He is wiry and compact and has a quieter, less flamboyant personality, so he seemed to take up less space.

I asked to hold the Sterling and, after ascertaining that it was unloaded, Jeremy placed it in my hands. The Sterling was the British-made successor to the Sten gun, little more than a metal tube with a big spring inside, like a beefy shock absorber. It had a folding metal stock and, projecting from the side, a long, curved magazine—a simple $7,500 device that probably cost less than a hundred dollars to manufacture.

"Did you hear me going *dink-dink-dink-dink*?" Marcey asked him. "I was hittin' 'em, but they weren't fallin' over!"

"A lot of us didn't bring hot enough loads today," Jeremy explained. He'd made all the ammunition with which he and Marcey were competing, assembling bullet, powder, brass casing, and primer into finished cartridges on a workbench in the garage at home. He gave me the calculations that went into finding the perfect combination of controllability and oomph for each cartridge, taking ten leisurely minutes to spool it out for the non-nerd, so long that I started thinking the sport was more about math than marksmanship. "Those Marcey were shooting were power factor 150, which is bullet weight times velocity divided by a thousand. I didn't want to load her up too hot, because she was using a borrowed gun and hot loads are hard on the lower receiver." The range officer called his name, and Jeremy took the Sterling from me, adjusting his hearing protectors as he approached the firing line.

Marcey slipped her arm through mine and asked, in a warm, big-sister way, if I had any questions. When I looked into her smiling eyes, I realized why she seemed so familiar. The hair, the rimless rectangular glasses, the smile . . . she was a dead ringer for Sarah Palin.

"That's not altogether accidental," she said in a deep, conspiratorial drawl, touching my forearm playfully. "I have an insurance agency out in rural Kentucky, so lookin' like Sarah Palin is not a bad thing."

As Jeremy shot, Marcey introduced me to Ed Varner, father of the sport of subgun. Varner was fit and tanned, wearing a red golf shirt with a submachine gun silk-screened on the breast and the kind of stylish mirrored sunglasses that impart an animatronic starship-trooper look that a certain type of guy enjoys. "We started it twenty-five years ago because we worried that the government might ask, 'Why do you need submachine guns?'" he said. "It might not be enough to tell the government that we collect them or like to shoot them. We thought it was important to be able to say, 'Well, we compete with subguns.'"

If the path to legitimacy in America ran through competition, I could imagine the next frontier: Claymore mines, perhaps, or hand grenade matches, with divisions for unassisted hurling and for rocket-propelled launchers.

There was a lot to subgunning, Varner insisted. Running a course with a loaded submachine gun required a nervous system that could sustain a surgeon's touch on the trigger during a whole-body bear hug of a bucking dynamo. And then there were the nonshooting skills: How fast could you swap magazines? How fast could you clear a jam? How well had you maintained your firearm and selected—or made—ammunition for it? Most of all, subgun called for a cool head. In a split-second lapse in concentration, you could kill several spectators and the poor son of a bitch holding the timer.

I nodded politely, but what I was thinking was, *Sure. If what you want is a test of physical agility, marksmanship, small-motor control, and judgment, there are plenty of ways to find that without a submachine gun.* If the four-thousand-to-forty-thousand-dollar price tag wasn't discouraging enough, there was the bureaucratic hassle of acquiring one, the precautions needed to store and transport it, and the ordeal of getting the ATF's permission every time you wanted to take it across state lines. Want to test your physical agility and small-motor control? Try Ping-Pong.

I didn't say that, of course. It was clear that competition was only part of it. Like Robert and the machine-gun enthusiasts in Arizona, the Knob Creek competition was about love of the gun. It was about getting together with other enthusiasts to look over one another's firearms, discuss their history, debate how they worked best, see where their technology was going, and have fun using them. *That* I totally understood. If becoming expert in the safe and accurate handling of firearms set a person apart, doing so with a submachine gun made a man—or a woman—a gun-guy Jedi. And ever since popping that stick of dynamite at the Wikieup shoot, I'd been carrying the deliciously guilty secret that few inanimate objects are sexier or more fun to play with than a hot tommy gun.

Marcey and Jeremy were soul mates and lovers, but most of all they were *playmates.* From their first date, they'd liked big, noisy, gasoline-powered fun, the kind that messed up Marcey's hair and stained their clothes—ear-shattering dirt-track meets, a gigantic Honda touring motorcycle, ATVs, a big Checkmate water-skiing boat, and a vintage Shelby Cobra that could blow the doors off anything on the road. Between Marcey's insurance agency and the mining-equipment company Jeremy had started with his dad, money was never a problem, and because the doctors had told them that children weren't in their future, neither was time. Weekends were played at top, four-barrel volume—bombing around Kentucky's winding back roads, steering chopped-up cars around a dirt track, or roaring through the woods. In the first seven years of their marriage, guns were just about the one noisy toy that didn't figure into their fun. Jeremy would hunt deer and bobcat in the fall, but then he'd lock away his rifles and not think about them again.

In 2006, he was at the bank discussing a loan for his business when Cliff, his banker, got up from the desk and closed the office door with a mischievous smile. "Look at this here," Cliff said. From the closet, he took an AR-15 and put it in Jeremy's hands.

For a gearhead like Jeremy, the AR-15 was a bar of candy. He loved the way the thing snapped apart and fit together; he admired the small number of moving parts and its limitless fungibility. "Come by the gun club Saturday," Cliff said. "We got a match."

Jeremy and Marcey hadn't known there was a gun club up there at the end of Barnhill Road. As they pulled in, the place looked more like a genteel horse farm than the roar-and-fume venues where they usually played. Vast, grassy ranges stretched in every direction, with neat, sun-shaded shooting platforms at the head of each. Men—and a few women—were stretched out on the platforms, aiming rifles downrange. Others stood laughing and talking, holding rifles in cases. But for the occasional snap of a gunshot, it was quiet enough to hear birds singing.

Holding hands, Marcey and Jeremy made their way around the periphery of the action, unsure of the protocols. The folks they were used to at ATV parks and dirt tracks could be a pretty rough bunch—macho, swaggering, harshly competitive, and frequently inebriated. Who knew what gun people were like?

"Hey!" A fit older man in a tight golf shirt and ball cap smiled broadly, hand outstretched. "Glad to have you." He introduced himself as Pete and explained the different stages of the match—one hundred, two hundred, and three hundred yards, shot prone, kneeling, sitting, and standing. "Like to join in?"

"I don't have a rifle."

Pete laughed. "One thing we're not short of here is rifles. You can use one of mine."

Jeremy and Marcey glanced at each other; ask a guy at an ATV track to ride his rig and you might get your face torn off.

Pete led them to a bench and introduced them around. "Welcome!" "Glad you're here!" On the bench lay several black AR-15s. Jeremy noticed that every time Pete touched one, the first thing he did was open the chamber to make sure it wasn't loaded. Even if he'd touched it only seconds before, he ran through the same routine. As a guy who made his living serving safety-minded coal miners, Jeremy was impressed.

Pete gave him a quick rundown of how the rifle worked and said he could start on the one-hundred-yard range. "How about you?" he asked Marcey.

"No! I mean, thank you, but not this time. I think I'll just watch."

Pete led Jeremy through the stages, adjusting his position with little nudges and teaching him to breathe properly. The more Marcey watched, sniffing the burned cordite, her ears a-crackle with the gunfire, the sorrier she was that she'd passed up a chance to shoot.

"I think I'm going to get me one of these," Jeremy told her when he was done, placing the warm AR-15 in her hands. She sighted down the barrel. "And you *know* what *I* want for Christmas," she said.

They each bought a bare-bones AR-15 and started shooting the monthly match at Tri-County. Pretty soon, they were driving to regional matches in Kentucky, Tennessee, and Indiana and finding everywhere the same inclusive, tender community of sport shooters. Something about the open, thoughtful people and the clean, disciplined geometry of shooting got under their skin.

They bought more guns, which meant a bigger safe, and store-bought ammunition started getting expensive. So Jeremy set himself up with two $2,500 cartridge-loading machines, and after working out the mathematics of bullet weight and powder grain, he'd sit down after supper and crank out six hundred specially formulated rounds an hour, for a few pennies apiece. Given the cost of factory-made ammunition and how much practicing Jeremy liked to do, he'd make back his investment quickly. But more than that, the techno-geek in him loved having that much more control over his shooting. Craving more range time, he hired a bulldozer to level a swath of forest behind their house—his own hundred-yard range, with no range fees and no wait times. He and Marcey realized one day that it had been months since they'd taken the motorcycle, the ATVs, the boat, the dirt-track car, or the Shelby Cobra from the garage.

They were sitting around one afternoon, drinking sweet tea at a match in southern Indiana, when a wiry guy in his twenties started talking about "running and gunning." He was passionate about shooting on the move, instead of standing still or lying down.

"Look here," he said, pulling some gun cases from the back of his truck. Inside were the weirdest guns Jeremy and Marcey had ever seen. One was obviously an AR-15, but it was anodized red, not black. Its magazine well was flared like the bell of a trumpet; Jeremy could see instantly that the shape would make it faster to reload. The pistol, too, had a flared magazine well. Its grip was unnaturally large, and its slide was extra long, perforated with a row of round, space-age cutouts; riding along the top was some kind of weird electronic optic. As for the pump-action shotgun, its stock was a bright, flashy white instead of dull black, and on the underside, a big blue scoop, like a shark's fin, was supposed to guide shells into the magazine faster. It was like getting a glimpse of Buck Rogers's arsenal.

Jeremy and Marcey looked at each other and smiled.

I'd arranged to meet up with them again at the third annual Blue Ridge Mountain 3-Gun Championship, in Bowling Green. The weather was hot and steamy as I made my way down U.S. 31W from Louisville through the tourist-brochure scenery of central Kentucky—storybook farms, lush meadows, gamboling horses, and thick stands of hardwood forest. On the radio, Miranda Lambert sang her hit "Gunpowder and Lead," about an abused woman loading her shotgun, lighting a cigarette, and waiting for her man to come home so she could "show him what a little girl's made of." Gun country-rock: perfect background music.

The Park Mammoth Resort had once been the region's premier golf destination, before Interstate 24 siphoned traffic away, and from the parking lot it still looked grand. A towering stone arch framed the front door of the hotel, and perfectly manicured swaths of lawn were visible beyond a line of oaks. Inside, though, the hotel's decline was evident in the worn carpet, peeling paint, and dim lighting. A couple of young brothers had recently bought the resort with an eye toward renovating; they were transforming it into Rockcastle, the first destination shooting resort in the United States. The Blue Ridge Mountain 3-Gun was their kickoff.

In the lobby, big men wearing Lycra jerseys emblazoned with corporate logos—Bushnell, DPMS, MGM Targets, Adams Arms—laughed and called to one another in a giddy, wifeless way, delighted to be coming together again. The Blue Ridge championship was one of many on a circuit they traveled all year long. On a roster tacked to the wall, the shooters had been divided into squads, each beginning on a different stage. An eager young man in a beige Park Mammoth golf shirt and cap put in my hands a map of the twenty stages, along with a rule book. If I hurried, he said, I could get to Stage 4 before Jeremy and Marcey's squad started shooting.

The directions carried me up a dirt road into the woods. As a shooting resort, Rockcastle had a ways to go; the road was a rutted ribbon of mud. I parked and took a look at the license plates on the other cars and pickups. They'd come from as far away as Michigan and Ontario—a thousand miles or more—to run and gun. To my great relief, the bumpers were mostly devoid of political bumper stickers—no KEEP HONKING, I'M RELOADING, no McCain-Palin, not even any NRA stickers. Might I have discovered an Elysium, a gathering of apolitical gun guys? The only potentially political sticker was plastered on two of the trucks: GOD BLESS OUR TROOPS. ESPECIALLY OUR SNIPERS.

Marcey and Jeremy were among the thirty-odd people milling around the start of Stage 4. Jeremy had his starship-trooper look going, wearing slick Wiley X glasses and a gray-and-white jersey bearing the logo of Benelli shotguns; he'd arranged to get guns at a discount in exchange for wearing the logo, which made him a semi-pro. Benelli's reputation depended, in part, on how well he shot today, and he looked nervous. He didn't notice when I waved to him. He was in a kind of trance, walking the stage with his hands up in shooting position, twitching his trigger finger and whispering *"pah, pah,"* as he planned each step, each swivel, looking for the most efficient combination of twists and footsteps.

Marcey, in a blue windbreaker over a hot pink polo shirt, looked fabulous. She gave me a big, relaxed hug; she was shooting entirely for her own amusement. "I am geetered out with excitement," she said. "This is a huge match for Jeremy." Around her waist, a thick Cordura belt held a long stainless-steel space-ranger pistol—not in a holster but mounted on a kind of quick-release rack that made it faster to draw. The pistol was big and ungainly, nothing anyone would carry for self-defense. You wouldn't want to stand in front of it, but by Greg Hepp's definition, you couldn't really call it a weapon. The belt also held an organ-pipe array of shotgun shells and two plastic pouches for pistol magazines, stuffed with shiny brass cartridges.

"I'm *so* happy Jeremy's switched over to the Benelli," she said in the same breathless veranda drawl other Southern women use to discuss their drapes. "In his last match, he was having jams, and I said, 'That thing is a boat anchor, honey; you need to get rid of it.'"

"What are you shooting?" I asked her.

"Look over there in the rack. You can tell mine." She walked me over, and it was like approaching an Army gun rack while high on LSD. All the rifles were recognizably AR-15s, but each was wildly distorted by swooping grips, stocks, and free-float tubes and decked out in colors the Lord never intended weapons to be—yellow, teal, scarlet. Marcey's was actually one of the plainest—all black but for the telltale feminine swirl of makeup on the stock. I got down close. It smelled like a girl's gun.

The range officer called us to order and explained the stage in the faux-military manner often adopted around guns, presumably on the assumption that unless one used a tone stern enough to make men's testicles retract, they'd devolve into twelve-year-old boys. "Shooters will start out with pistol and shotgun fully loaded, chambers empty! Shotgun leaning against this here stump and pistol holstered!" And so on. The rifle was to be positioned downrange, to be picked up after all the pistol and shotgun targets were hit. Shotgun, pistol, rifle: the holy trinity of three-gun.

Jeremy went first. After an intricate ceremony of loading and safing his guns, holstering the pistol, and leaning the shotgun just so, he stood, rotated his shoulders and neck like a boxer in the ring, and nodded at the range officer. Another man raised his arm toward the back of Jeremy's head; for a second it looked as if he was going to execute him. But it was a timer he held, not a pistol. The timer beeped, and Jeremy snapped into motion.

He snatched the shotgun from the stump and blasted left and right. *Blam! Blam!* The targets, clay pigeons held in wire frames, shattered satisfyingly. Marcey and I walked along behind him as he advanced down the clearing, wasting not a millimeter of motion. He swiveled on his hips as he walked, left *blam*! right *blam*! left *blam*! right *blam*! He hit every target, but really, I thought, shotguns are made for hitting running or flying things, not stationary targets twenty-five feet away, so how hard was it? The second I asked myself the question, Jeremy answered it: The shotgun part of the contest was less about shooting than gun handling—specifically, how fast a competitor could reload. After eight shots, Jeremy's left hand zipped between his belt and the belly of the gun faster than I could follow it; it looked as if the gun was sucking up shells. *Blam! Blam! Blam! Blam!* He finished with the shotgun targets, plunged the hot gun muzzle-down into the blue barrel, and unhooked the pistol from his belt in one fluid motion. Both arms straight out, pivoting left and right, he nailed every steel target with a satisfying *plink!* as his legs carried him forward, smooth and precise as an icon in a video game. "If you miss one, that's a penalty," Marcey said in my ear. "If you forget to shoot at one completely, that's a bigger one."

Jeremy plinked the last of twenty-one pistol targets, cleared his pistol, set it in a wooden box, and swung the rifle from where it lay up into shooting position. Another reason for mixing in the shotgun, I realized: His hands had to shed the muscle memory of the other long gun and adapt instantly to this one. Jeremy crisply put a bullet through each of the rifle targets—stylized squared-off silhouettes, made of brown cardboard and spread through the tall grass like a platoon of robots waiting in ambush. He ejected his magazine, wrenched open the rifle's action, and yelled, "Clear!"—a three-gun rock star.

Soldier of Fortune, the magazine for mercenaries and mercenary wannabes, is said to have held the first formal three-gun competition in the 1980s. To shooters who'd been taught to stand as still as possible and concentrate on a single target, running and gunning was a revelation. By the time I was watching it, the sport had branched formally into three-gun, subgun, and two different categories of practical pistol shooting (involving such arcane conventions as whether, in reloading, an empty magazine had to be returned to a pocket or could be dropped). There were also the historical categories of Cowboy Action Shooting—basically three-gun played with period guns and Western costume—and Zoot Shooting, which called for participants to dress in spats and fedoras or flapper dresses and wield the 1920s-vintage Colts, sawed-offs, and tommy guns that John Dillinger might have used. I'd tried a little practical pistol shooting in Boulder—with my first concealed-carry range officer, the anesthesiologist. We did things like open a door with one hand and shoot with the other while passing through, snatching up a gun from a desk and shooting while seated, and scooting from station to station while felling steel targets and reloading on the run. It was a lot of fun—so much so, in fact, that I found it pretty hard to go back to standing still in a lane, popping off at a single target.

Running and gunning was a marksmanship sport, no doubt about that. But there was no denying that it was also practice for joining the military, a SWAT team, or an end-of-the-world gang with Mel Gibson. "What's this all about, *really*?" I asked Marcey and Jeremy the next morning at breakfast in the lodge. "Is it a sport, or are you practicing to kill people?"

"We don't have any *thoughts* of killing," Marcey said, digging to the bottom of a plate piled with eggs, grits, and country ham. "It's a sport, like tennis or golf. That's why we call them 'guns.' We don't call them 'weapons.'"

I was pretty sure that the U.S. Army shooting team competing against Marcey and Jeremy, in their matching yellow Go Army jerseys, saw their guns as weapons. Ditto the many cops and deputy sheriffs who attended—some at their departments' expense—to polish combat-shooting skills.

"What we do out on the course would get you killed in a gunfight," Jeremy said, concentrating on his iPhone, on which he seemed to be doing calculations.

"What do you mean?"

He looked up. "We're not doing any of the things you do in a gunfight. We're not assessing threats and engaging them in order. We're not finding cover. We're not shouting commands."

"Or running away," said a voice on my other side, "which is the best thing you can do in a gunfight." I turned, and a stocky man with a craggy, copper-colored face put out a hand like a catcher's mitt, introducing himself as Clark Kennedy. "Any time you're practicing speed and accuracy, it's going to help you if something real happens," he said. "But hell, out here we're dropping mags! You don't do that in a gunfight in the military, because ammunition isn't issued in magazines! You're going to *need* those puppies." He leaned across me and asked Jeremy, "What you coming up with?"

Still poking at his iPhone, Jeremy said, "I think I'm going to hold two feet high and two feet left."

He was figuring out how to make the longest shot of the day—a 560-yarder coming up at Stage 3—using an app called Ballistic: Field Tactical Edition ($19.99). He rotated the phone so I could see what he was doing. "I put in the characteristics of my ammo, plus wind speed, wind direction, wind angle, relative humidity, our altitude here, and upwind velocity. What this is telling me is to hold two feet high and two feet left."

"You really think you're going to hit a target at 560 yards?" I asked. Jeremy and Clark both laughed.

"That ain't far. Clark and I shoot sniper matches out to two thousand yards."

"You guys are snipers?"

"No. We shoot *sniper matches.* Super long-range."

"Two thousand yards is more than a mile," I said.

"Tell me about it," Clark said, his smile crinkling up his face like an Indian chief's. Jeremy gestured at his iPhone.

"Shooting that far, you also got to punch in spin drift and Coriolis."

"Which are?"

"If your bullet spins clockwise, spin drift will carry it off to the right some. At 2,200 yards, spin drift can take you off three feet at target. Coriolis is the rotation of the earth."

"Get out of here."

"Real long shots, you got to figure it in, because by the time your bullet reaches the target, the earth will have moved some."

They told me the story of Corporal Craig Harrison, a British sniper who in November 2010 killed two Taliban fighters with two consecutive shots at a mile and a half. Clark said, "He was using the Accuracy International L115A3 in .338 Lapua"—a high-tech rifle that looks like a deck gun from a Klingon battle cruiser. "He did all his calculations and aimed six feet high and two feet to the left."

"The bullet took two and a half seconds to arrive," Jeremy said. "In that much time, the earth moved enough to affect the shot. If he hadn't figured in Coriolis, he'd have missed."

"So what's with all this *sniper* business?" I asked, remembering those GOD BLESS OUR SNIPERS bumper stickers. "Pretty hard to say your sport isn't about killing if you're going to call them 'sniper matches.'"

"It's just a name," Clark said. He sat back in his chair and peered down his nose at me. "But what you got against snipers?"

"Well, it's one thing to face an enemy in battle and another to hide and pick people off at safe distance." I was old enough to remember Lee Harvey Oswald and Charles Whitman, and *Life* magazine's chilling photo renderings of what they saw through their telescopic sights.

"Which would you rather?" Clark asked. "Put a missile into a building and kill a bunch of kids along with your bad guy? Or send in a sniper to shoot one bullet? A sniper gets the guy that needs killing and doesn't touch anybody else. If you don't like collateral damage, you got to love your snipers."

My mind drifted to the second of those two Taliban fighters. What must he have been thinking when his friend slumped over—and two seconds later, when the sound of the shot arrived? Or was he dead by the time the sound of the first shot arrived? "It must be terrifying," I said, "to have a bullet come out of nowhere."

"That's the whole idea," Clark said. "One sniper shot can wreck the morale of a whole company—of a whole division. You want the enemy scared, not knowing where it's safe to stand, not knowing when the next bullet's coming in."

"Imagine, though," I said, "looking through the scope and seeing the face of the man you're going to kill."

"That's not the worst thing," Clark said. "The worst thing is lying in your own shit for five days waiting for the shot."

Jeremy and Marcey shot five stages that day. Some required only two guns—pistol and shotgun, say, or rifle and pistol—and some all three. One diabolical stage called on shooters to hunt down and blast shotgun targets hiding in tall brush, then hit a rifle target rotating on a big wheel; another had them move through and around an old cinder-block building while shooting pistol targets, like cops in a hostage situation. Most of the shooters were men, but several squads had at least one woman, including a skinny sixteen-year-old girl being coached by her dad. She was awesome—lithe, quick, and coolheaded; not a girl to mess with. Her dad, a big, solid guy who asked me not to interview or identify her, said he couldn't think of a better way than three-gun to get a girl through her teenage years. "You got to take and put so much discipline into this, you can't be thinking of getting into trouble," he said. "She's got friends drinking, and messing around, and she's not into any of that. After school and weekends, she's on the range with me, with her mind focused."

One of Marcey and Jeremy's squad-mates was a bearded young man named Hendrik, who'd come from Sweden to compete. Tall and handsome, he wore a vest so encrusted with shotgun shells that he looked like a suicide bomber. Speaking in English more grammatical and less accented than that of most people at the meet, he told me it was hard getting three-gun off the ground in Europe because of restrictions on guns and ammunition. "You are very lucky here," he said. It was unfortunate, he added, that the FAA limited passengers to only eleven pounds of ammunition in their checked luggage. Eleven pounds would barely get a man through one stage. Like everybody else who'd flown to the match, he'd shipped his ammo ahead of time.

We stood and watched Stage 7. "Running and gunning" was overstating it slightly; a shooter had to run only a couple hundred yards, and not fast enough to break a sweat. Because Hendrik was the image of sculpted youth, I suggested creating three-gun for real athletes. "You know, where you run a mile and scale a cliff with your guns on your back, and *then* start shooting."

"There wouldn't be enough people to support it," he said. "Look at these guys. They're not the top athletes. What they do well is shoot. I know a range where guys use golf carts to get from the hundred- to the three-hundred-yard bay. They put their guns on the hooks for the golf clubs. Those guys aren't going to climb a cliff before shooting, and the guys who can climb cliffs aren't good shots, so it wouldn't be fun for them."

On Stage 3, Jeremy hit the 560-yard target on the first shot, somehow flinging a sixty-four-grain piece of metal—not much bigger than a grain of rice—a third of a mile, in a crosswind, to the exact spot he intended. I'm sure all the math he did helped, but that shot also involved a hefty dose of juju—knowing in your bones where your bullet is going to go and then willing it to the target. Jeremy had juju. Marcey, on the other hand, was disgusted with herself all day. She kept scolding herself as she shot her way through the stages—"You're no *good*," "Calm *down*," "Come *on*, girl"—while Jeremy walked along behind her, muttering, "Run your mouth less and shoot the gun."

That evening, I sat for a while in a folding chair in front of the hotel with two guys from Maryland.

"I'm thinking of taking four clicks of elevation out of it."

"You're an inch and a half high at fifty, 'cause you're zeroed to two hundred."

"I have a table in the truck; it'll tell you where you'll be."

"I got 'er loaded to a minute of angle at one hundred."

"You guys," I interrupted, "are more about math than anything else!"

"It's Zen, too," said the older of the two men, who had an intelligent eastern European face and an accent from somewhere north. "Shooting is a martial art, and it takes the same qualities that archery or tae kwon do or karate take: fitness, breath control, concentration, discipline. You have to connect yourself with your target; you have to breathe your shot there."

"Do you hunt?"

"Used to. Gave it up."

"Do you carry a gun?"

"Lord, no. You're missing the point. This whole thing you're seeing here has nothing to do with any of that. Imagine while you're here that you're at, I don't know, a kung fu tournament or a yoga retreat. It's the same thing—mastery of the mind, mastery of the breath, mastery of your concentration onto one distant point." Juju.

I found Marcey and Jeremy sitting in a big, laughing circle in the hotel's lobby, watching NASCAR on a huge flat-panel and shouting each other down about gun handling in the movies. Steven Segal was pretty good, one guy said, and another countered that Segal had lousy muzzle control and was always letting his muzzle sweep the girl. Bruce Willis, everybody agreed, had a creepy tendency to bring his gun up close to his face, and, in *Last Man Standing,* an irritating way of ejecting dozens of magazines onto the floor. "If they were mags like mine," a chubby young bald guy said, "that's about eight thousand dollars' worth." Everybody laughed and clinked beer cans; a good pistol magazine could cost eighty dollars. Jeremy ventured in his diffident way that he thought Bruce Willis was pretty good, but Marcey shouted over him, "Don't listen to him! When we go rent a movie, you know what he wants? *Chick flicks,* like *The Notebook* and . . . what? *Princess Bride*!" Everybody laughed, and Jeremy held up his hands in surrender and chuckled, "That's true, that's true."

"I'll tell you what movie got it right," Marcey said. "*Mr. and Mrs. Smith.* Brad Pitt and Angelina Jolie. You could just tell they had someone on the set who *knew* what he was doin'!"

A young man put down his can of Busch beer and raised both arms over his head in a victory salute. "I shot three-gun all day!" he yelled to nobody in particular, "and now I'm drinking beer and watching NASCAR without my wife yelling, 'Get your ass up here and help me put the kids to bed!' Shoot me now. It won't ever get any better!" As though on cue, his cell phone rang, and he jumped up and walked out of the room, mumbling, "Yeah, yeah, honey, I'm having a good time." He disappeared through the front door, the rest of the group razzing his back.

I had to make miles in the morning, so I excused myself. Marcey and Jeremy walked me across the parking lot to my distant wing of the resort.

"I can't decide," I told them, "if this is a really cool, harmless sport or if you're all pretty weird."

"I can see that," Jeremy said judiciously. "Maybe it's a little of both."

"I went to a Pampered Chef party this one time, and all the ladies talked about what they liked to do," Marcey said. "This one talked about her dogs. That one talked about flower arranging. Everybody was in their Sunday best; very girly. When I said, 'I travel around the country and shoot competitively,' you'd have thought I said we were Satan worshippers." Jeremy laughed; he loved that story.

"But I don't go into this with a killing mentality," Marcey said again.

"I go into it as therapy. After a week's worth of bullshit, shooting is better than the most expensive psychiatrist there is."

"And how is it different from fencing?" Jeremy said. "I mean, what's fencing if not sword fighting—as you say, 'practicing to kill people'?"

"Or javelin," Marcey said. "Or archery. Nobody thinks those guys are weird."

True that. Maybe the difference was that fencing, javelin, and archery recalled outdated battlefields—though why that should matter wasn't clear, given the millennia of slaughter that preceded the advent of firearms. Maybe the difference was, as Larry Zanoff had said, that wielding a sword, spear, or arrow required more physical strength than pointing a gun and pressing its trigger, and that overweight pseudo-warriors didn't lift the soul like beautifully sculpted pseudo-warriors. Maybe the difference was in the aesthetic of the tool: Guns were noisy, while swords, spears, and arrows were silent. Whatever it was, while I'd enjoyed watching the gunners at Rockcastle test a matrix of skills—jogging through the woods with rifles, semi-automatic pistols, and pump-action shotguns, joyfully blasting at man-shaped silhouettes—I had a feeling the match would have sent a lot of people reaching for their smelling salts.

Being comfortable enough with guns to play with them put Marcey and Jeremy on one side of the great gun divide—a high, treacherous frontier that few ever crossed in either direction. Either you liked guns or you didn't, as Greg Hepp had said, and no amount of jawing about hand-eye coordination was going to change that. I was glad that America was big and diverse enough to make room for something like three-gun. It was noisy; it imitated violence; you might reject it on a hundred different aesthetic levels. But it was harmless, and I hoped nobody would mess with it by, say, mounting another stupid campaign to ban the AR-15. I mentioned to Marcey and Jeremy as we threaded among the parked cars and trucks that this was the first place I'd been in rural America where I hadn't seen a single gun-rights bumper sticker.

"We're not all eat up in the head about gun rights," Jeremy said. "We just like to shoot."

Maybe. Or maybe three-gunners were simply less angry in general. Anybody who could afford such guns, ammo, and travel had one fewer reason to be.

12. FRIEDRICH AND BARNEY

The great body of our citizens shoot less as time goes on. We should encourage rifle practice among schoolboys, and indeed among all classes, as well as in the military service by every means in our power.

—President Theodore Roosevelt

Margaret was flying to Cincinnati to join me on the road for a few weeks. I was in a hurry to get to a campground and do a load of laundry before her plane landed. But I wasn't going to pass a cozy little farmhouse outside of Overton, Kentucky, that bore the sign GENERAL STORE, RESTAURANT, GUN SHOP.

Inside, it smelled of cinnamon candy and homemade rag dolls. The shelves were crowded with fudge, taffy, packaged summer sausage, smoked cheese, postcards, wooden toys, and doilies. I could picture a truck from Amalgamated General Store Supply LLC pulling up to off-load the exact same array of goods it had delivered to tourist-destination general stores from Maine to San Diego. I asked the man for some vanilla ice cream, and with a hearty cry of "Coming right up!" he began shoveling scoops into a quart-size Styrofoam container. "Uh, where are the guns?" I asked. He looked up, sweating and panting as he packed the container tight. "Downstairs. Feel free to have a look." He handed me the container; it must have weighed three pounds. "That'll be two dollars," he said.

The cellar looked as though it had been dug to hide shoats from the Yankees. The staircase was no wider than my shoulders, very steep, listing precariously to the left, and low; I bumped my bald head painfully on the way down. Rubbing my bruised pate, I found myself in a room of white-painted brick about twelve feet square and barely tall enough for me to stand up in. A single naked lightbulb dangled blazingly at eye level.

But what nice guns stood lining the four walls! Most of them were midcentury long-barreled pump-action shotguns—Winchesters and Marlins. The rest were either lever-action carbines or bolt-action hunting rifles that looked to have been passed down since Teddy Roosevelt's day. Their metal parts had acquired a comfortable brown patina that almost matched the walnut of the stocks. Not an AR-15 in the mix.

In the corner stood a comically tall rifle that I recognized immediately as a Mosin-Nagant—the Russian army rifle from the time of the czars through what the Russians called the Great Patriotic War. It was a good eight inches longer than any other rifle in the room, and this one had its regulation eighteen-inch bayonet, which made it look like a pike. I'm more than six feet tall, and when I set the rifle's butt plate on the floor, the tip of the bayonet reached my ear. I held it under the lightbulb: A sickle and hammer was etched into the top of the receiver, along with "1943," which was two years after Hitler invaded the Soviet Union. I tried to imagine how hurriedly this one had been thrown together at the Izhevsk Machine Building Plant, out there in the Udmurt Republic at the foot of the Urals, far from the reach of the Wehrmacht. It was sticky with brown grease, which meant it had never been issued. Price: $130.

I worked the rough-metal bolt and imagined a seventeen-year-old soldier shivering at Dukla Pass with nothing but this clumsy piece of furniture between his beating heart and the Nazis. Old guns worked on my imagination like a time machine.

"I'll take it," I told the white-haired man as I approached his ice cream counter with the Mosin-Nagant.

"A hundred and twenty-five out the door," he beamed, putting out a hand and introducing himself as Tom. "And I've got the sling, cartridge belt, and oiler for it, too. All brand-new and unissued. I've even got thirty rounds of ammo I'll give you."

He didn't have to run the computerized background check. Because I had a concealed-carry permit that Kentucky recognized, the state assumed I had been background-checked. "Yes, indeed," Tom said, "if you're ever stopped by the police, hand them your permit with your license."

"I don't know. Telling a cop I carry a gun? Seems like a lot could go wrong."

"He may know it anyway; it may come up on his computer when he runs your plate. He'll probably ask if you're carrying, and if you are, just tell him yes and keep your hands on the wheel. But he won't be afraid of you. You've been checked out. In fact, it will probably make him *more* relaxed." It had never occurred to me that a concealed-carry license could serve as a kind of good-citizen ID.

I filled out the 4473, handed him my credit card, and stepped out the door with my gigantic new rifle. I was a little worried about whether it would annoy Margaret to have to shoehorn into the overstuffed car a greasy firearm the size of an oar. But it wouldn't have been a proper gun trip if I didn't buy a gun.

As Margaret stepped into baggage claim, I realized how much I'd been missing her. We'd done lots of journalistic traveling together before Rosa was born, and now that Rosa was studying Arabic in Cairo for the summer, we were looking forward to this new window of roaming together-ness. As we walked to the car with our arms around each other's waists, her hand fell on the holstered Colt hidden under my shirt.

"Oh, for Christ's sake," she said. "Have you been wearing that thing?"

"Everyplace. I'm getting into the gun-carrier head. I'm trying to see if I get used to it."

"Well, don't get *too* used to it."

Margaret was going to be good to have along, in more ways than one.

We were in Cincinnati to experience a gun tradition entirely divorced from man-killing but central to cultural identity—that of the German immigrants who'd created the modern city of Cincinnati. From what we'd read, Schützenfest—which means "shooting party"—was a big deal: three days of wursts, beer, oompah bands, and stylized target shooting that harked back 150 years or more. Nobody in the Winton Woods Campground, two miles from the site of Schützenfest, had heard of it.

Winton Woods was an enormous tract of forest smack in the middle of Cincinnati, with bike trails and a grassy car-camping complex alongside a murky-green but lovely lake. It was car camping at its most American and, in many ways, its best—with clean shower blocks, a food store, laundry, and WiFi. Margaret set up the tent on soft lawn and inflated the air mattress while I cooked our standard road dinner: rice, cabbage, carrots, and onions boiled in a pot on the little camp stove, seasoned at table with a mixture of crunchy peanut butter and Sriracha hot sauce. The air was as thick and hot as dog's breath, the mosquitoes plentiful. As night began to fall, an old pickup truck with Michigan plates pulled into the space beside us, and out climbed a shirtless man who looked hollowed out by either overwork or crystal meth, a gelatinous woman in pink spandex shorts, and a pale, sunken-eyed boy of about four. They set up a McMansion of a tent—room enough for a dozen to sleep and tall enough to stand in. The mom and boy went off to look at the lake while the man took a pack of cigarettes from the waistband of his oily gym shorts, lit up, and exhaled luxuriously. I hadn't heard them say a word the entire time.

"Here for Schützenfest?" I called to him.

"Nope. Monster Truck."

His name was Vic. He'd driven seven hours from central Michigan to watch comically jacked-up pickup trucks with tractor-size tires crush lesser vehicles. Tickets were fifty dollars apiece. When I asked Vic if he had a gun, he patted the pockets of his shorts. "Not on me, no," he said, as though I'd asked him for a cigarette lighter or a pen. "Got one in the truck." He gestured with his body that way, as if to say, *If you need one, I can fetch it.*

"You don't worry about having a gun and a four-year-old in the truck?"

"He knows not to touch it. That's Daddy's."

"Think you need it?"

"Got a jack in the truck. Got a flashlight in the truck."

"Got other guns?"

"Lots of them. Deer season in the fall. Then ducks."

I asked him why he thought Americans liked guns. He scratched his unshaven chin, pleased to be asked his opinion. "Oh," he finally said, "probably because they piss off the liberals so much."

We laughed.

"I don't know," he went on. "When I was growing up, my friends and I would take our .22s out in the woods, and you could tell the kids who came from families that didn't have guns. There was something, I don't know, weak about them. Not weak maybe, but, well, yeah, *weak*. Afraid, kind of. You'd hand them a gun and they'd get all nervous. Guns are scary, I guess, and I'll tell you something else: They're part of what makes me different from my wife. She won't touch one. I got to keep them out in the garage. When I want to be with her, I can be with her. When I want to be with the guns, I can go out in the garage."

She and the boy were back. "Vi-ic," she called, and he excused himself.

A man drifted over from the campsite on the other side. "Heard you talking about guns," he said, introducing himself as Mark. He was buff, shirtless, and, like the rest of us, shining with sweat. Behind him, his wife was getting two tiny girls ready for bed. On the lake, a pair of ducks glided past.

"My dad loves guns," Mark said.

"Not you?"

"They're okay. Dad's *really* into them, though," he said, as though it burdened him.

"*Scary* into them?"

"No, no. It was always just 'Come on, boy, come shoot this *gun.*' " He laughed. "I guess I didn't catch the bug."

"Where you from?"

" 'Cross the river." Meaning: Kentucky.

"You don't hunt?"

"Oh, yeah, but I bow hunt."

"Really."

"There's a lot more to it. You got to get closer. A rifle, it's, you see a deer and *bang*—game over. With a bow, you got to stalk, and get right up on them."

"How'd you get into it?"

"I gun hunted with my dad, but when I started hunting with friends, they all bow hunted. And I got into *Western Extreme*. You watch that?"

"Never heard of it."

"On the Outdoor Channel. Check it out." His wife shooed the girls into the tent, and a television came on. For the first time, I noticed a wire running from an RV hookup box across the grass and into their tent. We said good night, and Mark joined his family for an episode of *10 Things I Hate About You.*

Cincinnati was home to so many Germans by 1861 that it raised entirely German-speaking regiments for the Union Army. By all accounts, they did Ohio proud, their guttural battle cry and efficient ferocity raising hell among the rebels from the first bayonet charge of the war. Those who survived came home to organize, in 1866, the first Cincinnati Schützenfest.

Their *schützen* rifles could never have been confused with weapons; they looked more like a cross between a firearm and a cello. Great swooping curls of polished wood surrounded an extra-long octagonal barrel. A hooked lever operated a massive falling-block breech. An elaborate rear sight rose high from the tang like a railroad signal. And they fired a tiny bullet. They were entirely for target sport, as different from Army muskets as ballet dancers were from coal miners.

By the time I got to Cincinnati, an organization called the Catholic Kolping Society was hosting the Schützenfest. Kolping societies started in nineteenth-century Germany as networks of hostels where Catholic journeymen working far from home could find a clean bed, good food, and the spiritual guidance of a priest. The Cincinnati Kolping had grown far beyond that, into a youth-sports and civic booster club with a vast complex of meeting halls and athletic fields carved from the forest. Schützenfest was the Kolping's annual bash.

Margaret and I were traveling with Dahon bicycles folded into the trunk of the Camry, and as we pedaled to the Kolping Center, we could hear the festival from ten minutes out, especially the tubas. Families with toddlers and strollers streamed toward the entrance to pay their three dollars. Up close, Schützenfest looked and smelled a lot like a state fair, the hot, damp air heavy with meat smoke, sugar, and perspiration. It was obvious, though, that this fair was German, because instead of funnel cakes and corn dogs, the booths along the midway offered Limburger-and-onion sandwiches, grilled mettwursts, and *goetta,* a mild patty sausage of pork, beef, pinhead oats, and bay leaf, said to be available only within fifty miles of Cincinnati. It came on rye bread, and when I asked for mustard, the big-armed lady behind the counter cried, *"Wha-a-a-at?"* and handed me a squeeze bottle of Log Cabin syrup. It was good, like breakfast, but while I was sure it was authentic, I wasn't sure it would keep me from venturing farther than fifty miles from Cincinnati. The Limburger-and-onion sandwich, though, was inspired. Margaret asked for a bite, and I practically had to wrestle her to the ground to get it back.

There must have been six or seven thousand people milling about, maybe a third of them wearing traditional German attire. The women were ornamental in ballooning dirndl skirts, push-up bodices, and aprons, with their hair in Heidi braids. The men wore lederhosen—and the vaguely sinister, self-satisfied air I associated with them. Most also wore green felt Tyrolean hats covered with ornamental cloisonné pins and floppy *gamsbarts,* the goat beard that blooms skyward like a huge shaving brush. Trudging around like that on a steamy day must have been rough. No wonder everybody was drinking so much beer.

A dirndled fräulein, breasts thrust to the top of her bodice like cream in a cannoli, shoved beneath our noses a fragrant stack of hot pretzels, impaled on a wooden dowel. They were crunchy without, chewy within, and delicious. Margaret wouldn't think of ordering beer mid-morning but was happy to drink half of mine. A man staggered by in a T-shirt that read THE LIVER IS EVIL AND MUST BE PUNISHED.

A *jagdhorn* band, in full *deutsche* regalia, raised their curved hunting horns to their lips and played a stirring and lugubrious call from the Alps. Then an oompah band set up, so perfectly outfitted that it looked like a tin windup version of itself. It played a medley of German tunes, including one that was oddly familiar. I stopped to listen, and they circled back to it: the theme from *Hogan's Heroes.* A Schwaben Schuhplattler troupe danced its way onto the floor in front of the band, rhythmically stamping and slapping their shoes until one young man turned the color of Pepto-Bismol and tottered as if he was going to collapse of heatstroke. It was altogether about as full-throated an ethnic festival as I'd attended, more German, say, than New York's Feast of San Gennaro is Italian or Denver's Cinco de Mayo is Mexican. These people were into it. The muggy heat, though, made it feel like a festival of German colonists in the Amazon.

At the far end of the big, woods-shaded patio was a metal pole, on the top of which a carved wooden eagle spread two-foot wings. He was a beauty—holding a scepter and an apple in his claws, glowering downward, every feather on his outstretched wings vivid in the dappled sunlight. He wore a radiant crown and was obviously the product of many hours of painstaking work. We were here to watch men shoot him to pieces.

The rifles lay on a table—no longer the gorgeous *schützen* rifles of yore but ordinary Remington bolt-action single-shot .22s. Paul Weinkamp, youthful in a Tyrolean hat with *gamsbart,* was filling plastic drinking cups with cartridges, and I asked how many shots he thought it would take to shoot the eagle apart.

"About three thousand," he said. "But it depends on the wood. Last year, the guy who carved it used poplar, and it kind of shredded instead of shattered. By the end, there was a big brush up there."

The rite of mauling a bird of prey, as Paul told it, commemorated the long-ago heroism of a hunter who, with a single shot, saved a baby from being carried off in an eagle's talons. It was a mystery to me why this story, whose protagonist and date nobody could remember, should have inspired an annual festival throughout the German-speaking world. This wasn't shooting to commemorate the hunting of food for the table, or shooting to commemorate warfare. It was shooting to commemorate defense against wildlife—an odd type of shooting around which to build an annual festival. My guess was that men liked shooting things apart with guns, and needed some pleasant folklore to win their wives' approval. That the story involved saving a baby was the giveaway.

A drumroll interrupted us, and we all stood for "The Star-Spangled Banner" and "Deutschlandlied"—the German national anthem, which is "Deutschland Über Alles" without the Nazi-tinged words of the original first verse. Then Paul loudly introduced three florid, smiling Kolping officers, who stepped up for the honor of the first shots. Wearing Tyrolean hats and clutching steins of beer the size of paper-towel rolls, they looked like burghers from a George Grosz painting. Each set his stein on a shelf beside his cups of cartridges, brought the little rifle to his shoulder, pointed high in the forest, and began firing.

Wood chips came flying off the eagle with a racket impressive for such small guns, like firecrackers at a Chinese New Year parade. Nobody wore hearing protectors or, for that matter, shooting glasses. But the eagle was a good ways off, and the splinters drifted harmlessly to the forest floor. When the officers finished, the eagle showed little damage.

This was going to take a while.

A long line of men, members of the men-only *schützenverein,* or shooting club, had been waiting, and now they cycled through the firing line, three abreast. A great shout went up as the last piece of crown tumbled through the poplar leaves. As we understood it, those who shot off the last piece of crown, the last piece of scepter, the left wing, and the right wing would each get a prize. But he who knocked the last shard of wood off the pole would be crowned king of Kolping for the whole year—a dubious honor, as we would come to learn.

We found a place at a long table in the deep shade with two sweaty brothers named Tom and John, who wore T-shirts that read LIVING WITH A GERMAN BUILDS CHARACTER! and I GOT SCHÜTZENFACED AT SCHÜTZEN-FEST. They were eager to explain to out-of-towners that just because Cincinnati looked dull and unsophisticated didn't mean locals didn't know how to rock out—within reason. "It's like that book, *The Millionaire Next Door.* People here live below their means. But they party! The beer consumption, the sausage consumption—it's off the charts. People here know how to party, but they don't get out of hand!"

"Look! You got kids here! Families! But we don't get out of hand!"

"Hitler, you know, didn't want to fight in the west," Tom said suddenly. "All he wanted was lebensraum for the German people."

Margaret and I stared at him for a long moment. Where did *that* come from?

Maybe it was the heat, or the beer, or the racket of the guns. Margaret suddenly stood, cocked her head toward me, and casually said to them, "Dan here? Jewish." Then, to me: "Gotta pee." And off she walked.

The brothers flew into a panic. "I've got a Jewish friend! Great guy!" "They say the DA of Cincinnati is Jewish! Great guy!"

A shout went up; someone had shot off the last piece of the scepter. A hearty man in full *deutsche* garb plunked himself down next to me and thrust out his hand. "Mike Rademacher," he said, with Babbitt-like vigor. He had a Vandyke that was starting to whiten and brown eyes that sparkled behind heavy glasses. His hat was so coated with cloisonné pins, and sported a *gamsbart* so enormous, that it was a miracle he could hold his head upright.

"That's one hell of a hat," I said.

He laughed, sweat pouring down his face. "In my family, ethnic was uncool. We kids would ask where our family was from, and my grandfather would say, 'That depends who won the last war.' I grew up with no Germanness."

"So how did you discover your inner kraut?"

"I married Kathy, whose grandfather was chief genealogist for the Mayflower Society! They could trace their family back to the year 800. For them, family history was everything. I looked at all that and said, 'Our kids aren't going to know anything of my side.' So I started connecting with my German past." He took a long pull of beer and wiped his beard with the back of his hand. "Kathy and I got invited to a polka dance at Kolping in 1988 and started attending functions. We learned to drink Jägermeister, and we got acquainted with senior members. They'd say, 'You're a *Rademacher* and you don't speak the language? What's the matter with you?'"

Mike was a member of the *schützenverein* and had already taken his mandatory shots at the eagle. The last thing he wanted, he said, was to win the contest and become king. "It'll cost you about twenty thousand dollars, if you do it right. You throw a *lot* of parties. My wife says I can shoot for king once we've made our younger daughter's last tuition payment. But then someone will want to get married, and I'll have to put it off again." He took a sip of beer. "It's okay. I can go to my grave without being king. It would be a long year."

"So why shoot at all?"

He shrugged. "It's a social thing. Want to see the shooting room?"

Of course. He took Margaret and me inside to a long room that looked more like a stretched classroom than a rifle range, with wood-paneled walls lined with books and framed certificates. At one end was a sloping steel wall over a sand pit: the bullet trap. At the other end was a wooden countertop. "Practice opens at six, and we start shooting at seven-thirty after everybody's had a few beers," Mike said. "Men only in here. You and your five-man team shoot once. You put your belly to the table and you shoot standing. You get all the time you want to shoot eight shots, of which the top six count."

"You're drinking beer while you're shooting," Margaret said.

"No beer in this room; when you're not shooting you're out in the fellowship halls with the wives. You want to shoot early so you're not drunk." Shooting nights were once a month.

Mike didn't even like guns, he said. Just about the only ones he'd ever shot were the club's .22s. "I have no tradition of seeing people go shooting. I like hiking. I like the outdoors. But buying a gun and shooting is a serious choice. You have to be shown how. I never thought it was attractive or necessary. In a life of limited choices, am I going to shoot guns?"

"Yet this you like."

He spread his hands. "It's like Fred and Barney at the Water Buffalo Lodge. I like the shooting, but mostly it's a social thing. We drink beer. We smoke cigars. We talk. And we shoot. It's helped connect me with my German heritage. And there are some great moments. One shooting night in June 1994, the fiftieth anniversary of D-day, a friend was telling the story of his father, a merchant marine who was bringing men to shore, how scary it was knowing every German up on the cliff was aiming at him. So he's telling this, and from down the bar an old-timer calls"—here Mike put on a heavy German accent—"'Yeah? Vell vat do you think it vas like to look out and see all those fucking ships?'"

Mike laughed. "Everybody went silent, and we went back to our beers."

Getting back to the beers seemed to be the point of the *schützenverein,* not the shooting. Three-gun had been real competition. Here, the rifles were really just bigger, noisier barroom darts—fun things to play with while drinking beer and telling stories with the fellas. It wasn't exactly shuffleboard, though. Because it involved guns, it divided the men from the women. We'd evolved enough as a society to understand that if the gunplay was about skill and scoring points, we couldn't very well exclude the women any more than we could exclude blacks or the disabled. But if it was all about Fred and Barney at the Water Buffalo Lodge, then the rifles of *schützen* could be the equivalent of the needles at a sewing circle or the eyeliner at an Iona Cosmetics party—tools for giving a single sex cover for enjoying its own good company. For all the lederhosen and cloisonné hat pins, the fact that *schützen* gave Mike Rademacher "a chance to connect" with his German heritage seemed incidental to the pleasure of hanging with the fellas.

We walked out into the social hall—a vaulted room with exposed beams in faux Bavarian-castle style, draped with the colorful flags of the German states. At big round tables, families were bravely hunched over plates of steaming sauerbraten and spaetzle. If I'd tried to eat such winter food on a stifling day like this, I'd have seized up like a tube of caulk.

When we reached the garden, everybody who had been lounging at the tables was standing, crowded at the rail, watching eagerly. Next to me, a teetering young man wore a beer-sloshed T-shirt silk-screened with a picture of Jesus over the words IF YOU DON'T SIN, I DIED IN VAIN. All that remained of the eagle was a tiny matchstick. Instead of three men firing at once, the shooters were taking turns, one bullet at a time. *Pop! Pop! Pop!* A roar went up as a toothpick fluttered earthward: Long live the king! We moved in a solid wave—hundreds of us—toward the beer kegs, where the king was hosting free beer for everybody, the start of his twenty-thousand-dollar year.

13. HE UPPED, I UPPED

Affluent Americans care not one whit what happens to their trashier
neighbors, and it is hypocritical, at best, to suggest that we are
improving their lives by depriving them of their guns.

—Robert Sherrill, *The Saturday Night Special*, 1973

For a guy who didn't look the part and had to depend on camouflage, I'd been having pretty good luck getting people to talk about their gun lives. People like sharing their hobbies, and that proved true even of conservative gun guys who knew my politics. Many shared a belief that liberals and the media were institutionally hostile to guns and gun people. Most of them were delighted finally to be approached.

But not all.

That book I'd found at the Grand Island gun show, about caching guns, made me want to learn more about why people would take an expensive firearm and bury it. On AR15.com, I found a forum devoted to burying guns in preparation for what participants called TEOTWAWKI— the end of the world as we know it—an acronym that, pronounced as a word, sounded like an upstate New York summer camp. The guys on the forum discussed TEOTWAWKI and SHTF—shit hits the fan—coming in the form of bird flu, the circuit-killing electromagnetic pulse of an ionospheric North Korean nuke, the eruption of the Yellowstone caldera, an asteroid strike, peak oil, nuclear war, and starvation brought about by climate change. None of which were beyond the realm of possibility. What puzzled me was why guns topped the list of things one might need at such a time. I'd been through the immediate aftermath of Hurricane Katrina in New Orleans and had never felt the need for a gun. Despite the purple press reports about marauding predators and babies being raped in the Superdome, people at the height of the disaster were a lot more focused on helping one another than on preying on one another. (Yes, I saw looting. But as Rebecca Solnit aptly writes in *A Paradise Built in Hell*, about the way disaster brings people together instead of turning them into savages, "Who cares if electronics are moving around without benefit of purchase when children's corpses are floating in filthy water and stranded grandmothers are dying of heat and dehydration?") It turned out that just about the only wanton killing during the Katrina disaster was done by the New Orleans Police Department.

That, of course, was the other possibility cited by the "Arfcom army" on AR15.com: that government, in the form of the police, the Army, or the black-helicopter forces of tyranny, would become the people's enemy and start rounding up all the guns. As with the teachers of my concealed-carry class, the gun guys on Arfcom made it hard to delineate between preparing for disaster to strike and praying for disaster to strike. After all, if you've gone to the expense and trouble to buy and bury guns and ammunition and then you never need them, you've wasted a lot of time and treasure.

I learned a lot from reading the forum. A Chinese SKS rifle is cheap, short, powerful, and easy to hide. Smearing its workings with grease and putting desiccants in the tube will prevent rust. The PVC tube containing it should be buried vertically to make it harder to find with a metal detector. Forgetting where it's buried is a real danger. After reading the forum for a while, I wanted to interview a cacher. I was smart enough to know that anybody burying his guns wouldn't want to go public about it but not smart enough to realize that, even offering anonymity, asking people about something as secretive and sensitive as TEOTWAWKI preparations was offensive, threatening, and, well, stupid.

The cachers went completely crazy. In torrents of anonymous vitriol, they accused me of being an ATF agent, a gun grabber, a troll. They dug off the Internet pictures of Margaret and Rosa and called them ugly names. Then they found photos of us at Barack Obama's nomination-acceptance speech, which really sent them around the bend. It went on for weeks, at one point becoming genuinely scary. Even two years after, if I published anything about guns, these same guys rose up to denounce me en masse without reading what I'd written. "You're a brand," one gun blogger told me. It was awful. Even writing about it here makes me shudder, because I know that when this book appears, they'll be back.

There was another group of gun guys I wanted to interview who I figured would be equally resistant to exposure. Unlike cachers, though, these other ones weren't marginal to the gun-guy story but instead were at its absolute center: criminals. Even though crime wasn't "out of control" and was falling fast, the United States still experienced more than its share. Much of what was said and done about guns in America had to do with violent crime; millions of people owned and carried firearms to protect themselves from armed criminals, and the gun debate was all about whether, and how, to try to keep guns "out of the hands of criminals." Halfway through my year of traveling around talking to gun guys, I realized that I had a thug-shaped hole at the center of my story. Vicious armed predators risked becoming an unrepresented constituency. So I went looking for one to speak for the profession, as it were, to explain how it feels to use a gun in a life of crime.

This time, I trod more delicately. Unlike the cachers lobbing insults from the safety of the Internet, gangsters were accustomed to pointing guns at people and pulling the trigger. I quickly established that I wasn't going to find these guys in online forums; Thug.com was about music, and ExThug.com didn't exist. But I discovered that every major city had at least one organization either founded or assisted by former gangbangers, devoted to keeping young men from taking the same deadly path—Homeboy Industries in Los Angeles, Beyond Bullets in New York, Vision Regeneration in Dallas, the Miami-Dade Anti-Gang Coalition, CeaseFire-Chicago, and so on. I began calling them, asking if any of the former drug-dealing, baby-shooting savages standing around the office might want to unpack his entire criminal life for publication. "You paying?" asked one. When I said no, he hung up. But at least he didn't broadcast pictures of my daughter or call me an Obamatron libtard troll.

Finally, I got a call from a man named Tim White, who said that yes, he'd been in the life, had "done it all," and that, sure, he'd be willing to talk about it. Just to be sure he was the guy I wanted, I asked him if he'd used a gun in his criminal undertakings. He gave one of those short laughs that aren't intended to be funny.

"Lots of guns," he said on the phone. "Guns all the time. I've been shot twice, too, so I know 'em from both ends."

We met in a coffee shop near Chicago's Humboldt Park, in a neighborhood trying mightily to gentrify itself out of the odium of being simply

"West Side." Tim, at forty-six, was engaged in a related exercise: attempting a personal transformation through Christ to elevate himself to the role of elder sage. He worked with CeaseFire-Chicago, traveling around the city and the country trying to teach younger versions of himself to settle their disagreements in some way other than gunfire. "I'm not telling them to give up drug dealing or anything like that," he'd told me on the phone. "I don't make judgments. You got to do what you got to do. I'm all about, 'You got a problem, you settle it some other way.' Violence is a learned behavior. If you can learn it, you can unlearn it."

For a man who claimed to have been so fearsome, he was awfully benign-looking—stocky, with baby cheeks and a wide, toothy smile. He wore a black ball cap and a Raiders hoodie. When he sat down, he laid his smartphone on the table where he could see it, indicating that while he was willing to talk, he wasn't going to interrupt his important business for our conversation. He reminded me of a riverboat gambler casually placing a derringer beside his chips—not making a big deal of it, just letting everybody know what's what.

I started to ask a question, but he already knew where he wanted to take the conversation, and without preamble pulled up his hoodie to expose a muscular torso of milk-and-coffee brown. "This is where his bullet hit me; see that red mark?"

A young white woman at the next table glanced over, and quickly away. Tim's fingertip found a raspberry-colored pock on the outboard side of his left pectoral, then slid to another at the center of his sternum. "It bounced off my rib and came out over here."

Pulling the hoodie back down, he started at the beginning. Tim had grown up at Kedzie Avenue and Ohio Street, in deep West Side. But his wasn't a typical story of a neglected, fatherless childhood. Just the opposite, in fact, which may have been the problem.

"It was ghetto for sure, but I grew up in a good family. Didn't want for nothing. My father was a minister; I never saw him smoke or drink. My mother was first lady of the church. There was seven of us kids—three girls and four boys, and I'm second to the last. Until I was twelve or so, I did the thing—went to school, played drums in the church, all that. Them streets, though, man. Them streets. When you're eleven, twelve years old, they call to you."

His phone buzzed. He put it to his ear, listened for a moment, said, "I'm doin' the interview," and set it back on the table.

"Dad was always gone, building the ministry," he went on. "Mentally, me and him didn't connect. He was all fire and brimstone, and I didn't understand that. He had a way of talking, not listening. Like, 'This is how it's going to be.' And I'd say, 'Not with me.' I was like, 'No matter how much you whip me, preach to me, I'll be walking away.' This is when I'm like twelve years old, and my father's always talking, talking, talking. But what you want at that age is a family that *listens.* So I went out and found one in the streets."

In 1977 and '78, roller disco was big, and the hot hangout for people Tim's age was a rink called Hot Wheels, at the corner of Chicago and Pulaski. "Everybody from everywhere went there. You skate. You dance. You get into fights with them from other neighborhoods. That's where we formed our identity—who could fight and who couldn't.

"My dad, he'd say, 'You can't go to that devil place,' and I'd say, 'I'm going.' I'd get home and my dad would be like, 'Gimme a shoe.' I'd say, 'You can go ahead and whup me, but I'm going back there tomorrow.' The whuppings became numb to me."

Tim, at least, had parents. "Other kids' parents, they were, like, gone. This one's dad's in jail, that one's mom's on aid, or she's using. So these cats would be way out there, staying out late, showing around big wads of money. They was daredevils. This one boy, Curt, I seen him snatch a chain off a lady's neck on a bus. He pulled the cord and snatched that chain, and I was, like, shocked. We ran, and I was all 'What you *doin*'?' Man, he showed me that money, and my eyes was like *baseballs.*"

The phone buzzed again. "Yeah, man, I *said.* I'm doin' the interview *now,* and I'll get wit' you later." He took a moment to remember his place in the story. The speed with which it was tumbling out of him told me it was a tale he'd told many times before. It was the rap he carried around the country with him, spreading it like the Gospel to any young man who'd listen.

Anybody living on the West Side in those days was presumed to be a member of the Vice Lords gang, but that was like being a member of the AFL-CIO. What mattered was one's clique. "Ours we called KO. One day you start wearing the hats, wearing the colors. And now you got power and respect. Hats was important. We wore ours to the left. Disciples wore theirs to the right. Colors was black and gold, but we weren't really tripping about the colors. The Latinos, they're way into colors. And graffiti. They love that shit. Us, we'd tag our territory, but then people knew our territory and we didn't bother no more."

Being a Vice Lord, though, involved more than just wearing a hat the right way. It was work. "What it is, when we were coming up, everybody took a path. Some dudes became pickpockets. Some were shoplifters. Some became stickup men. Everybody tried to choose their paths; we knew all them facets of life.

"I was never a *robber* robber. I didn't get off on that. Some dudes, they like to see fear in people, they'd come back and be all 'I liked to put them in their place.' I didn't say nothing; it wasn't my thing. Seemed they always went after people weaker than them, littler than them, people who didn't have no gun. I'd be like, 'I don't like seeing you take from niggers you can beat. I see the punk in you. If you're so tough, why don't you take from *him*.'" He gestured at an imaginary bruiser.

He stopped and looked at the woman at the next table, who was leaning on her elbow and listening to us talk. She nervously turned back to her laptop.

"That's all right, listen up," he told her with a gentle laugh. "What I got to say, I want everybody to hear." He was being genuine, but from the way she studiously ignored him, gazing into her laptop, she seemed to think he was being sarcastic. He smiled at the side of her head a moment longer, then turned back to me with a shrug.

"What I was, I was a hustler. I had a niche for it," he continued. "Buy. Sell. People trusted me. I *served* them."

But what about the guns? I asked. *When did you start carrying a gun?* His first, he said, he came by the old-fashioned way. He stole it.

"One day, we were cleaning out the backyard of a neighbor across the street, and when my friend went in to use the bathroom, the little girl who lived there showed him a shotgun up in a closet. He went back in later and took it. I said, 'It's too long,' so we cut it off. You could get it up under your clothes then."

Chicago made it harder to get a gun legally than almost anywhere else in the country, but Tim never had trouble getting guns, even as a young teenager. "You had these guys go to Memphis, where it's easy to get, and bring them back here, where it's hard. Maybe it's a white guy addicted to narcotics. A businessman. He starts partying a little too much, comes into the ghetto, and gets hooked. So he brings a proposition: 'You guys buy guns?' And we'd be like, 'Can you get guns? Go get them and bring them back here.' That guy, he's straight. He got no record. He can buy a gun any damned place. Guys would come back from down south and sell them out the trunk of their car. Get whatever you liked.

"I liked a revolver. I had a lot of them, but my favorite was a .41 Magnum. The big guns were *famous*. Magnums. Forty-fives. Nine-millimeters. The bigger the gun you got, the more powerful you were. Cost you anywhere from one to five hundred dollars, depending on what it was and how it looked. Big guns were the thing. I'd use a girl to carry mine. The man-police at the door of the club can't search her, so she has the gun, and when we're inside it's like, 'Go in the bathroom and get it out and bring me my gun.'"

"So how much of what you were doing was about the gun?" I asked.

"For me, the gun was exciting at first, but I grew out of it. I don't know when or how; just having so many of them, I guess. It was a tool. If you needed it, you needed it. But it wasn't like I was all *about* the guns, like some dudes. You could tell who was way into the guns and who wasn't. Some dudes, they was *addicted*. Always asking, 'Lemme see the gun, lemme see it.' And I'd be like, 'What are you always asking to see the motherfucking *gun*?'"

Even in Tim's criminal world, then, some people liked them, while others could take or leave them.

"There'd be guys you wouldn't give the gun," he went on. "Like there'd be guys you wouldn't let drive the car or hold the money. Some guys you can trust with shit like that; some you can't. After trial and error, you learn who not to give a gun to. We'd be somewhere and something would happen that you could settle with fists, and out of fucking nowhere it's *Boom! Boom! Boom!* And I'd be like, 'What the fuck you do *that* for? Gimme that fucking gun.'"

I'd had dealings years earlier with a reformed drug dealer from Washington, D.C., who'd told me that he and his friend shot their guns all the time in the course of doing business but that most of the time they hadn't really tried to hit anybody. Gunfire for them—in 1990s Washington—had mostly been language. They'd blast a few rounds in the general direction of a rival to send a message. If they hit him, that was fine. But mostly they used gunfire simply to make a point. When I ran this past Tim, he looked at me like I was nuts.

"That's not how we did," he said. "If we shot at someone, we was sure as hell trying to kill the motherfucker."

The woman at the next table banged shut the lid of her laptop, slid it into her shoulder bag, and walked off without a glance at either of us. Tim watched her go. He seemed to be wondering how he'd ever connect with people like her, so that he could spread his message that much further. When he turned back to me, he quit the bouncy raconteur act he'd been using and dropped his voice to a deeper, slower, more serious register.

"That Curt, who snatched the chain off the lady? Later on, he tried to rob a guy's radio—also on a bus. Shot the guy and killed him. I saw him in jail and asked him, 'What the fuck?' He said, 'The guy grabbed the gun.' It was the guy's birthday, he'd just gotten the radio and wouldn't give up. Curt said, 'I'm not playing; give me the radio,' and the guy grabbed the gun. 'But why you shoot him?' I asked, and all Curt said was, 'The guy was a little bit bigger than me. He grabbed the gun.' Curt, man, he's still doing thirty years.

"There's a lot of *isms* in our neighborhood," Tim said quietly. "Some people are mentally disturbed but aren't diagnosed. Never *been* to a doctor. Guy starts shooting when he doesn't need to be doing no shooting, you know he's crazy in the head. Guy who'd shoot at a cop: crazy. He's not a person you can violate physically, but you can *manipulate* him. 'You fucked that up; now you owe me.' 'You like shooting? Okay, then; you do him over there.' Everybody else know he's crazy, too. So a guy doesn't pay, all you got to say is, 'I'm going to get Crazy Larry.' Everybody knows Crazy Larry likes to shoot."

He stopped for a moment, looking sad. Then, he shuddered visibly, willing himself back to his story.

"I was straightforward," he announced with renewed vigor. "My word was my *bond*. I was a trusted man on the street, someone people looked up to. I had a good heart because of my mother and father. Really, I shouldn't have been in the street life, but since I was, I had that preacher upbringing to draw on, and people knew they could trust me. Some people run the street with fear, some people run the street with love."

"Love," I said, "and a .41 Magnum."

"People weren't afraid of me. They knew that if I was coming, I was coming. But not if I didn't have no reason. I had a large following. I took the Vice Lords to another level in my neighborhood, financially and organizationally. Everything happened fast. Millions of dollars passed through my hands. Forty thousand dollars a day. Paid for an apartment six months in advance and put my money in there. Parked a car in a garage with the trunk full of money. Or I'd take the car in to get painted, and then tell them, 'I changed my mind; paint it again,' just to leave it there because it's all stuffed with money and I got no place else to put."

He sat back, chuckled, and slapped his belly contentedly with both hands. "It's funny that my dad being a preacher and all helped me in the life," he said.

Then a shadow crossed his face, as though his little hurricane of braggadocio had blown itself out. His voice pinched down again; we seemed to be coming to a place he didn't want to go but knew he must.

"Some guys, though, they don't want to work their way up," he continued. "They wait until you do all the work and get up there, and then they stick you up. Guys come home all buff from prison. They have tattoos, they're talking about taking over. But I'm like, 'You don't have the finance and you don't have the *guns*.'

"The guy I'd started out hustling with was a dude called Shank. We was close. I'd sleep at his house, eat with him and his mama. We was hustling well together. Shank, though, he didn't understand what they meant when they said, 'Don't get high on your own supply.' He fell into the hype of being somebody. And he was living above his means. I was like, 'Man, you spent *how* much last night?' I chose to walk away, and he messed up with his connect because he couldn't pay his bills.

"Then he focused on me. He was like, 'I know who got some money; I'm going to *get* that nigger.' He told someone he knew where my safe house was, and he wanted to pop me off.

"So this one night, I'm in my Mercedes and pull up at Augusta and Keeler and he's right there with a gun and told me to get out the car. He upped with his gun and busted me upside the head. He was going to take me in the house, where the money at.

"I told him, 'Hold up, let me get my keys,'" and I upped with *my* gun. He shot. I shot. I knew right off I'd been hit. I jumped back in the car and tore it up getting out of there. I could see blood coming out my chest, and I thought I was dying. That's the thing about getting shot: It hurts, yeah, but you're more scared than the pain—that unknown, are you going to make it? I was telling my friend in the backseat, 'If I die, make sure that nigger die, too.'

"Turned out, the bullet hit the sleeve of my big coat, went in the side of my chest, hit that rib, and bounced back out. Hurt like a motherfucker. Doctors thought it was two bullets, and turned me over, looking for where they went. I heard them yell, 'Didn't exit!' They were about to cut me open when they figured it out.

"My dad came in while they were working on me and whispered, 'That boy died. Be quiet. Don't talk.'

"Shank shot me with a .380. I shot him with a .22. Mine went in and bounced around inside him. He'd parked a couple blocks away so I wouldn't see his car, and when he ran to it, he pumped out all his blood.

"At the preliminary hearing, the judge said to the prosecutor, 'You said this was premeditated, but this look more like self-defense.' Gave me a year for UUW—unlawful use of a weapon, firearm in the city limits, all that."

After all my time in concealed-carry classes and talking to gun guys about defensive gun use, this was my first encounter with someone who'd actually used one to save his own life—and he was a crook, shooting another crook. I'm not sure why, but until this moment it hadn't occurred to me that one drug dealer shooting another could make the claim of self-defense.

I figured it was getting shot in the chest and having to kill a friend that had woken Tim up to the error of his ways and driven him into the arms of Jesus. Nope.

"They sent me to Sheridan Correctional Facility, minimum security. I knew a lot of people there. Now I had status: I'm a killer. That validated me as being authentic. I do what I say I do. If you do me, you're set to leave this world in a coffin. When I got out, I was an even bigger man on the street."

His ten-year sentence in federal prison, for conspiracy, came later. It was eighteen months into that when he realized how tired of the life he'd become and accepted Christ as his personal savior—"went crazy for Jesus" is how he put it. Upon his release in 2006, he came home and preached a sermon in his father's church. Then he started working for CeaseFire.

His phone buzzed, but this time he let it go. He was sorry about Shank, he told me, but given the circumstances they were both living at the time, it couldn't have played out any other way.

"You live by the sword and you get what you get. 'You came to hurt me; you got hurt. Them are the rules. You came to stick me up and fumbled the ball.' Shank had friends, yeah. But: 'You got a problem with it, you can join him. You violated my space, I ought to get you, too.'

"Poor Shank was broke and starving. He went to my house to stick me up and got killed. End of story. Two months later, I called his mother and apologized. We were tight; I'd eaten her food. I told her the truth, that this wasn't my intention. She said, 'I know you didn't want it. I'm a Christian woman and I have to find it in my heart to forgive you.'

"Shank, he was on a death wish. His mother and me, we're close now."

Among the many lies I'd always assumed Hollywood taught us was that people can walk away from killing someone in a gunfight psychologically unscathed. One hardly ever sees a protagonist affected by the killing he does on-screen. James Bond? Marshall Dillon? Do we ever see them wringing their hands afterward and blubbering in guilty self-doubt? If you totaled up all the people shot dead on-screen by Steve McGarrett on *Hawaii Five-O*, for example, he'd have a higher body count than Jeffrey Dahmer. At the end of each show, he walked away calmly from the corpse he'd just created, and in the next episode he seemed perfectly well adjusted.

In reality, of course, police officers who kill in the line of duty are often disarmed and withdrawn from the street until not only an investigation of the shooting can take place but a psychological evaluation as well. The Army is starting to recognize that a soldier who kills on the battlefield is likely to be a psychological casualty. Even the NRA has acknowledged that killing somebody with a gun is a traumatic event, no matter how justified the shooting, and is likely to haunt the shooter forever.

For all the blathering I'd heard about defending oneself with a gun, Tim was the first person I'd met who'd actually done the deed—and he surprised me by seeming more like McGarrett than the reality I expected. He was sorry that he'd had to kill Shank, but he didn't seem tortured by the experience. Maybe if the circumstances had been more ambiguous, Tim would have spent a lifetime wondering if he'd really had to pull the trigger. But I imagine taking a .380 slug through the brisket was pretty convincing. "Them are the rules," he'd said, as though that's the code of the street thug. It seemed a pretty good rule for everybody, though: If someone shoots you, shoot him quick before he can pull the trigger a second time. Even the Dalai Lama, when asked in 2001, said he was down with that.

I wasn't carrying my gun in Chicago; it wasn't permitted. But I looked forward to putting it back on once I had reached a more permissive jurisdiction. This probably wasn't the lesson with which Tim wanted to leave me, but hearing firsthand from someone who'd actually defended himself with a firearm made me believe not only that I'd be able to do it but that—provided the need was as clear-cut as Tim's—I'd also be able to live with having done so.

14. GUN SHUL

Dominic: What do you think will happen?

Finch: What usually happens when people without guns stand up to
people with guns?

—*V for Vendetta*, 2005

Everybody we meet—*everybody*—has a gun story," Margaret said as we unfolded our napkins at a little restaurant near Lake Michigan's northern shore. "And a gun figures into the most important moment of their lives."

"You want a gun story?" said a voice from the next table. Margaret and I sighed. A young man with a buzz cut and eyelashes so blond they sparkled leaned eagerly toward us. "I didn't have toy guns as a kid. My dad said, 'When you're old enough, I'll let you have a gun and teach you to use it.' But no toy guns. He caught me once playing with a friend's pop gun, and he threw it over the fence. That was my dad's way of teaching me they're not toys."

The waitress set down our orders, big crockery vessels of cheese-beer-and-bratwurst soup—Wisconsin in a bowl—but the man at the next table kept talking. "He'd fill a milk jug with water and red food coloring and have me shoot it with a .30-06. That made a big impression on me. That's what a bullet can do."

There seemed no way to avoid a conversation. "You have guns now?" I asked.

"Oh, sure. Lots."

"What do you do for a living?"

"Maintenance for the county parks department."

"Mind if I ask who you voted for in the last election?"

"McCain."

"How come?"

"Who else? Obama?" He snorted, cutting into his steak.

"Why do you say it like that? Workingman like you—I'd have guessed you were a Democrat."

"Not as long as they want to take my guns, I'm not," he said. He tucked a chunk of steak into his cheek and talked around it. "You can't go on a college campus and find a lot of professors who support gun rights. There's an elitism—that guns are for the unwashed. The yokels. The people who like Sarah Palin."

Among the guns with which we were traveling was a clever little back-packers' .22 rifle that came apart and fit into a short nylon case. I wanted to buy an inexpensive telescopic sight for it, and when we passed a huge chain store, Gander Mountain's Gun World, in Germantown, Wisconsin, I begged Margaret's pardon and pulled into the parking lot.

Gander Mountain's Gun World was overwhelming—two floors of clothing, canoes, sleeping bags, fishing gear, and camp-cooking sup-plies, and an entire room devoted to guns. Margaret went to look for a tent-patch kit and camp-stove fuel; I sidled up to the optics counter. Two salesmen stood with their backs to me about twenty feet away. One glanced over, ran his eye up and down my clothes, and turned back to his colleague. They may have been engaged in urgent business, but I didn't get that vibe. The clerk had seen a wimpy-looking middle-aged man in pleated pants and glasses, reeking of the metropole, and decided I wasn't a member of the tribe. (I wasn't wearing the NRA cap.)

I waited him out, and eventually—reluctantly—he detached himself and walked over. He was a big man with a deeply creased face; he'd have looked at home in a bunkhouse.

"Yes?" he said, crossing his arms.

I told him what I wanted, and, sighing, he unlocked the case, reached in, and put a scope on the counter. "Register's in the front," he said, turn-ing away.

"How did you pick this one?"

"You said you wanted a scope for a .22. That's a scope for a .22."

"Is that the only scope you have for a .22?"

He narrowed his eyes. "Just what is it you want?"

"I want a scope for a .22. I don't want to spend too much. I'd like it to be fairly small, so that it fits in the gun's case. I was hoping to look at several and decide."

"How much do you want to spend?"

"I don't know. Fifty bucks?"

"That one there's the only one costs less than fifty dollars. Register's up front."

"I think not. Thank you."

Without so much as a shrug, he put the scope back in the case and returned to his friend.

"Hey," I called to his back. "How about a holster for my carry gun?"

He stopped and returned, all smiles. A licensed gun carrier: Now I was part of the clan. "What kind of gun you carrying?"

"Never mind," I said, and headed for the door.

It wasn't the first time I'd been treated that way in a gun store, and for a long time I thought it was something about me personally. But the National Shooting Sports Foundation was sufficiently aware of the rude tendency of gun-store clerks that its monthly magazine, *SHOT Business,* was running a feature that summer called "The Undercover Shopper," in which a potential customer, sometimes a woman, would go into three or four stores pretending to be a newbie—and record the clerks' reception.

Again and again, clerks treated the undercover shopper with open contempt. If she didn't know the nomenclature, they embarrassed her. If the undercover shopper was a man who asked greenhorn questions, they shrugged him off. If, in other words, customers weren't already part of the club, gun-store clerks didn't want them around.

One theory circulating was that the attitude went back to the years after the Second World War, when any man who had to ask questions about guns revealed himself as someone who'd evaded battle and was therefore beneath contempt. To me, though, it felt like that same old gun-guy anger. You're one of us or you're not—and we can tell by your clothes and by the questions you ask. For gun-store clerks to circle the wagons against potential new customers seemed like rage that overpowered self-interest—especially since it was the opposite of the welcome I received at most gun ranges.

Gun-guy anger was becoming so tedious that I found myself expending a lot of energy fending it off—driving past gun stores, walking away from gun guys starting to puff themselves up with fury, avoiding the gun bloggers and online forums. Gun politics all but ruined my enjoyment of firearms. Although the vitriol surrounding gun politics was what had first attracted me to this project, it was the cultural division represented by the politics that I'd set out to explore. The bickering about this or that "gun right" was something I'd hoped to avoid entirely.

But turning my back on the fight over gun rights completely didn't feel right, either. That gun-rights zealots could be rude didn't necessarily invalidate their argument. Data about the effects of gun-control measures were available to examine and interpret. Philosophical points of view could be compared and contrasted. When it came to whether restrictive gun laws did good or did harm, reasonable people could disagree.

Finding reasonable people was the problem.

But I decided, finally, to try. I'd cease pushing the absolutist gun-rights community away and approach it willingly—even if I had to do it with a chair in one hand and a whip in the other. But, being weary of the bullies, the haters, and the shouters, I went looking for an honest, reasonable, and soft-spoken gun-rights activist to take me by the hand and explain his worldview in detail. I confess that I expected such a man to be a compromiser—someone who could feel the pain of those most horrified by gun violence and delineate gun-control measures that might save lives from those that would merely inconvenience people and restrict liberties, one who would be seeking a negotiated solution. When I found him, though, he turned out to be anything but. The man best able to give me the gun-rights viewpoint without raising his voice was the founder of an organization widely revered by gun-rights activists as so absolutist that it made the NRA look like a bunch of milk-and-water sissies. He was a courtly, learned, likable man of sixty-four named Aaron Zelman, and when I first heard the name of his organization I thought it was a joke: Jews for the Preservation of Firearms Ownership.

He was born in Winthrop, Massachusetts, in 1946, not long after his father, the schlemiel, abandoned his mother. Grandma took over, carting a bereft daughter and fatherless baby to a dirt road at the edge of Tucson, where, her doctors said, the dry air would do her arthritis good. *Such a place for Jews,* their friends in Winthrop said, but the Zelmans liked it. Plenty of Jews lived in Arizona; the Goldwassers, for example, might have anglicized their name to Goldwater because it looked better on their department store, but that didn't fool anybody. Most of all, the Mexicans lived their way, the cowboys theirs, the Indians theirs, and the Jews theirs. You worked, you obeyed the law, you kept to your own, and you got on fine. Nobody bothered anybody simply because of who he was, and that meant a lot to Grandma; tattooed on her arm, she carried a numbered keepsake of a different place and time.

Aaron grew into a tall, grave boy. At school, he liked history, and certain lessons stuck with him, perhaps because the movies he liked reinforced them. Again and again, one group of people set up another to be dominated by taking away its guns. The British marched on Lexington to seize the colonists' powder and shot, the Union blockaded the Confederacy to disarm it, the cavalry hanged men who sold Winchesters to the Indians, the British—*again*—disarmed India. "Among the many misdeeds of the British rule in India," Mahatma Gandhi wrote in his autobiography, "history will look upon the act of depriving a whole nation of arms as the blackest."

And, of course, the Nazis had hewed strictly to the letter of their laws as they stripped the Jews of their guns, homes, businesses, and, ultimately, their lives. It was the 1938 ban on Jews owning guns that, as Aaron saw it, made the Holocaust possible. At his bar mitzvah—a dark, mumbling affair at Tucson's stuffy Orthodox shul—one of Grandma's ancient friends gripped his arm with a veiny tattooed claw and rasped, "Understand, we couldn't defend ourselves." His breath smelled like the bottom of a well.

In Tucson during the Eisenhower and Kennedy years, though, guns were simply objects, with no particular moral or political significance. Western Auto, Sears, and Montgomery Ward sold them as freely and easily as tools or auto parts—pick them out of the case, pay your money, and walk out, no paperwork. The Browse Around Store had barrels of military surplus rifles for ten or fifteen dollars apiece, and if you wanted a gun that none of the stores carried, you could order it by mail from Sears, Roebuck and have it delivered to your house, parcel post. Aaron and his friends thought nothing of roaming the town with their BB guns or .22s, shooting pigeons. If they were going quail hunting after school, they'd carry their shotguns in the morning and stow them in their lockers. Aaron wasn't much of a shooter, except at the rifle range at Jewish summer camp, but he finally bought a gun when he was sixteen, at Stan's Swap Shop. He laid a few dollars on the counter and walked out with an old British Webley revolver. Legally, he should have been eighteen, but he was so tall and somber, like a young Abe Lincoln, that Stan didn't bother asking. It must have been obvious to him that Aaron was as responsible as a man needed to be to own a gun.

And that, in a nutshell, was what Aaron came to love about firearms and the freedom to own them: It was all about responsibility and respect. The fact that anybody could walk into a store and buy a powerful weapon with no questions asked, or order one through the mail, bespoke a rational esteem for adults' self-possession and sense of right and wrong. If you could be trusted to walk down the street, you could be trusted to own and carry a gun. And the converse was equally true: If you couldn't be trusted to own a gun, perhaps you shouldn't be on the street.

Sure, there'd be a shooting in Tucson every now and then, but never among the people in Aaron's world. It was the bad element getting up to no good, and they did that whether they had guns or not. Nobody suggested a connection between the availability of guns and the occasional shooting. You might as well have argued that barbed wire caused windstorms.

Aaron met me at the Mineshaft, a big saloon-style restaurant in downtown Hartford, Wisconsin, about an hour from Milwaukee. He was six foot seven and achingly thin; in a big straw hat, he looked a little like Pete Seeger. Behind thick glasses, his eyes were huge and mournful. He sat with a slight groan. Bad enough being sixty-four years old and spindly; he also had a problem with his *kishkes* that needed surgery. A chubby blond waitress took our orders with chirpy single-mindedness, high on either Jesus, methamphetamine, or the sheer joy of being alive at six in the morning. I hated to do it, since I was breakfasting with a conservative Jew, but I ordered the Gold Digger—three eggs, a six-ounce smoked pork chop, and home fries. Margaret and I, economizing madly, were camped in a state forest at the edge of town and for a week had been eating nothing but the single-pot rice-and-cabbage gruel that we could cook on our camp stove. I was starting to digest my own stomach. Aaron, for all his plumbing trouble, ordered the Golden Skillet: three eggs over American fries, ham, green pepper, onion, and mushroom, topped with hollandaise sauce. Hold the ham.

"I bought all that business about seeing the world and joined the Navy in 1964," he said with a faint trace of a smile. "I never got any farther than Oakland. They made me a corpsman at the Oak Knoll medical center. The amputee center was there—Vietnam was getting started—and I had the chance to see eighteen-year-olds like me missing their arms and legs, with colostomy bags hanging . . ." His face darkened, and he flapped a hand to shudder away the memory. "It made me very anti-violence. Not a pacifist—not against the war. Being raised right after World War Two, I grew up with a strong sense of needing to fight evil, and I believed the domino theory."

For Aaron, freedom wasn't just a slogan to go along with a bunch of silly flag waving. Freedom was the mechanism for raising mankind to its full potential, because when people were truly free, power wasn't concentrated in a few leaders. Everybody, in charge of his own destiny, became his own leader. Rejecting violence and supporting the war against the Communists' attempt to subjugate South Vietnam by violence, then, weren't contradictory. They were part of a unified vision in which nobody allowed himself to be a victim, and every man rose to the challenge of managing his own affairs. It wasn't a matter of choosing between the sovereignty of the individual and the good of the collective. A society composed of confident, self-reliant individuals was a naturally more efficient and just collective, in the same way that a machine worked better with high-quality parts.

"I left the Navy in 1966, and all I wanted to do was veg for a while. I remember sitting in a barbershop in San Francisco and picking up a copy of *Guns & Ammo.* I wasn't such a big gun lover—I didn't even own a gun by then—but I needed something to read. In it was a piece about what became the Gun Control Act of 1968. I couldn't believe it."

Frightened by the mid-sixties riots and the assassination of President Kennedy, Congress was planning to ban mail-order gun sales and gun sales to those who had a criminal record or who had received psychiatric care. To make that possible, the feds would require gun buyers to fill out a government form with their name and address.

What infantile nonsense, Aaron had thought as he waited for his haircut—to pretend that government could confront violence by making rules about guns. Guns didn't cause violence, and the people who committed violence with guns didn't respect laws. If the country was so violent, why was Congress trying to make it harder for citizens to defend themselves? Worst of all, the National Rifle Association was helping write the law.

Aaron stopped talking and looked at me, waiting for a question, but I was distracted by what was going on outside the picture window behind him. It seemed to be getting darker, not lighter, as the morning progressed. "So that's when you got involved?" I finally asked.

"No. I had a career to start. I got a job selling brassieres. Did very well. So well, they offered me my own territory: Detroit or Milwaukee. Detroit in 1967—imagine. I came here."

Our breakfasts arrived, food enough for twelve on plates the size of manhole covers. Aaron stared at his steaming plate, sighed, picked up his fork, and couldn't bring himself to use it. He seemed to enjoy ordering big breakfasts more than eating them; perhaps he'd been a robust eater and was still surprised by his new lack of appetite.

"Every time there was a push for more gun control, the people behind it were Jews," he said. "Howard Metzenbaum, Charles Schumer, Dianne Feinstein—she's the granddaughter of Polish Jews! That they could support the disarming of civilians, after what had happened to Jews in Europe, always seemed to me the worst kind of myopic self-delusion. Jews have been on the wrong end of the gun, the crossbow, and the sword forever." He set down his unused fork and took a sip of water. "It's that fawning desire for acceptance that's always our downfall. Oh, please, *like* us! The Democratic Party is very anti-gun, the Jews want a home in the party, so they go along."

It took Aaron until he was forty-five to get started as an activist. One night in 1991, after doing the dishes and putting their sons to bed, he and his wife, Nancy, sat at their farmhouse kitchen table and talked. "She asked me, 'What is it you really want to do?' And I said, 'I want to destroy gun control.' Not resist further restrictions on guns; not negotiate easier concealed-carry permits or fewer gun-free zones; not mince around with 'common-sense' gun laws. What I wanted was to do away with all gun laws, *period*." Appetite momentarily summoned, Aaron picked up the fork and took a mouthful of eggs.

He wanted the world back the way it was when he was a kid—when you could go into a store and buy any gun you wanted and walk out with it without asking anyone's permission. When you could carry a gun openly or concealed, as you saw fit. When you could pick a gun out of a mail-order catalog and have it sent to your house with nobody keeping a record of it. Not because he was such a lover of guns, but because free access to firearms was, for him, the ultimate sign of respect for the individual.

The NRA, he knew, was never going to bring about such a world. It had helped write the Gun Control Act of 1968, after all, and its opening position was "Let's enforce the gun laws we have." Aaron didn't want to enforce the gun laws. He wanted to wipe them off the books. "The NRA doesn't want to end gun control; then where would it be?" he said to me, looking around on his plate for something he could tolerate putting in his mouth. "The NRA cares about one thing only: the NRA."

What the American gun debate needed, he'd decided back in 1989, was an anchor—one organization about whose position nobody ever had to guess, a place where people could go for scholarly, historical evidence of the evils of gun control.

I started to ask about his interpretation of the Second Amendment, but he cut me off.

"Second Amendment this, Second Amendment that. What if the Second Amendment were repealed? I'm talking about something that precedes the Second Amendment by eons. I'm talking about something that comes from *God*. I'm talking about preserving *life*. For Jews, that's more than a right; in the Bible, it's an obligation."

"So *no* gun law? Not even, I don't know, keeping felons from getting them?"

"*I* never thought felons shouldn't be able to get guns," Aaron said, as though to imply, *What idiot would?* "First of all, ex-felons are just that. Ex. They've paid their debt and shouldn't be considered second-class citizens with fewer rights than you and I enjoy. Second, when did a criminal ever have a problem getting a gun? By definition, the only people impacted by laws are the ones who obey the law. Criminals aren't hamstrung by the system at all."

What Aaron wanted to show the world was that not all American Jews were as willing to shuffle off to the boxcars as Charles Schumer apparently was. So he called his new organization Jews for the Preservation of Firearms Ownership. Its logo—a red-white-and-blue Jewish star flanked by a musket and a machine gun—was electrifying when it appeared in his first propaganda attack: a full-page ad in *Gun Week* that read "Not all Jews are stupid and pro-criminal, but Charles Schumer is both." He put a fragment of potato in his mouth and chewed it thoroughly, framed by that oddly dark window. No doubt about it: The sun seemed to be setting at 8:00 a.m.

Aaron had no illusions about how a lot of *Gun Week* readers felt about Jews—especially given that Jews led the fight to take away peoples' guns. He figured that his ad would be a wake-up call for gun guys everywhere. They'd see that not all Jews wanted guns taken away, even if the most visible Jews did. It was time to make Jews the gun guy's friend, Aaron felt, instead of his enemy. That was the path to the Jews' long-term survival.

"The point we want to make is that those who support gun-control schemes rely on man's law to justify what they're doing," Aaron said, leaning urgently across the table. "By bringing up God's law, we're putting God's law and man's law at loggerheads, which puts Sarah Brady and Charles Schumer in the position of saying that God's law means nothing." *Well,* I thought, *when it comes to federal legislation, God's law does mean nothing.* At least that's how I read the First Amendment.

The waitress came around with the coffeepot. "Y'all hear about the tornado coming?" she said.

I jumped up. Margaret was in the campsite, probably asleep, with no car and no radio. I threw money on the table and asked Aaron if we could continue later. *This is what I get,* I thought, *for questioning the supremacy of God's law.*

No tornado hit, but we endured a morning of biblical rain from which Margaret and I hid in a movie theater. Among the others taking refuge was a studious-looking man of about forty, with glasses and a Vandyke.

"I don't have a gun, but I've been thinking I should get one," he said.

"Why?"

"I don't know. It just seems like a good skill to have. Seems like something I ought to know how to do."

"You thinking rifle or handgun?"

"Oh, a rifle. I grew up in New Hampshire, where everybody hunted except my family."

"So you're thinking you might hunt?"

"No, probably not. It's more wanting to know how to shoot. I'd like my son to know, too. I think of it as something we could do together. Not knowing how to shoot makes me feel a little inadequate as a man."

I wondered whether to take that as an expression of Wisconsin norms or what the feminists called phallic projection—or maybe simply the efficacy of gun advertising. It was mawkishly candid, though, and from a complete stranger in a half-lit movie theater.

"I can't own a firearm," said a voice to our left. We turned to find a clean-cut-looking man in his late twenties, wearing a jeans jacket and a blond Brylcreem bouffant.

"Why not?" Margaret said.

He frowned at us so long, I felt like a fool.

"Something in your past?" Margaret said.

"Duh. But we're filing the papers. I mean, once you've paid, you've paid, right?"

"Can you vote?" I asked. The Supreme Court had upheld felony disenfranchisement in 2005, and nine states temporarily barred ex-felons from voting, while both Kentucky and Virginia struck them from the rolls for the rest of their lives.

"I'm from Michigan," he said. "You can vote there once you're off paper. No guns, though. Forever. Can you believe it?"

I could.

"I mean, imagine you're told no First Amendment rights forever, just because you did something stupid once. Who'd put up with that?"

"I guess they figure guns are dangerous and words aren't."

He rocked back in exaggerated alarm. "What happened to 'The pen is mightier than the sword'?" He leaned forward. I thought I smelled whiskey, at 11 a.m.; maybe he wasn't so clean-cut. "Can't have it both ways, can you?" he whispered nastily.

The lights went off, and we were blasted with an overamplified and explosive trailer for *Harry Potter and the Deathly Hallows, Part One.* By the time its two minutes and forty seconds were over, I felt like I'd spent the morning outside in the storm.

When we stepped outside two hours later, the world looked as though it had brushed its teeth. Everything sparkled in extra-vivid relief. The sky was cloudless, the air scrubbed of its moisture. I could count individual leaves on trees a block away. Within an hour, though, the heat started rising and the morning's rain began evaporating in visible tendrils. Margaret was irritated by *The Kids Are All Right*—for all its au courant lesbian-marriage setting, she thought it reinforced a stultifying *Leave It to Beaver* morality. She was in a surly mood that probably wasn't improved by being left to rebuild camp alone in a sea of muddy pine needles. By the time I drove back into town to meet Aaron, the sky was ashen. We'd chosen Hartford's other restaurant, a dark Chinese place with a murky fish tank by the door. He ordered wonton soup and a bowl of boiled rice; I, wincing again in apology, a plate of spicy ginger pork.

Launching Jews for the Preservation of Firearms Ownership before the dawn of the Internet was largely a matter of churning out newsletters and monographs, printed as cheaply as possible on thin newsprint with smeary ink. Aaron stumbled on to Theodore Haas, a Jewish survivor of the Dachau concentration camp, who couldn't have been a more perfect poster child for the fledgling organization had Aaron created him from clay with his own hands like a golem. "There is no doubt in my mind that millions of lives could have been saved if the people were not 'brainwashed' about gun ownership and had been well armed," Haas told Aaron in a clipped *mittel* european accent. As far as Aaron knew, Haas was the first Holocaust survivor publicly to draw a connection between German gun control and the horror that followed it.

Little by little, Jews for the Preservation of Firearms Ownership began attracting members, and, to Aaron's satisfaction, most of them weren't Jews. They were *goyim,* discovering a different kind of Jew than the one they'd expected. Aaron tried hard to keep the language of the newsletter, even letters to the editor, cordial. Readers began submitting articles, and Aaron insisted that they be footnoted; he was amazed to discover how many amateur scholars were out there, waiting for a chance to share their knowledge. A reader named Gus Cotey Jr. attempted to get inside the heads of those who would ban guns, identifying "The Seven Varieties of Gun Control Advocate" as Elitists, Authoritarians, Criminals, the Fearful, Ideological Chameleons, Security Monopolists (who want citizens disarmed "so that they can command high fees for protecting the citizenry"), and the Dysfunctionally Unworldly ("To them, tyranny and crime are things that happen in other places far removed from their 'civilized' universe"). A Utah psychiatrist named Sarah Thompson argued, in a paper Aaron published, that gun haters believe the worst about gun owners because they wouldn't trust themselves with a gun. She urged gun owners to be gentle and non-argumentative when confronting them. Use "the mirror technique," she advised, feeding back what they say "in a neutral inquisitive way," then asking, "what makes you think that?"

"This was the plane onto which I wanted to elevate the gun debate,"

Aaron told me as he spooned up broth and avoided the wontons. "There was too much pointless shouting going on. I wanted to win the other side over, not merely enrage them."

For all his theoretical interest in guns, Aaron had little practical interest in them. But since he was going on about the need to defend oneself, he figured he ought to go shoot. One afternoon in the early nineties, he dutifully drove to a nearby range and unpacked a few of his guns onto a shooting bench. The usual suspects—hefty *goyim* in overalls and feed caps—blasted away with the rifles and slug-loaded shotguns with which they'd hunt deer. But then, from off to the left, came the unexpected rip of a machine gun. Everybody stopped and peered down the line. Chopping away at his target with a big black machine gun of some kind—Aaron was never good on technology—was a fellow Jew, unmistakable by the nose, the beard, and the black suit. When the man took a break to reload, Aaron walked over and introduced himself. "Good afternoon," the man said with a smile, and as he extended his hand, his jacket fell open to reveal two pistols jammed into his waistband.

"This was some Jew," Aaron said with a wisp of a smile. "He didn't have any accent, but he told me he'd been raised in Israel and said that American Jews were like the old joke. You know, two Jews standing against the wall, the Nazi soldiers are counting down, and one guy yells, 'Hey, I want a blindfold.' The other says, 'Shush, Hymie, you'll make them angry.'" Chuckling, Aaron spooned up a little rice, dipped the spoon into his broth, and brought it to his lips.

The Jew set down his machine gun, Aaron recalled, and began popping away with his pistols. First one hand, then the other, talking all the while. "My family"—*bang!*—"moved from Israel to a rough neighborhood of Cleveland"—*bang!*—"when I was just a kid"—*bang!* "All the Jews had already fled the neighborhood"—*bang!*—"so I stood out"— *bang!* His guns clicked empty, and he cocked his arms like a baseball player awaiting a pitch. "I started carrying a bat. 'Mess with me and you're going to die,' I told the hoods, and I could see them thinking, *Is it worth messing with this crazy guy?*"

"It was all I could do not to kiss this guy," Aaron told me. "When I mentioned JPFO, he said, 'I like the sound of *that*.' His name was Gideon Goldenholz. *Rabbi* Gideon Goldenholz. Said he had a shul in Mequon, which was something in itself. Mequon was where the country club used to have a sign: NO JEWS OR DOGS."

Aaron started attending synagogue for the first time in years, to hear

Goldenholz talk the talk from the bimah. "There is a strain of Judaism that yearns for peace at any cost," Goldenholz told the congregation one Friday evening as Aaron sat in the pews. "Such Jews think that being powerless proves that they're good in the eyes of God. Like, 'We're victimized because we're a great people.'" Goldenholz leaned across the pulpit. "Well, let me tell you: I can be a *victimizer* also." Aaron was thrilled.

Jews for the Preservation of Firearms Ownership produced its first book in 1994: *Death by "Gun Control,"* examining nine twentieth-century genocides—in Cambodia, China, Guatemala, Nazi Germany, Rwanda, Ottoman Turkey, Uganda, the Soviet Union, and Zimbabwe—and the gun bans or restrictions that preceded them. Working with an attorney, Aaron carefully footnoted every chapter so that nobody could accuse him of making up facts. Time and again—as in his childhood history lessons, as in the movies—one group disarmed another before annihilating it. *This,* he thought, as he shipped boxes of *Death by "Gun Control"* around the country, *will blow open the gun-control debate like nothing before it. This,* he thought, *will give the lie, once and for all, to the fallacy that gun control saves lives. Death by "Gun Control"* was as solid as stainless steel, Aaron felt: factual, dispassionate, unignorable.

It was ignored.

Not by JPFO's faithful, of course. They loved it. But the media—even the conservative media—didn't touch it. Aaron was floored. He produced, next, a series of comic books about a kindly white-haired man named Gran'pa Jack, which included such titles as *Will "Gun Control" Make You Safer?, The United Nations Is Killing Your Freedoms!, Is America Becoming a Police State?, "Gun Control" Is Racist!* and *Do Gun Prohibitionists Have a Mental Problem?* He also self-published a novel, *The Mitzvah*—about a Jew who awakens to the cause and arms himself—and commissioned an attorney friend to write *Dial 911 and Die: The Shocking Truth About the Police Protection Myth.*

Then Aaron stumbled upon what he felt was the greatest imaginable smoking gun: a letter from Lewis C. Coffin, law librarian at the Library of Congress, to Senator Thomas Dodd of Connecticut, on July 12, 1968. "Dear Senator Dodd: Your request of July 2, 1968, addressed to the Legislative Reference Service, for the translation of several German laws, has been referred to the Law Library for attention." Dodd, who had been a prosecutor at the Nuremberg trials after the Second World War—and who had been pushing for gun control since President Kennedy's assassination—had asked the Library of Congress to *translate Hit-*

ler's 1938 gun-control laws into English. Aaron couldn't believe it. Four months after Dodd got his translation, Congress passed his Gun Control Act of 1968, the first big federal gun law. When Aaron got ahold of the Library of Congress's translation and compared it with the American law, he was aghast at the similarities. Both assumed that gun ownership was a government-granted privilege. Both required people to prove they were "reliable" before buying a gun. Both prohibited certain classes of people from doing so. Both required store owners to keep gun-sale records; the Nazis had used those records to round up privately held guns. Dodd seemed to have lifted whole phrases of the Nazi law word for word.

Zelman put together a book—*"Gun Control": Gateway to Tyranny*— that opened with a photograph of Coffin's letter to Dodd, so that nobody could question his linking of Nazi law to the Gun Control Act. On facing pages, he printed a translation of the Nazi law and the relevant text of the 1968 law so that readers could compare them. What could be clearer? America's premier gun-control law was based on laws the Nazis had written to disarm the Jews before exterminating them. It was a solid-gold slam dunk.

Nobody paid attention.

Aaron sent it to Fox News. Nothing. He sent it to the *Washington Times.* Nothing. He sent it to Glenn Beck's producers. "We'll get back to you." But they never did. Even the NRA ignored it. Aaron thought he understood: If the country acknowledged the Nazi roots of gun control, it would have to scrap it, and nobody wanted to do that. Even the supposed opponents of gun control, like the NRA, got too much out of it.

"He's making two points," I told Margaret that evening at the campsite as we boiled our cabbage and rice. "The first is that the gun is a symbol of how society regards the individual. To trust everybody with something that lethal is to bestow the ultimate in respect."

"You think that respect is warranted?" she asked. "Those guys shooting the rocks at Green River?"

"I think Aaron would say that they acted like children with their guns because society treats them like children when it comes to guns."

She looked at me over the top of her glasses.

"He wants to elevate society, I think, by elevating respect for the individual. He'd probably say it's a slow process, but that you start by summoning everybody to his most responsible adult self."

"How about you summon your most responsible adult self and go get some water," Margaret said, extending a jug. I hoofed it to the communal tap and back.

"His other point is that people are going to try to slaughter each other, and the way you prevent that is by . . ."

"Making sure *everybody* has guns."

"Well, yes. Like the old mutually assured destruction."

"How about *nobody* has guns?" Margaret asked. "Then this group can come throw rocks and that group can throw rocks back, until everybody gets tired."

The rice was finished. We ate.

How *about* nobody has guns? It sounded good. No guns, no gun accidents. No guns, no gun murders. Two problems, though. One was that the country was saturated with guns, and they almost never wore out. Were government to impose the ultimate gun controller's victory—a total ban on the manufacture, import, and sale of firearms—we'd still have about 270 million guns floating around—for decades. What if everybody were ordered to turn them in? Many wouldn't. Then what? A nationwide door-to-door warrantless search?

And even if we could somehow rid ourselves of guns, how much good would that do? Russia had a murder rate four times that of the United States, with no legal private guns in circulation. I didn't know how they were killing each other, but clearly the Russians' breathtaking murder rate had little to do with their gun laws. Maybe ditto our higher-than-average murder rate.

The ubiquity of firearms in America tripped me up whenever I thought about ways to "control" them. The cold truth was that, given the number of guns in America and their longevity, there was no surefire way to keep guns from falling into the wrong hands. We could throw up obstacles—registration, waiting periods, background checks at gun shows—but would they do any good? Or rather—and this was a better way to ask the question—would they do *enough* good to make it worth alienating and enraging the 40 percent of Americans who liked guns enough to own them? Someone intent on evil would, for the next hundred years, probably be able to find a gun. And as Timothy McVeigh demonstrated so convincingly with his van full of heating oil and fertilizer—a gun wasn't necessary.

Maybe Aaron was on to something by trying to change how we thought about who we were as citizens and people, instead of how we regulated inanimate pieces of metal.

At our last breakfast at the Mineshaft, Aaron seemed discouraged. "We have a Jewish newspaper in Milwaukee, the *Chronicle,* that's written negative articles about me," he said. "The Jewish Federation doesn't like me. The ADL doesn't like me." He took a joyless sip of water. "At the shul we belong to now, I make a point of not talking about what I do, because there are Holocaust survivors there who argue with me, and I'm tired of having the argument. 'Guns wouldn't have made a difference,' they say." He shrugged, looking pained. "They won't talk to me anymore."

He set down his water glass and drove a long forefinger into the table, leaning across his untouched eggs. "But you know, in all the time we've been doing this, nobody's ever said, 'Oh, Zelman, you're wrong, and here's the proof.' Time after time, the gun laws were there. The laws were enforced. And the genocides happened. Bodies don't lie. And people who think it can't happen here? Ask Japanese Americans, the American Indians, the African Americans. They'll tell you it *can* happen here, because it already has."*

---

* Aaron Zelman died on December 21, 2010.

15. HOGZILLA

One does not hunt in order to kill; on the contrary, one kills in order to have hunted.

—José Ortega y Gasset, *Meditations on Hunting*

Then said he unto them, But now, he that hath a purse, let him take it, and likewise his scrip: and he that hath no sword, let him sell his garment, and buy one.

—Luke 22:36

When I called the Texas Parks and Wildlife Department in January of 2011 to ask about pig-hunting regulations, the lady who answered the phone said, "There aren't any."

"Excuse me?"

"You need a hunting license; a five-day will cost you forty-eight dollars."

"What's the season?"

"Year-round."

"What's the bag limit?"

"Ain't none. Shoot all you want."

"Males? Females?"

"Take them all, big and small."

"Wait. Have I reached the Texas Department of Wildlife?"

"Yes, sir."

"Any restrictions on what kind of gun I can use?"

"Nope."

"Do I have to wear orange?"

"It's a good idea, but not required."

"Time of day?"

"Jack them at night with a spotlight for all we care. As long as you shoot a lot of them. What you want to do is take and shoot the sow first. The piglets will stand around for a minute, and you can pick all of them off, too."

She directed me to an online pamphlet called "The Feral Hog in Texas." It read less like a wildlife primer than a multicount indictment in a death penalty case. It established straight off that hogs had no business running wild in Texas in the first place. They'd descended from barnyard stock that first escaped from settlers' pens three hundred years ago. The malevolent DNA of Russian boars, imported for hunting in the 1930s, had seasoned the stock, making them big, mean, and wily.

The result: as many as a million and a half feral hogs rampaging through Texas, growing as big as sofas, tearing up farmland and creek bottoms with their root-rooting snouts. They gobbled up baby lambs and caused car wrecks. They carried pseudorabies, swine brucellosis, tuberculosis, bubonic plague, tularemia, hog cholera, foot-and-mouth disease, kidney worms, stomach worms, liver flukes, trichinosis, roundworms, whipworms, dog ticks, fleas, hog lice, and anthrax. Their tusks were "razor sharp," the pamphlet said, and their gallop as fast as "lightning." Lest some shred of sympathy stay my hand from indiscriminate slaughter, the pamphlet threw in the lurid detail that feral sows had been known to eat their own young. No spirit-worshiping, tobacco-rubbing sanctimony here. By the time I finished reading about Texas feral hogs, I was drooling on my shirt and growling, "Lemme at 'em."

Until the early seventies, a banner hung over Stonewall Street in Casey Gunnels's hometown: WELCOME TO GREENVILLE. THE BLACKEST LAND, THE WHITEST PEOPLE.

"That's how it was," he said as he steered his car through town on the way to his grandpa's land. "I'm not sure if I remember seeing it with my own eyes, or if I just saw pictures and heard stories." Casey, a twenty-four-year-old high school Spanish teacher, was broad-shouldered, with a substantial belly he'd acquired in college and hadn't yet gotten around to losing. He had a round face, almond-shaped eyes, and spiky black hair. "People always ask me, 'You Asian?' I know there's Indian or a Mexican back there somewhere," he said. "That must be it."

Casey invited me down after we met through TexasHogHunter.com, and I figured that as we drove to his family's hunting cabin, he'd teach me tricks for finding wild swine. Instead he wanted to talk about the Church of Christ, in which he'd been raised, and detail the rigors of a faith that took the Bible literally. No alcohol, no instrumental music in church, and no church suppers—for didn't Paul ask in Corinthians 11:22, "What? have ye not houses to eat and drink in?"

"We'll have whiskey at the cabin, don't worry," he added with a quick laugh. "I believe the Bible forbids only drunkenness. It's full of references to wine."

He lapsed into a pained silence—it was his opinion about alcohol that had set off a recent swivet at church, and I got the impression that one reason he'd brought me down was to process it with someone from outside—an agnostic East Coast Jew seemed to fit that bill. The civil war at church had touched off when he taught his interpretation of the alcohol question to a Sunday school class. The congregation, already divided over whether God used the terms "thee" and "thou" when addressing mere humans, had blown up over Casey's apostasy. His parents, disgusted by the vitriol of the anti-Casey and pro-thee-and-thou factions, had decamped with half the congregation to another church, many miles away. Casey's wife, Megan, though—whom he'd known from church since they were four years old—wanted to stay put with *her* parents. Sundays were excruciating. I told him the joke about the lone Jew stranded for years on an island, whose rescuers can't understand why he'd built two synagogues. "That's the one I go to," he tells them. "And that's the one I *don't* go to." Casey laughed and laughed. "That may be the first Jewish joke I've ever understood," he said, wiping his eyes.

As Casey piloted the truck through the rolling East Texas country between Greenville and Cooper, he tried to play the redneck he figured I'd expected. He told me stories about dipping snuff, driving big trucks, and shooting guns, but his heart wasn't in it. The cantankerous intellectual in him kept rearing its head. The master's thesis on which he was working posited that football was ruining high school education in Texas, a topic that was likely to get him tarred and feathered. At a gas stop, he took off his jacket and rolled up his sleeve to reveal a big tattoo: NOT ALL WHO WANDER ARE LOST, from *Lord of the Rings.* And he kept bringing up Dante's *Inferno,* which he'd first discovered in ninth grade and devoured. "Being a hell-bound sinner is a big concept in the Church of Christ," he said.

Casey was a living, breathing exception to the rule laid out in the *Industry Reference Guide:* an enthusiastic young shooter unlikely to lose his firearms ardor. He'd fallen for guns when visiting his Uncle Charles in Amarillo as a little boy. He would disappear for hours into the attic, where he pored over fragrant and tattered back copies of the *American Rifleman, Shooting Times,* and *Guns & Ammo.* Even before he could read, he loved sitting cross-legged on the floor in his short pants, leafing through 1950s ads for Marlin rifles and Colt revolvers. Everything about the shooting world appealed to Casey long before his dad let him hold a gun. Firearms were for serious, virtuous, and technically competent adults of the type Casey wanted to be—like his dad. The men who smiled at him from the pages were rugged and wholesome. The accounts of hunting and target matches were stirring and cinematic. And the guns themselves, rendered in crisp black-and-white photos, were complex, elegant, and manly.

Dad kept a loaded five-shot .38 Smith & Wesson Chief's Special in the house. He showed little Casey where it was—on top of the bottom pair of blue jeans on Dad's closet shelf—and while Casey was forbidden to touch it on his own, he had only to tell Dad he wanted to look at it and Dad would stop what he was doing, unload it, and place it in Casey's small hands. If Casey wanted to shoot it, Dad would take him out behind the barn and let him knock cans off a fence. There was no fear attached to the gun, and no taboo. It was a piece of equipment, like the cream separator or the baler, and Dad was happy to have Casey know how to work it. He drew the line, though, at letting Casey join Grandpa in the ramshackle trailer he kept as a poor man's hunting cabin. It wasn't the guns that bothered him; it was the thought of Casey's young lungs cooped up in that little trailer with the thick miasma of cigarette smoke that followed Grandpa everywhere.

"Grandpa drove a truck for Safeway his whole life, and saved a little bit out of every paycheck to buy land. He had parcels all over," Casey said as he turned off the highway onto a long dirt road. When, at age eleven, Casey was finally allowed to join his grandpa on a deer hunt, it was like being baptized all over again. They stalked the woods as the sun rose and returned to the trailer for a big breakfast of bacon, eggs, biscuits, sausage gravy, and coffee, which they ate standing outside under a cottonwood. It was Casey's earliest lesson in what it meant to be a man in Texas: to lean your rifle against a tree at dawn and, in reverent silence, sop gravy from a tin plate with other men.

Casey received a Remington 870 shotgun for his twelfth birthday, then bought with his own money a sporterized 1891 Argentine army Mauser that he used to kill his first white-tailed deer the following year. He waited until ninth grade, though, to buy his first handgun: a stainless-steel Smith & Wesson 686 .357 Magnum revolver. He was too young to buy it himself, but Dad was willing to do the paperwork and buy the gun with Casey's savings—a violation of the "Don't Lie for the Other Guy" rule, but hell, this was Texas, and Casey was a responsible boy. Dad imposed no rules on Casey when he handed him the revolver. He didn't order him to lock it up or shoot it only under adult supervision. A man's guns were his own business, Dad believed, and caring for them safely was part of what it meant to be an adult in a free country. One day, a kid announced in class that he'd captured a wild hog, and the class decided to barbecue it. Casey brought his .357 to school in his backpack the next day to dispatch the pig, and though it was only a year after the Columbine High School massacre, in Colorado, it didn't occur to anybody to draw a connection. This was Greenville, Texas, after all—a million miles from places where teenagers misbehaved with guns.

Casey said he saw no contradiction between his love of guns and his love of Jesus. Portraying Jesus as a skinny little pussy was a lie, he felt; a first-century carpenter would have been a big, strong man accustomed to felling trees with an ax, splitting them with a hammer and wedge, and sawing them into boards by hand. Jesus understood the uses of violence; he'd chased the money changers from the temple with a whip, after all, and, according to the Gospel of Luke, he'd told his apostles to prepare to defend themselves. "He that hath no sword, let him sell his garment, and buy one." Turning the other cheek, Casey was convinced, didn't mean letting people beat you up; it meant moving into a defense posture.

The cabin stood in a clearing at the end of a muddy driveway—one room, with a sheet-metal roof and, inside, unfinished plywood walls. Casey lent me a lever-action .44 Magnum carbine that his grandpa had given him. It was no longer than my arm; it had a shockingly big bore; and its cartridges were as plump as baby carrots. He shouldered a scoped AR-15. "I'm trying this out," he said with a sheepish shrug. "I'm still not sure about these things."

As we stepped outside, Casey inhaled deeply. "Smell them?" he asked, waggling his fingers in front of his nose. "Nothing else smells like that." I smelled nothing.

The land around Grandpa's cabin was a lovely expanse of open oak-and-hackberry forest, but the trees were laced with thorny vines that tugged at clothing, at exposed skin, and, I feared, at the exposed triggers of firearms. We hadn't walked a hundred yards when four dark shapes sizzled through the fallen leaves to our left. My heart burst through the roof of my mouth. By the time I recovered, the monsters were gone.

Casey was in full stalk, crouched forward, gun up, urging me forward with commando hand gestures. He froze and passed me his rifle. "Use this one; they're about sixty yards out," he whispered. I raised the scope to my eye, but with all the foliage, I couldn't find the pigs.

"Come on, come on, *Jesus*!" he whispered as I feverishly tried to place crosshairs on swineflesh. The pigs vanished with nary a rustle. As I handed back the rifle, I expected Casey to unleash that vilest of Texas insults— *For Christ's sake, you're hunting like a middle-aged Jewish man from New Jersey!*—but he was a paragon of politesse. "Not a problem, not a problem. I just want to get you one."

The pigs may have vanished, but their handiwork was everywhere. Great swaths of forest looked stomped by giants, the earth so thoroughly churned that small trees had toppled. "They can tear up a ten-acre corn-field in a single night," Casey said. "They'll kill this forest if we let them. My grandmother's hiring a guy with a helicopter next week to come shoot as many as he can. Last year, he got twenty-four." He smiled, his round face lighting up like a little boy's. "I imagine it would take a very long time for *that* to get boring."

Casey jerked to a halt and pointed at a swishing stand of ragweed canes about fifty yards ahead. A sow and half a dozen hefty piglets emerged, sunlight glinting off their backs. "Nice blond one," Casey whispered, taking a knee. "I'm going to count 'one, two, three,' and we'll shoot on three." But there was a tree blocking my shot, and then a tree blocking his. We waited and waited, and finally I landed my sights on a tan flank. I pulled the trigger and up went a squealing like old truck brakes. Pigs exploded in every direction. Casey leapt to his feet, ejecting brass shells into the blue sky—*Bam! Bam! Bam! Bam!*—as a huge, shovel-faced black sow made the fatal mistake of dashing across a clearing to Casey's left. He followed her with his rifle and shot once. The sow shoulder-rolled beside a big oak and didn't move again.

All God's children got wings, but this one also had brush-bristle fur caked in mud and crawling with bugs, jagged three-inch tusks emerging from a ripply grimace of a mouth, and the aroma of a musk-and-feces milk shake.

Of the pig I'd shot, the only sign was a tablespoon of blood on crispy leaves. I began walking in outward concentric circles, searching. "They're not like deer," Casey said as he got down on one knee beside his pig. "They've got a layer of fat that seals up the wound and makes them hard to track." I kept at it, loath to let a wounded animal get away, while Casey did something that nobody I knew would dream of doing with a dead deer. He used his dead sow to test ammunition.

Standing over her, he shot several bullets into her flank, then several more, of various types. "Nice," I heard him say as he dug with a knife through the meat of her hip. "That cheap Russian hollow-point fragmented like I wanted her to!"

I was relieved to find my pig, a young male three feet long, about a hundred yards away, dead of a lung shot. He was proportioned like a smallmouth bass—about one-quarter head—and heavy as a sack of Quikrete. Casey estimated he was two months old. I'd have gutted, skinned, and hauled him out, but Casey said not to bother. "If you want meat," he said, "just take the backstraps."

I opened the piglet's hide like a valise and sliced out the backstraps—the tender fillets that run along the spine. I didn't enjoy the feeling. Where I came from, a carcass stripped only of backstraps was the work of a poacher.

All million and a half of Texas's pigs lived within a mile radius of us, it seemed. As I packed up the fillet meat in a Ziploc bag, another clan came crashing out of the brush in a long line. Accustomed to quiet stalking and single-shot placement, I was amazed to see Casey take off after them at full tilt, firing into the underbrush as he ran. I caught up with him as, panting, he drew his pistol on a writhing pig. "I'm wasted on cross-country!" he laughed, quoting Gimli from *Lord of the Rings*. "We dwarves are natural sprinters, very dangerous over short distances!" He leaned over and casually shot the pig between the ears.

I looked back as we walked away. The pig lay on its belly, looking comfortably asleep. Leaving a dead animal unprocessed: again, a strange feeling. We ran into another hog family down by the creek, and Casey killed two more before I could even raise my carbine to my cheek.

For about ten minutes, I stalked a deep rustling in the brush, until a foot-long armadillo came waddling out, laughing at me. Then a big sow materialized from nowhere and, for once quicker on the drop than Casey, I took a shot and seemed to hit her; after some squealing and scuffling in the scrub, a deep moaning echoed through the woods. It was late now; the sun filtering through the oaks made long, spooky shadows. I couldn't place the direction of the moaning, and as I crisscrossed the area, it stopped. Casey called to me to come on—there was one more spot he wanted to try before we lost the light.

My every impulse was to keep searching, with a flashlight if necessary. The worst thing a hunter could do, according to the hunting ethic I'd learned, was lose a wounded animal: It was cruel, it wasted meat, and it messed up game management, because no tag went on the kill. But, good Sunday school teacher that he was, Casey explained patiently and repeatedly: "That's not what we're about here." To reinforce his point, he pulled me from the woods into a pasture thoroughly bulldozed by hogs. If it had been my pasture, I'd have wanted the hogs dead, too.

"It's primal; we like to kill things," Casey said of our species as we headed back to his cabin in the gloom. "You got to be careful how you say it, but it's true. It doesn't make us sick. It's just the way we are. The reason I like pig hunting is, I get to kill a lot of pigs. It's the distilled essence of the thing. If you told someone you went out and killed seven deer and let them lie there, they'd put you in jail. You tell them you killed and let lie seven pigs, they're like, *'Badass!'*"

My mistake may have been to think of Texas pig hunting on the same spectrum as Georgia or Montana deer hunting. All of the outward elements were there—tramping the woods with a gun, figuring out the nature of the quarry, reading sign, and of course the shooting and the blood. I'd started hunting because of the gun, but I realized with Casey that my reasons for loving the hunt had changed. For me, the shooting and the killing were no longer, as Casey would say, "the distilled essence of the thing." I still loved being in the woods with a rifle in my hands. But for me, hunting was more about the unworldly relationship with one special animal that gives himself over in return for the care you've taken to understand him and his habitat. Then his flesh becomes your flesh, sealing the bond.

At the same time, though, I couldn't find anything wrongheaded or immoral about the way Casey hunted pigs. Through carelessness, people had created the problem of the feral hog, and now it was up to people to ameliorate it. To focus on the cruelty of shooting individual pigs, when we were ruining habitat and causing extinctions from the Arctic to the Great Barrier Reef, seemed a little silly. And a state dependent on agriculture couldn't afford an overpopulation of flesh-and-blood bulldozers. Somebody had to kill them, and it made more sense to let sportsmen pay and enjoy it than to spend public dollars to have rangers cull the herd, as Rocky Mountain National Park had done recently to manage an oversupply of elk (to the outrage of Colorado hunters). The pity in Texas was that tons of useful protein—local, free-range, organic, lean pork—rotted in the woods because a raft of laws banned the selling of wild meat.

Gunning down Texas pigs with Casey was, in the end, a gas—the greatest moving-target shooting I'd ever done, even if it wasn't, for me, *hunting*. It was more like football—our team against theirs, with a score posted at day's end.

We walked on, doubling back past the spot where I'd lost my sow. A sinister rustling came from our right, and a dozen buzzards rose heavily into the treetops like a panel of black-robed judges. "They found your pig," Casey said. "You can stop worrying about it now."

16. THE ARMED BONEHEAD

Note the relationship between the words casual and casualty.

—Posted on a NorthwestFirearms.com forum by Deavis

Christ almighty, the noise in the Benoit house as the kids got ready for school! Imagine four huge boys—Jackie, Robert, Paul, and Peter—tumbling out of bunk beds in their tiny room, clawing their way into clothes, and fighting to make it first down the narrow hall to the single bathroom. Then the girls, Jean and Judy, too young for school, jostled out of sleep by the tumult, standing in their cribs in the next room, loudly demanding their share of attention. Lucky for everybody, Dad was at his post office job before they all woke, leaving nothing but the smell of his cigarettes lingering in the family's four rented rooms. He couldn't stand too much noise, and his temper wouldn't have done anyone good at seven in the morning. Somehow, with a baby on her hip and another yelling from a high chair, Mom would churn out enough pancakes to stoke the boys, and off they'd thunder to Fletcher Elementary School, smack between MIT and Harvard but culturally a million miles from either.

Cambridge in the 1960s was a rough-knuckled town full of undersupervised kids. By neighborhood standards, Peter was a pretty good boy. He helped out with the cooking, hauled the family laundry to the coin-op up the street, and accompanied his mom to Irish dances above the police station. Sure, he cut school sometimes, broke a few windows playing stickball, but it wasn't like he was getting picked up for shoplifting. Somehow, though, Dad had it in for Peter special, and he was quick with the strap. Even after Peter was hit by a car walking home from the Laundromat and was hobbling around in a cast, Dad didn't let up. Peter suspected that Dad was toughest on him because he was the littlest boy; the bigger boys wouldn't have stood for it. Benoits could be tough bastards.

It wasn't that Dad was a drunk, or even particularly mean. He was just an old-school Catholic who demanded things his way, like a lot of the hardworking dads in Cambridge. He'd fought in the Battle of the Bulge and, along with bits of German shrapnel buried in his body, had a pile of German guns and bayonets in the back of a closet. He'd shown them to Peter a couple of times, but, at precisely the moment the boys got big enough to find weapons interesting, Dad sold them. Cambridge didn't need the Benoit boys running around with a bunch of Lugers and Hitler Youth knives.

Although Peter was a minor track star in high school and got A's and B's, nobody talked to him about college—not his parents, not his teachers, not his guidance counselors. At Rindge Technical High School, victory amounted to getting a diploma and finding a job. Peter majored in auto repair, did a stint in the Marines, and came home to the neighborhood at loose ends.

The summer of 1980 was hot and dreamy. Peter hung out with his friends listening to Bob Seger, Van Halen, and Pink Floyd's *The Wall*; going to see *The Shining* and *The Empire Strikes Back*. He was in a car wreck a couple of days before his twenty-first birthday, and his brother Robert cheered him up by finding a girl he thought Peter might like. He put a piece of paper in Peter's hand with her name and address. "I met her over on Beacon. Happy birthday." Peter had two black eyes from the wreck and looked like a raccoon, but he thought, *What the hell*. Robert didn't often turn him on to girls; this one must be something. He walked over to meet her, delighted to find that her house lay in the morning shadow of Fenway Park. She stood out front, talking to an old man; she was tall, with wild reddish hair that stood up all over the place. She wore some kind of ankle-length tie-dyed muumuu and looked a little like Janis Joplin, truth be told, which ordinarily wouldn't have been Peter's thing, but something about her drew him across the street and into a conversation, and within two minutes Peter knew this girl was for him. She seemed to know it, too—he could tell by her eyes and the deep, comfortable register of her voice. Monica, her name was; Peter moved in with her that night.

He had never known anything like their immediate, intimate romance. It was as though they'd been looking for each other for years without knowing it. Everything about being together was easy and pleasant; he wondered sometimes if they'd known each other in a prior life. And such an admirable person, holding down three different restaurant jobs—a breakfast place in Faneuil Hall, a lunch place in Kenmore Square, and a dinner shift at the Teak House, in Brookline. On top of everything else, Peter ate well.

Monica had endless energy. A bicycle trip up the coast of California? Who'd ever think of such a thing? But it was cool. They rode their bikes up Highway 1 to San Francisco, eating from the boxes of vegetables that farm trucks dropped along the way and making love in that magical Pacific fog.

Back in Boston, Monica came up with another of her wild ideas. *Let's move to New Orleans; it'll be fun.* Peter thought, *What the hell.* Boston winters were getting old. So off they went, Monica finding no end of restaurant work and Peter laying carpet, earning enough to buy a splintery house on St. Roch Avenue for $36,000. Peter loved New Orleans—the food, the music, the booze, the easygoing fuck-up lifestyle. He didn't have to worry about his working-class Boston Catholic accent, because white working-class New Orleanians had a meaty Irish-tinged accent a lot more like his than like characters in *Gone with the Wind*. The only weird thing was having to change how he said his last name. He'd always pronounced his name Ben-*noyt*. When he'd spell it in New Orleans, though, people would say, "Oh! Ben-*wah*!" So that's how he started saying it—a new place, a new life, a new name.

Monica had enough energy at the end of her restaurant shifts to work with Peter, cleaning the carpets he laid. It was a nice domestic life—maybe too domestic for a Benoit boy newly transplanted to the City That Care Forgot. In 1987, Monica invited him on another bicycle trip, through Italy to visit her relatives, and Peter said, *Nah, you go. I'll stay here and keep the money coming.* The minute he put her on the plane, he bought a motorcycle from a tattooed drifter at a wacky three-house commune on Mandeville Street, and while making the transaction, caught the eye of a cute black-haired girl who called herself Kalisch. When Monica got back in September, she took one look at him with his new motorcycle, tattoo, mustache, and that black-haired girl hanging on him and she was out of there. The love of Peter's life: gone.

Without Monica, Peter spent the next two years wallowing in the hippie and biker scenes, hanging at the commune on Mandeville, getting drunk or high, and grooving on an endless parade of colorful drifters. He hung a lot with a big, tough biker named Greg who was the walking embodiment of the bad boy Peter imagined himself to be; Greg wore a leather motorcycle jacket, inhaled beers by the can, and seemed ready at any moment to tear somebody in half. It was fun, and shit, man, he was about to turn thirty, so why not have a little fun? Pretty soon he'd have to settle down anyway: Kalisch was pregnant.

One of the crazy dudes from the commune, Harold, came up with a funny idea one weekend in 1988: *Let's drive to the Metairie gun show!* Guns didn't interest Peter much, but the show would be amusing. They piled into Harold's old car and toked up as they trundled along Veterans Highway. At the show, they grooved on the old fat white guys drooling over firearms. It was a riot. Trolling the tables, Peter spotted a neat little .38 revolver with a seventy-five-dollar price tag. He stopped and picked it up. It felt good in his hand. "Fifty dollars out the door," the old man behind the table said, and Peter thought, *What the hell.* Lots of bad shit was happening in New Orleans. He was going to have a family to protect. A gun might be a good thing to have around. He laid his money down, and the man asked if he needed ammo.

"Sure."

"Plus-P? Hollow-point? Full metal jacket?" He gestured toward a stack of colorful boxes.

"Whatever's cheapest," Peter said.

The vendor threw in a little zippered case.

Harold thought it was hysterical: Peter Benoit buying a gun. And when Peter took it home and showed it to Kalisch, she giggled, too. A gun! He loaded it, then thought, *No, I'll be safe.* He pulled out one cartridge—the one that would move under the firing pin when the cylinder rolled clockwise. That way, if one of their drunk or stoned friends picked up the gun and pulled the trigger, that empty *click* would give him a chance to think twice. He zipped the gun into its case, put it in the top dresser drawer, and forgot all about it.

Kalisch delivered Callan, a healthy boy, on Peter's thirtieth birthday, in 1989. It didn't much slow them down. Callan slept most of the time, and he didn't seem to mind the rock and roll, the rumble of motorcycles revving, or the heavy musk of incense and weed. But something was changing between Peter and Kalisch. They bickered, and grew more distant. Peter started wondering whether they'd make it, or whether he'd be one of those guys who never sees his kid. On November 29, they put five-month-old Callan to bed and had a few drinks. Peter did a couple of lines of coke, but they were both in a bitchy mood and argued. They went to bed and lay back to back, quietly seething. Peter, never one to hold a grudge long, started drifting off to sleep. But then the bed moved, and he realized Kalisch was up. He heard her moving in the dark, heard the top drawer open, heard the sound of a zipper. *Fuck,* he thought. *She's getting the gun.* He threw off the covers, walked across the rolling wooden floor, and turned on a light. Sure enough, Kalisch was standing next to the open dresser drawer, the revolver in her hand. He threw out his arms and thrust out his chest. "What are you going to do, shoot me?"

She swiveled toward him.

He saw the tips of the bullets in the open ends of the cylinder, and as her finger tightened, he watched the cylinder start to turn. *All right,* he thought. *The first chamber is empty. We'll have a good laugh.* But . . . what? The cylinder wasn't rolling clockwise; it was rolling counterclockwise.

I first met Peter in New Orleans almost sixteen years later, on August 31, 2005, two days after Hurricane Katrina. Four times, as I'd walked through the oak-strewn Garden District covering the disaster, I'd encountered white people with guns. They seemed frozen in a kind of apocalyptic panic, as though all the wrongs committed by white folks since the time of the Middle Passage were going to be paid back on that day.

This was long before I'd gotten a concealed-carry permit, but on the way in, my ears full of dire—and false—reports of violence in New Orleans, I'd asked a friend in Baton Rouge if he thought it was a good idea to borrow one of his guns before plunging into the disaster zone. He'd just chuckled. "They have lost everything in that city," he drawled. "But they *will* find a jail cell for a Yankee reporter with a gun."

Thousands of people were gathering at the Convention Center, which was up on the river levee and unflooded. I bought a bicycle someone was shedding as he evacuated and pedaled through the dry part of the Ninth Ward. At the corner of Burgundy Street and St. Roch, a man in a wheelchair sat blinking in the murky sunlight. He had wide-spaced eyes that turned down at the corners, giving his face a sad, contemplative cast. I introduced myself, and he asked where I was from before giving his last name. "Good," he said. "With you I don't have to say Ben-*wah*."

I joked that he was the first unarmed white man I'd encountered all day. "I won't touch them," he said. "It was a gun put me in this chair." We wandered around together for an hour, I on my bike and he using the heels of knotted-up hands to push his chair along. Then he rolled off in his direction, and I in mine.

When Kalisch's bullet hit him, Peter went down like a dropped marionette. He never lost consciousness, though. Kalisch stood there looking at him. At least she didn't raise the gun and shoot him again.

"Call 911," Peter said, and someone must have, because a while later—it seemed a very long time—the police came in. Lying on the floor, Peter could feel a cold draft that told him they'd left the front door open. They didn't seem to be in much of a hurry, and they were surly. "They got a baby, and feel how cold it is in here," one said. "Let's take the baby." Peter tried to say, "Hey, you left the door open. That's why it's cold." By then, though, he wasn't able to speak.

Though he could see his legs stretched out, they felt odd, as though they were doubled up under him. It was painful. "Straighten my legs," he tried to say. "Straighten my legs."

It was at Charity Hospital that Peter gradually came to understand that his walking life was over, that there would be no more bicycle trips up the California coast. As doctors and nurses raced around frantically, he kept hearing the words "cervical," and "cord," and "no response." Then he looked past the nurses and saw big, tough Greg from Mandeville Street standing in his leather jacket, crying wetly. That was when Peter knew he was fucked.

"You're lucky," the nurses told him when they got him into a ward bed after hours in the ER. "You're a C7; you'll have your hands." He could move his arms, but the hands were curled up. They'd be usable, but not for any finer work than picking up a fork between the flat of his thumb and the side of his palm. He lay in his charity bed and sobbed. If only he hadn't met Kalisch. If only he hadn't thrown away Monica's love. If only he hadn't bought that fucking gun.

At first he thought the only silver lining was that he'd bought cheap ammunition. Had he bought something more powerful, he'd be dead. They eventually drilled holes in his skull, fitted him with a steel halo to immobilize his head, and carted him over to rehab. The skin on his hips broke down from bedsores, and he lay there in his own stink, immobile, penniless, and lost. He had to have skin grafts to heal the bedsores, and he endured repeated operations until the grafts took. He found himself wishing he'd bought the better ammunition after all.

Then one day he looked up, and there stood Monica.

"It's not like I took him back right away," Monica said in a deep Boston accent as she dug her spoon into Peter's macaroni and cheese. We were having lunch at the Cafe Reconcile, on Oretha Castle Haley Boulevard in New Orleans; I'd driven here to meet them after hog hunting with Casey Gunnels. Monica had stopped in to the restaurant "for a minute" as she sped from one home-health-care job to another. She didn't have time to order her own lunch, only enough to eat Peter's. He smiled and slid his plate a little closer to her.

Monica was bigger than I expected, attractive and at the same time mannish in the way she held her shoulders and moved her hands. Her hair was straight and dark red, and her smile was so wide, it seemed to extend beyond the line of her cheeks.

"He went back to Kalisch!" she said with a laugh, around a mouthful of mac and cheese.

"Kalisch didn't go to prison?"

"Nah," Peter said, flapping one of his crumpled hands. "She went to jail for a couple of days, but I dropped the charges. The nurses thought I was crazy." He smiled ruefully.

I was starting to think maybe the sadness in his face had predated the injury—a product of his hard-knocks Cambridge upbringing. Or maybe it was just the shape of his face. Either way, despite his obvious delight in the way things had turned out, he never lost that sad, knowing cast—even when smiling.

"I thought Kalisch and I would go home and live happily ever after," Peter was saying. "And we had Callan. I thought, if Kalisch goes to jail, maybe Callan ends up a ward of the state; maybe he gets sent to some abusive foster home."

Monica lofted her eyebrows and nodded as though to admit that she approved—as though to say she'd have loved to see Kalisch punished but that the best thing wasn't necessarily the obvious thing.

"We go back to the commune," Peter said. "Nobody made a big deal about my being shot and paralyzed; it was like, *That kind of thing happens.* These were motorcycle people, remember. They got racked up all the time. For Callan's sake, Kalisch stopped smoking and drinking and started eating right. But I think she realized, *Well, Peter is disabled now, he can't do stuff, things are different.* She started going out, leaving me and Callan sitting there looking at each other. I did the Irish Catholic thing, like my mother would have: Don't say anything and maybe everything will work out. But I was really depressed. Charity gives you a handful of diapers and Valium and says, 'See you later.' I wasn't taught how to take care of myself properly, how to keep myself clean. I wasn't practicing nutrition.

"I got sick. I was sweating, with chills, huddling over the space heater. My brother Paul came up from Atlanta and took me to the hospital. They took one look at me and said, 'He ain't leaving; he's going into isolation.' I had TB. I probably got it from one of the people passing through the commune."

The Cafe Reconcile was created to give at-risk teenagers a chance to learn how to work in a restaurant, and a six-month internship was a treasured opportunity. Our cornrowed waiter, a hulking young man in a red Cafe Reconcile T-shirt, loomed over our table and told us, with great solemnity, that Bananas Foster Bread Pudding was on the menu. Peter and Monica locked eyes for a second. "We'll take one, with two spoons," Monica said.

"It was when Peter was sick that I got back in the picture," Monica said, reaching across the table and taking his twisted hand.

Monica moved him to her house and got him set up with proper home care. She got him involved in wheelchair rugby, which helped him recover physical and mental strength. And she supported him through a college degree and helped him develop a carpentry career.

I asked Peter whether Kalisch had ever apologized.

"She said once that she wasn't in her right mind," Peter answered. "And three years after, she said, 'It's unfortunate.' Not 'I'm sorry,' just 'It's *unfortunate.*'"

"He bought me a little diamond ring," Monica purred. "I asked him, 'What is this, honey?' and he said, 'Uh, uh, uh, it's a, uh, friendship ring.'" She laughed a deep, satisfied laugh. "When commercials come on for diamond rings now—showing those lovey-dovey couples?—Peter laughs and says, 'I guess other people know what a diamond ring means.'"

Peter's story was a catalog of arguments for gun control: loosey-goosey rules at a gun show, the casual purchase of a handgun without learning how it worked, and a loaded gun tossed unsecured into a dresser drawer.

Closing the gun-show loophole wouldn't necessarily have saved him; his record was clean. But had he been required to get in line at the gun show for a background check, pay an additional ten dollars, and wait around until the results came back, he might have said *to hell with it* and walked off into a sunnier future.

A lot of gun guys would say that was precisely what the endless parade of nitpicking new regulations was intended to do: not weed out criminals, but discourage law-abiding people from buying guns, like driving people away from cigarettes by making them stand outside in the rain to smoke. And for every Peter Benoit, who would have been better off without a gun, they'd point to someone who was raped and murdered in her apartment because she either couldn't get a gun or was daunted by the bureaucratic hoops through which she'd have had to jump.

But the story of Kalisch shooting Peter pointed to another, more pervasive problem with how Americans thought about gun violence. Gun-control advocates liked to speak of "keeping guns out of the hands of criminals." Those who favored gun rights talked of protecting themselves from "criminals" and of punishing "criminals" harder to discourage them and get them off the street. You'd have thought that "criminals" were a distinct community, like pilots or bus drivers, a card-carrying profession whose members could be identified by their striped shirts, Lone Ranger masks, and newsboy caps. But a lot of shootings were just like Peter's or Brandon Franklin's—done by people who were law-abiding until the moment they picked up the gun.

Lots could have been done to make such shootings less likely. The problem was that both sides of the "gun debate" could think no further than what government might do—gun controllers calling for more restrictive laws, and gun guys gnashing their teeth over same. As the two sides bickered, people continued to die. Meanwhile, steps that might actually have reduced shooting deaths and injuries wouldn't have involved government at all.

As *individuals,* the majority of gun guys were achingly responsible with their guns. They locked them up, kept them clean, practiced with them, and obeyed the Five Cardinal Rules about treating guns as loaded and keeping them pointed in a safe direction. As a *community,* though, gun guys were lethal—so focused on how "criminals" and government were the villains that they had forgotten to examine how they, who knew guns better than anybody, might have helped reduce the number of people killed and injured by them.

The wrongest of wrong hands weren't necessarily those of "criminals" but of curious children and depressed teenagers. If it seemed like every other week the nation learned of a little kid accidentally shooting himself or a playmate, it was because it happened somewhere in America about that often, and everybody in the cable-television-and-Internet-connected country heard about it. The chance of a kid dying by gunfire was one in a million, but in a country with forty million children under age ten, that was a lot of dead kids. Accidental child death was one of the few gun statistics that had grown worse since 1999. Teenage gun suicide was a lot lower than it had been in 1999, but still high. Almost half the teenagers who killed themselves in 2007 did so with a gun, and, unlike those who tried it with pills, car exhaust, razor blades, or a rope, those who attempted suicide with a gun almost always succeeded.

Where were those children and teenagers getting the guns? Not from gun stores—the minimum age to buy a long gun was eighteen, and twenty-one for a handgun. Not from gun shows, either, unless they were getting an adult to buy them. And not from some murky "illegal gun market." They were getting them, by and large, from their parents, who left them around, loaded, where immature hands could find them.

The same went for criminals. In the mid-1980s, a pair of sociologists surveyed almost two thousand violent felons in prison about their gun lives. Almost half the guns that the felons described having used were stolen. Add to that the ones they thought were "probably" stolen, and it jumped to 70 percent. Most were stolen from households. At the time I was writing this, an estimated half a million guns a year went missing one way or the other.

To the legislatures of twenty-seven states and the District of Columbia, the solution to both problems seemed obvious: pass laws that required guns either to be stored separate from their ammunition, locked up, trigger-locked, or some combination of the three. A lot of gun guys hated those laws. They argued that a gun that was separated from its ammunition, disabled, or locked away was useless if needed in a hurry.

Not true. I kept my handgun loaded in the bedroom, in a metal safe the size of a toaster that popped open the second I punched in a three-button code. I bought it on eBay for twenty-five dollars. It solved both problems. The gun was secure, but instantly available to me alone. A lot of gun guys used such safes. They just didn't want to be *ordered* to use them.

Neither did a lot of gun guys want to be ordered to report a stolen gun to the police. In 2012, the Judiciary Committee of the Pennsylvania House of Representatives voted to penalize any town that required gun owners to report stolen firearms to the police. Other states had likewise succumbed to pressure from gun guys, who considered it tyranny to have to tell the police anything about their guns. Only seven states and the District of Columbia made reporting a stolen gun mandatory.

The real question was: If gun guys were the paragons of civic virtue that they claimed to be, why did they have to be *ordered* to lock up their guns or report a gun theft to the police? Wouldn't a responsible citizen have done so anyway? Gun guys were operating under a double standard. They wanted to be left alone to buy, use, and carry guns because, they said, they understood firearms better than any bureaucrat. But at the same time, enough of them behaved so carelessly that thousands of people were needlessly killed, injured, or victimized every year by guns left lying around.

Was a gun guy who kept his guns properly secured responsible for some knucklehead who didn't? If the NRA was consistent in its logic, the answer was yes. Solidarity was a constant theme of the NRA, whose e-mails, mailings, and magazines exhorted members to support the community of gun owners by writing to their representatives about gun-related legislation, voting out anti-gun legislators, and voting in those who were pro-gun. But that's where service to the community ended. For the NRA to have suggested that law-abiding gun owners take responsibility for the cads would have shattered the notion that "criminals" were a separate class. So while the NRA trained people in gun safety and published books about gun care, it—like every other gun-rights group—avoided drawing a connection between the carelessness of law-abiding gun owners and America's still high rate of needless gun death.

What could the NRA and the community of responsible gun owners have done to reduce gun deaths without government intervention? They could have made irresponsible behavior socially unacceptable, just as it had become unthinkable, among most Americans, to smoke inside another person's house, say words like "nigger," or make lascivious comments about underage girls. It would have taken time, but it could have been done, and some were trying. Robert Farago, who wrote a funny and popular gun blog called *The Truth About Guns,* ran a regular feature called "Irresponsible Gun Owner of the Day"—often a YouTube video of some young man acting stupid or a news item about a needless tragedy. After Arizona instituted "constitutional carry"—allowing any adult to carry a concealed gun with no training or permit—a group called TrainMeAZ.com organized to exhort citizens to get trained and to help them find trainers. Farago and TrainMeAZ, though, were lonely voices. The big dog, the NRA, had for decades run a monthly feature in its magazines called "The Armed Citizen," about people successfully defending themselves with firearms. Had it called its members to a higher standard of responsibility with a complementary column called, say, "The Armed Bonehead," it would have reached millions more people than either Farago or TrainMeAZ. Most of all, I enjoyed imagining how gun culture could have changed—and lives could have been saved—if, say, gun guys refused to hang out or go shooting with those who left loaded guns lying around their houses. "Sorry, dude. I'm not shooting with you until you clean up your act." Or if gun guys refused to shop at a gun store that sold home-defense handguns without insisting that buyers also take electronic safes to keep them in. Little by little, shooters and gun stores would have gotten the message, and the problem of unsecured guns—the main source of gun tragedy—would have withered away. Government would have been out of the picture, so there would have been nothing to resent and nothing to fight about. Both sides would have gotten what they said they wanted.

Gun guys were right to object to government officials who proposed bans without understanding what they were banning. But until they took responsibility for the gun violence that continued to frighten and desolate their fellow Americans, they were setting themselves up for more of it. Taking collective responsibility for social problems is not the same thing as knuckling under to a tyrannical government. In fact, it's the exact opposite.

It felt pretty weird talking to Peter Benoit, the bullet pock still visible on his throat, with a loaded revolver under my clothes. But then, as I'd discovered a few months earlier at Brandon's funeral, everything about wearing a gun in New Orleans was complicated. I loved the city, but hideous things happened to people even in "good" parts of town. It was one of the few places on my gun-guy walkabout where I was glad I was licensed to carry a gun.

At the same time, carrying made me feel guilty. Perhaps because of the violence in their streets and the levee disaster in their recent past, New Orleanians had developed a culture of sweetness and tenderness toward one another that was unlike anything I'd seen elsewhere. It was a kind of hippie aesthetic—the easygoing, huggy closeness of a big mourning family. A musician friend, Paul Sanchez, had painted on the front of his guitar THIS MACHINE SURROUNDS SADNESS AND FORCES IT TO SURRENDER. When I saw that, all I could think was: The machine under my jacket *creates* sadness. To be carrying around the device that had wreaked so much horror on the people of New Orleans felt like betrayal. Even if it made me feel safer, it made me lonely. The gun had lowered a screen between me and the people I loved. It made me careful how I hugged. It made it hard to take off my jacket in a hot restaurant. It made me feel like a traitor to all that New Orleanians were trying to accomplish. The thought of having to send more bullets whizzing through its fragrant, damp air was almost unbearable.

I left Peter Benoit in the early evening and wandered over to listen to the Jazz Vipers at the Spotted Cat. Standing outside with some friends was Tommy Malone, lead guitarist of the Subdudes. We talked awhile, and when I said I was headed to a bar in an especially rough neighborhood, Malone said, "Whoa. Got a pistol?"

"I do," I replied, and everybody laughed.

17. DEAD AGAIN

It's not always being fast or even accurate that counts. It's being *willing*.

–John Wayne, in his last film, *The Shootist*, 1976

’d been wearing either my Colt or my Smith & Wesson .38 everywhere I could legally do so, and the thrill was wearing off. I no longer felt like James Bond. For most of the day, the gun was an uncomfortable lump of metal jammed between my waistband and my love handle or a paperweight dragging on my right front pocket. Had I been spending more time in New Orleans, I might have seen it differently, but you feel pretty dumb walking around Minot, North Dakota, or Boulder, Colorado, armed to kill.

One aspect of the gun life still pleased me: The rituals of safety slowed me down. I couldn't rush out of the house wearing a gun as I had when my only accessories were a cell phone and sunglasses. I enjoyed getting the gun out of the electronic safe, checking it to make sure it was loaded and functioning, and tucking it away. Out on the street, I felt vigilant, aloof from petty animosities: a modest equal to death. After practice at the range, I liked gingerly unloading the gun, laying the cartridges in a bowl, swabbing out the barrel and chambers, applying a thin sheen of oil. All that satisfaction, for the four-hundred-dollar price of a revolver.

But I was also increasingly aware of my inadequacies. I could punch holes in paper pretty well and handle a gun safely on the street as long as I didn't actually need it. But in the event of a shoot-out with a bad guy, I was not likely to prevail. Could I draw and fire accurately into the flesh of a fellow human being while ducking for cover from whizzing bullets? No way. And if not, why was I carrying?

When I complained to other gun carriers that the classes I'd attended to get the permit had been a joke, they urged me to get more training. The country was full of shooting instructors, from freelancers like Rick Ector, in Detroit, to the 2,000-acre Gunsite Academy, in Arizona, which Jeff Cooper founded and which advertised a fifteen-hundred-dollar, five-day pistol course and a chance to shoot more than a thousand rounds of ammunition at stationary and moving targets, indoors and out.

The company that I finally chose, American Shooters, was housed in a gigantic gray concrete cube of a building on Arville Street, in Las Vegas, about a mile west of the Strip. I signed up for a daylong course, "Defensive Pistol," and showed up at 8:30 a.m. on a sparkling Tuesday.

The facility was a shooter's heaven—not only lots of shooting lanes but a big store and a rental counter stocked with every pistol, rifle, shotgun, and submachine gun one would ever want to sample. The clerks, all dressed in identical golf shirts, showed me into a windowless cinder-block classroom, where two other pupils were already waiting.

I wasn't wearing my gun. Nevada doesn't honor a Colorado permit, and the instructors had asked me to bring it unloaded, in a bag. The other guys had their range bags out on their tiny school desks. I took a seat and introduced myself.

Reid, a professional baseball player, was slim and fit. Tom, a Mercedes dealer, was strong and stocky. Both were surprisingly taciturn. Like the people in my concealed-carry class, they seemed embarrassed to be there. "You actually going to carry?" I asked them. *Probably not,* they both said. "I want to know what I'm doing in case I do," mumbled Reid. Tom dragged his eyes from his smartphone for a second. "I just bought it," he said distractedly. "All I want is to know how to use it."

The door banged open, and Jack Hawley strode in, trim and muscular, looking as though he was about to bust out in a dance number. He had icy-bright blue eyes, raptor features, and a shaven head under a beige ball cap. He was dressed for combat: desert combat boots, desert-camo cargo pants, a desert-tan T-shirt over his washboard belly, and a Beretta nine-millimeter semi-automatic in a black duty holster. Like those camp counselors who had terrified me when I was five, Hawley was all man, and it was our job to live up to him.

"This class is about *how* to use a pistol in a gunfight," he announced.

"We assume you know the *when*—that you learned your legal, financial, ethical, and moral responsibilities in your concealed-carry class. Let me start by saying that the best way to win a gunfight—really the *only* way to win a gunfight—is not to be there when it happens. You got that? Your best move, always, is to retreat. Run away." He raked us with those icy blue eyes. "This class is about what to do once you've decided you cannot retreat and you must take the gun from the holster and fire it."

Hawley was now the third gun teacher to tell me that the best strategy in a life-or-death situation was retreat. Gun guys always said the same thing; even the bloggers did. Yet the gun community, led by the NRA, had pressed hard for "stand your ground" and "castle doctrine," laws that said a person has no legal duty to retreat from a dangerous situation if he is in a place he is allowed to be. Almost half the states had some form of stand-your-ground law, including Illinois, the last state to forbid carry permits under any circumstances. Gun-guy logic, I suppose, was this: It's a *good idea* to retreat, but the state has no business telling you that you must.*

Hawley planted his fists on his hips. "I am going to teach you how to fight with a gun. And it's a *fight.* If you're taking your gun from your holster, somebody is going to die. We don't want it to be you." He looked around, as though daring us to ask a question on *that* topic.

"The world is dangerous," he said loudly. "Carry a gun; two is better. Carry extra ammo; more is better. Carry a light; two is better."

I raised my hand. "That's a lot of weight."

"Less than a coffin," he said.

"I can understand a policeman carrying two guns or extra ammunition. But do you really think people like us need to?"

Fixing me with those sky-blue eyes, he pulled his gun, pressed the magazine release, and caught the empty magazine in midair. "The magazine is the component of the firearm most likely to malfunction," he said, holding it high. "You may not need the extra rounds, but if your magazine malfunctions and you don't have a replacement, you will die."

"I carry a revolver."

---

* The nation got a lesson in stand-your-ground law in March 2012, when a twenty-eight-year-old neighborhood-watch volunteer in Florida named George Zimmerman shot dead an unarmed seventeen-year-old black boy named Trayvon Martin and was not initially arrested because the local police chief insisted that Zimmerman was protected by Florida's stand-your-ground law.

"Five shots?"

"I'm told most gunfights are over in a second, with at most two or three shots fired."

"That's true," he said, reholstering his gun. "*Most* gunfights. What if *your* gunfight isn't that way? What if *your* gunfight goes on awhile and you run out of ammunition in the middle of it? I'll tell you what happens: You die. You and the people you're with."

He smiled, his blue eyes changing from drill-sergeant tough to school-teacher kind. He wasn't a hard-ass; it was all an act. "I'm just sayin' . . ." He snapped back into drill-sergeant mode.

"You perform differently under stress. You engage your five-million-year-old lizard brain when someone is trying to kill you. You dump adrenaline. The blood is gone from your hands, and they go numb. Your ears shut off. You get tunnel vision. And it all happens instantly."

He led us down a hallway to a deserted indoor range. Directly in front of us were the shooting bays: little booths from which one shot toward a target. He opened a shooting bay—normally an alarming transgression—and led us through, down to where the bullets usually fly.

It was eerie walking down that gloomy cement cavern, looking back at where the shooters normally stand. We gathered at the end, and Jack repeated aloud the Five Cardinal Rules. "Treat every gun as though it's loaded! Never let your muzzle cross anything you're not willing to destroy and pay for! Keep your finger off the trigger until your sights are on the target and you're ready to fire! Be sure of your target and what's beyond it! Maintain control of your firearm!

"They apply to everybody, everywhere, all the time!" he shouted. "Four-man entry team in Fallujah, jungles of Vietnam, here on the range, or in your family room. The five rules *always apply.*"

He hung a target for each of us—a life-size man silhouette with a six-inch circle over the chest, two-inch circles on the hips, and an inverted triangle on the face. "This is center mass," he said, putting his hand on the big circle on the chest. "This is where your shots are most likely to stop the threat."

Still down at the far end of the shooting lanes, we stood seven yards from our targets and did some shooting. Reid had a nine-millimeter Smith & Wesson M&P semi-automatic like Rick Ector's. Tom had an extremely complicated double-and-single-action Heckler & Koch pistol festooned with safety, de-cocking lever, slide release, and an external hammer—a lot to keep track of. Their guns held fourteen shots or more. My five-shot

.38 revolver seemed puny, but, standing still and shooting slowly, we all did fine.

"I'm going to give you commands," Jack said. "'Standard response' means two shots center mass. 'Nonstandard response' means two shots center mass and one shot in each hip to break bone and bring him down. 'Failure to stop' means two shots center mass and one in the white zone." He pointed to the triangle on the face.

As we hung fresh targets, I considered the words "failure to stop." A man keeps coming with a knife, despite bullets ripping into his chest. *Yeesh.*

Jack barked alternating commands. "Failure to stop!" "Standard response!" "Standard response!" "Nonstandard response!" The faster and louder he got, the more nervous I became and the more I dropped cartridges while reloading. Reid and Tom, with their big semi-automatics, kept shooting and shooting, and when they needed to reload, it was magazine out, magazine in, *zip-zip,* done.

Even under the minimal pressure of Jack's yelling, that triangle and those little circles on the hips were hard to hit. And I kept dropping the damned cartridges. When we were finished, my shirt was damp and the floor around my feet was littered with live ammunition. God forbid *my* gunfight went on for more than five shots. I'd be toast.

During a break, Jack took me by the shoulder and walked me up to my target. "See this?" he said, pointing to a hole that was half an inch outside the silhouette's head. "That is everything you own, everything you've ever worked for, everything you'd hoped to leave to your children. That bullet went on to hit a seven-year-old girl, or a mother of three, or a heart surgeon. You own every bullet you fire, and you can't call them back."

He turned to Reid and Tom. "Regardless of what I tell you, if you press the trigger, you own it. We're grown-ups. The decision is yours, not mine."

I already felt a little light-headed, a little heart-fluttery, like at the top of a roller coaster. Talk of thugs running at me as my bullets hit bystanders had me convinced this wasn't for me. Then we got serious.

Jack had us shoot while walking toward the targets, while backing away, and while walking across them, putting two shots into each. To ready us for being wounded in our strong hand, he taught us to shoot with our weak one. He taught us to reholster slowly—"reluctantly," as he put it—while looking around behind us, because people are often shot when they think the fight is over.

We played a kind of quick-draw game that Jack called "The Initiator."

Two of us stood side by side, facing targets, with our guns holstered. One had his hands at his sides; the other held his arms out straight in front of him. It was up to the one with his arms up to start moving toward his gun. As soon as he did, the other could draw. First one to put two shots into center mass won. The initiator, with his arms out, had the advantage of knowing when the game would start. The other had the advantage of starting with a hand close to his gun. We played over and over; neither player had a clear edge.

We shot for hours, burning through about four hundred rounds apiece. We hardly spoke; it was all shooting. Jack walked behind us, adjusting our positions like a yoga instructor. We drew and fired, drew and fired, drew and fired, trying to etch the actions into muscle memory. By the end of it, I was bushed.

But I wasn't finished. After the other students went home, Hawley handed me off to an instructor named Billy—a short, powerfully built man of about sixty with an egg-bald head and a murky Special Operations past in the brown-water Navy during Vietnam. Billy had a gravelly voice and hands that could probably tear a beer can in half. He wore a .45 automatic on his hip and kept a folding knife the size of a harmonica in his pocket. After we shook hands, he smiled, reached down the front of his jeans to a hidden pocket, and came up with a hammerless stainless-steel .44 Special revolver. It seemed to me that clawing that thing out during the panic of a gunfight would be a good way for Billy to shoot off his wedding tackle, but he laughed that off. "You get as old as I am, and see as much as I have, and you get pretty good with your gear."

He put his arm around my shoulders and chuckled in a vaguely malevolent way. "We're going to do something for you we don't usually do," he said. "Ready to have your mind blown?"

No, actually. I was ready for a beer and a nap.

"We're going to put you on the Prism machine, which is really here to train police." Billy led me to a range that had no shooting bays. Instead it had a booth at the back end in which a young man sat at a big computer console. He said hello with the kind of smirk that indicated that something unpleasant was about to happen.

Billy walked me downrange until we were standing only a few feet from what appeared to be a bedsheet that someone had stretched across the range like a screen. He told me to remove my holstered revolver, then fixed around my waist a gun belt on which hung a holstered Glock 19—a compact nine-millimeter. He handed me three loaded magazines and told me to put them in my left pants pocket.

"What's going to happen is, you're going to see a scenario played out on that screen, and you have to decide whether or not to shoot." Once again, something about the exaggerated manliness of Billy and the potential lethality of our project reeled me back to the fright and excitement of Hank Hilliard's rifle range at Camp Sunapee. I could really blow it here; I'd better not.

"I shoot at the screen?"

"It's made of rubber. Here's what's so cool: The heat of the bullet passing through it cauterizes the hole and seals it up. Sensors aimed at the back of the screen detect your hits, the computer analyzes them instantly, and, depending on where your bullets hit, the people on the screen react. They'll either fall over or not. Is that cool? The whole thing is run by the kid in the booth. You ready?"

"I've never shot a Glock before."

Billy had me take it from the holster. It wasn't fancy, like Tom's Heckler & Koch—no de-cocker, no external hammer, not even a safety catch. It was the pocket camera of firearms: point and shoot. But it was heftier than my .38, and it held three times as many cartridges. I loaded it, pulled the slide, and returned it to the holster.

"These are what we call 'active shooter' situations," Billy said. "You have an unknown number of active shooters in a building—your typical university or office-building situation. You ready?"

The range went dark, the screen came to life, and I was in some kind of school building. Because I was standing only about ten feet from the screen, it filled my vision. Up came the sound, realistically loud: people screaming and, in the distance, muffled gunshots. I drew the gun and held it with both hands at low-ready. This was nothing like playing a first-person shooter game on a computer. I was *there* among the cinder-block walls, the bulletin boards, and the office doors with cartoons tacked to them. And it wasn't a cheap plastic controller in my hand, but a real gun loaded with live ammunition.

My heart was somewhere up around my collarbone. My hands were sweating. I found myself moving down a hallway and realized how many places there are in the average building for a bad guy to hide. That doorway! That cranny! Behind that fire extinguisher! I checked each one as I passed: nothing.

I turned and moved through a door. Loud screams: Someone came running toward me from the gloom at the end of the hall—a young woman, crying and pointing behind her. Another person came running up the hall from back there—someone chasing her? I raised the gun. No, another screaming person, with empty hands.

Up ahead, a body sprawled on the floor, and something lay near his hand. A pistol? Was he alive? About to pick it up and shoot me? Should I shoot him? No, it was an open cell phone that looked like a gun. Christ, I could have shot a victim.

While I was looking at the body, another person appeared in the hallway, and I jerked the gun up: another empty-handed innocent. I was gasping audibly, my torso rigid with fear. Yet for all that, I was amazed to find that my index finger still lay along the slide, not on the trigger. Rule Three: Keep your finger off the trigger until your sights are on the target and you're ready to fire. Such was the value of good training; it held even under pressure.

I kept moving down the hall. I turned left into a classroom. People were lined up against a blackboard, crying. On the floor lay at least one body, maybe two. Standing directly in front of me was a big woman with her arm around another woman's neck and a gun to the woman's head.

I froze.

The big woman with the gun was yelling at me. Everybody else was screaming; the noise was overwhelming, the tableau so terrifying that my brain locked up. I don't know how long I stood there, frozen, before the screen went dark.

Billy appeared at my shoulder. "You should have shot her."

"What?" I squeaked. I felt like I'd been plugged into a wall socket. "I was afraid of hitting the hostage."

"The hostage is dead already," Billy said calmly, and fixed me with the kind of level gaze I imagined him using in combat when delivering such news as "The leg has to come off" or "You're dying." I must have been trying to break eye contact, because he moved his head sideways a little to keep me locked in. "You've got bodies on the floor," he said. "*Look at me.* Bodies on the floor shows *intent.* The woman with the gun has demonstrated she is willing to kill and she's going to kill again. You have only three options: You can back away; she kills the hostage. You can shoot and maybe hit the hostage. Or you can freeze, like you did, and she kills the hostage and you both. Either way, the hostage is already dead; you have to save yourself and everybody else in the room."

"Christ." I blinked and shook my head, like a dog shaking off water.

"It's the real deal. We stopped it because we didn't want to overload you too soon. She was about to shoot you and then the hostage. Want to do it again?"

No. I wanted to cry until I stopped shaking.

"Yeah," I said.

Billy murmured into his walkie-talkie, and the scenario restarted. The doors, the gunshots, the screaming, the running people. I moved into the room where the woman with the gun was behind the hostage, yelling at me. Two-thirds of her face was hidden behind that of the hostage; I could see one of her eyes. I raised the Glock and shot once. She collapsed like a silk scarf drifting to the floor. The screen went dark.

"Good shooting!" Billy growled.

My heart was going like crazy and I was gasping air, but I felt terrific—like a superhero who had saved the day. I felt not a trace of remorse for having killed a woman. At that moment, in the seconds after it happened, it only felt good. The threat was over, because I'd kept my head and shot perfectly. I'd kept people from getting killed.

I had no memory of either the shot or the recoil. Although it was the first time I'd fired a Glock, I'd made an incredibly difficult shot. Whether that said something about the gun or performance under pressure, I couldn't say. But it was the second time I'd shot well with one of the high-tech guns I'd so disdained. The first had been the kid's AR-15 at the Family Shooting Center. Gunmaking had come a long way.

Billy spoke into his walkie-talkie, and the screen showed a still image of the moment I'd shot, with a blue dot on the woman's left eye, where my bullet had struck. "You hit her in the white zone," he said, using two blunt index fingers to define the triangle on his face: eye, eye, middle of upper lip. "The shock wave takes out her medulla oblongata, and it's impossible for her to pull the trigger. It's the perfect shot—the white zone is the only shot that really ends a situation." Odd, I thought, as I used my sleeve to wipe sweat from my forehead. In the gun world, white has contradictory meanings: the lowest condition of readiness, and the ultimate bullet strike. "Your alternative was to shoot the hostage here," Billy continued, pressing a finger into his own shoulder. "That's a nonfatal wound. She falls, and you have a clear shot at the shooter. Ready?"

The screen lit up, and I was in an office building, with even more hiding places than the college—cubicles, closets, hallways. People were screaming and crying, running all over; it was impossible to tell which might be the shooter. A door burst open to my right, and I jerked up my gun. Again, Jack's training kept my finger from moving onto the trigger. I didn't yet have a target. I wasn't about to shoot.

People poured toward me and around me. I moved through a door and found myself at the top of a stairway. Two people came running up. A man in a yellow hoodie appeared on the landing, gun in hand. I shot, and, to my immense relief, he collapsed.

"Notice the blood spatter on the wall," Billy whispered in my ear, proud of the realism.

I continued down the stairs, stepping around the body, and eased through a door into another floor of cubicles. Bodies lay on the floor. I didn't know if this was the work of Yellow Hoodie or if there were more shooters. The machine kept me moving down a hallway. Slowly.

I looked left. Sitting at a computer, a man in a dark jacket had his hands up. In one hand was a gun, pointed straight at the ceiling.

I put my sights on him and moved my finger to the trigger. He started to lower the gun, and I shot him.

From down the hall, about twenty-five feet away, a third gunman advanced.

I shot and shot and shot, and he kept coming, firing his gun, the muzzle flashes as big as basketballs. The screen went dark.

"You're dead," Billy said.

A still image appeared on the screen: the man in the long hallway shooting at me. Five blue dots made a perfect ring around him, one quite close to his head. None on him. I'd missed every time.

"Shooting fast isn't always the best thing," Billy said. "You can't miss fast enough to win a gunfight. Take that extra half second to aim. Chances are he'll miss with his first shots. And even if you're hit, chances are you won't die; if you keep your head, you can still shoot back."

As I was absorbing the grisly lesson, Billy added, "That guy on the stairs? I'd have put another one in him as I went past. You don't know if he's dead, if he's faking, if he's wounded. He could pick up the gun and shoot you as you walk past."

"Isn't that murder?"

"It's a gunfight. A gunfight is to the death—yours or his. It's what you have to remember, over and over, if you're going to carry a gun."

The screen lit up, and I was in a shopping mall. More screaming people, more distant gunshots. Two young women came running toward me.

Suddenly, between them and me, a man in a Raiders jacket stepped out, holding a rifle. He turned toward them; I put my sights on his back but didn't shoot.

Rule Four: Be sure of your target and what is behind and around it. If I shot, I might have hit the girl in the white sweatshirt.

Mistake: The man fired, and the girl in the white sweatshirt fell dead. I shot him twice in the back.

The slide on my gun locked back: empty. As fast as I could, I dropped the empty magazine, found a new one in my pocket, rammed it in, grabbed the slide, hauled it back, and released it forward. I turned left into a corridor and came face-to-face with a young man holding a gun.

I put the sights on him and pulled the trigger . . . Nothing happened. I pulled and pulled. Nothing. My gun was dead. The man lifted his gun at me and fired. The screen went dark.

"The loudest sound you'll ever hear in a gunfight is *click*." Billy laughed sardonically. "Your slide was out of battery," he said, meaning it hadn't returned all the way forward after I'd released it. "I could see that. I wanted to see what you'd do. Here's something you won't forget again, I'm sure: When you release the slide forward, give it a little bang on the back to make sure it's seated."

Shit. Jack had taught us that. I'd forgotten, and I was dead again.

I went through about a dozen scenarios: a high school, the Las Vegas City Council Chambers, a patrol in Afghanistan. By the end, I was soaked in sweat and needed to sit down and eat something with sugar in it.

Billy was kind. He said I'd done well. In most of them, though, I'd died.

My day with Jack and my hours on the Prism left me with two powerful impulses. One was to get a better gun. I couldn't have done as well on the Prism with either of my .38s. I couldn't have shot as far, as accurately, or as fast. Reloading—fumbling individual rounds into the cylinder after only five or six shots—would have gotten me killed even more often than I'd died with the Glock. Rick Ector's motto finally made sense.

Capacity, capacity, capacity. I'd been carrying those .38 revolvers because I "liked" them, because they pleased me historically and aestheti-cally. Now my taste in guns seemed dilettantish and irresponsible. If I was going to carry a gun, it should not be a fashion statement. I should carry only if I believed I might someday have to use a gun to defend my life or someone else's. In that case, what I needed was the weapon that was most likely to get the job done.

After a lifetime of buying used guns, I finally bought a brand-new one—a Glock 19, the same as I'd shot on the Prism, the same gun Angelina Jolie used in *Mr. and Mrs. Smith*—as well as the one with which Jared Loughner shot twenty people, killing six and injuring Arizona representative Gabrielle Giffords. It was a terrifically ugly thing, as graceless as a stapler, utterly without charm. It had black plastic in all the places that wood should have been. The slide was shaped like a stick of margarine, with none of the sweep and styling of an early-twentieth-century pistol. It lacked any engraving save the Glock logo. It wasn't much of a fashion accessory, but it put bullets where I wanted them to go. It was no bigger than the six-shot Colt, and yet it held sixteen cartridges. I picked out a suede inside-the-pants holster, slipped the unloaded Glock into it, and, standing at the gun-store counter, tucked it in place over my right kidney. It was instantly apparent how much more comfortable the Glock was going to be. With no bulging cylinder, it didn't poke me in the love handle.

But something about this transaction was making me uneasy. Signing the credit card slip with the Glock in place on my belt, I found myself crossing a threshold. I wasn't merely playing now; I was genuinely arming myself to kill someone in a gunfight, and paying $438 for the privilege. My little experiment in going armed was taking on a life of its own. Was I carrying the gun, or was the gun carrying me?

At home, I opened a box of Golden Saber nine-millimeter hollow-points—specialty self-defense ammo at a breathtaking twenty-four dollars for a box of twenty—and loaded the Glock. Pointing it at the floor of my garage, I pulled the slide, chambering a round and cocking the firing pin. It instantly felt swollen to bursting. A semi-automatic is a different animal from a revolver. It's more mysterious, because its moving parts and its ammunition aren't visible from the outside. It requires more trust in the hardware than a revolver does. A Glock may not have a hair trigger the way some semi-autos do, but to a revolver guy like me, the thing—hot, cocked, and ready to go—felt especially dangerous in the hand. Holding it was one thing; slipping it into my pants completely freaked me out.

I found myself walking on tiptoes with my hips thrust forward, prancing along like a marionette, lest I put pressure on the trigger and blow off my right buttock. I removed it from my pants and set it on my garage workbench, wondering how anybody carried such a thing.

Finally, on the advice of some guys on the GlockTalk.com chat board, I tried an experiment. I unloaded the gun, pulled the slide to cock it, and returned it to its holster. Then I massaged the holster with my fingers every which way, as hard as I could, and found that I couldn't make the trigger click no matter what I did. Part of what makes the Glock so popular is that, although it doesn't have a manual safety catch, it's designed with three internal safeties that prevent it from firing unless the trigger is deliberately pulled. Somewhat satisfied, I reloaded it, holstered it, and stuffed it down my pants with a tremendous sense of misgiving. If the Colt had been unignorable, the Glock practically shrieked in my ear every minute I carried it.

What, exactly, had I gotten myself into? Those scenarios on the Prism system's screen had lodged somewhere in *my* medulla oblongata. I was a believer: Nightmares happened, and in the most mundane of places. For weeks after, I imagined "active shooter situations" everywhere I went—at Safeway, in the library, at the movies. What would I do if all hell broke loose right now? What would I use as cover? How would I position myself so as not to hit a bystander? And this was after one hour on a simulator. *The guys coming back from a year in Iraq and Afghanistan,* I thought. *How do they stand it?*

If I wasn't *well* trained after Las Vegas, at least I was *better* trained. And now I had a gun that might actually do me some good in a horrible situation. Now that I was minimally competent and properly equipped, the other powerful impulse that overcame me after Vegas was to continue with my training. I pictured an attack at Boulder's annual United Nations' Day celebration—a place where it was entirely possible to imagine some SinCity2A type showing up to war-paint his face with liberals' blood. What would I do? Run away? If I did that, with my gun on my hip, how would I live with myself if people were murdered? I'd be like a doctor who walked away from a stranger having a heart attack.

But if I ran toward the sound of the guns, with my one piddly day of training, I could easily be killed—or kill a bystander. So what exactly were my choices? I could stop carrying the gun and run away with impunity. But if I was going to carry, I needed to train more and practice more. I had willy-nilly bought in to something from which retreat seemed possible only if I gave up the gun. But if I did that, was I abdicating a responsibility to keep myself and the people around me safe? Or did I have no such responsibility?

No wonder hard-core gun guys felt superior to their unarmed brethren and enraged by their contempt. Who else among us willingly took on such life-and-death challenges? One might call such people testosterone-poisoned death freaks, which is how they were often portrayed by those who would have disparaged gun culture. But another word might be "warrior." And society had always had a place for he who would willingly take up the sword and place himself in harm's way. It's a peculiar specialty, requiring a certain personality, a certain worldview, a certain combination of physical and emotional courage, and a certain way of organizing questions of morality in one's mind.

For the most part, we love those guys. They're the ones we make movies about. And one can't drive fifty feet without seeing a bumper sticker urging us to SUPPORT OUR TROOPS. What I'd discovered during my gun-guy walkabout was that warriors walked among us, on our own soil and out of uniform. Not every gun guy was a warrior. Not even every person who'd obtained a concealed-carry permit was necessarily a warrior. But while I met relatively few of the six million Americans who'd done so, every one I encountered was serious about the undertaking. They'd decided, on some level, to be one of society's warriors. The question for me, after Las Vegas, was whether it was a role I wanted to play.

18. TRIBES

I'm sorry, I can't hear you. Don't fire the gun while you're talking!

—Leslie Nielsen, as Lieutenant Frank
Drebin in *The Naked Gun*, 1988

As much as I'd wanted to avoid gun politics, Washington, D.C., was like the drain at the bottom of the bathtub. Like it or not, I was already circling it. And every time somebody mentioned the Second Amendment, I inched a little closer.

The Second Amendment was a problem—for me, for the anti-gun crowd, even for the NRA. Its maddeningly vague, awkwardly punctuated and capitalized text reads: "A well-regulated Militia, being necessary to the security of a free State, the right of the people to keep and bear Arms, shall not be infringed." No other amendment was as opaque as the Second. Nobody had ever had a ghost of a clue what the framers meant by it.

Scholars, lawyers, and politicians had argued for decades about whether the Second Amendment conferred an individual right to own and carry a gun or whether its preamble limited it to a collective right of the people to organize when necessary into well-regulated militias. For years, the tide of the Second Amendment argument flowed in the direction of the collective-militia analysis. Then it washed up against Antonin Scalia. In 2008, he wrote the lead opinion in *District of Columbia* v. *Heller*, striking down the federal district's thirty-three-year-old handgun ban, reversing long-standing precedent, and establishing that the Second Amendment indeed guaranteed an individual right to be armed. Writing for the 5–4 majority, Scalia declared that gun bans were "off the table" in the federal district. A year later, in *McDonald* v. *Chicago,* the Court extended Scalia's ruling to the entire nation.

I naively expected it to be a healing moment. The Court had taken gun bans "off the table," so I waited for the NRA and its allies to abandon their insane scaremongering that even the mildest gun regulation was a step toward forcible disarmament. For their part, I expected the anti-gun side to recognize that the game had changed and give up attempts to deprive people of firearms. Silly me.

The NRA's *American Rifleman* magazine warned, bizarrely, that after *Heller,* "our firearm freedoms may be in *greater* danger." As for Washington, D.C., and Chicago, their city councils passed catch-22 laws that hewed to the letter of the Court's decisions while making handgun possession all but impossible—with the predictable result that both faced multiple lawsuits they could ill afford and would probably lose.

The framers had written the Second Amendment awkwardly in order to get it ratified by mutually hostile infant states, and the perpetual bickering over the paragraph's meaning depended on attempts to divine what the white-wigged men were thinking at the time. Whole shelves of books had been devoted to describing the political and economic conditions of 1791 and how the framers would have been responding to them. The more conflicting interpretations of intent I read, and the more I tried my own hand at intercentury mind reading, the less relevant the whole exercise came to appear.

In the absence of certainty about the framers' intent, gun guys had invented a pantheon of ersatz framers and, like ventriloquists, made them say the damnedest things. Get this widely disseminated howler, allegedly from Benjamin Franklin: "Democracy has been defined as two wolves and a sheep discussing plans for lunch. Liberty is a well-armed lamb contesting the vote." The quote appeared nowhere in Franklin's writing, and the word *lunch* wasn't in popular usage until 1820, thirty years after Franklin's death. Gun guys often quoted John Adams as saying, "Arms in the hands of the citizens may be used at individual discretion for the defense of the country, the overthrow of tyranny or private self-defense," when what he said was the exact opposite: that privately held guns "demolish every constitution, and lay the laws prostrate, so that liberty can be enjoyed by no man." Poor Thomas Jefferson probably had more guns stuffed into his long-dead mouth than anybody. I particularly liked one, found on any number of posters and T-shirts at gun shows, attributing to Jefferson the paranoid use of the sinister gun-guy "they": "The beauty of the Second Amendment is that it will not be needed until they try to take it." Total hooey.

The slurry of invented quotes concealed the obvious. The framers couldn't foresee the AK-47 any more than they could foresee women and African Americans in the voting booth. They couldn't imagine how the widespread ownership of rapid-fire rifles might affect cities that contain four times as many people as lived in the entire United States at the time they were writing. Since we had no way of knowing exactly what the framers wanted the Second Amendment to mean, the wretched paragraph did naught but make rational discussion of gun policy impossible.

Certainly if we were looking for reasons that gun guys clung zealously to their firearms, we could take off the list their expressed fealty to the Second Amendment. Not that they didn't *like* the Second Amendment; they did. But despite their protestations, none had guns in his life primarily to fulfill a perceived duty to protect and defend it. Many of the same guys who could go on ad nauseam that the Second Amendment *must not be infringed* supported public-school prayer in defiance of the First Amendment's prohibition against establishing a state religion; objected to closing the prison at Guantánamo Bay—a city-size violation of the Fifth, Sixth, and Eighth amendments—and were willing, in the name of the war on terror, to submit to all manner of physical and electronic Fourth Amendment intrusions. It wasn't so much the Constitution or its authors that gun guys loved; it was guns. Which was okay with me. I loved them, too. But as my gun-guy walkabout was winding down, I was growing tired of the breast-beating about James Madison.

Still: Could I really spend eighteen months trying to figure out gun guys without visiting the temple of the Second Amendment—NRA headquarters? I'd certainly hoped so. I read the NRA's magazine every month. I knew what the organization had to say. The thought of being trapped in a D.C. cubicle with a functionary and listening to the NRA's endlessly repeated talking points made me want to take a nap.

Back in the spring, after carrying a gun for a couple of months, I'd published an article in *Harper's Magazine* about the experience. A lot of strangers wrote to me, many of them working through their own conflicted feelings. My favorite e-mail, from a frank woman in Seattle, illustrated the deep well from which feelings about guns spring—much deeper than the level of statistics, studies, or other people's experiences. "I disagree with everything you wrote," she wrote. "But I can't tell you why."

A couple of weeks after the article appeared, my phone rang, and a man introduced himself as Sean Thornton of the National Rifle Association. I braced for a blast of vitriol. My *Harper's* piece had argued that, as scary as widespread concealed carry sounded, the data demonstrated that the NRA was right to say that it was not a threat to public safety. But I'd criticized the NRA-approved classes I'd taken, and in my experience, political gun guys like those at the NRA brooked no disagreement on anything. Waver a millimeter from the party line and they flew into a foaming rage. So when this fellow Thornton introduced himself, I was sorry I'd picked up the phone. "I was pretty disappointed to read your piece," he said mildly. "NRA-sanctioned classes should be a lot better than that. Can I ask you a few questions?" It turned out Sean wasn't one of the NRA's ideological enforcers. He was from the political wing's forgotten stepsister, the Education & Training Division.

"At any time, did you see live ammunition in the room?" he asked.

"Yes." I mentioned the instructor who hadn't known that her .38 was loaded.

"Were you trained in how to keep an attacker from taking away your gun?"

"No."

"Were you counseled in the extreme emotions of regret and remorse you're likely to feel even after a justified shooting?"

"No."

He apologized for the lousy classes and offered to help me find a better one. Imagine! The NRA was talking about safety and training. It was like a phone call from 1954.

As I flew home from Las Vegas, I had one of those lightbulb-over-the-head moments: I could visit the NRA I liked and not the NRA I didn't like. I could visit Sean Thornton.

The NRA used to house itself on Second Street in downtown Washington, but in 1994, having outgrown those offices, it commissioned a gigantic modernist building in deepest Fairfax, Virginia, more than a mile from the nearest Metro. I arrived late and perspiring, my laptop heavy as an anvil. It was like visiting Microsoft or General Motors: two steel-and-glass towers with underground parking and a vast outdoor lot. Carved in stone above the door were the words THE RIGHT OF THE PEOPLE TO KEEP AND BEAR ARMS SHALL NOT BE INFRINGED—the Second Amendment conveniently shorn of its troublesome militia preamble. Like Scrooge seeing Marley's face where the door knocker should have been, I pictured a different motto carved above the door of the nation's "premier gun-safety organization": SAFETY RULE ONE—TREAT ALL GUNS AS THOUGH THEY ARE LOADED.

The NRA may have been sufficiently tone deaf to build a twenty-first-century headquarters in a place reachable only by car, but it was smart enough to make its first greeter an African American woman, the demographic least represented among shooters. She sat behind a reception desk as high and imposing as a judge's bench. I handed up my name and took a seat in the lobby, scanning back copies of the *American Rifleman*. On the coffee table sat something I hadn't seen in an office in years: an ashtray.

"We're an organization devoted to personal freedom," Sean Thornton said with a shrug when he showed up a few minutes later. He was a short, semi-bald, worried-looking man in his thirties, wearing a fashionably clipped beard and a royal-blue shirt with a royal-blue tie. Towering over him, hulking and impassive, with a thin beard and shop glasses, was his colleague Andy Lander. Together, they looked like George and Lenny from *Of Mice and Men*. Neither smiled as they shook my hand; the initial vibe was like a Korean prisoner exchange at the 38th parallel.

To break the ice, Sean suggested we tour the NRA National Firearms Museum. "One of the world's best," he said. As we walked, I asked if they didn't feel like poor country cousins to the Institute for Legislative Action—the NRA's thunderous political wing. "No. No, I don't," Sean said, frowning thoughtfully. "Just to let you know, I'm not the typical NRA guy. I'm married to a black woman. I voted for Barack Obama. But when it comes to the Second Amendment, I guess I'm a purist. I'm not saying that you're not. But I believe it's a right."

"We oversee about 75,000 instructors worldwide," Andy said. "We do everything from policing them to developing new curriculum."

"And how many of you are there?"

"In training and education?" Sean asked.

"Yeah."

"Five guys."

"And how many in the ILA?"

"Oh, hundreds." He shrugged and smiled.

The museum took up most of the building's first floor. At the threshold, a case held what looked like a rusty pipe lashed to a rotting fence post—a Spanish hand cannon, perhaps the first firearm ever brought to North America. Beside it hung a matchlock from the *Mayflower.* For a gun-guy history buff, these were like fragments of the True Cross. And it only got better from there.

We looked at nineteenth-century double-barreled rifles and a wildly impractical but utterly beautiful double-barreled *bolt-action* rifle. We saw an air rifle with which Lewis and Clark killed an elk—after fifteen hundred priming strokes. The guns of the Old West were a lot cruder than the reproductions used in cowboy movies. We looked at a flintlock designed to keep its powder dry in the rain. "Its inventor demonstrated it on Boston Common during a storm," Andy said, looming over me at the case. "He fired it three times, and before he could get off a fourth shot, he was hit by lightning and killed."

"You see?" I said. "Guns are dangerous and must be banned!" Sean and Andy looked at me like Mount Rushmore; wrong joke for the NRA, even its Education & Training guys.

"So why do we like these things so much?" I asked, moving along to a case full of First World War guns. Sean and Andy frowned in thought; gun guys never could resist the question.

"A gun that went to San Francisco in the Gold Rush, you can pull out of the case and fire today," Sean said. "We do it here all the time. The guns you see in this room get fired." He pointed to a Broomhandle Mauser—one of the first practical semi-automatic pistols. "They're better designed than clocks. They had to be, because people's lives depended on them."

Andy said, "For me it's really an emotional thing. My grandfather carried a Thompson submachine gun on D-Day. He had a couple of guys coming at him, and if he hadn't had a Thompson, he wouldn't be here. So my dad wouldn't be here. So I wouldn't be here. The first time I saw my father cry was when I put a Thompson in his hands and had him shoot full auto. I can take that gun and see my genealogy in it."

I was getting impatient. Had I really trekked halfway across Fairfax to hear the same bromides I'd heard everyplace else? Here I was in the temple of the firearm, where people had been thinking seriously about guns for years. And this was all they had? "Yeah, yeah, I get it," I said roughly. "History. Craftsmanship. Family lore and blah-de-blah. I've heard it all before. But let's face it: We're not talking about old kitchen tools or cameras here. These things are about *death*."

It was an inside pitch, a little dirty, and I expected Sean to whiff, deny-ing that the attraction to firearms had anything to do with killing. Instead he calmly stepped back and put it over the right-field wall.

"Absolutely," he said, touching my chest with the tip of an index finger. "These are about *death*! That's a *huge* part of the attraction. They're about *mastering* death. Mastering the fear of it. You're not just in awe of death. You're accepting responsibility for taking death in your hands, something that a lot of people don't even want to *think* about."

"Yup," Andy said, nodding. "Yup."

"When people think of America, they think of the cowboy and his Peacemaker," Sean said. "But you can find an equivalent in every cul-ture: the knights of Europe, the samurai warrior. That respect, that awe that every culture has for the warrior, for the man who will take it upon himself to be a master of *death*—that's a *lot* of what goes into the love of firearms. It's romantic. We love the science, the art, and the beauty. But there's also that macabre element. There's also the *death*."

Well, that was a surprise: The most honest and uncomfortable answer about firearms attraction I'd yet received, and inside the walls of the NRA. Sean wasn't apologizing. He wasn't saying, "Yeah, it's too bad that our enjoyment of shooting sports and our admiration for the mechanical elegance of these devices is bound up with men slaughtering one another." He was saying that the grisly business that lay behind firearms was part of their attraction, that a dark streak ran through humankind, and that we who liked guns should be proud of confronting it.

Despite Marcey Parker's protestation, then, guns were not merely to gun guys what golf clubs were to golfers or sauté pans to cooks. They were also what fast cars were to race drivers or parachutes to sky divers: a means of approaching and staring down death, of walking the edge of the abyss dividing this world from the next. Gun guys got a little contact high from the grim reaper. They stood apart from those who misunderstood or dis-liked firearms and said, essentially, *I am master of this death-dealing device, and you are not. I am prepared for and capable of surviving the kind of situa-tion you can't even bring yourself to think about.* No apology necessary.

We were by now standing in front of a case of guns used in movies, a mini-monument to Americans' conflicted love affair with violent death: John Wayne's Winchester, Dirty Harry's .44 Magnum, a Humphrey Bo-gart .32 Colt, a Smith & Wesson 639 from *Reservoir Dogs*. The cowboy, the cop, the spy, the gangster . . . We *loved* this stuff.

"You want to talk about fascination with death?" Sean said. "Come look at this." A silver-plated and elaborately engraved Colt Detective Special nestled in a black, coffin-shaped box with a tiny mirror, a glass vial of water, six odd-looking bullets, and what appeared to be a mahogany chopstick. "Vampire gun," Sean said. "See the death's heads carved into the bullets? They're silver. You've also got a vial of holy water, a mirror—so you're sure you're shooting at Nosferatu—and a wooden stake in case the fight goes hand to hand."

The set was so gorgeously and expensively crafted that I couldn't tell whether it was meant as a joke.

"You're right about one thing," Sean said, gazing down at the coffin-shaped box. "This is some complicated shit."

Those who wanted guns more tightly controlled had, since the 1970s, placed blame for America's loose gun laws on "the might of the gun lobby" and politicians whom *The New York Times* never tired of accusing of knuckling under to the NRA. It was more comforting, I suppose, to imagine the enemy as a goliath who played dirty than to face the reality: that gun laws were loose because that was the way most Americans wanted them.

Although the NRA had never been bigger or richer than it was in 2010, it was, for all its bluster, a middling player by Washington standards. Its membership of four million was no bigger than that of the National Wildlife Federation. It fielded no former congressmen or administration officials as lobbyists. It didn't even give out much money. NRA contributions to congressional candidates were about half that of the pipe-fitters' union—and when was the last time politicians cowered before the pipe fitters?

Most members of Congress didn't need NRA money or pressure to toe the pro-gun line. They, and their constituents, were already on board. Gallup had been asking people about stricter gun control for decades; in twenty years, support had fallen by a third, to less than 50 percent.

Of course, polling on gun control was distorted by how strongly those who answered the questions felt about the issue. Unlike the rest of the population, gun guys thought about their guns—and about efforts to take them away—every day. If 90 percent of victory was showing up, NRA members were going to win the gun-control fight every time.

But even if the numbers were imprecise, the trend was clearly toward less and less public support for gun control. The big drop in crime probably explained a lot of that. NRA propaganda might have helped, too. But there was also this uncomfortable reality: It was almost impossible to prove that the measures we thought of as "gun control" saved any lives. The *American Journal of Preventive Medicine* took a swing at it in 2005, examining dozens of studies of gun-control effectiveness. In many cases, the researchers found flaws with the studies themselves. But the *Journal* was prepared to be declarative about a few gun-control measures. Gun registration, for example, rarely helped police solve crimes, because people so rarely committed a crime with the guns they'd registered. It was stolen guns, or guns in underground circulation so long that any registry would have missed them, that did the killing. Canada's national long-gun registry ate up more than sixty million dollars a year and yielded so few practical results that in October 2011 the Parliament voted to scrap it. Gun licensing, banning classifications of weapons (assault rifles, Saturday night specials, etc.), waiting periods, one-gun-a-month laws, and paperwork requirements all yielded similarly ambiguous results at best. Usually they had no effect at all. Yes, gun crime fell after passage of the Brady Law . . . but it was already falling before. New York City had tough gun laws and, as the second decade of the twenty-first century began, remarkably low crime. But Chicago had even tougher gun laws, and lots of violent crime. Gun crime was almost nonexistent in Vermont, which had some of the loosest gun laws anywhere, and relatively high in California, with some of the strictest. While it was easy to argue that California and Chicago needed tougher gun laws than Vermont because they had more crime, arguing it that way reversed causality—that the crime rate spawned the laws, not the other way around. That high levels of violence continued despite the tough laws only weakened further the "guns cause crime" argument.

It's possible that Chicago and California would have been even more violent had their laws been looser, and that gun crime wouldn't have fallen as fast had the Brady Law never passed. But it was impossible to know—and therefore easy to sow doubt about the gun-control exercise.

The most useful way to think about gun laws was as an analogue to marijuana laws. Both let citizens and policymakers feel like they were "doing something." Both were ineffective at achieving their stated goals. Laws like the assault-rifle ban responded not to a real public safety threat but an imaginary one, which reminded me of drug prohibitionists excoriating marijuana not as a hazard unto itself but as a "gateway drug." Blaming guns for crime was as dishonest an exercise in avoidance as saying that teenagers were alienated because they smoked pot—not because they were overstressed by competition, underfunded and unimaginative schools, and the divorces of their overworked parents. How much more convenient was it to ignore the totality of the lives lived by young black urban men—the group most likely to die by gunfire—and focus instead on taking away their guns?

Most of all, though, what both marijuana laws and gun laws did best was express disapproval of a lifestyle and the culture that enjoyed it.

NRA executive vice president J. Warren Cassidy once told a *Time* magazine writer, "You would get a far better understanding if you approached us as if you were approaching one of the great religions of the world." Guns may have been fun, useful, nostalgia-inducing, and mechanically intriguing, but in the America I was touring, they also stood in for a worldview that, broadly defined, valued the individual over the collective, vigorous outdoorsiness over pallid intellectualism, certainty over questioning, patriotism over internationalism, manliness over femininity, action over inaction. The gun was the physical manifestation of the tribe's binding philosophy. It was the idol on the altar. The tribe exalted it and invested it with supernatural powers—to stop crime, defend the republic against tyranny, turn subjects into citizens, make boys into men.

The opposing tribe, which tended to value reason over force, skepticism over blind certainty, internationalism over American exceptionalism, multiculturalism over white-male hegemony, income leveling over jungle capitalism, and peace over war—liberals, for lack of a better word—recognized the gun as the sacred totem of the enemy, the embodiment of his abhorrent worldview. They believed that they could weaken the enemy by smashing his idols—by banning the gun if possible and, if not, by forcing it into an increasingly small box with as many restrictive laws as they could pass.

The elite soldiers of the anti-gun tribe were those of the Brady Center to Prevent Gun Violence, Washington's premier gun-control organization, and the disparity in strength between them and the NRA was apparent even before I entered their offices. While the NRA filled those two soaring towers in Virginia, the Brady Center had stuffed itself into a cramped warren of cubicles in a downtown D.C. building that also housed a fusty collection of anti-genocide, anti-war, and anti-racism nonprofits.

Dennis Henigan, the Brady Center's legal director, was fifty-nine years old and had the weary, exhausted manner of a man who knew that the war he'd been waging would continue long after he'd left the field. He had an enviable head of hair; big, 1970s-style eyeglasses; and long fingers that he pressed together as he spoke. As we took seats in his office, I asked a very D.C. question: Who's winning, your side or the other guy's?

"My view," he said, "is that we're at a stalemate."

Dude, I thought, *are you joking?* If what most concerned the Brady Center to Prevent Gun Violence was gun *violence,* Henigan should have been taking a victory lap. Gun violence was falling faster and landing lower than at any time in American history. The only way to see a stalemate was to accept the gun-guy view that what people like Henigan wanted was not only to get rid of gun violence, but to get rid of guns.

By that standard, the NRA was cleaning Brady's clock. Gun laws were looser almost everywhere than they'd been twenty years earlier. The Supreme Court had settled the meaning of the Second Amendment in the gun guys' favor. Six million Americans had obtained licenses to carry concealed weapons. Hundreds of thousands more guns were going into circulation every year. One could logically argue that if the Brady Center's goal was to reduce gun violence, perhaps the thing to do was declare victory and close up shop. But good luck convincing a D.C. nonprofit that it was time to turn out the lights and send back the contribution checks.

"I was raised just outside D.C., in Springfield, Virginia," Henigan told me as we made tea in the Brady Center's windowless break room. "You know—tract houses, shopping centers, the classic 1950s suburb." Henigan's father, a debate coach at George Washington University, was an Adlai Stevenson liberal who'd died young—"the same age I am now," Henigan said. "He was a smoker; I'm very passionate about tobacco, too."

We walked back to Henigan's office through narrow hallways festooned with blowups of gun-control magazine ads going back to the 1970s; it had been a long fight.

"My father clearly had no use for guns," Henigan said. "I had all the Davy Crockett accoutrements, cap guns and water guns. But my father wouldn't allow me to have a BB gun, because they were real. You could put your eye out." Henigan's only childhood experience of guns was when a neighbor his family knew well was cleaning his gun in the kitchen and shot his wife in the leg. "I do remember how shocking that seemed to me and my parents," Henigan said as we took seats in his office, "the notion that someone even had a gun. After that, she walked with a really pronounced limp."

The incident made Henigan wonder whether even well-intentioned people could handle guns safely at home. "All it takes is a single lapse in judgment," he said. "It's human not to be perfect."

After law school, Henigan enjoyed work as a corporate litigator but found pro bono work more exciting. In 1989, he answered an ad in *Legal Times*: Handgun Control Inc. was looking for an attorney to bring the tactics of Thurgood Marshall–style public-interest law to the gun-control cause.

"From the first day I walked in, it was drummed into me that we were moderates," Henigan said. "They didn't want us to evoke an image of left-ists or hippies or anything like that." Pete Shields, who founded Handgun Control, was a Republican DuPont executive whose son had been the last victim of the Zebra killers, who shot random people with pistols in San Francisco in the 1970s. Charlie Orasin, another founder, was also Repub-lican. They realized that restricting such a popular product as guns ran counter to the Republican impulse toward personal freedom, and they wanted a conservative, clean-cut organization. Spokesmen for the group cut their hair short and looked sharp. An American flag stood in the lobby. Shields and Orasin had zero tolerance for hostile or elitist com-ments about gun owners. And Handgun Control would never promote a ban. It changed its name to the Brady Center in 2001, in honor of James Brady, President Ronald Reagan's press secretary, who had been crippled with a handgun during an attempt on Reagan's life.

Henigan had tried shooting a gun once, he told me. In the mid-1990s, his nephew and some friends invited him out for a day of practice in a field in rural Maryland. He didn't like the Magnum or the shotgun, but "When we got down to the .22, I could understand the fun of shooting one. It was educational to be around people who enjoyed it, to hear them talk about it. They fascinate me, the gun people. I want to get into their heads."

Though not enough to try shooting more than once every twenty years.

"I think my nephew was surprised to find neither I nor the Brady orga-nization was in favor of banning guns," Henigan said.

"Wait," I said. It was the third time he'd mentioned that neither he nor Brady supported gun bans, yet reinstating the assault-rifle ban was the Center's main legislative goal.

"We do say that there are kinds of guns that are significantly distin-guishable from others, so ought not to be in civil society," Henigan said, tenting his fingers.

"So you support a gun ban."

"Of assault weapons."

"So why do you keep saying that Brady doesn't support banning guns?"

He spread his hands and looked at me through the bottom of his glasses as though I'd just fallen off a turnip truck. When Brady said it didn't support gun bans, most of its friends in the Capitol understood that they meant guns that good Americans wanted. Assault rifles, with their pistol grips, barrel shrouds, long magazines, and sinister black plastic stocks, were evil and murderous—an entirely different category.

I thought of all the gun stores I'd been to in the past year, all the gun shows, competitions, and rifle ranges. The AR-15—an assault weapon, by Henigan's definition—was so prevalent, so widely accepted as a hunting and sporting rifle, that to make a distinction between it and what Henigan called "other semi-automatics" seemed ridiculous. "When's the last time you visited a rifle range?" I asked.

"I've never visited a rifle range."

We met again the following day, and he clarified. "We understand here at Brady that you have to be careful when talking about banning a class of firearms. It's just very difficult to make the case that you need to be able to fire thirty rounds in five seconds." He swiveled in his chair and looked out along I Street, like an admiral surveying the sea. "It's not that you can't imagine legitimate uses," he said. "You can take an AR-15 out on the range and have a good time. You can use it in competitions." He swiveled around to face me and frowned at his desktop. "It is simply risk versus benefit. It would be a lot of fun to drive 120 miles an hour on our roads, but we have speed limits. Our position is—and you may disagree—that it's more important to protect people from being shot by criminals than to allow gun owners to enjoy an AR-15. We have limits on enjoyable activity in this society because some would threaten death and serious injury to other people."

It made sense in theory, and had we been speculating about what might happen if people were allowed to have such weapons, he might have convinced me. But we didn't need to speculate: We had data.

The FBI's annual Uniform Crime Report was as "hard" a set of numbers as could be found in the gun debate. It wasn't a survey that depended on how questions were asked; it simply tallied the crimes that police departments were required to report to the FBI. And what it showed was that assault rifles were not a public safety problem—and hadn't been even back when the original ban was passed. The FBI didn't delineate assault rifles from other rifles in its murder statistics. But in 1993, the year that the first assault-rifle ban was being debated, rifles of all kinds were used in only 3 percent—754—of the 23,271 murders committed. So the entire, polarizing assault-rifle debate was over a problem that, however telegenic and symbolically potent, barely existed. By 2004, when the ban was up for renewal, murder had fallen by a stunning 64 percent, and rifles of all kinds were responsible for the same 3 percent. Since then, rifles' portion had fallen half a percentage point, with assault rifles only a fraction of that.

It made me wonder why the Brady Center refused to support a ban on handguns. Handguns killed almost twenty times more Americans than rifles of all kinds did in 2009. Assault rifles, though, were just as powerful symbolically as they were ballistically. A renewed assault-rifle ban would really smash the enemy's idols. And politics was the art of the possible. Depending on whom you chose to believe, support for a handgun ban didn't rise above about 35 percent, while anywhere from two-thirds to three-quarters of Americans supported reinstating the assault-rifle ban.

Henigan looked at his watch; he had a meeting to attend.

As we rose, I asked if he'd ever subjected his desire for stricter gun control to a cost-benefit analysis. The benefits were murky, but what about the costs? I mentioned all the serious work Americans needed to do to arrest climate change, expand access to health care, reduce a crippling income gap, and regulate the financial sector. I told him about all the working guys I'd met on my trip who wouldn't even listen to such talk, because they didn't trust Democrats when it came to guns. Given that assault rifles—scary-looking as they were—didn't seem to pose a public safety threat, wasn't Brady doing the liberal tribe a disservice by needlessly handing the Republicans a big, fat cudgel with which to beat senseless the progressive agenda?

Henigan was the wrong guy to ask. I might as well have asked an infantry sergeant under fire in a Kandahar foxhole to explain his role in managing America's relationship to global Islam.

"I don't care what it does to the *progressive agenda*," Henigan snapped. "We're a single-issue group. Which is not to say that our typical supporters are not progressives. But we're here to advance a gun-control agenda, period."

Descending toward I Street in the elevator, it seemed to me that Dennis Henigan was as much of a problem for liberals as was Wayne LaPierre, the NRA's shrill and ubiquitous executive director. Henigan, in fact, may have been a bigger problem.

And he wasn't the only one. Using the law to diminish the gun was only one tactic in the campaign to smash the enemy's idols. Another was to attempt to expunge the gun from public consciousness. The San Francisco Municipal Transportation Agency wouldn't allow Columbia Pictures to advertise the Will Ferrell/Mark Wahlberg comedy *The Other Guys* in its bus shelters until it rolled out a poster that changed the guns in the actors' hands to badges and pepper spray. Capital One bank invited customers to "Personalize your card with an image of your choice" but refused to let a New Jersey woman use a photo of her husband hunting; no "death imagery," Capital One said. The Maplewood, New Jersey, Little League wouldn't let a gun store called Constitution Arms sponsor a team, though it accepted sponsorships from stores selling tobacco, alcohol, and Cluck-U Chicken ("Large Breasts, Juicy Thighs, Luscious Legs"). Twelve-year-old Zachary Fisher of Roseville, California, was sent home from school for wearing a T-shirt commemorating his victory in a trapshooting competition. Lots of cities did buybacks to get guns off the street, but Providence, Rhode Island, also did *toy*-gun buybacks, trading dolls and board games for toy guns. If gun guys could be like the Taliban in their absolute intolerance of even a slight disagreement, well, so could those on the anti-gun side. And if Sean Thornton's experience was any indication, teachers apparently believed that it was better to pretend that guns didn't exist than to teach kids how to stay safe around them.

The year before I met him, he'd set up a booth at the National Education Association's annual conference to try to interest teachers in the NRA's Eddie Eagle GunSafe Program, which taught kids four things to do if they happened upon a gun: *Stop. Don't touch. Leave the area. Tell an adult.* Not particularly sophisticated, perhaps, but simple and apolitical. "That whole weekend, I had maybe six people come up who were open to the idea," he said. "The majority were very upset with us—that we were even there, that we were the NRA. They wouldn't even listen." I asked a Boulder friend who taught third grade how she'd feel about Eddie Eagle, and she was adamant. "I don't want the NRA in my classroom getting kids all excited about guns." She sounded like the right-wing parents who opposed sex education because they felt it would encourage kids to have sex. I didn't tell her that, though. She didn't seem ready to listen.

If liberals thought they were weakening the enemy by smashing its idols, they had it exactly wrong. It was hard to think of a better organizing tool for the right than the left's tribal antipathy to guns. From the kid at the Family Shooting Center in Colorado to Infidel in Nebraska, from Biff in Louisville to the sparkly-eyelashed parks worker in Wisconsin, America was full of working people who wouldn't listen to the donkey party—about anything—because of the Democrats' identification with gun control.

The Democratic strategists Paul Begala and James Carville recognized this trap when they wrote of the gun-show loophole in their 2006 book *Take It Back.* "Democrats risk inflaming and alienating millions of voters who might otherwise be open to voting Democratic. But once guns are in the mix, once someone believes his gun rights are threatened, he shuts down." The NRA and Republicans knew it, too, of course, and were doing all they could to whip up hatred of the "elitists," "liberals," and "gun grabbers" in the Democratic Party—the same "effete corps of impudent snobs" that Republicans had been invoking to consummate the awkward marriage of working people to the GOP since the time of Spiro Agnew.

But the tactical damage that reflexive anti-gun sentiment did to the Democratic Party was the least of it. At a time when the economy was plummeting and the electorate was polarizing, vilifying gun owners seemed simply, and needlessly, *impolite.* The historian Garry Wills wrote in the Baltimore *Sun* that handgun owners were "accessories to murder" who had implicitly "declared war on their neighbors." Newspaper editorialists called gun owners "a ridiculous minority of airheads," "a handful of middle-aged fat guys with popguns," and "hicksville cowboys" with "macho" hang-ups. For Gene Weingarten of *The Washington Post,* gun guys were "bumpkins and yeehaws who like to think they are protecting their homes against imagined swarthy marauders desperate to steal their flea-bitten sofas from their rotting front porches." Mark Morford of *SF Gate* called female shooters "bored, under-educated, bitter, terrified, badly dressed, pasty, hate-spewin' suburban white women from lost midwestern towns with names like Frankenmuth." It was impossible to imagine getting away with such cruel dismissals of, say, blacks or gays, yet among a certain set, backhanding gun owners was good sport, even righteous. When I told an elderly friend of my mother-in-law—a generous and civic-minded Unitarian—that I was interviewing gun people, she spat, "I certainly hope you're going to condemn those *awful people.*"

Which ones? I thought. Marcey Parker? Casey Gunnels? Rick Ector? Most of the gun guys I'd met were admirably careful, sober, self-reliant individuals. They had taken up the responsibility to handle incredibly dangerous weapons with great care, and were doing so safely. Even the unpleasant ones I'd encountered weren't doing any harm. For that matter, the one guy I'd met who'd actually shot someone—Tim White—had devoted his life to keeping others from doing likewise. The community of gun guys had work to do in getting its members to keep their guns locked up, and no doubt awful people existed among the ranks. But I was alarmed at the breadth of the brush my mother-in-law's friend was willing to deploy.

In the fall of 2011, I called an energetic gray-haired woman whom Margaret and I had met at the Iron County Fair, in far northern Wisconsin, more than a year earlier. Her name was Janet Bewley, and when we met her she was campaigning as a Democrat for a seat in the Wisconsin State Legislature. She'd won, and since then Wisconsin had scrapped its long-standing prohibition on concealed carry and had gone all the way to being a shall-issue state. I wanted to know whether Bewley had voted for or against.

"For," she told me in the chewy, countrified accent I remembered well. "I don't like guns. I wasn't raised with them. But you don't pass laws based on what your gut says. You pass laws based on the Constitution and what's best."

Before casting her vote, she looked next door at Minnesota, which had become a shall-issue state two years earlier. "The sky didn't fall there," she told me. "We haven't seen a wave of shootings there. My constituents, by and large, were for it. They said, 'It's in our culture. Don't turn it into a big liberal agenda.'"

The gun debate reminded her of another issue important to northern Wisconsin: snowmobiles. "People want to be able to drive their ATVs through town to go ice fishing, and there's a whole lot of people against it because they don't like *those people*. Some people are just so anti-gun their brains explode when you try to talk about it. Same thing; it's *those people*. My own husband, he's a UCC minister and he says, 'I don't like guns.' And I tell him, 'It doesn't matter what *you* like or don't like. That's not how we make law!'" I wished her a long and productive political career—a politician who could see past her own prejudices.

Given that the vast majority of gun owners hurt nobody, and that most traditional gun-control measures couldn't be proven to have saved lives, what good came of insulting, belittling, and maligning *those people*—the 40 percent of Americans who owned guns? Where was the public benefit in blaming them for "blood-soaked streets" and an "epidemic of gun violence" that in most of America didn't really exist? By 2010, gun owners—rightly or wrongly—were feeling put-upon, marginalized, and tarred with everything from Columbine to the Mexican drug cartels. Wasn't escalating the culture wars toxic for the nation and antithetical to the notion of "liberal"? As Sarah Palin put it at the 2011 NRA convention, "Those left-wing groups are supposed to be so tolerant of everybody's lifestyle, but they're intolerant of *our* lifestyle." How about this for a bumper sticker, borrowing a phrase from the abortion-rights movement: DON'T LIKE GUNS? DON'T HAVE ONE.

EPILOGUE: SAMBA!

Always forgive your enemies; nothing annoys them as much.

—Oscar Wilde

One winter evening, I went with Margaret to hear the Brazilian music at the Laughing Goat. It's a place with a menu heavy on fair-trade coffees, herbal teas, local artisan goat cheese, and vegan soups—a hard place for a guy on a low-sanctimony diet, but lovely nonetheless. My experiment in stepping out armed still had some weeks to run. I wore the Glock under a heavy wool sweater and a tweed sport coat. As soon as we got inside, it was clear what a dumb idea it had been to come packing. The place was crowded and heating up fast. I stood in a corner, back to the wall, and in fast motion I stripped off my jacket, shrugged off my sweater, and pulled the jacket back on. After dancing for about twenty minutes, I was ready to keel over. "Aren't you hot?" Margaret shouted above the din, plucking at my bristly tweed lapel. I retreated to the men's room, tucked the holstered Glock into the front of my pants—where I'd never carried before—and untucked my shirt over it. Slow dancing was out, and I had to be careful not to bump up against anybody. Most of all, though, it was disconcerting to dance samba with a loaded, cocked 9-millimeter handgun pressing against my penis.

This obsession with guns was never going to leave me; it was time to lay down the burden of decoding it. I didn't have the time, money, or competitive urge to go running and gunning with Marcey and Jeremy. I didn't have a group of Ashkenazi homies with whom to shoot apart a carved eagle. I'd never have the dough to assemble a rare and valuable collection. I didn't sense tyranny and genocide behind every tree, so I felt no need to stockpile rifles as an antidote. I was under no illusion that I had to take my gun samba-dancing to feel safe.

If I had it to do again, would I have trained my obsession instead on guitars or cameras? Probably. Either might have satisfied that male craving for exquisite machinery, and it certainly looks like more fun to bring music or art into the world than to cozy up to a device that wreaks such misery. But I yam what I yam, neither the first gun guy nor the last. Psychoanalysts have argued since Freud's time about whether it's love of guns or fear of guns that signals retarded sexual development. I prefer to withhold judgment on a person's pleasures, as long as no harm is done. Guns will be with us for a long time. People will continue doing evil and stupid things with them. Would that we could weigh the physical harm they inflict against the political and social damage we do by vilifying those who feel about them differently than we do.

The community of gun guys turned out to be more complex than I'd imagined. I didn't necessarily enjoy every encounter, but for the most part I found my fellow gun guys passionate, responsible, and fully aware of the tremendous power they wield every time they pick up a firearm. That was true even for the screamers. They convinced me that handling guns can, if done right, impose a welcome discipline on one's life and, properly supervised, can be particularly healthy for young people. I came to regret the way guns and the people who like them are mocked and excoriated. It can't be pleasant to feel oneself on the losing end of a demographic trend, and castigated in the bargain.

I'm no less a Democrat than I was when I started. But I did come away with a greater appreciation for the way many Americans feel overmanaged and under-respected. And once my ear was tuned to that frequency, I began hearing that same frustration in other contexts. I ran into a friend one day in Boulder who, as a mountain biker, was locked in a struggle with hikers over access to trails outside of town. "They don't understand mountain bikes, and they can't be bothered to understand the people who ride them!" he fumed. "They have preconceived ideas of who we are and what mountain bikes do to trails, and want to sit back and dictate based on their prejudices!" Swap mountain bikes for guns, and mountain bikers for gun guys, and he sounded a lot like Bernie Herpin or Wayne LaPierre.

Then a friend who is a neonatal nurse in California told me that her state legislature had ordered locked away emergency drugs that had always been readily to hand. Worried that an addict might get ahold of them, the legislature imposed a complicated process that nurses must go through to get access—a process my friend argued might cost a baby's life. "We're nurses!" she cried. "We're responsible professionals! We know how to take care of our medications!" Again, substitute a word or two and she might have been any ordinary gun guy—who is certain that *his* guns will never be a public safety problem—railing against laws that restrict and infantilize everybody because a tiny percentage of miscreants *might* do something ugly. Which isn't much different, when you think about it, from racial profiling. After my year among the gun guys, I was hearing echoes of the gun-guy complaint everywhere. As the second decade of the twenty-first century began, it seemed, one did not have to be a gun guy to feel messed with, ignored, micromanaged, and disrespected. Unlike most of us, though, gun guys had found a way to focus that resentment into one manageable issue, and had big, well-funded organizations to stoke and amplify their rage.

We've settled into a nice middle-aged marriage, my gun and I. I finally bought one that imposes no physical penalty for wearing it—a tiny .380 automatic, so small and flat that I can slip it into the front pocket of my trousers less obtrusively than a wallet. It carries only seven shots and has less knockdown power than the Glock, but it isn't heavy; it doesn't restrict how I dress; I don't have to worry about exposing it accidentally. It reduces the cost of carrying a gun to near zero.

Even Margaret has grown accustomed to it. I don't tell her when I'm pocketing my gun; she wouldn't like it. And if I told her I was getting rid of all my handguns, she'd be thrilled. But we were riding bicycles in Miami one evening and found ourselves in a neighborhood that felt a little scary. She cocked an eyebrow and asked with a smile, "You packing?" She wasn't really hoping I was, but if I happened to have the little gun under my clothing, she wouldn't entirely have disapproved.

The thing is, I hardly ever carry a gun anymore. My ardor for going armed burned itself out. Most mornings, I open the safe and close it again, leaving the gun untouched. I'd have liked to have had it in some of those dicey jurisdictions where those who obey the law go unarmed: while wandering Tim White's world on the West Side of Chicago; riding the Metro through southeast Washington, D.C.; taking night walks through Harlem, Brooklyn, and Queens; driving around south-central Los Angeles. But I don't carry anymore in Boulder. I don't even carry very often in New Orleans. The stress was too much for me. I never learned to take my mind off the gun. It rarely made me feel safer. Perhaps more training would have fixed that, but I couldn't summon the enthusiasm to spend the time, money, and energy. Turns out I'm not much of a warrior, at least in that sense.

But I begrudge nobody the right to get licensed and trained to carry a gun. Given how little effect widespread carrying seems to have on crime rates, either positively or negatively, it is more an aesthetic choice than anything else. Besides, if I can ask you to accept abortion and gay marriage, you have a right to expect me to accept your gun thing. That's one of the pleasures of living in a country as complicated and diverse as ours. I just hope that those who carry will do everybody a favor and be discreet and careful about it.

I don't plan to let my carry permit lapse. And I plan to continue taking my carry guns to the range from time to time. Carrying a gun is a skill and a privilege I value, even if I don't exercise it daily. I am fully aware that there's almost no chance I will ever need my gun. I no longer imagine armed crazies lurking in every doorway or behind every Dumpster. But circumstances change. I may find myself traveling to a high-crime city that honors my permit. I might start getting death threats from an angry reader. Violent crime could spike again. After carrying for a year, having the skill and legal right to keep a gun in my pocket feels little more ridiculous than keeping a health insurance card in my wallet or a fire extinguisher in my kitchen. In the extremely unlikely event that I'm in a convenience store when a crackhead barges in, waving a gun, having my own gun means I won't have to leave it up to him whether I die.

I am grateful also to my gun for teaching me about the difference between Condition White and Condition Yellow, and about the value of vigilance, whether I'm armed or not. Carrying a gun tightened the laces on my life a bit. I like that.

Giving up full-time concealed carry doesn't mean I've given up guns (or become a baseball star). I still take the old ones from the safe to clean and shoot them—the Luger, the break-top Smith & Wesson, the Krag. They're as elegant and evocative of their day as they ever were. I still stop at gun stores and gun shows to look for old and interesting firearms. But I haven't touched the Glock in months.

A few days after samba-dancing with my Glock, I happened to be wearing it when I stopped at my bank to make a deposit. Because there was a line for the tellers, I moved over to the ATM. After punching in my code, I fed a stack of checks into the machine's stainless-steel maw. They disappeared. I waited. Nothing. No acknowledgment of the deposit, no receipt, nothing. The machine had eaten $2,200 in checks without so much as a burp.

This, then, is the epitaph for my year of living dangerously: I walked into a bank with a gun, and the bank robbed me.

POSTSCRIPT

On July 20, 2012, a man opened fire with an AR-15 rifle in the Century 16 theater in Aurora, Colorado, killing twelve people and wounding fifty-eight. Five months later—just as this book was going to press—Adam Lanza used an AR-15 to murder twenty first-graders and six adults at Sandy Hook Elementary School, in Newtown, Connecticut.

Maybe it was the collective sorrow of so many tragedies in quick succession; maybe it was the heartbreaking age of the Sandy Hook victims; but suddenly gun control, a back-burner issue throughout the election season that had just ended, was front and center. The little bodies were still at the morgue when Senator Dianne Feinstein of California announced that she would introduce an assault-rifle ban and a prohibition on magazines holding more than ten rounds. President Obama said he would support both and assigned Vice President Joe Biden to represent the White House in negotiations. Dick's Sporting Goods pulled AR-15s from its shelves. The private-equity group Cerberus Capital Management announced that it would sell its stake in Freedom Group, whose cluster of corporations includes the one that had built Lanza's rifle. Columnists suggested repealing the Second Amendment. Longtime Senate opponents of gun control said they were wavering. Even Rupert Murdoch and the *New York Post* became voices for tougher controls on guns.

It was a natural reaction, but I remember thinking, *There goes another year of potential progress on climate change, immigration reform, and income inequality.* Despite all the challenges the country faced, we were now going to spend months in a bitter fight over a new assault-rifle ban.

The public grieving brought to mind the awful spring of 1986, when a University of Maryland All-American basketball player named Len Bias dropped dead after using cocaine. The country was already distraught over the dawn of the crack epidemic; Bias's death touched off a long-pent-up reaction. "Write me some goddamn legislation!" House Speaker Tip O'Neill thundered to his staff, and what they came up with, in the heat of the moment, was mandatory minimum sentencing—a policy that would fill prisons, waste billions, and ruin countless lives.

By the time Sandy Hook happened, the country was battered by the Aurora massacre, the Sikh temple murders, the shooting of Representative Gabrielle Giffords, the Virginia Tech killings, Fort Hood, and many other mass murders stretching back to Columbine High School, in 1999. A familiar-sounding cry for "some goddamn legislation" made me hope that whatever Congress did in Sandy Hook's emotional aftermath wouldn't come back to haunt us.

It was easy to argue that banning assault rifles and high-capacity magazines wouldn't do any good. Banning things that lots of Americans want—from alcohol to marijuana to guns—has never worked well for long. Millions of assault rifles and big magazines were already in circulation and—just as they had the last time Congress debated a ban, in 1994—gun guys were stocking up like crazy. Once again, talking about a ban was putting more fast-shooting guns and high-capacity magazines on the street. And even if we could somehow get control of such weapons, the ban probably wouldn't make us much safer statistically. Despite the high-profile incidents, assault rifles were hardly ever used in homicides.

But so what? Even if a ban wouldn't magically evaporate the nation's supply of assault rifles, it would at least slow the commerce in military-style weapons. Eventually the old ones would wear out, and America's arsenal in closets and garages would become a little less lethal. A ban might not radically alter crime rates, but it might save a life. Wouldn't that be worth it? Mandatory minimums weren't a perfect comparison; they'd wasted billions of dollars and destroyed countless lives. What harm would an assault-rifle ban do?

The way I came to see it, the harm was in opportunity cost. If we did the instinctive thing and made gun owners the enemy, we couldn't do the smart thing and make them allies in the struggle against gun violence. When we demonized good people like Casey Gunnels, Marcey Parker, and Rick Ector, we deprived ourselves of their expertise. We made gun owners like them the enemy by threatening to ban their guns. We demonized them by implying—when we inveighed against "gun culture" and "America's love affair with guns"—that they were somehow to blame for

Sandy Hook. We alienated them by asking why any "sane" or "decent" person needed an AR-15—the most popular gun in America, enjoyed harmlessly by millions of law-abiding citizens.

Not that most of us gun guys were attractive allies after Sandy Hook. The website, Twitter feed, and Facebook page of the National Rifle Association went dark for a week, and when the organization resurfaced in a much-hyped press conference, it offered only to help put more guns in schools, in the form of armed volunteers. On the blogs, many gun guys got no further than rage. Even before any gun-ban legislation was introduced, one of my favorite bloggers, often a nuanced writer, referred darkly to "the post-Sandy Hook Elementary School massacre anti-Second Amendment witch hunt."

What a wasted opportunity. Gun guys—who knew guns better than anybody—should have had a lot more to offer. Although there was a cold logic to Wayne LaPierre's insistence that "the only thing that stops a bad guy with a gun is a good guy with a gun," suggesting that we turn schools into armed bunkers was tone-deaf a week after Sandy Hook, as was his bleating that the NRA, successful at nearly every turn for decades, was a victim of the "media" and the "political class."

Such is the nature of what passes for a "debate" over guns—sanctimony and name calling on one side, a snarling defensive crouch on the other. If we could have kept our hands off the gun-control hair trigger a moment longer, we might have been able to enlist gun guys—or the least doctrinaire among them—in coming up with measures that might have made a statistical dent in gun violence.

The NRA wing of gun-guy America believes that all regulation is illegitimate, that to consider any new law is to start down a slippery slope toward gun confiscation. But some regulations work. They improve public safety without infringing on what the U.S. Supreme Court has deemed an individual right to keep and bear arms. They make it possible for the non-gun-owning public to shape the way our firearms affect them. (And our guns *do* affect them; let's start by accepting that.) Instead of blindly rejecting any new laws, gun guys ought to come up with ones they like. At the risk of putting my head in the lion's mouth, here are three modest suggestions to start a conversation:

Responsibility. If gun owners knew they would be criminally liable for crimes committed with guns stolen from their houses, they'd gradually get more serious about locking them up. Adam Lanza might have been using guns his mother had left unsecured. Quick-access safes make guns available to their owners in emergencies, so there's no excuse for not requiring gun owners, through criminal penalties, to obey Rule Five: Maintain control of your firearm. We're obviously not doing a good enough job of it on our own. If gun-rights extremists want to mount an argument against keeping guns safely stowed, let them. (They'll answer to Jeff Cooper someday.) The rest of us should not mind criminal consequences for those who leave guns lying around where children, troubled teenagers, and thieves can find them.

Training. Some gun guys object to stiffer training requirements for concealed carry. Some don't think a permit should be required at all; they believe in "constitutional carry," which is the law in Arizona, Vermont, and Alaska. But take it from someone who's done it: Packing without good training is a bad idea, both practically and politically. Every gun guy urges every other gun guy to get properly trained before carrying, so why not mandate it? Training is not an infringement of Second Amendment rights; it's an *enhancement* of Second Amendment rights—a well-trained armed citizen is more effective in a crisis. The NRA offered to train a cadre of armed volunteers for schools, so why does it object to more stringent training requirements for everybody who carries? The non-gun public fears concealed carry. Gun owners should be leaders in making the practice safer, more effective, and easier for our neighbors to accept.

Background checks. Closing the gun-show loophole—requiring background checks at gun shows—is a no-brainer. It is no great burden on anybody, and it would give us one less thing to fight about. I live in a state that has closed the loophole, and I have bought plenty of guns at shows with little inconvenience. My gun rights are intact.

But what of the 40 percent of gun sales that buyers and sellers arrange privately, outside of gun shows? President Obama and a large segment of the population want to subject such sales to background checks. Forcing every buyer and seller to drive to a gun store and pay for a background check, though, wouldn't work; many people wouldn't bother, and there's a cost to passing laws that lots of people won't obey. In rural areas and in metropolitan areas with few gun stores, driving to a store would be a genuine burden. So why not put the FBI's National Instant Criminal Background Check online, where everybody can access it? We could require private sellers to keep a paper copy of the approval for a set number of years, the way gun stores do, so that if the gun turns up at a crime scene, they can demonstrate that the sale was legal. (And woe unto he who can't produce the paper.) As with the current background-check system, the FBI computer would keep no record of the check, preventing the creation of a de facto gun-registration database.

Yes, it would be a bother to background-check every sale and hold on to a piece of paper for a decade or so, but inconvenience is not infringement. It would comfort the non-gun-owning public to know that all sales are background-checked, and, frankly, it should comfort gun guys as well. It won't stop truly hard-core criminals from trading guns, but if everybody's firearms were locked up and none were leaking out of the law-abiding community through unchecked private sales, the pool of criminal guns would shrink over time.

None of these ideas is perfect. I'm open to suggestions. In fact, I insist upon them. American gun culture will have to be creative, compassionate, and thoughtful if it wants to respond to a demographic calamity and attract young people back to the shooting sports. When gun guys speak with the caustic, affronted voice of the NRA, we turn people off, and turn them against us. After the transformative horror of Sandy Hook, growling from the sidelines will no longer cut it. If gun culture is to survive, gun guys will have to get in the game. If we want to hold on to our guns, we'll have to be part of the solution, helping to instruct Americans how to live safely alongside 300 million firearms.

Lacking a national church, Americans have few ways of expressing our public morality except by saying, "There oughta be a law." Even good laws, though, have their limits. Guns make acts of criminal lunacy more deadly, but as a nation we haven't even started trying to figure out why ours is so much more violent than other countries, why we seem to produce more than our share of alienated, homicidal crazies. A year of arguing about which features make guns more deadly, and how many rounds in a magazine is too many, isn't likely to get us much closer to figuring ourselves out. *The New York Times* mocked President Obama, six days after Sandy Hook, for criticizing a "culture that all too often glorifies guns and violence" and saying that action should begin "inside the home and inside our hearts." But he was right. Something in the American character seems to make us more violent, and it's not good enough to say, "That's just the way we are."

ACKNOWLEDGMENTS

Thanks are due, I suppose, to Hank Hilliard and Chucky Blau, for setting the gun hook deep inside me when I was in kindergarten. Though it must be said that I'm not altogether sure whether, if I saw either of them again, I'd shake his hand or punch him in the nose.

Certainly the following have my unalloyed gratitude, for sharing their gun lives with me so generously: Craig Menteer, Laura Millin, Rick Ector, Robert the machine-gun collector, Howard Davis, Tom Beitling, John Beitling, Charlie Zix, Helen Zix, Jeffrey Baum, David Needham, Tom Daniel, Bernie Herpin, Tom Fashinell, David Stegman, Charlie Anderson, Erin Jerant, Marcey Parker, Jeremy Parker, Marty the First Edition Saloon bartender, Paul Weinkamp, Parry Sarto, Biff, Andy Pottgeier, Rick Freeman, Mike Rademacher, Robin Bryant, Mark Mann, Dale Albert, Steven Simons, Andrew Lisko, Walter Neumann, Scott Hawkins, Dale Kaspar, Kathy Poling, Paul Paradis, Dale Worth, Tom Taggert, Frank DeSomma, Richard Linke, Manfred Schnetzer, Peter Moskos, Tim White, Mike Hanson, Eric Simon, Roger Sprava, Garen Wintemute, Richard Sanders, Tony Wendling, Aaron Zelman, Ed Hope, Julie Moser, Tom Rompel, Tommy Rompel, Charlie Rollins, Mark Kelem, Gideon Goldenholz, Krista at AA Guns, Tony Walker, Vanessa Walker, Terri Proud, Greg Hepp, John Titsworth, Joe Sirochman, Anna Hackett, Robert Smith, Jeff Crank, Syd Stembridge, Larry Zanhoff, Karl Weschta, John Feinblatt, Chris Harris, Debra Hellwig, Mike Papac, Janet Bewley, Justin Raber, Jack Hawley, Arkadi Gerney, Bill Stojack, Bob Zelinski, Jerry Hunnicut, David Fencl, Nick Dranias, Clark Kennedy, Hope Parrish, Dustin Lohof, Oliver Mazurkiwiecz, Andy Blaschik, Sean Thornton, Andy Lander, Bill Newell, Peter Benoit, Casey Gunnels, Gwendolyn Patton, Maggie Leber, Dennis Henigan, and the many gun guys of both sexes who told me their gun stories whether I wanted them to or not.

In addition to those I met in person, I am indebted to many whose wisdom on firearms reached me from arm's length, either through phone calls or written correspondence. They include: Becca Knox, Teja van Wicklen, Dan Churchman, Cory McDonald, Tom Bowers, Andrew Betts, Ashley Peacock, Bill Brassard, Brian Malte, Mark Damian Duda, Justin Harvel, Dan Hixson, Jeffrey Folloder, Jack Jackson, Marilyn Marbrook, Ken Baker, Michael Schuyler, Shannon Whitler, Siddhartha Sharma, Brandon Campbell, Todd Pegg, Eric Wold, Neil McMillan, Howard Snyder, Gail Hayes, David Hemenway, Eugene Volokh, Robert Farago, Gary Kleck, Jack Dolan, James D. Wright, Kim Johnson, Jason Huss, Jay Corzine, Ryan Roberts, Jens Ludwig, Massad Ayoob, Roy Hill, Bruce Hallman, Stephanie Skaff, Alan Korwin, Ken Kolosh, Ted Novin, Philp J. Cook, Robert P. Hartwig, Rosanna Ander, Eric Washburn, Howard Nemerov, Abigail Kohn, Steve Shapiro, Frank Askin, Ladd Everett, Sam Friedman, Benjamin Blair, Klaus Eckman, Juha Hartikka, Ted Martin Vick, Yih-Chau Chang, Will Kiersky, "Old Bear," Chris Hamilton, Dan Parker, David Southall, James Finley, John Wagonseil, Peter Jackson, Joe Bageant, Tom Smith, Harry Lu, Kristen Rand, Ginger Couden, Ben Piper, Nadine Strossen, Tom Diaz, Mike Stollenwerk, David "Mudcat" Saunders, and John Howard.

Most of my friends and relatives hate guns—or at least say they do. Though many of them shuddered visibly when I told them about this project, all of them were supportive. Thank you, all.

Get a group of writers together, and in addition to low pay and kill fees, they'll complain about their agents. I must fall silent in such conversations, because I have been superbly served by the Wylie Agency—in particular Sarah Chalfant, Jeffrey Posternak, Matthew Bloomgarden, Andrew Wylie, Adam Eaglin, Scott Moyer, James Pullen, Caroline Smith, and Edward Orloff. They are tireless advocates; they return phone calls; they find me work. I couldn't ask for better and they have my boundless gratitude.

The other thing writers whine about is the quality of the editing they receive, and I have little to add to those bitch sessions, either. Andrew Miller at Knopf knows and cares less about guns than just about anybody I've ever met, but his open-mindedness and curiosity were vast, and his unfamiliarity pushed me to explain things more fully than I might have otherwise. He prodded me constantly to go deeper, reach harder, and take more chances. I was lucky to work with him. Similarly, the copyediting of Will Palmer was superb. Gratitude as well to Luke Mitchell, who commissioned and edited the story about carrying a gun that I wrote in 2010 for *Harper's*. Like Andrew, Luke urged me to swing for the bleachers.

For twenty-five years, Margaret has been administering a steady, gentle, loving ass-kicking to my writing. She is the best editor anywhere. Nobody knows better than Margaret how to home in on the meaning of a passage and then express it in as few elegant words as possible. This time, Margaret had a dog in the fight, because while she tolerates my gun thing, and even participates gamely in hunting, she really hates guns and everything they represent. So she was particularly useful in both the research and the writing of this book. If I could make gun guys sympathetic to Margaret, and the gun-guy point of view comprehensible to her, I knew I was over a hurdle. Margaret made that hurdle very high indeed, and I thank her for it. She makes this writing life lots of fun, and takes good care of me. Thank you, too, to our daughter, Rosa, a stalwart supporter of all we do, who performed the best service a child can to her freelance-writer parents: She won a four-year full scholarship to a great college.

NOTES

The studies and data cited here are obviously not the entirety of the wisdom on the subject of guns and crime. They are the ones I encountered and found useful. Do other studies exist that show different results or make different points? Certainly. I include this disclaimer because in my experience, everybody who cites *this* study ends up being chastised for not considering *that* study.

PROLOGUE: BIG BANG

The NRA sends members two magazines every month: *American Rifleman,* which carries a political editorial but is mostly about guns and shooting, and *America's 1st Freedom,* which is entirely about gun politics. The line on page 9 about sipping tea and nibbling biscuits appeared in the January 2010 issue of *America's 1st Freedom.*

CHAPTER ONE: BARBIE FOR MEN

The reasons people bought guns that are cited on page 12 are from *Gun Ownership and Use in America,* a Gallup survey published on November 22, 2005. Two-thirds of gun owners cited crime as the reason they keep guns, almost identical to target shooting. Fifty-eight percent said they kept guns for hunting.

Anybody who hasn't played *Call of Duty 4* or any of the other shooter games should give it a try. It is harder than it looks. Whether it acculturates young people to killing was a source of perpetual debate. I did, though, have the opportunity in 2004 to ask a Fort Benning infantry trainer, Captain Tim Dunnigan, if young men who played shooter video games were quicker on the trigger, better shots, or got over moral qualms about killing more easily. "The effect of video games is huge," Dunnigan said. "The young man today is physically bankrupt! He is soft. He is useless. We have to do a tremendous amount of work with him just to get him to where he can do ten push-ups. Young men today don't go outside. They don't move. They sit on the couch and play XBox. That's the effect. Whatever hand-eye skill is involved does nothing to condition the young man to help him here."

The National Shooting Sports Foundation is the firearms industry trade group. While it opposed most new restrictive gun laws, it focused more on the business of guns instead of the politics. In 2010, it published a report called *Modern Sporting Rifle (MSR): Comprehensive Consumer Report* that examined the market for the AR-15, and the people who used it, from many angles. It was the surveys done for this report that turned up the news that the AR-15 was for shooters who were younger, more urban, and more multicultural than the norm. That AR-15 owners shoot more often than owners of other guns comes from a press release issued by the National Shooting Sports Foundation, "Modern Sporting Rifle Owners Are Most Active Shooters Says NSSF/Responsive Management Survey," April 19, 2010.

Gun Store Finder has since disappeared from Apple's App Store.

CHAPTER TWO: CONDITION YELLOW

The gun wearing in Starbucks described on page 26 was reported by the Associated Press in "At Starbucks, Gun Owners Push Right to Bear Arms," on February 28, 2010. People wearing openly holstered guns, and at least one man with a slung rifle, showed up at an event including President Obama in Phoenix on August 17, 2010, according to Bloomberg.com and other news sources.

The Firesign Theatre joke is from *Don't Crush That Dwarf, Hand Me the Pliers*, released in 1970.

The woeful state of crime in Florida and the rest of the United States at the time Florida instituted shall-issue is detailed in the Uniform Crime Report of 1987, available from the FBI on its website. The UCRs held a special place in the gun debate, because they were the one set of numbers that nobody ever seemed to question. A lot of studies had been done on crime, violence, and the role of guns in the United States, but most of it was problematic when it came to forming public policy. Many were flawed, or the right data weren't being gathered, as the *American Journal of Preventive Medicine* discovered in 2005 when it examined them ("Firearms Laws and the Reduction of Violence: A Systematic Review," by Robert A. Hahn, et al., *AJPM* vol. 28 (2005): 40. Worse, though, was that people were rarely convinced by studies that didn't reinforce their own beliefs. Instead they impeached the research—*this question was asked the wrong way, that question wasn't asked, etc.*

The UCRs weren't without their own problems. They counted on police chiefs to report crimes to the FBI, and one chief's boys-will-be-boys might be another's aggravated assault. Moreover, the FBI's tabulation of statistics wasn't always perfectly useful. It didn't break out assault rifles in its homicide statistics, for example. And, as pointed out by James Alan Fox and Mark L. Swatt of Northeastern University, in their paper "The Recent Surge in Homicides Involving Young Black Males and Guns: Time to Reinvest in Prevention and Crime Control," published by the Bureau of Justice Statistics, homogenized national statistics don't always give the full picture. "It is not that the FBI figures tell an inaccurate story about crime trends in America. Rather, they obscure the divergent tale of two communities—one prosperous and safe, the other poor and crime-ridden." Still, while I'd had people criticize almost every study out there, I'd hardly heard anybody challenge the reliability of the UCRs, especially when it came to tracking trends.

That statistics and studies were hopeless in moving the gun debate was well argued by Donald Braman and Dan M. Kahan in their *Emory Law Journal* article "Overcoming the Fear of Guns, the Fear of Gun Control, and the Fear of Cultural Politics: Constructing a Better Gun Debate," vol. 55, no. 4 of 2006. "The gun debate appears to hinge on a narrow factual question: whether more guns make society less safe or more. . . . But so long as statistics continue to fund the parties' arguments, the gun debate, we believe, will remain bankrupt. . . . For one segment of American society, guns symbolize honor, human mastery over nature, and individual self-sufficiency. . . . For another segment of American society, however, guns connote something else: the perpetuation of illicit social hierarchies, the elevation of force over reason, and the expression of collective indifference to the well-being of strangers."

America continues this fruitless argument, they write, because it's easier than the alternative. "Many politicians and policy analysts no doubt realize that the gun debate is really about culture, not consequences. But precisely to *avoid* committing the law to picking sides in the struggle between the egalitarian and solidaristic proponents of control, on the one hand, and the hierarchic and individualistic opponents of it, on the other, they prefer the seemingly neutral idiom of econometrics."

A lot of the political energy in favor of shall-issue laws derived from examples of egregious favoritism. The California Senate, for example, voted in June 2011 to exempt its members from the near impossibility of obtaining a carry permit in California, according to "One Law for Us, Another for You," an editorial that ran on June 6, 2011, in *The Washington Times*. And on February 18, 2011, *The New York Times* published an article, "The Rich, the Famous, the Armed," that detailed how such wealthy and well-connected people as Roger Ailes, Morgan Stanley chair John J. Mack, and talk-show host Sean Hannity—none of whom even lived in the city—had been able to obtain concealed-carry permits in New York.

That thirty-seven states had gone shall-issue comes from USACarry.com, which has interactive maps showing where one's carry permit is valid. The laws change constantly; it's worth checking.

For a quick look at what the Justice Department believed happened to homicide in the United States from 1975 to 2005, see *Homicide Trends in the U.S., Age, Gender, and Race Trends,* published by the Bureau of Justice Statistics on January 17, 2011. More complete data on the drop in crime comes from the Uniform Crime Reports. For a quick glance at the trend over time, see Table 1 of "Crime in the United States: 2010," which shows both the numbers and rates of violent crime overall and also breaks it down by murder, rape, robbery, property crime, burglary, motor vehicle theft, and larceny-theft. The rate of violent crime per 100,000 people fell from 758.2 in 1991 to 403.6 in 2010. The murder rate fell from 9.8 to 4.8, rape from 42.3 to 27.5, robbery from 272.7 to 119.1, and aggravated assault from 433.4 to 252.3.

Some states published the number of concealed-carry permits they issued. Others did not. The National Shooting Sports Foundation estimated in 2011 that 6.8 million people, out of an adult U.S. population of 230 million, had concealed-carry permits.

Evidence of the relative good behavior of concealed-carry permit holders comes, ironically, from an organization that strongly opposed concealed carry: the Violence Policy Center. According to its 2010 report *Concealed Carry Killers,* 402 people had been killed by people holding carry permits from May 2007 to the end of 2010. A few were multiple killings, and a few were murder-suicides, but for the sake of argument, let's assume one killer for each murder. Given that about six million people had concealed-carry permits then, that means that in round figures, one carry-permit holder in 15,000 had committed murder during that time. How does that compare with the rest of the adult population? In that same period, about 56,702 murders took place in the United States.[*] Assuming again one murderer per murder, if you divide the murders into 200 million, which was about the size of the adult population, you get, in rough figures, one murderer in every 3,500 adults. That means that, according to the VPC's figures, concealed-carry permit holders were four times *less* likely to commit murder than members of the general adult

---

[*] In 2008, 2009, and 2010, there were 46,712 murders. To get a rough figure for June–December 2007, I took the 2007 total—17,128—divided by 12, and multiplied by 7, to get 9,991, making a rough murder total, from May 2007 to the end of 2010, of 56,702.

population. Even if you consider that only about half of all murders are committed with guns, that still makes concealed-carry holders half as likely to kill with a gun as the general population. Perhaps the Violence Policy Center, instead of resisting concealed carry, should have been fighting to make it mandatory.

The high priest of the "more guns, less crime" theory was John Lott, an independent researcher who started out at the American Enterprise Institute and wrote the book *More Guns, Less Crime.* Lott and his book were lauded by the NRA and its allies and vilified by those supporting stricter gun control. Professor John J. Donohue III of Stanford, in the July 2003 edition of *Criminology and Public Policy,* published a detailed essay titled "The Final Bullet in the Body of the More Guns, Less Crime Hypothesis," which only proved that when it comes to research on the effects of guns on crime, nothing is ever the final bullet. Nine years after Donahue's article, Lott continued to be quoted by the gun-rights community, Fox News, and many media outlets. Setting aside the validity of his research, Lott himself was an odd duck. In 2003, a blogger named Julian Sanchez, tracing IP addresses, discovered that one of John Lott's tireless defenders in online forums—a woman identifying herself as Mary Rosh—was in fact John Lott himself.

Regarding the dispute described on page 32, Gary Kleck published his findings of 2.5 million annual defensive gun uses as "Armed Resistance to Crime: The Prevalence and Nature of Self Defense with a Gun," in *Journal of Criminal Law and Criminology,* vol. 86, no. 1, 1995, and defended them in such articles as "Carrying Guns for Protection: Results from the National Self-Defense Survey," in the May 1998 issue of *Journal of Research in Crime and Delinquency.* David Hemenway published his rebuttal to Kleck in, among other places, the Spring 2009 Harvard *Bulletin* ("Comparing the Incidence of Self-Defense Gun Use and Criminal Gun Use") and *The Journal of Criminal Law and Criminology* ("Survey Research and Self-Defense Gun Use: An Explanation of Extreme Overestimates," vol. 87, no. 1, 1997).

The National Research Council attempted to evaluate the Kleck/Hemenway defensive-gun-use dispute in its book *Firearms and Violence* in 2005. After churning through both researchers' work, the NRC's conclusions boiled down to this, on page 150: "The committee concludes that with the current evidence it is not possible to determine that there is a causal link between the passage of right-to-carry laws and crime rates."

A great analysis of the whole brouhaha over defensive-gun use can be found in "A Call for Truce in the DGU War," by Tom W. Smith, in *The Journal of Criminal Law and Criminology,* vol. 87, no. 4, 1997.

A related disagreement continues over whether a family is safer with a gun in the home or without it. Gun-control advocates often argued that a family was "47 times safer" without a gun, a figure lifted from an article in the *New England Journal of Medicine* by Arthur Kellerman and Frederick Rivara, titled "Gun Ownership as a Risk Factor for Homicide in the Home" (October 7, 1993, vol. 329, no. 15, pages 1084–1090). Kellerman and Rivara found that people keeping guns at home were forty-seven times more likely to kill a friend or family member than an intruder. The problem with their reasoning, from the point of view of gun-rights proponents, is that people who keep guns at home rarely kill the intruder. Usually, the gun is used to frighten off the intruder, and sometimes to wound. Also, gun guys say, Kellerman wasn't making distinctions. Guns properly locked up or left loaded in the nightstand? Homes with children or without? Guns owned by careful and trained shooters, or guns bought to stick under the mattress and never practiced with? Gun guys also pounce on this quote from Kellerman in *Health* magazine, vol. 8, no. 2, page 52: "If you've got to resist, your chances of being hurt are less the more lethal your weapon. If that were my wife, would I want her to have a thirty-eight special in her hand? Yeah."

In an earlier paper, Hemenway, along with Sara J. Solnick and Deborah R. Azrael, both of Harvard's Injury Control Center, argued that while more than half of gun owners say they own guns for self-defense, their guns lowered the *perceived* (their italics) safety of others in the community. "This Article provides suggestive evidence that possession of firearms imposes, at minimum, psychic costs on most other members of the community," they wrote in "Firearms and Community Feelings of Safety," in *The Journal of Criminal Law and Criminology,* vol. 85, no. 1, 1995. Senator Dianne Feinstein apparently agrees. The Associated Press quoted her on November 18, 1993, as saying, "Banning guns addresses a fundamental right of Americans to feel safe."

Robert Bork tried out a similar argument in 1971 in defense of prosecuting such victimless crimes as drug abuse. In "Neutral Principles and Some First Amendment Problems," in *Indiana Law Journal* (Fall 1971, page 20), Bork argued that "knowledge that an activity is taking place is a harm to those who find it profoundly immoral." It was as bad an argument when Hemenway and Feinstein made it as when Bork made it. We may not like it that other people are doing things we revile—smoking pot, enjoying pornography, making gay love, or carrying a gun—but if we aren't adversely affected by it, the Constitution and common decency argue for leaving it alone. People may have *felt* less safe because people kept guns in their homes and on their persons, but the data suggested that they weren't less safe.

On the other hand, although gun carriers felt safer when armed, they may not have been. In Philadelphia in 2009, five researchers from the University of Pennsylvania surveyed 677 people who had been shot in an assault between 2003 and 2006, and 684 control participants. Their conclusions, published in the *American*

Journal of Public Health, vol. 99, no. 11, November 2009, as "Investigating the Link Between Gun Possession and Gun Assault," were that people carrying a gun were 4.46 times more likely to be shot than someone unarmed, and 5.45 times more likely to be shot if they had a chance to resist the assault.

And widespread concealed carry may actually have made criminals *more* dangerous. More than half of the felons surveyed by James D. Wright and Peter H. Rossi, when researching *Armed and Considered Dangerous: A Survey of Felons and Their Firearms,* said the chance their victim might be armed was a very important reason for carrying a gun during a crime.

Regarding how it could be possible that guns are used defensively as often as the research suggested without any of us hearing about it, I turned to John Lott. Lott is problematic for a lot of reasons, but he makes two good points on page 224 of his 2003 book *The Bias Against Guns.* "While the government releases an annual report on the top ten crime guns, there is no corresponding list of top ten guns used defensively." And "each year the government releases reports on the number of crimes committed with guns, but the government surveys don't directly ask people the other side of the issue, whether they have used a gun to stop crime."

The rates for gun accidents come from two sources. The first is a report from the Centers for Disease Control dated November 19, 1999, called *Nonfatal and Fatal Firearm-Related Injuries—United States, 1993–1997,* which found that fatal and nonfatal gun injuries decreased almost 41 percent in that period, from 40.5 per 100,000 people to 24. My second source was a chart generated on the CDC's website, which has a fabulous feature called Web-based Injury Statistics Query and Reporting System, or WISQARS. One can punch in many parameters—type of injury, age of injured, relevant years—and it will generate a chart. One that I generated, titled "1999–2006, United States Unintentional Firearm Deaths and Rates per 100,000," showed the rate, for deaths only, dropping from .3 in 1999 to .22 in 2006.

It must be said, though, that according to another WISQARS chart I generated, the rate of nonfatal gunshot injuries from assault rose from 2001 to 2008, from 14.4 per 100,000 to 18.62, even while the CDC's count of fatal gun accidents and the UCRs' count of gun murder both fell during the same period. A downturn in marksmanship might explain it, or, more likely, an improvement in emergency medical care. It's possible, then, that more people were shooting each other as the first decade of the twenty-first century elapsed but that fewer were dying, because responses were quicker and care was better.

And when I generated a chart called "1999–2006 United States Homicide Firearm Deaths and Rates per 100,000," I got a very different picture than that reported by the UCRs. According to CDC figures, the gun-homicide rate went up from 1999 to 2006, from 3.88 per 100,000 people to 4.05—not a lot, but a big discrepancy from the UCRs.

The number of carry permits issued in Boulder comes from the Boulder County Sheriff's Office.

That Boulder had a higher concentration of advanced degrees than other cities (page 33) comes from *Forbes*, October 20, 2011, in "In Pictures: America's Smartest Cities," which reported that 52.92 percent of Boulder's residents over age twenty-four had bachelor's degrees or higher, and 3.97 percent had Ph.D.s.

Despite what our police instructor says on page 39, Massachusetts does not require citizens to retreat from their own homes in the face of a burglary. Section 8a, Chapter 278, Title II, Part IV of the state code states in its entirety: "In the prosecution of a person who is an occupant of a dwelling charged with killing or injuring one who was unlawfully in said dwelling, it shall be a defense that the occupant was in his dwelling at the time of the offense and that he acted in the reasonable belief that the person unlawfully in said dwelling was about to inflict great bodily injury or death upon said occupant or upon another person lawfully in said dwelling, and that said occupant used reasonable means to defend himself or such other person lawfully in said dwelling. There shall be no duty on said occupant to retreat from such person unlawfully in said dwelling."

The line about never being in Condition White without being at home with the alarm on and your dog at your feet comes from "State of Awareness, the Cooper Color Codes," by Tom Givens in *Sharpen the Blade*, 05-2004, published by the American Tactical Shooting Association at teddytactical.com.

The increase in residential robberies from 2004 to 2008 and the number of people killed in such incidents are from Table 7 of *Crime in the United States, 2008*, Uniform Crime Reports. The number of households in America—114 million—is from *State & County QuickFacts*, U.S. Census Bureau, http://quickfacts.census.gov/qfd/index.html.

In 2008, twenty-seven people were killed by lightning, and 303 injured, according to Struckbylightning.org.

The law that placed the tax on silencers, sawed-off shotguns, and machine guns was the National Firearms Act of 1934. Congress apparently did not believe it had the authority to ban such weapons. It figured that placing an astronomical tax on them would solve the problem. That the tax hadn't risen in seventy-five years seems extraordinary. Some people told me that it is the only federal tax that has never risen since being instituted, but I was not able to confirm that.

A farmworker earned an average $27.17 a week in 1934, according to the *World Almanac and Book of Facts 1935*.

Directive 2003/10/EC of the European Parliament, with its language about silencers, can be found in the *Official Journal of the European Union,* L 42/38, February 15, 2003.

The 1990 killing spree that started at the shooting place outside Boulder was committed by a prison escapee named Michael Bell. One can read about him in "Police Catch Prison Escapee Suspected in Killing Spree," which ran in *The Washington Post* on August 26, 1990.

CHAPTER THREE: THE iGUN

The assault-rifle ban was contained in H.R. 3355—Violent Crime Control and Law Enforcement Act of 1994—a gigantic grab bag that contained funding for judges' training, rewriting of federal prison rules, grants to police for various purposes, substance-abuse funding, and on and on. The ban was contained in Title XI, Sec. 110101 and 110102, which went by the smoke-and-mirrors title "Public Safety and Recreational Firearms Use Protection Act."

This is how the final law defined an "assault weapon":

18 U.S.C. § 921 (30): The term "semiautomatic assault weapon" means—
   (A) any of the firearms, or copies or duplicates of the firearms in any caliber, known as—
        (i) Norinco, Mitchell, and Poly Technologies Avtomat Kalashnikovs (all models);
       (ii) Action Arms Israeli Military Industries UZI and Galil;
      (iii) Beretta Ar70 (SC-70);
      (iv) Colt AR-15;
       (v) Fabrique National FN/FAL, FN/LAR, and FNC;
      (vi) SWD M-10, M-11, M-11/9, and M-12;
     (vii) Steyr AUG;
    (viii) INTRATEC TEC-9, TEC-DC9 and TEC-22; and
     (ix) revolving cylinder shotguns, such as (or similar to) the Street Sweeper and Striker 12;
   (B) a semiautomatic rifle that has an ability to accept a detachable magazine and has at least 2 of—
        (i) a folding or telescoping stock;
       (ii) a pistol grip that protrudes conspicuously beneath the action of the weapon;
      (iii) a bayonet mount;

      (iv) a flash suppressor or threaded barrel designed to accommodate a flash suppressor; and

      (v) a grenade launcher;

(C) a semiautomatic pistol that has an ability to accept a detachable magazine and has at least 2 of—

      (i) an ammunition magazine that attaches to the pistol outside of the pistol grip;

      (ii) a threaded barrel capable of accepting a barrel extender, flash suppressor, forward handgrip, or silencer;

      (iii) a shroud that is attached to, or partially or completely encircles, the barrel and that permits the shooter to hold the firearm with the nontrigger hand without being burned;

      (iv) a manufactured weight of 50 ounces or more when the pistol is unloaded; and

      (v) a semiautomatic version of an automatic firearm; and

(D) a semiautomatic shotgun that has at least 2 of—

      (i) a folding or telescoping stock;

      (ii) a pistol grip that protrudes conspicuously beneath the action of the weapon;

      (iii) a fixed magazine capacity in excess of 5 rounds; and

      (iv) an ability to accept a detachable magazine.

18 U.S.C. § 921 (31): The term "large capacity ammunition feeding device"—

(A) means a magazine, belt, drum, feed strip, or similar device manufactured after the date of enactment of the Violent Crime Control and Law Enforcement Act of 1994 that has a capacity of, or that can be readily restored or converted to accept, more than 10 rounds of ammunition; but

(B) does not include an attached tubular device designed to accept, and capable of operating only with, .22 caliber rimfire ammunition.

The Dianne Feinstein quotes about spray-firing and light triggers appear in *The Congressional Record—Senate,* May 8, 2003. You can watch Representative Carolyn McCarthy say "a shoulder thing that goes up" on YouTube. The interview with Tucker Carlson took place on April 18, 2007.

The Eric Holder comment about reinstituting the assault-rifle ban was reported by, among others, Jason Ryan on *ABC News,* February 25, 2009. His backpedaling was reported as "Holder Dials Back His Commitment to Pushing Ban on Assault Weapons," by Sam Youngman in *The Hill,* November 15, 2009.

A list of the companies making AR-15s can be found at AR15.com.

The *Gun Digest* article on Frank DeSomma's AR-15 ran in the July 2009 edition.

CHAPTER FOUR: BLOWBACK

The price of a 1934 Thompson submachine gun comes from a reproduction of the Thompson gun catalog from that year.

This is the way Thomas, the Library of Congress online service, summarizes the provisions of Public Law 99-308, the Firearms Owners' Protection Act of 1986:

Amends the Gun Control Act of 1968 to redefine "gun dealer," excluding those making occasional sales or repairs. Exempts certain activities involving ammunition from current prohibitions.

Permits the interstate sale of rifles and shotguns, provided: (1) the transferee and transferor meet in person to accomplish the transfer; and (2) such sale complies with the laws of both States. Presumes the licensee to have actual knowledge of the laws of both States.

Repeals certain recordkeeping requirements for the sale of ammunition (but retaining such requirements for armor-piercing ammunition).

Revises the current prohibition against the sale of firearms or ammunition to certain categories of individuals by: (1) prohibiting such sales by all persons (current law covers only licensees); and (2) including as additional categories illegal aliens, dishonorably discharged members of the armed forces, and U.S. citizens who renounce their citizenship. Extends the prohibition against shipping firearms or ammunition in interstate or foreign commerce to include such individuals.

Makes it unlawful, with certain exceptions, for any individual to transfer or possess a machinegun.

Excludes pawnbrokers dealing in ammunition from current licensing requirements. Declares that a licensed dealer's personal collection of firearms shall not be subject to recordkeeping requirements in specified circumstances.

Permits the Secretary of the Treasury to revoke a license only where the holder "willfully" violates a provision of this Act. Bars the Secretary from denying or revoking a license based on violations which are alleged in criminal proceedings in which the licensee has been acquitted. Allows the Government to voluntarily dismiss such charges before trial and still proceed with revocation.

Requires the Secretary to obtain a warrant, based on reasonable cause, to examine a licensed importer's, dealer's, or manufacturer's records, firearms, or ammunition. Provides certain exceptions from the warrant requirement, including a permissible annual inspection to ensure compliance with the recordkeeping requirements.

Requires licensed collectors to maintain records of the receipt, sale, or other disposition of firearms.

Requires all licensees to report all multiple firearms sales.

Requires records maintained by a licensee who has discontinued business to be delivered to the Secretary.

Allows the Secretary to require additional recordkeeping and reports when necessary.

Permits licensed importers, manufacturers, and dealers to conduct business at temporary locations other than the one specified on a license (for example, gun shows).

Establishes either a "knowing" (scienter) or "willful" requirement with respect to general violations of this Act. Makes it a misdemeanor for any licensee to knowingly violate the recordkeeping requirements of this Act.

Imposes additional penalties, under certain circumstances, for: (1) the use of a firearm during certain drug trafficking crimes; (2) the use of a machinegun during the commission of a crime; and (3) the use of a firearm equipped with a silencer during the commission of a crime.

Amends the forfeiture provision to require that a firearm be "involved in or used" (instead of "involved in or used or intended to be used") in a knowing violation of the Gun Control Act. Directs the court to award attorney fees to the prevailing party (other than the United States) in such forfeiture actions.

Imposes a mandatory sentence of not less than 15 years imprisonment and a fine of not more than $25,000 for individuals with three or more prior convictions of robbery or burglary who are convicted of illegally shipping firearms in interstate or foreign commerce. Prohibits the court from: (1) suspending such sentence; or (2) granting parole or probation.

Permits any person prohibited from possessing, shipping, transporting, or receiving firearms or ammunition to apply to the Secretary for relief from such prohibition. Permits any person denied such relief to seek de novo judicial relief in Federal court.

Makes the authority of the Secretary to permit the importation of certain types of firearms nondiscretionary. Makes it unlawful to import any frame, receiver, or barrel of a firearm which, if assembled, would be prohibited.

Amends the rulemaking authority of the Secretary to provide that no regulation may require: (1) the transfer of records required under this Act to a facility owned, managed, or controlled by the United States or any State; or (2) the establishment of any system of registration of firearms, firearm owners, or firearm transactions. Requires a 90-day public comment period for proposed regulations.

Prohibits the Secretary from prescribing regulations which require purchasers of black powder to complete affidavits or forms attesting to their exemption from certain provisions of the Federal criminal code.

Permits the interstate transportation of unloaded firearms by any person not prohibited by Federal law from such transportation regardless of any State law or regulation.

Imposes additional penalties for the use of armor-piercing ammunition during the commission of certain drug trafficking crimes.

Amends the National Firearms Act to include within the definition of "machinegun" any part designed and intended solely and exclusively for use in converting a weapon to a machinegun. (Current law includes only a "combination of parts" within such definition.)

Among the local Republican Party chapters that have used machine-gun shoots as fund-raisers is that in Manchester, New Hampshire, as reported in "N.H. Republican Fundraiser to Feature Machine Guns," Reuters, July 24, 2007.

CHAPTER FIVE: FUDD LIKE ME

Howard Dean's comment about hunters not needing AK-47s appeared in "Dean Walks a Tightrope Over Positions on Gun Control," by Adam Nagourney and Jodi Wilgoren, in *The New York Times,* October 31, 2003. John Kerry's comment was reported in "Kerry Takes Aim at Dean Position on Guns," by Mike Glover of the Associated Press, October 31, 2003. The Bill Clinton quote was reported by Karen Gullo of the Associated Press in her November 16, 1997, story "'You Don't Need an Uzi' to Hunt Deer—Clinton Explains Ban on Import of Assault Rifles." One can watch Cass Sunstein call for a ban on hunting on YouTube: "Cass Sunstein Wants to Ban Hunting."

On page 90, I refer to the "40 percent of American households that owned guns." This comes from a May 1997 Research in Brief bulletin from the National Institute of Justice called "Guns in America: National Survey of Private Ownership and Use of Firearms," by Phillip J. Cook of Duke and Jens Ludwig of Georgetown. They found that 40 percent was a decrease from the 1960s.

On October 26, 2011, Gallup reported in "Self-Reported Gun Ownership in U.S. Is Highest Since 1993" that 47 percent of American adults had a gun in their home or on their property, which was down from a high of 54 percent in 1993 but higher than at any time since. More than half (55 percent) of Republicans said they owned a gun, as opposed to 40 percent of Democrats. Gun ownership was highest in the South (54 percent of households), lowest in the East (36).

CHAPTER SIX: FLICKED OFF

One can read about the killing of Brandon Franklin by Ronald Simms in such stories as "Suspect in Hollygrove Shooting Turns Himself In Sunday," by Richard Thompson, in *The Times-Picayune,* May 10, 2010; "Hollygrove Shooting Victim Took Leadership Role in Classroom and in Band," by Lauri Maggi of *The Times-Picayune,* May 10, 2010; and "Brandon Franklin of T.B.C. Brass Band Murdered," in *Offbeat,* May 12, 2010.

The effectiveness of waiting periods was evaluated in "Firearms Laws and the Reduction of Violence: A Systematic Review," by Robert A. Hahn, et al., *AJPM* vol. 28 (2005): 40.

The court case that established that police have no constitutional duty to protect citizens from crime was *Castle Rock* v. *Gonzales,* 545 U.S. 748 (2005).

CHAPTER SEVEN: THE RUBBER-GUN SQUAD

The Great Train Robbery was directed and photographed by Edwin S. Porter—Thomas Edison's former cameraman—in 1903. Ten minutes long, it was filmed in Essex County Park and along the Lackawanna Railroad in New Jersey.

For excellent articles on Stembridge Gun Rentals, I refer the reader to "Shoot for Effect," by John Fasano in the October 1998 issue of *Guns* magazine, and, even better, "7,000 Guns for Hire," by Bob Thomas, in the January 1969 issue of *True* magazine ("For Today's Man").

Not all goes smoothly in the Hollywood gun business. *USA Today* reported on December 12, 2011, in "Weapons Reportedly Meant for Brad Pitt Film Seized," that Hungarian authorities had confiscated about a hundred live weapons headed for the set of *World War Z,* Pitt's zombie-war movie.

Anybody interested in wasting many hours could visit imfdb.com—the International Movie Firearms Database—which attempts to list every firearm used in every movie. If you need to know, say, how Jack Bauer armed himself in the second season of *24,* what Jimmy Stewart used to shoot Liberty Valance, or which pistols gunned down Marlon Brando in *The Godfather,* you can look them up. You can answer for yourself the question that inevitably arises as gun guys sit in the dark before a flickering screen: What *is* that gun? The database is cross-referenced, too; type in the name of a gun and imfdb will tell you every movie in which it has appeared. The Bernardelli Model 60? *Dawn of the Dead* (1978) and the first six episodes of *The X-Files.* The Haenel-Schmeisser? *Metropolis* (1927). My Glock 19? Too many to list.

Imfdb.com is one of those realms of arcana that the Internet was practically invented to foster. It tries to identify guns in movies you'd have thought contained no guns—the Colt New Service that flashes by in the international trailer for *Water for Elephants* or the Remington 700PSS seen for a nanosecond in *Up in the Air.* Imfdb is where you go to learn that the first time an M16 appeared in a movie was in *Seven Days in May,* in 1964, or that until the Soviet Union collapsed in 1989 and its weapons became available to Hollywood, almost all the Soviet guns in movies were mocked-up American guns disguised with plastic and sheet metal. Woe betide the Hollywood director who commits the sin of anachronism or inaccuracy. The makers of the 2002 Mel Gibson film *We Were Soldiers* get high marks from imfdb for scattering shell casings from live rounds on the ground; they look different from the crimped casings made by blanks. But imfdb dismisses the overall effort this way: "Many rifles used in this movie were not actual XM16E1s. The historical XM16E1s had only a partial magazine fence. Many rifles were actually M16A1s mocked up to look like XM16E1s, modified with chromed bolt carriers and 3 prong flash hiders." *Well!* I must not have been much of an arma-cinephiliac; I was impressed that the filmmakers had gone to the trouble of modifying guns with chromed bolt carriers and 3-prong flash hiders. And for the record, gun guys aren't the only ones policing movie props with obsessive compulsion. Witness these websites: the Internet Movie Cars Database, the Internet Movie Plane Database, Watches in Movies, and Rotary Action (helicopters in movies). Even The Fountain Pen Network maintains a page to track—and argue over—movie sightings.

CHAPTER EIGHT: BRING IT ON, GOD DAMN IT!

This is how Thomas, the Library of Congress's online service, summarizes the Brady Act of 1994:

Title I: Brady Handgun Control—Brady Handgun Violence Prevention Act—Amends the Federal criminal code to: (1) require the Attorney General, within five years, to establish a national instant criminal background check system (system) for firearm licensees to contact for information on whether receipt of a firearm by a prospective transferee would violate Federal or State law; and (2) establish an interim five-day waiting period for handgun purchases and procedures for checking with the chief law enforcement officer of the place of residence of the purchaser (police official) for such information.

(Sec. 102) Prohibits, under the interim procedures, any licensed importer, manufacturer, or dealer from transferring a handgun to an unlicensed individual unless: (1) the transferor has received a statement of eligibility from the individual, verified the individual's identity, and notified the police official and during the next five business days the transferor either has not received information that the transfer would violate the law or has received notice that the transfer would not violate the law; (2) the individual has presented a statement from the police official that he or she requires a handgun because of a threat to a family member; or (3) applicable State law requires, before any transfer, verification that possession of a handgun by the purchaser would not be unlawful. Requires notified police officials to make a reasonable effort to make the relevant determinations within five days.

Prohibits the transfer of a firearm to an unlicensed individual after the system is established unless the transferor has verified the individual's identity and contacted the system and either: (1) the system has provided the transferor with a unique identification number for the transfer; or (2) three business days have elapsed and the system has not notified the transferor that the transfer would violate the law.

Permits a transfer (before or after the system is established) if: (1) the individual has presented a permit issued in the past five years by a State that verifies that the individual is legally qualified; (2) the Secretary of the Treasury has approved the transfer under specified provisions of the Internal Revenue Code; or (3) the Secretary has certified that compliance with the applicable background check requirements is impracticable.

Requires the destruction of records pertaining to any transfer to an eligible individual.

Sets penalties of up to a $1,000 fine, imprisonment for not more than one year, or both, for violations of this Act.

(Sec. 103) Directs the Attorney General to: (1) determine a timetable by which each State should be able to provide criminal records on an on-line capacity basis to the system; (2) expedite the upgrading of State records in the Federal criminal records system maintained by the Federal Bureau of Investigation (FBI), the development of hardware and software to link State systems to the national system, and the FBI's revitalization initiatives for technologically advanced fingerprint and criminal records identification; and (3) notify each licensee and the chief law enforcement officer of each State upon establishment of the national system.

Provides for the correction of erroneous information in the system and for regulations to ensure the privacy and security of system information.

Prohibits any Government entity from using the system to establish any system for the registration of firearms, except with respect to persons prohibited from receiving a firearm.

Authorizes appropriations.

(Sec. 106) Amends the Omnibus Crime Control and Safe Streets Act of 1968 to permit the use of formula grants under the drug control and system improvement grant program for the improvement of State record systems and the sharing with the Attorney General of specified records for the purpose of implementing this Act.

Directs the Attorney General, through the Bureau of Justice Statistics, to make grants to States for the creation of a computerized criminal history record system or improvement of an existing system and for assistance in the transmittal of criminal records to the national system.

Title II: Multiple Firearm Purchases to State and Local Police—Requires each Federal firearms licensee to submit a report of multiple sales or other dispositions of firearms to the department of State police or State law enforcement agency of the State or local law enforcement agency of the local jurisdiction in which the sale or other disposition took place. Prohibits agency disclosure of any such form or contents and requires each such department or agency to: (1) destroy any form containing such information and any record of the contents within 20 days after such form is received, except with respect to a purchaser who is prohibited from receipt of a firearm; and (2) certify to the Attorney General (at six-month intervals) that no disclosure contrary to such requirements has been made and that all such forms and records have been destroyed.

Title III: Federal Firearms License Reform—Federal Firearms License Reform Act of 1993—Amends the Federal criminal code to prohibit any common or contract carrier from requiring or causing any label, tag, or other written notice to be placed on the outside of any container indicating that it contains a firearm.

Prohibits: (1) any common or contract carrier from delivering in interstate or foreign commerce any firearm without obtaining written acknowledgement of receipt of the package containing the firearm; and (2) stealing or unlawfully taking or carrying away from a licensed firearms importer, manufacturer, or dealer any firearm in the licensee's business inventory that has been shipped or transported in interstate or foreign commerce (subject to penalties of up to a $10,000 fine, ten years' imprisonment, or both, for violations).

(Sec. 303) Increases license application fees for firearms dealers who do not deal in destructive devices.

Regarding states that have closed the gun-show loophole, the Violence Policy Center, which supports closing the loophole nationally, reports this on its website:

"Only six states (California, Colorado, Illinois, New York, Oregon and Rhode Island) require universal background checks on *all* firearm sales at gun shows, including sales by unlicensed dealers. Three more states (Connecticut, Maryland and Pennsylvania) require background checks on all handgun sales made at gun shows. Eight other states (Hawaii, Iowa, Massachusetts, Michigan, Missouri, New Jersey, Nebraska and North Carolina) require purchasers to obtain a permit and undergo a background check before buying a handgun. 33 states have taken no action whatsoever to close the gun show loophole. In two states, voters themselves closed the loophole when their legislatures refused to do so. On November 7, 2000, the citizens of Colorado overwhelmingly voted 70%–30% in favor of Amendment 22, closing the gun show loophole in their state. The referendum followed the tragic shooting at Columbine High School on April 20, 1999 (the guns used in the shooting were purchased from private sellers at Denver gun shows). In Oregon, voters also voted overwhelmingly, 62%–38%, in favor of Measure 5, effectively closing the gun show loophole in their state."

The study referenced on pages 127 and 128, which found that gun shows, with or without the loophole, had little or no effect on violent crime, was published in *The Review of Economics and Statistics,* MIT Press Journals, as "The Short-Term and Localized Effect of Gun Shows: Evident from California and Texas," by Mark Duggan of the University of Maryland, Randi Hjalmarsson of the University of London, and Brian Jacob of the University of Michigan, September 9, 2010.

That nearly a third of gun sales are private and therefore don't involve a background check at a federally licensed firearms dealer comes from *Guns in America: Results of a Comprehensive National Survey of Firearms Ownership and Use,* by Philip J. Cook and Jens Ludwig for the Police Foundation in Washington, D.C., 1996.

When I assert on page 128 that gun controllers didn't talk much about banning private gun sales, one exception would be Democratic National Committee chair Debbie Wasserman Schultz, who, according to the article "New DNC Chief Wants to Screen All Gun Sales," by Mike Lillis, in the April 18, 2011, edition of *The Hill,* told a rally sponsored by Mayors Against Illegal Guns, "It is outrageous that gun buyers evade the background-check system every day, even in broad daylight." She could point to such cases as Eduardo Sencion, a man with a documented history of mental illness who—according to an item titled "Carson City IHOP Shooter Fired About 60 Rounds from Fully Automatic Rifle," on RGJ.com on October 5, 2011—bought his gun in a private sale. Even though he broke the law by possessing a full-auto weapon without going through the steps required by the National Firearms Act of 1934, buying a gun privately was perfectly legal. Representative Carolyn McCarthy of New York was "expected" to introduce a bill requiring all gun sales to pass through a background check, though if she did so, it seems to have gone nowhere.

James D. Wright and Peter H. Rossi discovered, when researching *Armed and Considered Dangerous: A Survey of Felons and Their Firearms,* that only 16 percent of the felons they surveyed said they got their guns from gun stores, in all likelihood because their criminal records made them "prohibited persons." And Wright and Rossi conducted their survey in 1986, eight years before the Brady Act would mandate computerized background checks.

Ross Douthat's column arguing that Christianity is punching below its weight was "A Tough Season for Believers," *The New York Times,* December 19, 2010.

CHAPTER NINE: CONDITION BLACK

One of Rick Ector's inspirations was Kenneth Blanchard, author of the book and podcast *Black Man with a Gun.* His book, whose subtitle is *A Responsible Gun Ownership Manual for African Americans,* begins with "A Letter to My Sisters," addressing African American women, who are among the strongest adherents of gun control.

"You will unknowingly contribute for the first time to the destruction of our people," Blanchard writes. "Proof that you have been targeted for manipulation is that gun control groups use your tears and your suffering as sound bites in commercials and in public hearings. . . . You are being used to disarm African Americans by allowing the increase of senseless and repetitive laws."

There's a connection, Blanchard writes, between the high rate of murder among young black men and the strict gun-control laws that exist in many majority-black cities. "We are allowed to destroy ourselves because this negative image is profitable. . . . The people that want us unarmed and helpless don't have a hard time convincing us. . . . Racially motivated violence is not the only threat to which blacks are more vulnerable. An African American has at least a forty percent greater chance of being burgled and a one hundred percent greater chance of being robbed than a white person."

If young black urban men liked guns so much, the gun blogger Robert Farago had a solution: train more of them to shoot. He argued in a March 26, 2012, posting titled "Guns and Inner City Kids: A Modest Proposal on Guns" that disciplined, supervised firearms instruction might satisfy these young men's natural fascination with guns, teach them safe gun handling, and demystify guns to the point that they don't feel a need to carry. Moreover, he argued, by holding out the prospect of getting a permit to carry legally if they stayed straight and passed their gun-handling classes, training young men to get their concealed-carry licenses might actually make better citizens of them. "If you can convince inner city kids on a rifle team that staying out of trouble will allow them to carry a gun legally when they reach adulthood *and make it happen,* you will create a new corps (in the non-military sense) of trained, responsible gun owners within inner city communities. People ready, willing and able to defend themselves and the rule of law. How great is that?"

While most black civil rights groups support gun control, the big exception is the Congress of Racial Equality, founded in 1942, which pioneered the Freedom Rides, among other achievements. CORE, whose national chairman, Roy Innis, was a member of the NRA board, frequently took the gun-rights side in writing amicus briefs; one example is its brief in *Edward Peruta* v. *County of San Diego,* a 2011 case. CORE opened its argument with a historical argument. "CORE's interest in this case stems from the fact that the Second Amendment right to keep and bear arms for self defense is an important civil right that was denied to African Americans under the antebellum Slave Codes, the Black Codes passed just after the Civil War, and under the Jim Crow regimes that persisted into the twentieth century."

Readers might also enjoy reading "The Second Amendment: Toward an Afro-Americanist Reconsideration," by Robert J. Cottrol of Rutgers School of Law and Raymond T. Diamond of Tulane University Law School, in *Georgetown Law Journal,* vol. 80 (1991–92): 309.

Representative Bobby Rush's son Huey was shot dead in Chicago in 1999.

According to the website OnTheIssues.org, which tracks the positions political leaders take, Rush has voted against reducing the waiting period to buy a handgun, voted against laws that would indemnify the gun industry from product liability lawsuits, voted in favor of closing the gun-show loophole, and has an F rating from the NRA.

CHAPTER TEN: IT'S NOT GOING TO BITE

Jeff Cooper wrote in *Jeff Cooper Commentaries,* vol. 5, no. 7 (June 1997), "I coined the term 'hoplophobia' in 1962 in response to a perceived need for a word to describe a mental aberration consisting of an unreasoning terror of gadgetry, specifically, weapons. The most common manifestation of hoplophobia is the idea that instruments possess a will of their own, apart from that of their user. This is not a reasoned position, but when you point this out to a hoplophobe he is not impressed because his is an unreasonable position. To convince a man that he is not making sense is not to change his viewpoint but rather to make an enemy. Thus hoplophobia is a useful word, but as with all words, it should be used correctly."

Jeff Cooper's classic volume is *Principles of Personal Defense,* published in 1972 but reissued many times since.

CBSNews.com reported Robert Reza's shooting as "Emcore Shooter Robert Reza Kills Two, Self, Say Police," on July 12, 2010.

The statement on page 159 that support for gun control among the public is dropping comes from a Gallup report on November 26, 2010, "In U.S., Continuing Record-Low Support for Stricter Gun Control." In 1990, 78 percent of Americans thought gun laws should be made more strict. By 2010, that was down to 44 percent.

President Obama's decision to allow holders of concealed-carry permits to wear their guns in national parks was reported in *The Washington Times* on February 22, 2010, by Stephen Dinan, as "Parks Open to Holders of Concealed Guns."

The National Shooting Sports Foundation's annual report, *Industry Reference Guide,* is a trove of information about the gun business and gun-guy demographics. All of the information about the aging of the shooting community comes from the *Industry Reference Guides* of 2010 and 2011. The line about the future of shooting sports being "precarious" comes from the second paragraph on page 1 of *The Future of Hunting and the Shooting Sports: Research-Based Recruitment and Retention Strategies,* published by the National Shooting Sports Foundation in 2010.

To the extent young people are hunting, they are more and more doing it with bows. Archery was the one type of shooting sport that the *Industry Reference Guide* reported to be on the rise. Everyplace Margaret and I traveled, we found lots of floor space in gun stores given over to archery. On the approach to Belle Fourche, South Dakota, for example, we encountered Triggers, a compact store wedged into a roadside strip mall. Inside were only about twenty-five rifles and ten handguns, while dozens of bows hung from the ceiling in long, colorful echelons. Really, Triggers was an archery store with a little bitty gun annex.

"Young people are all over archery," said Justin Raber, the fit and eager young owner. "It starts when they're little. The 4H has an archery program, but no riflery. And look at the hunting shows on the Outdoor Channel—they're all about archery. It just looks better on television than gun hunting—the string being pulled back, the arrow flying through the air—you can see it hit the deer. There's more to watch than when a guy puts a gun to his shoulder and goes *bang*."

Archery season always comes before rifle season, he said. Young people want to be out when the weather is good and the elk are bugling. It's warmer. It's easier to camp. "And young people don't want to do what their fathers did," he said. "They want more of a challenge."

He took a bow off the wall. "Tell you something else: There's no hassle to buying a bow. No 4473s. No bullshit with the ATF. You put down your money and you walk out with it." He placed the bow in my hands. It was light, made of carbon fiber. With pulleys at either end and an electronic red-dot sight, it seemed less like a throwback to Indian times than something issued by NASA. "That's the future you're holding there," Justin said.

Given that the National Shooting Sports Foundation is the trade group for the firearms industry, it's surprising how many gun guys ignore it so completely. When I quoted the figures from the *Industry Reference Guide* in an article about the AR-15 business called "Guns Gone Wild," published on Kindle Singles in September 2011, the gun blogger Robert Farago of *The Truth About Guns* took off after me as though I'd quoted Charles Schumer or Sarah Brady, and judging from his readers' comments, most agreed. I sent Farago the pages from the *Industry Reference Guide,* but if he looked at them, he didn't respond. Six months later he was still going about it, telling his readers, "Dan Baum Is Still Wrong, But You Knew That," even though I'd published nothing further on the subject. I was reminded of the wisdom of the sociologist C. Wright Mills, in his 1959 book *The Sociological Imagination*: "First one tries to get it straight, to make an adequate statement. If it is gloomy, too bad. If it leads to hope, fine."

The point isn't the insults against me. What's striking is the refusal of many gun guys to acknowledge the demographic problem that their own trade group has identified. As someone who likes to shoot and thinks that firearms instruction, properly done, can be good for young people, I'd like to see the shooting sports continue. While I assume most gun guys would say likewise, many seem to prefer the defensive crouch to acknowledging that something about guns and shooting is failing to appeal to young people. The hostile, defensive crouch may well be it.

The article about young people turning away from automobiles and driving is "To Draw Reluctant Young Buyers, G.M. Turns to MTV," by Amy Chozick in *The New York Times*, March 22, 2012.

CHAPTER ELEVEN: SPIN DRIFT

Those who participate in practical shooting—running and gunning—insist that standing still and squeezing off aimed shots at a target is useless practice for defending yourself with a gun. "You take Olympic shooters, and they practice all the time, and they can hit a fly off a cow's nose from 100 yards," a retired New York police commander told Al Baker of *The New York Times* in the December 9, 2007, article "A Hail of Bullets, a Heap of Uncertainty." "But if you put a gun in that cow's hand, you will get a different reaction from the Olympic shooter." Typical New Yorker: He thinks cows have hands.

That the magazine *Soldier of Fortune* held the first three-gun contest in the 1980s is common wisdom, but I was never able to document it.

CHAPTER TWELVE: FRIEDRICH AND BARNEY

One can read about Cincinnati's German regiments in the Civil War at cincinnati .com and about the Kolping Society at kolpingcincinnati.com.

CHAPTER THIRTEEN: HE UPPED, I UPPED

For information about police killings during the aftermath of Hurricane Katrina, readers are referred to the case of the Danziger Bridge, in which eight officers of the New Orleans Police Department were involved in the killing of two unarmed civilians on September 4, 2005. Although state charges were originally dismissed, five of the officers were convicted in federal court on August 5, 2011, on charges related to covering up the shooting and deprivation of civil rights.

Here is a sample of the invective directed against me on AR15.com after I asked if any gun buriers would like to be interviewed anonymously. First someone discovered this passage I had written in a 2010 blog about the Tanner Gun Show:

The weapons at this Denver show seem to have been designed by Klingons. Many are short, black, high-tech semi-automatics—ARs in the jargon—the civilian version of the rifles American soldiers carry in Iraq and Afghanistan. They fire a bullet unsuitable for most hunting, and are crusted with combat-ready lasers, flashlights, night-vision scopes, and red-dot sights. They start at around a thousand dollars. The tables that don't cater to the AR crowd hold other modern man-killers: rough-finished Yugoslav AK-47's for three hundred dollars apiece; Barrett .50-caliber rifles capable of penetrating an armored limousine; brand-new stainless-steel semi-automatic pistols with fifteen-shot clips selling for upwards of eight hundred dollars; tinny chrome-plated pocket pistols for less than a hundred bucks. There's also plenty of body armor, web gear, combat fatigues, silencers, stacks of thirty- and fifty-round magazines. It feels less like a "show" than an arms bazaar in Peshawar.

The guy who posted this said I was being "overly dramatic and deliberately putting out false information." I'm still not exactly sure what it was about this paragraph that got him so upset. Nothing in it was untrue; I even avoided the mistake, which gun guys hate, of calling magazines "clips." Maybe the line about "man-killers." Several people took exception to the reference to Klingons.

It wasn't until someone discovered a *Washington Post* story about Margaret and me getting cheated out of a D.C. apartment we'd rented for Barack Obama's inauguration that the "Arfcom army" went completely wacky. Range_Officer posted in tall red letters, "THIS GUY IS AN OBAMA SUPPORTER," and then the vitriol really flowed. Someone went to my website and posted a picture of me with Margaret and Rosa. Wrote Meadowmuffin: "Is nice that obango lickers were the first to get bent over financially after his inauguration [*sic*] then the rest of the country after them. That family pic looks just like a poster for liberal types, go write about your hero the kenyan and wookie instead." Added Fxntime, "I put forth the motion that said liberal troll-turd be banned as the worthless commie obama butt kissing socialist mangina he is."

This went on for about two weeks, and then I was banned from AR15.com by its owner, Edward Avila of Rochester, New York.

The Dalai Lama quote about shooting back was taken from "Dalai Lama Urges Students to Shape World," which ran in *The Seattle Times* on May 15, 2001. Reporter Hal Benton paraphrased the Dalai Lama this way: "The Dalai Lama said acts of violence should be remembered, and then forgiveness should be extended to the perpetrators. But if someone has a gun and is trying to kill you, he said, it would be reasonable to shoot back with your own gun. Not at the head, where a fatal wound might result. But at some other body part, such as a leg."

CHAPTER FOURTEEN: GUN SHUL

Gus Cotey's and Sarah Thompson's articles on the mentality of gun-control proponents, and the Theodore Haas interview, can be found on the website for Jews for the Preservation of Firearms ownership.

I confirmed the story of meeting Gideon Goldenholz with Goldenholz himself, in a telephone interview on January 6, 2011.

The number of privately owned guns in the U.S. is always a guess. According to "U.S. Most Armed Country with 90 Guns Per 100 People," a Reuters story by Laura McInnes on August 28, 2007, the Geneva-based Graduate Institute of International Studies estimates 270 million. This isn't too far from the estimate of David Hemenway et al., who in an article titled "The US Gun Stock: Results from the 2004 National Firearms Survey," in the journal *Injury Prevention,* vol. 13 (2007): 15–19, estimated at least one privately owned gun for every adult.

That Russia has a murder rate four times that of the United States comes from *Seventh United Nations Survey of Crime Trends and Operations of Criminal Justice Systems,* covering the period 1998–2000 (United Nations Office on Drugs and Crime, Centre for International Crime Prevention). The U.S. had a 2008 murder rate of 4.2 per 100,000 people, and Russia's was 20. Ireland, Switzerland, Indonesia, Greece, Hong Kong, Japan, Saudi Arabia, and Qatar were all around 0. Colombia topped the list at 61.

But not all Americans are necessarily equal. Writing in *American Psychologist in* April 1993, Richard E. Nisbett of the Institute of Social Research at the University of Michigan argued in *Violence and U.S. Culture* that guns aren't the best predictor of violence; white Southerners are. "There is a marked difference in White homicide rates between regions of the United States, such that homicide is more common in the South and in regions of the country initially settled by Southerners." And it's not that the South was poorer than other regions, either. "Although differences in poverty are associated with higher homicide rates, regional differences in homicide are by no means completely explained by poverty, because Southernness remains a predictor of homicide even when poverty differences between regions are taken into account." Why were Southerners more violent? They "are more likely to endorse violence as an appropriate response to insults, as a means of self-protection, and as a socialization tool in training children," Nisbett wrote.

The Anti-Defamation League had no use for Aaron Zelman or Jews for the Preservation of Firearms Ownership. In "Revolution and Reality: A Transcript and Analysis of Mark Koernke's 'Time is Running Out,'" published as part of ADL's *Militia Watchdog* series in 1998, it backhanded JPFO as a "small extremist group." JPFO, the ADL wrote, a "radical pro-gun group, which ironically consists of mostly non-Jews, shrilly makes the (unsupportable) claim that the Holocaust was caused by gun control."

CHAPTER FIFTEEN: HOGZILLA

The term "Hogzilla" refers to a giant pig that may or may not have been a hoax. Certain subjects are perfect for research on Wikipedia, and this seems one of them. This is what Wikipedia says:

> Hogzilla is the name given to a male hybrid of wild hog and domestic pig that was shot and killed in Alapaha, Georgia, United States, on June 17, 2004 by Dr. Eliahu Katz on Ken Holyoak's fish farm and hunting reserve. It was alleged to be 12 feet (3.7 m) long and weighed over 1,000 pounds (450 kg). It was originally considered a hoax.
>
> The animal's remains were exhumed in early 2005 and studied by Dr. Oz Katz and his father, Dr. Eliahu Katz for a documentary and a book they wrote together. In March 2005, these scientists confirmed that Hogzilla actually weighed 800 pounds (360 kg) and was between 6.9 feet (2.1 m) and 8.6 feet (2.6 m) long, diminishing the previous claim. DNA testing was performed, revealing that Hogzilla was a hybrid of wild boar and domestic pig (Hampshire breed). However, compared to most wild boars and domestics, Hogzilla is still quite a large and extraordinary specimen.
>
> Hogzilla's tusks measured nearly 28 inches (71 cm) and 19 inches (48 cm).

A story about the question of whether to allow hunters to cull the elk herd in Rocky Mountain National Park or to have rangers do the job ran on ABCNews .com as "Officials Consider Ways to Cull Wildlife," by Jim Avila, August 26, 2006.

CHAPTER SIXTEEN: THE ARMED BONEHEAD

The data on children shooting themselves and each other, the rising rate of teenage suicide, and the methods by which teenagers attempted suicide all come from charts generated on the CDC's WISQARS website and also from *Protect Children, Not Guns 2010,* published by the Children's Defense Fund.

In their article "Prevalence of Household Firearms and Firearm-Storage Practice in the 50 States and the District of Columbia: Findings from the Behavioral Risk Factor Surveillance System, 2002," in *Pediatrics,* vol. 116, no. 3 (2005): e370–e376,

Catherine A. Okoro et al. wrote that two million American homes have loaded guns lying around unlocked. Similarly, a group of CDC researchers found in 1996 that about one in ten Oregon adults lived in a home that always or sometimes contained a loaded and unsecured gun ("Population Estimates of Household Firearm Storage Practices and Firearm Carrying in Oregon," by David Nelson, Joyce A. Grant-Worley, Kenneth Powell, James Mercy, and Deborah Holtzman of the CDC, published in the *Journal of the American Medical Association,* vol. 275, no. 22, June 12, 1996).

Even the Department of Homeland Security can't keep track of its guns. *Washington Post* reporter Spencer S. Hsu wrote on February 18, 2010, in "Report Tracks Lost Firearms at DHS," that DHS agents had lost 289 handguns, shotguns, and automatic rifles between 2005 and 2008. Some were left on car trunks, others in restaurant or bowling alley restrooms and in clothing-store fitting rooms.

The study of felons and their firearms was published in 1986 as *Armed and Considered Dangerous: A Survey of Felons and Their Firearms,* by James D. Wright and Peter H. Rossi. It makes terrific reading. The half a million annual missing guns comes from a fact sheet issued by the Bloomberg School of Public Health at Johns Hopkins University, undated.

The story about the Pennsylvania legislature on page 238 was reported in "Municipalities May Be Forced to Rescind 'Missing Gun' Reporting Laws," by Linda Finarelli in *Montgomery News,* February 24, 2012. The seven states that required gun owners to report stolen guns to police were Connecticut, Massachusetts, Michigan, New Jersey, New York, Ohio, and Rhode Island, according to *Regulating Guns in America: An Evaluation and Comparative Analysis of Federal, State, and Selected Local Gun Laws* (Legal Community Against Violence, February 2008).

CHAPTER SEVENTEEN: DEAD AGAIN

That twenty-three states had some form of "stand your ground" law comes from a *ProPublica* article, "The 23 States That Have Sweeping Self-Defense Laws Just Like Florida's," by Cara Currier, published on March 22, 2012. Those states were Alabama, Arizona, Georgia, Idaho, Illinois, Indiana, Kansas, Kentucky, Louisiana, Michigan, Mississippi, Montana, Nevada, North Carolina, Oklahoma, Oregon, South Carolina, South Dakota, Tennessee, Texas, Utah, Washington, and West Virginia.

A gunfight is an imprecise enterprise. As reported in "A Hail of Bullets, a Heap of Uncertainty," by Al Baker, in *The New York Times,* December 9, 2007, New York City Police who fired at a person in the line of duty in 2006 hit their target only

28.4 percent of the time. But that was an improvement over 2005, when their hit rate was 17.4 percent. Los Angeles Police officers hit their targets 40 percent of the time, "which, while better than New York's, still shows that they miss targets more often than they hit them."

CHAPTER EIGHTEEN: TRIBES

According to the Legal Community Against Violence, which advocates for tougher gun laws, state and local governments from New York to Hawaii, in addition to Chicago and Washington, D.C., were, as of April 2, 2012, facing forty-four "significant" lawsuits challenging gun laws after *Heller* and *McDonald*. Readers are directed to LCAV's *Post-Heller Litigation Summary*.

Guncite.com is a website devoted to constitutional rights, particularly the Second Amendment. Its home page states, "Until the Second Amendment is treated as normal constitutional law, this web site will always be under construction . . ." So as a gun-guy ally, it is to Guncite's credit that it maintains a page devoted to "Bogus Quotes Attributed to the Founders," usually bogus quotes that would support the gun-guy position. The bogus quotes on pages 256 and 257 come from Guncite.

That the NRA is not a particularly big lobby comes from "What Sort of Lobby Is the NRA?" by Timothy P. Carney in the January 13, 2011, edition of *The Washington Examiner*. The statement on page 262 that support for gun control had fallen below 50 percent comes from a Gallup report on November 26, 2010, "In U.S., Continuing Record-Low Support for Stricter Gun Control."

My assertion on page 263 that it was almost impossible to prove that the measures we thought of as "gun control" saved any lives is obviously a contested issue. In addition to the "Firearms Laws" article in the *American Journal of Preventive Medicine*, I relied upon *First Reports Evaluating the Effectiveness of Strategies for Preventing Violence: Firearms Laws*, published by the CDC in October 2003. The CDC evaluated fifty-one studies on everything from the effectiveness of gun bans to laws requiring gun locks. On banning types of guns or ammunition: "Certain studies indicated decreases in violence associated with bans, and others indicated increases." On laws restricting who can get a gun: "some studies indicated decreases in violence associated with restrictions, and others indicated increases." On waiting periods: "some indicated a decrease in violent outcome associated with the delay and others indicated an increase." On registration, shall-issue concealed-carry, child-access-prevention laws, and zero-tolerance gun policies in schools, the studies were either too few or poorly designed, so no conclusions could be reached.

That researchers kept finding that studies were inadequate for evaluating the effectiveness of firearms laws may not have been entirely the blame of those who conducted the studies. Michael Luo of *The New York Times* made a compelling case that the NRA unduly influences how research on gun violence is conducted and funded, in "N.R.A. Stymies Firearms Research, Scientists Say," January 25, 2011.

And some studies have indeed shown links between guns and violence. Handguns bigger than .32 caliber seemed to be associated with higher homicide rates in Dallas from 1980 to 1992, for example, but whether those weapons were semi-automatic or not seemed to make no difference, according to Christopher Koper of the Crime Control Institute, who published the study "Gun Density Versus Gun Type: Did the Availability of More Lethal Guns Drive Up the Dallas Homicide Rate 1980–1992?" (final revised report submitted to the Firearms and Violence Program, National Institute of Justice, 1997).

The Canadian Parliament's canceling of the country's long-gun registry was reported as "Long-Gun Registry Scrapped," by CTV.ca, on October 25, 2011.

When I write on page 263 that crime fell after the Brady Law but it was already falling before, the FBI's Uniform Crime Reports make that clear. Two of my favorite gun-crime researchers drilled more deeply into the question, though, in 2000. Jens Ludwig of Georgetown and Philip J. Cook of Duke, whom I've never met, are among the very few researchers on the gun/crime nexus who don't seem to come at the question with preconceived ideas, and are equally willing to gore oxen on both sides. Writing in the *Journal of the American Medical Association*'s August 2, 2000, issue, they examined data from the National Center for Health Statistics and concluded that the Brady Act seemed to be associated with a reduction in suicide among people fifty-five or older, but that it had no effect on homicide rates. That their article appeared in *JAMA* is significant. Many people have attempted to discuss guns as a public health issue, as Arthur Kellerman did in the *New England Journal of Medicine* article described in the notes to chapter two. But Abigail Kohn, in her terrific book *Shooters: Myths and Realities of America's Gun Cultures,* makes a strong argument that the public health approach when it comes to guns is suspect. I quote her here at length because the gun-control argument so often relies on the rhetoric of public health.

> Public health rhetoric provides the aura of scientific fact to the political agenda of gun control. It avoids the more obvious and politically fraught good guy/bad guy dichotomies, rests moral authority on medical science, presents antigun ideology as logical reasoning and empirical fact. Within the public health paradigm, there are no overt bad guys, only average people who engage in risky, dangerous behavior. [page 134]

The public-health approach to gun violence is particularly toxic, she writes, because it both blinds the anti-gun camp and needlessly inflames gun guys.

> Having these beliefs legitimized by public health advocacy also provides liberal supporters of gun control with certain material benefits. They don't need to pay more taxes or radically rework operational social welfare programs to help reduce gun violence. All they need to do is vote for tighter gun restrictions or bans on certain kinds of guns. [pages 134–35]
>
> As far as shooters are concerned, this kind of gun-control advocacy exists not only to inform them of their own ignorance and naiveté but also to convince them that owning a gun will transform them into murderers or suicide victims. These messages run so contrary to what shooters know about guns, and what shooters know about *themselves*, that they reject these messages outright as ludicrous and insulting. . . . When control advocates promote the ubiquitous dangerousness of guns, gun enthusiasts hear ad hominem attacks. [page 135]

The Warren Cassidy quote on page 264 appeared in *Under Fire*, by Richard Lacayo, in *Time*, June 24, 2001.

More about the deadliness of the assault rifle: In 2010, the Brady Center published a list: "Examples of Assault Weapon Violence Reported Since Ban Expired in 2004." The list included 410 incidents, some of which—like the September 15, 2007, birthday party in New Orleans, where twenty-eight bullets were fired from an AK-47, killing one man and wounding three children—were horrifying. But a closer examination of the list showed that several of the incidents were accidents; several more were suicides; and twenty-five involved the popular Chinese military rifle called the SKS, which held only ten rounds, had no pistol grip, barrel shroud, or collapsible stock, and was an "assault rifle" under the law only because it had a bayonet—not a widely used murder weapon. Of the 410 incidents, only thirty-nine involved more than ten bullets being fired. Ten was the maximum size of a gun's magazine under the Clinton-era assault-rifle ban. Even if one adds in the seven others that mentioned "spraying" bullets, in only forty-six of the incidents that "involved" assault rifles was the fact that the weapon involved was an assault rifle relevant. The rest of the shootings could have been done with any gun. Forty-six incidents in five years and three months is, undeniably, forty-six tragedies. But nobody at Brady seemed to be asking whether it was worth cleaving the country down the middle yet again to prevent them.

For an example of what drives gun-rights activists around the bend, get ahold of the conclusion of *Assault Weapons and Accessories in America*, published by the Violence Policy Center. "The weapons' menacing looks, coupled with the public's confusion over fully automatic machine guns versus semi-automatic assault weapons—anything that looks like a machine gun is assumed to be a machine gun—can only increase the chance of public support for restrictions on these weapons." In other words, never mind that these weapons aren't much of a public-safety threat; the guns are scary-looking enough to fool people into supporting a ban. And the report's last words are positively ghoulish in their palpable desire for political victory. "Recognizing the country's fascination for exotic weaponry and the popular images and myths associated with guns, it may require a crisis of a far greater proportion before any action is taken."

Another useful document is *Updated Assessment of the Federal Assault Weapons Ban: Impacts on Gun Markets and Gun Violence, 1994–2003*, published by President George W. Bush's Justice Department in July 2004, when Congress was considering renewing the ban. It makes the point that it wasn't so much the weapons but the large-capacity magazines that mattered in gun crime—though not very much, since so many were grandfathered in under the ban that the ban itself did little to reduce their prevalence on the street. Overall, the report concluded, "Should it be renewed, the ban's effects on gun violence are likely to be small at best and perhaps too small for reliable measurement."

The lack of support for a handgun ban referenced on page 268 comes from "Record-Low 26% in U.S. Favor Handgun Ban," by Gallup, published October 26, 2011. That was down from 60 percent in 1959.

The role of the American Civil Liberties Union in the gun debate has always been a puzzler. To gun guys, it has always seemed crazy that an organization that stood up for the rights of Nazis to parade through Skokie, Illinois, wouldn't stand up for citizens' Second Amendment rights. On March 4, 2002, the ACLU published a bulletin disagreeing with the Supreme Court's reasoning in *Heller*, which wasn't unexpected. "The ACLU interprets the Second Amendment as a collective right," the online bulletin said. "As always, we welcome your comments."

Hoo boy, did it get them. The vitriol went on for months, some of it typical bashing from the right but most from people identifying themselves as long-time ACLU members. "I don't know why this is the only constitutional right the ACLU doesn't defend," wrote TexasCivilLibertarian. "The Bill of Rights protects the rights of INDIVIDUALS, so the idea that the Bill of Rights protects a 'collective right' is absolutely preposterous." SuperNaut wrote, "I just took the money I had slated to re-up my lapsed ACLU membership and used it to re-up my NRA membership. Sorry ACLU you lost me." A lot were like those of MadRocketScientist: "I've often found myself defending the ACLU to other conservatives and have supported many of your legal actions, but this I can not abide. You need to explain why you continue to refuse to defend the 2nd amendment as you do the others." I counted about thirteen hundred comments, mostly from people who claimed to be members or supporters of the ACLU, and didn't find one of them in favor of the organization's interpretation.

I phoned Frank Askin, the ACLU's general counsel, who had served on the ACLU's national board for almost thirty years, from 1969 to 2007. "There's been almost no support in the national board that I recall for an individual right to own a gun," he said. "The major debate has always been over whether we should assert what is not a civil liberty. The ACLU has never taken a crime-control position. You could say that freedom from crime is a civil liberty but the ACLU hasn't gotten into that." He called "absurd" Scalia's reasoning that the Second Amendment protects citizens' right to violent revolution, and said conservatives usually make the opposite argument, when fighting regulations, that "the Constitution is not a suicide pact." "The other amendments say very clearly there should be no laws abridging free speech, and that we have a right to be free of unreasonable search and seizures. In the Second Amendment it's all backwards, with the well-regulated militia coming first." Even as we spoke, though, the South Dakota chapter of the ACLU was fighting to win Second Amendment rights for legal U.S. residents, as reported in "ACLU Challenges Citizenship Requirement for Concealed Weapons," by Nick Penzenstadler, *Rapid City Journal,* January 3, 2011.

On the Fourth of July, the left-leaning online publication *The Daily Kos* published an impassioned argument, "Why Liberals Should Love the Second Amendment," by Kalili Joy Gray. "This is an appeal to liberals, not merely to tolerate the Second Amendment, but to embrace it. To love it and defend it and guard it as carefully as you do all the others. Because we are liberals. And fighting for our rights— for *all* of our rights, for *all* people—is what we do. Because we are revolutionaries."

When presented with, say, the reality that President Obama had done nothing about guns in his first term except allow people to wear them concealed in national parks, gun-rights activists often fell back on what he, and other liberals, "really wanted" to do. They pointed to quotes like this one, from Sarah Brady in *The New York Times,* on August 13, 1993, in an article called "A Little Gun Control, a Lot of Guns," by Erik Eckholm, on the struggle to get the Brady Law passed: " 'Once we get this,' she said, 'I think it will become easier and easier to get the laws we need passed.' " Gun guys argued that Mrs. Brady had tipped her hand that she wanted to put gun policy on the "slippery slope" toward a total ban.

Dennis Henigan of the Brady Center had a good answer to the slippery-slope argument: What difference does it make what gun-control advocates really want? It's not like they're going to get their way just because they want something; we have laws. "Not only are we not talking about outlawing guns, but guns *cannot* be outlawed" after the *Heller* decision, he writes on page 40 of his 2009 book *Lethal Logic:*

Exploding the Myths that Paralyze American Gun Policy. On page 99 he continues, "In the final analysis, the slippery slope argument asks policymakers to forgo the life-saving benefits of sensible gun control policies because it is possible to dream up some hypothetical scenario in which such policies may increase the likelihood of a gun ban. This is sheer folly. In no other area of policymaking would we allow such rank speculation to defeat proposals that have concrete and demonstrable benefits."

The story on page 269 about the San Francisco Municipal Transportation Agency making the producers of *The Other Guys* change their poster came from "Altered Movie Poster Puts the Spotlight on a San Francisco Agency's Gun Ban," by Maria Wollan, in *The New York Times,* September 5, 2010. Capital One's refusal to allow a woman to put a picture of her husband hunting on her credit card was the NRA's "Outrage of the Week" on Friday, April 22, 2011. The story of Constitution Arms being denied the opportunity to sponsor a Maplewood, New Jersey, Little League team was reported as "N.J. Kids Baseball League Rejects Maplewood Gun Dealer's Sponsorship," by Philip Read, in the Newark *Star-Ledger,* March 5, 2010. Zachary Fisher's story was on CBS 13, Sacramento. The story about Providence's toy-gun buyback, "Disarming the Toy Box," ran in *The Boston Globe* on December 19, 2010.

The Carville/Begala quote is from *Take It Back,* pages 49–50.

The Garry Wills quote on page 270 comes from "Murders at One Remove," Baltimore *Sun,* September 5, 1994. "A ridiculous minority of airheads" was the work of Perry Young, in his article "We Are All to Blame" in *The Chapel Hill Herald,* April 24, 1999. The "popguns" line belongs to Eric Sharpe, from his article "Outdoorsmen Can't Ignore Gun Control," which ran in the Los Angeles *Daily News,* June 11, 1995. Gene Weingarten took after "bumpkins and yeehaws" in his *Washington Post* column, Get Me Rewrite, on October 14, 2010. Mark Morford's writing about women gun owners ran as "Pistol-Packin' Polyester," in *SF Gate,* March 21, 2001.

Sarah Palin's speech to the NRA was reported, among other places, on the *Huffington Post*'s Politics Daily as "Sarah Palin Tells NRA Convention Obama Would Ban Guns If He Could," by Mary C. Curtis, May 15, 2010.

Gun owners—even those who belong to the NRA—may not be as rigid in their thinking as they are frequently portrayed. In December 2009, the Republican pollster Frank Luntz surveyed 832 gun owners—401 who belonged to the NRA and 431 who didn't—on behalf of Mayors Against Illegal Guns and came up with some surprising results. The vast majority of both groups—85 percent of non-NRA gun owners and 69 percent of NRA members—supported closing the gun-show loophole. Support was even stronger in both groups for laws requiring gun owners to tell the police if their guns were stolen. Both groups were over 80 percent in their approval of background checks at gun stores.

SELECTED BIBLIOGRAPHY

Ayoob, Massad. *In the Gravest Extreme: The Role of the Firearm in Personal Protection.* Massad F. and Dorothy A. Ayoob, 1980.

———. *The Gun Digest Book of Concealed Carry.* Iola, Wis.: Gun Digest Books, 2008.

Bellesiles, Michael A. *Arming America: The Origins of a National Gun Culture.* New York: Alfred A. Knopf, 2000.

Benson, Ragnar. *Modern Weapons Caching: A Down-to-Earth Approach to Beating the Government Gun Grab.* Boulder, Colo.: Paladin Press, 1990.

Bijlefeld, Marjolijn, ed. *The Gun Control Debate: A Documentary History.* Westport, Conn.: Greenwood Press, 1997.

Blanchard, Kenneth V. F. *Black Man With a Gun: A Responsible Gun Ownership Manual for African Americans.* Baltimore: American Literary Press, 1994.

Burbick, Joan. *Gun Show Nation: Gun Culture and American Democracy.* New York: New Press, 2006.

Cassidy, Kyle. *Armed America: Portraits of Gun Owners in Their Homes.* Iola, Wis.: Krause, 2007.

De Becker, Gavin. *The Gift of Fear and Other Survival Skills That Protect Us from Violence.* New York: Dell, 1997.

Diaz, Tom. *Making a Killing: The Business of Guns in America.* New York: New Press, 1999.

Eddie the Wire. *How to Bury Your Goods: The Complete Manual of Long-Term Underground Storage.* Boulder, Colo.: Paladin Press, 1999.

Garbarino, James. *Lost Boys: Why Our Sons Turn Violent and How We Can Save Them.* New York: Free Press, 1999.

Halbrook, Stephen P. *The Founders' Second Amendment: Origins of the Right to Bear Arms.* Chicago: Ivan R. Dee, 2008.

Hemenway, David. *Private Guns, Public Health.* Ann Arbor: University of Michigan Press, 2004.

Henigan, Dennis A. *Lethal Logic: Exploding the Myths that Paralyze American Gun Policy.* Dulles, Va.: Potomac Books, 2009.

Kelly, Caitlin. *Blown Away: American Women and Guns.* New York: Pocket Books, 2004.

Kleck, Gary. *Targeting Guns: Firearms and Their Control.* New York: Aldine de Gruyter, 1997.

Kleck, Gary, and Don B. Kates. *Armed: New Perspectives on Gun Control.* Amherst, N.Y.: Prometheus Books, 2001.

Kohn, Abigail A. *Shooters: Myths and Realities of America's Gun Cultures.* New York: Oxford University Press, 2004.

Kopel, David B. *Guns: Who Should Have Them?* Amherst, N.Y.: Prometheus Books, 1995.

Levitt, Steven D., and Stephen J. Dubner. *Freakonomics: A Rogue Economist Explains the Hidden Side of Everything.* New York: Morrow, 2009.

Lott, John R. *More Guns Less Crime: Understanding Crime and Gun Control Laws.* Chicago: University of Chicago Press, 1998.

———. *The Bias Against Guns: Why Almost Everything You've Heard About Gun Control Is Wrong.* Washington, D.C.: Regnery, 2003.

National Research Council. *Firearms and Violence: A Critical Review.* Washington, D.C.: National Academies Press, 2005.

National Rifle Association. *NRA Guide to Personal Protection in the Home.* Fairfax, Va.: National Rifle Association, 2000.

———. *NRA Guide to Personal Protection Outside the Home.* Fairfax, Va.: National Rifle Association, 2006.

———. *NRA Guide to the Basics of Pistol Shooting.* Fairfax, Va.: National Rifle Association, 2009.

National Shooting Sports Foundation. *The Writer's Guide to Firearms and Ammunition.* National Shooting Sports Foundation, undated.

Nelson, Zed. *Gun Nation.* London: Westzone, 2000.

Schulman, J. Neil. *Stopping Power: Why 70 Million Americans Own Guns.* Mill Valley, Calif.: Pulpless, 1994.

Sherrill, Robert. *The Saturday Night Special and Other Guns with Which Americans Won the West, Protected Bootleg Franchises, Slew Wildlife, Robbed Countless Banks, Shot Husbands Purposely and by Mistake & Killed Presidents—Together with Continuing Debate Over Same.* New York: Charterhouse, 1973.

Sowell, Thomas. *Intellectuals and Society.* New York: Basic Books, 2009.

Stevens, Richard W. *Dial 911 and Die: The Shocking Truth About the Police Protection Myth.* Hartford, Wis.: Mazel Freedom Press, 1999.

Sugarmann, Josh. *Every Handgun Is Aimed at You: The Case for Banning Handguns.* New York: New Press, 2001.

Taylor, Alan. *American Colonies: The Settling of North America.* New York: Penguin, 2001.

U.S. Department of Justice. *Violent Encounters: A Study of Felonious Assaults on Our Nations' Law Enforcement Officers.* August 2006.

Walker, Tony. *How to Win a Gunfight: Gaining the Half-Second Advantage.* Conshohocken, Pa.: Infinity Publishing, 2007.

Weiner, Jon. *Historians in Trouble: Plagiarism, Fraud, and Politics in the Ivory Tower.* New York: New Press, 2005.

Wenger, Stephen P. *Defensive Use of Firearms: A Common Sense Guide to Awareness, Mental Preparedness, Tactics, Skills, and Equipment.* Boulder, Colo.: Paladin Press, 2005.

Wright, James D., and Peter H. Rossi. *Armed and Considered Dangerous: A Survey of Felons and Their Firearms,* expanded edition. New York: Aldine de Gruyter, 1994.

Wright, James D., Peter H. Rossi, and Kathleen Daly. *Under the Gun: Weapons, Crime, and Violence in America.* New York: Aldine de Gruyter, 1983.

Yewman, Heidi. *Beyond the Bullet: Personal Stories of Gun Violence.* Vancouver, Wash.: Dash Consulting, 2009.

Zelman, Aaron. *Gun Control, Gateway to Tyranny: Proof that U.S. Gun Law Has Nazi Roots.* Hartford, Wis.: Jews for the Preservation of Firearms Ownership, 2006.

Zelman, Aaron, and L. Neil Smith. *The Mitzvah: For Those Who Love Freedom and for Those Who Should.* Hartford, Wis.: Mazel Freedom Press, 1999.

Zelman, Aaron, and Peter Spielmann. *The Life Insurance Conspiracy Made Elementary by Sherlock Holmes.* New York: Simon and Schuster, 1976.

Zelman, Aaron, and Richard W. Stevens. *Death by "Gun Control": The Human Cost of Victim Disarmament.* Hartford, Wis.: Mazel Freedom Press, 2001.

INDEX